The History of the English Language

SECOND EDITION

THE
History
OF THE
English Language

A source book
SECOND EDITION

DAVID BURNLEY

An imprint of **Pearson Education**

Harlow, England · London · New York · Reading, Massachusetts · San Francisco
Toronto · Don Mills, Ontario · Sydney · Tokyo · Singapore · Hong Kong · Seoul
Taipei · Cape Town · Madrid · Mexico City · Amsterdam · Munich · Paris · Milan

Pearson Education Limited
Edinburgh Gate
Harlow
Essex CM20 2JE
England

and Associated Companies throughout the world

Visit us on the World Wide Web at:
www.pearsoned.co.uk

First published 1992
Second edition 2000

ISBN 0–582–31263–9 PPR

British Library Cataloguing-in-Publication Data

A catalogue record for this book is available from the British Library

Library of Congress Cataloging-in-Publication Data

A catalog record for this book is available from the Library of Congress

7 6
08 07 06 05

Set in 10.5/14.5pt Minion by 35
Printed in Malaysia, VVP

FOR RICHARD

CONTENTS

Modern English (1800–1920)

Appendix

LIST OF PLATES

ACKNOWLEDGEMENTS

We are grateful to the following for permission to reproduce copyright material:

Plate 1: *Cura Pastoralis* MS Hatton 20, fol. 1v; Plate 2: *Ormulum* MS Junius 1, folio 70v; Plate 6: Caxton's advertisement, Arch Ge 37, all used with permission from The Bodlian Library, Oxford.

Plate 3: *Troilus and Criseyde*, CCC MS, f.27.r, The Parker Library, Corpus Christi College, Cambridge.

Plate 4: *Caxton: The Faytis of Arms*, reproduced by courtesy of the Director and University Librarian, John Rylands University Library, Manchester.

Plate 5: extract from Milton's *Paradise Lost*, by permission of Sheffield University Library.

Plate 7(i): advertisement from the *Publick Adviser* (126B) and Plate 7(ii): from the *Daily Courant* (E922 PG 195) by permission of the British Library, London.

Plates 8 & 9: *Eno's Fruit Salts* used by permission of SmithKline Beecham, Brentford, Middlesex (intellectual property holders). *Eno's Fruit Salts* is a registered trademark of Beecham Group plc.

Plate 10: we have been unable to trace the copyright holders of this image, and would be grateful for any information that will enable us to do so.

We are indebted to Oxford & Cambridge University Presses for permission to reproduce extracts from *New English Bible*, Second Edition © 1970.

PREFACE TO THE FIRST EDITION

A source book does not try to usurp the role of a fully explanatory and discursive history of the language, nor replace the information and advice which can be offered to the student by a teacher. It seeks only to make conveniently available to students and teachers alike a resource which can be used to illustrate the development, and something of the variety, of the English language used in Britain through nearly thirteen centuries.

A variety of purposes and levels of competence among the users of this book is foreseen. Some very early dialect texts and classics of philological investigation (such as the *Ormulum* or *Ancrene Wisse*) are included, and the provision of a proportion of rhymed verse permits rhyme analysis. But the translation of earlier texts, and some marginal glossing, is intended to make analysis of the linguistic features of these texts more practicable for those whose purposes do not demand a reading knowledge of the earliest stages of the language.

The overall structure of the book sustains the consensus view of the development of the language through successive historical periods towards the goal of present-day standard English. Thus, apart from one letter from King James VI of Scotland, Scottish texts have not been included, since they are considered to belong to a distinct and specialised development. The progress of English is outlined in brief introductions to the texts of each period, as well as illustrated in chronologically contrasted and parallel passages from the Bible, situated in the final section of the book. Despite this arrangement, the main collection of texts facilitates an alternative view, which emphasises the stylistic and dialectal complexity of English and acknowledges the importance of variation in linguistic change. Among the possible topics which might be developed in using this collection are the relationship between dialect speech and the standard at various periods, and its social implications; the influence upon English of foreign languages; the occurrence of colloquial expression in writing; or the characteristics of Latin-based prose. The selection of particular types of writing from a range of periods permits the exploration of certain pathways through the history of English: scientific writings, from Ælfric to Darwin; the continuing art of letter writing; or the development of the language of a particular region. Attitudes to, and the understanding of, language from the fourteenth to the nineteenth centuries forms a connected theme, which emerges in the later selections in scholarly discussion of the study of language in general, and of English in particular. Lexicography, from an anonymous fourteenth-century concordance to Johnson and the editors of the *Oxford English Dictionary*, is particularly well represented.

Unless otherwise stated in the introduction to the text, excerpts of medieval origin have modern capitalisation and punctuation, and apart from *æ*, *þ*, and *ð* in Old English, and these with the addition of *ʒ* in Middle English, modern letter-forms are used. Abbreviations have been silently expanded. Later texts reproduce the spelling and punctuation of the originals, but with modern letter-forms. Facsimiles of some texts, manuscript and printed, are provided in order to demonstrate features of orthography and text presentation which cannot be appreciated from printed versions. I gratefully acknowledge the assistance I have received from the staff of the British Library, the Lambeth Palace Library, and the Imperial War Museum. I am grateful also to Mrs D. J. Finch for permission to print the letter of Private D. J. Sweeney and to Mrs Katherine Cleasby-Thompson for those of Captain Ainslie Douglas Talbot.

Without the willingness of colleagues in Sheffield to offer helpful advice and to cover during a term's study leave, of my students cheerfully to adopt the role of guinea pigs for some of the texts incorporated, and my wife and children to deliver coffee to the keyboard, the preparation of this book would have been much less pleasurable and much longer delayed. I should like to record my appreciation of them all.

JDB
University of Sheffield
September 1990

PREFACE TO THE SECOND EDITION

When this book was planned originally it was intended above all to be useful to those whose duty it was to teach the History of the English Language – not always the easiest role to adopt. It cast its net very widely, seeking to provide texts which would serve the traditional philological purpose, whilst at the same time facilitating a more recent stylistically-oriented approach, in which it is possible to trace the evolution of certain genres of discourse.

This second edition does not depart from that earlier intention, but it makes certain additions, and responds to some detailed suggestions received from users of the first edition. Notably, there is now an expanded outline of linguistic features at each of the main chronological divisions, to produce a very compact history of the language. In passages of Old English, the grapheme <ȝ> is printed rather than the more usual editorial <g>, which now permits better-informed comparison with later spelling practice. A sample of Kentish has been added to the Old English dialect section. *The Equatorie of the Planetis* has been removed from the Later Middle English section, and the space occupied by an example of an elaborate fifteenth-century formal letter, and an extract from a fifteenth-century text on phonetics, which joins the existing text on lexicography. Alongside the parallel passages from the Bible have been placed some examples of the English Marriage Service from the late fourteenth century to 1927.

An innovation in the theme of genre development is the introduction of some texts illustrating the language of advertising. This has a briefer history than either the language of the English Bible or of the Marriage Service, but it represents a peculiarly interesting register. In contrast to scriptural and liturgical texts, where the dominant influence has been conservatism in style and stabilisation of content, the language strategies, style and content of advertising have been subject to great variation and rapid evolution. Its language functions as a very direct communication between the advertiser and the presumed audience, and so is subject to interpersonal linguistic features which construct a social relationship between them. Furthermore, with the emergence of illustrated advertisements, language becomes part of a more complex context elaborated by the parallel message carried by the illustration. I have supplied some examples of these.

Acknowledgements are due to the same people and institutions mentioned in the previous edition, but it might have a special appropriateness here to record my appreciation of those who have bought, used, and commented on the earlier volume, so making a second edition possible.

JDB
University of Sheffield
May 2000

ABBREVIATIONS

AN	Anglo-Norman
BL	British Library
EDD	*English Dialect Dictionary*
EM	East Midland
EModE	Early Modern English
Fr.	French
CUL	Cambridge University Library
ME	Middle English
MED	*Middle English Dictionary*
Lat.	Latin
MDu	Middle Dutch
MLG	Middle Low German
MS	Manuscript
MSS	Manuscripts
OE	Old English
OED	*Oxford English Dictionary*
OF	Old French
ON	Old Norse
WM	West Midland
OSc	Old Scandinavian
Sp.	Spanish
WS	West Saxon

SYMBOLS

Phonetic symbols

The symbols of the International Phonetics Association are used to represent the sounds encountered in earlier stages of the language. In the chart
below, the words used as examples should be pronounced as in Received
Pronunciation (idealised Southern British English) unless otherwise stated.
The italicised portion in each word is the sound represented by the symbol.

Consonants

b	*b*ut	ʒ	vi*si*on
d	*d*id	ʤ	*j*u*dg*e
f	*f*oot	t	*t*in
g	*g*o	θ	*th*in
h	*h*it	ð	*th*is
j	*y*et	v	*v*ine
k	*c*an, *k*i*ck*	w	*w*ine
l	*l*et	ç	(German ni*ch*t; some Scots *l*i*ght*)
m	*m*an		
n	*n*o	X	(French *r*ouge, North Northumbrian *r*oad)
ŋ	si*ng*		
p	*p*in	x	lo*ch* (as in Scots or German a*ch*t)
r	*r*ed		
s	*s*et	ɣ	(German sa*g*en)
ʃ	*sh*e	z	*z*oo
ʧ	*ch*ip		

Vowels

Vowel quality only is represented by these symbols. Vowel length is indicated in the text by a colon (ː) following the symbol.

æ	h*a*t	y	(French t*u*)
a	h*a*t (Northern British pronunciation)	ɒ	p*o*t
		ɔ	c*o*rd
ɑ	p*a*rt	ʌ	c*u*t
e	(French c*e*s, cit*é*)	o	(French *eau*)
ɛ	(Northern and American English b*e*d, French b*ê*te)	ʊ	b*oo*k
		u	t*oo*
ɪ	h*i*t	ə	butt*er*, *a*long
i	b*ee*		

Diphthongs are represented by the combination of two vowel symbols: for example, aʊ (*ow*l), eɪ (d*ay*), aɪ (*eye*), and ɔɪ (b*oy*).

Other symbols

ø A null symbol, used to indicate a zero morpheme, as in the contrast between singular and plural *dogø*, *dogs*.

* An asterisk immediately preceding a cited form (*refrangere) indicates that the form in question has not been recorded in texts, but has been reconstructed. In some cases, the reconstruction may be ill-founded, and this is noted.

CHRONOLOGY

Ruler	Historical events	Literary events
400		
	Withdrawal of Roman forces (410)	
	Anglo-Saxon Settlement commences	
	Last Roman Emperor deposed (476)	
500		
Legendary King Arthur		
600		
Edwin, King of Northumbria (616–33)	Conversion of Kent to Christianity (597)	
Penda, King of Mercia (626–55)	Conversion of Northumbria (625)	
	Sutton Hoo ship burial (635)	
700		
Offa, King of Mercia (757–96)	Danish raids commence (787)	Cædmon's Hymn
800		
Alfred the Great, King of Wessex (871–99)	Dane-law established (886)	Anglo-Saxon Chronicle begun
900		
Æthelstan (924–40)	Unification of England	*Brunanburh*
Ethelred the Unready (978–1016)		West Saxon Gospels
1000		*Battle of Maldon*
Cnut (1017–35)	Death of Ælfric (1010)	
Danish Rule (1017–42)		
Edward the Confessor (1042–66)		
William I (1066–87)	Norman Conquest (1066)	
William II (1087–1100)		

Ruler	Historical events	Literary events
1100		
Henry I (1100–1135)	Oxford University established	*Peterborough Chronicle*
Stephen (1135–54)	(1167)	ends
Henry II (1154–89)		*Ormulum*
Richard I (1189–99)		
1200		
John (1199–1216)	Loss of Normandy (1204)	*Ancrene Wisse*
Henry III (1216–72)	Arrival of the Friars (1221)	
Edward I (1272–1307)	Annexation of Wales (1277)	
1300		
Edward II (1307–27)		
Edward III (1327–77)	Statute of Pleading (1362)	
Richard II (1377–99)		Wycliffite Bible
1400		
Henry IV (1399–1413)		*Canterbury Tales*
Henry V (1413–22)		
Henry VI (1422–61)	Loss of Gascony (1453)	
	Wars of the Roses (1455–85)	
Edward IV (1461–83)	Introduction of printing (1476)	
Edward V (1483)/		
Richard III (1483–85)		
	Discovery of America (1492)	
1500		
Henry VII (1485–1509)		Skelton
Henry VIII (1509–47)	Dissolution of the Monasteries	Tyndale's Bible
	(1536–39)	
Edward VI (1547–53)/		
Mary (1553–58)	Loss of Calais (1558)	
Elizabeth I (1558–1603)		
1600		
James I (1603–25)	East India Co founded (1600)	A. V. of Bible (1611)
Charles I (1625–49)	Union with Scotland (1603)	Shakespeare First Folio
The Commonwealth	First American colonies	(1623)
(1649–60)		*Paradise Lost* (1667)
Charles II (1660–85)		
James II (1685–88)		
William (1689–1702) and		
Mary (1689–94)		
1700		
Anne (1702–14)		Newton's *Opticks* (1704)
George I (1714–27)		*Rape of the Lock* (1714)
George II (1727–60)		Johnson's *Dictionary* (1755)
George III (1760–1820)	American Declaration of	
	Independence (1776)	
	First Australian colonies	

Ruler	Historical events	Literary events
1800		
George IV (1820–30)	First passenger railway (1830)	*Pickwick Papers*
William IV (1830–37)		
Victoria (1837–1901)	India under Crown rule (1858)	*New English Dictionary*
	Primary Education Act (1870)	(1884)
	First petrol-driven car (1885)	
1900		
Edward VII (1901–10)	Earliest aircraft (1903)	D. H. Lawrence
	First public radio broadcast (1906)	
George V (1910–37)	First World War (1914–18)	New English Bible
George VI (1937–52)		
Elizabeth II (1952–)		

OLD ENGLISH

(700–1100)

Old English, and Anglo-Saxon, are names used by modern scholars for the written version of a language used in England from the departure of the Romans until some time after the Norman Conquest. Its speakers referred to it as *Englisc*, the language of the Angles, who were the major ethnic group consistently identified among the Germanic settlers of Britain in early sources. These people must have spoken a language closely similar to that used by other Germanic peoples along the North Sea coast from Denmark to the Rhine, but in a period of some seven centuries following the earliest settlement their language underwent major developments. Direct written evidence of these is available only from the last four hundred years of this evolution, and indeed the vast majority of our information about Old English is preserved in manuscripts written in the tenth and eleventh centuries. Apart from the runic alphabet, which had been used in earlier Germanic society for inscriptions on all kinds of objects, from weapons to standing stones, the earliest speakers of English, despite artistic skills evident in archaeological discoveries like those at Sutton Hoo and from Kentish cemeteries, were both pagan and illiterate. The coming of Christianity in AD 597 introduced Latin literacy to England, which was followed by attempts to render the English language in the letters of the Latin alphabet – those which survive to the present day. Old English forms of the Latin letters in the Hiberno-Saxon script were very different from modern printed forms, as can be seen in the case of the <s> and <r> in the facsimile (p. 21), and in addition Old English used some letters no longer found in English: 'eth' <ð> and 'yogh' <ʒ> (the latter is usually printed as <g> in modern editions, but is retained in this book to permit a more valid comparison between the spelling systems of Old and Middle English) were derived from Irish Latin, 'thorn' <þ> and 'wynn' <ƿ> were runes (the latter printed as <w> in modern editions), and the Latin digraph 'ash' <æ>. Thorn and eth are equivalent to <th> in the modern spelling system and indeed <th> is not unknown in early Old English. The letters <v>, <z> and <q> were not normally used in Old English texts, and their roles were filled respectively by <f>, <s> and the digraph <cƿ>. The letter <j> was not used (Scragg 1974: 8).

The scribes who wrote the manuscripts which are our only source of information about Old English lived in various parts of England and wrote a version of the language which they spoke every day. Consequently OE manuscripts, especially from the earlier period, preserve evidence of dialectal variation in the pronunciation and grammar of the language. Modern scholars (Campbell 1969: 1–22; Toon 1992) have distinguished several groupings: West Saxon (the language of King Alfred and England south of the Thames but excluding Kent) is distinct from non-West Saxon, which includes both Kentish and Anglian. Kentish is phonologically separate from the other dialects, and Anglian is in turn divided into Northumbrian (spoken from the Humber to the Forth) and Mercian in the Midlands. No clear evidence survives for the languages of Sussex, Essex or East Anglia, and an unrelated Celtic language, closer to Welsh, was spoken until quite late in the Lake District, the Welsh marches, and the British kingdom of Elmet close to Leeds in the old West Riding of Yorkshire. From the late ninth century, England to the east of Watling Street (the old Roman road from London to Chester) was subject to intense linguistic influence from the settlement of Scandinavian invaders, but this is masked in the documentary record by the political and religious revival of Wessex. After about AD 975, as the result of West Saxon domination of the rest of the country, a degree of standardisation emanating from Winchester is to be found in Old English documents (Gneuss 1972; Hofstetter 1988). This means that the vast majority of surviving Old English literature, which post-dates this standardisation, is written in Late West Saxon. The excerpts in this book illustrate something of both the variety of dialects and the West Saxon standard.

By comparison with Modern English, Old English was written relatively 'phonetically'. Consequently, when reading, each letter in a word is individually sounded, even double consonants (compare the double pronunciation of [k] in the modern compound *book-keeper*) and those occurring in initial consonant clusters, as in <hrinȝ>, <hlaford>, <writan>, <ȝnornian> and <cniht>. Vowels, because of the origins of the spelling system, had a similar value to that in Latin or modern European languages. The digraph <sc> was pronounced as modern <sh>, <cȝ> as the consonantal sounds in *judge*, and <c> in the environment of a front vowel (*æ, e, i, eo, ea*) usually as modern <ch>. Following a front vowel <h> was pronounced very much as the <ch> in German *nicht*, and following a back vowel like the <ch> in Scots *loch*. The <ȝ> (usually written g in modern editions) was pronounced as modern <g>, except initially before most front vowels, where its palatal pronunciation was like modern <y->. In medial or final position, it had the velar value of the <g> in modern German <sagen>.

Like German, Old English possessed a complex inflexional grammar. The Nominal Group exhibited concord (agreement) between the article, modifier, and head, for number, gender and case. There were four cases (nominative, accusative, genitive and dative) and three genders (masculine, feminine and neuter). Traces of dual number and of instrumental case existed in the personal pronouns, and in the definite article and adjectives, respectively. Nouns possessed distinct sets of inflexional endings, by which they can be classified into separate categories as Strong or Weak nouns. In addition, according to the syntactical environment, any adjective could adopt a set of either Indefinite or Definite (Strong or Weak) inflexions. These Definite inflexions were selected when the adjective followed a demonstrative, definite article, or possessive pronoun. The declension of three Strong nouns together with the appropriate forms of the definite article and the Definite form of the adjective, is given here.

Masculine noun ('the long day')

	Singular	*Plural*
Nom.	se lanȝa dæȝ	þā lanȝan daȝas
Acc.	þone lanȝan dæȝ	þā lanȝan daȝas
Gen.	þæs lanȝan dæȝes	þāra lanȝena daȝa
Dat.	þǣm lanȝan dæȝe	þǣm lanȝum daȝum

Neuter noun ('the distant land')

	Singular	*Plural*
Nom.	þæt feorre land	þā feorran land
Acc.	þæt feorre land	þā feorran land
Gen.	þæs feorran landes	þāra feorrena landa
Dat.	þæm feorran lande	þæm feorrum landum

Feminine noun ('the old learning')

	Singular	*Plural*
Nom.	sēo ealde lār	þā ealdan lāra/e
Acc.	þā ealdan lāre	þā ealdan lāra/e
Gen.	þære ealdan lāre	þāra ealdena lāra
Dat.	þære ealdan lāre	þæm ealdum lārum

Similar paradigms for Weak nouns preceded by an Indefinite adjective after the indefinite article (or no article) are these:

Masculine noun ('a bold warrior')

	Singular	*Plural*
Nom.	ān beald wiȝa	bealde wiȝan
Acc.	ānne bealdne wiȝan	bealde wiȝan
Gen.	ānes bealdes wiȝan	bealdra wiȝena
Dat.	ānum bealdum wiȝan	bealdum wiȝum

Neuter noun ('a blind eye')

	Singular	*Plural*
Nom.	ān blind ēaȝe	blind ēaȝan
Acc.	ān blind ēaȝe	blind ēaȝan
Gen.	ānes blindes ēaȝan	blindra ēaȝena
Dat.	ānum blindum ēaȝan	blindum ēaȝum

Feminine noun ('a young lady')

	Singular	*Plural*
Nom.	ān ȝeonȝ hlæfdiȝe	ȝeonȝa/e hlæfdiȝan
Acc.	āne ȝeonȝe hlæfdiȝan	ȝeonȝa/e hlæfdiȝan
Gen.	ānre ȝeonȝre hlæfdiȝan	ȝeonȝra hlæfdiȝena
Dat.	ānre ȝeonȝre hlæfdiȝan	ȝeonȝum hlæfdiȝum.

The Old English personal pronouns were the most fully inflected of all words. Together with the definite article, they often serve to disambiguate the concord of Old English sentences, which may be obscure if interpreted purely in terms of noun and adjective inflexions.

First Person

	Singular	Dual	Plural
Nom.	ic	wit	wē
Acc.	mē	unc	ūs
Gen.	mīn	uncer	ūre
Dat.	mē	unc	ūs

Second Person

	Singular	Dual	Plural
Nom.	þū	ȝit	ȝē
Acc.	þē	inc	ēow
Gen.	þīn	incer	ēower
Dat.	þē	inc	ēow

Third Person Singular

	Masculine	Neuter	Feminine
Nom.	hē	hit	hēo
Acc.	hine	hit	hīe
Gen.	his	his	hi(e)re
Dat.	him	him	hi(e)re

Third Person Plural

All Genders

Nom.	hīe
Acc.	hīe
Gen.	hi(e)ra
Dat.	him

Verbs also fell into Strong or Weak types. The former indicated their preterite tense by a change in the root vowel, the latter by the addition of a dental suffix to the stem, thus *scīnan, scān*, 'shine, shone' and *lufian, lufode,* 'love, loved'. Strong verbs were conjugated according to the following pattern, illustrated by *bindan* 'to bind':

		Present	Preterite
Singular			
	1	ic binde	ic band
	2	þū bindest, bintst	þū bunde
	3	hē bindeþ, bint	hē band
Plural		hīe bindaþ	hīe bundon

The second and third person singular, present tense, has variant contracted forms. The subjunctive simply uses the stem of the infinitive (*bind-*) for the present tense, and the stem of the preterite plural to form the preterite subjunctive. In both cases the inflexional ending is *-e* throughout the singular, and *-en* in the plural. Weak verbs had the same inflexional pattern as Strong verbs, but marked the preterite by the suffix *-ed-*, *-od-* or *-t-* rather than by a change in stem vowel. However, a few Weak verbs, like *secan, sohte* 'seek, sought', do add a vowel change to the use of the suffix. New verbs were formed in historical Old English only on the pattern of the Weak conjugation, joining the Weak Class 2 verbs, which are distinguished by an infinitive in *-ian* rather than *-an* (*lufian* 'to love'), a present participle in *-iende* (*lufiende*) rather than *-ende*, and preterite and past participle forms with *-od-* (*lufode*) rather than *-ed-*. All verbs marked their past participle by the use of a prefix *ȝe-* (*ȝelufod*).

Like other languages, Old English expanded its vocabulary by means of external borrowing. Some of its word-stock can be traced to ancient borrowing from Latin in the centuries before the migration of the Germanic tribes to England: *strǣt* <strata via, 'paved road'; *weall* <vallum, 'stockade'; *wīn* <vinum, 'wine'; *ȝimm* <gemma, 'gem'; *dihte* <dictare, 'to order'; *mynster* <monasterium. Other words derive from the later Latin of the Church and of learning: *ǣstel* 'pointer' (< ?hastula, 'little spear'); *fers* <versus, 'verse-line'; *stǣr* <Irish *stoir* from Latin *historia* (Kastovsky 1992: 301–9). More important than its borrowing, Old English, like German, made much use of compounding and derivation in the creation of new wordforms. Thus the word *ealdorbiscop*, literally 'chief-bishop', is used by the translator of Bede's *Ecclesiastical History* to render the Latin *primus pontificum*, and Ælfric uses the form *leorningcniht*, 'learning-servant/boy', for 'disciple', and *hēahfæder*,

literally 'high-father', for 'patriarch'. Full use was also made of derivational affixes, so that the Latin *trinitas* is rendered *þrȳnes, ascensio, ūpāstiȝnes*, and *incarnatio, menniscnes* (literally, 'man + ish + ness').

Anglo-Saxon literature, which flourished largely under religious auspices but which still preserved a strong interest in heroic values, made fullest use of creative compounding. Poetic compounds for 'sea' include *swanrād*, 'swanroad', *hwælweȝ*, 'whaleway', and *hwælrād*, 'whaleroad' as well as the quasi-compounds *yða fūl*, 'cup of the waves' and *ȝanetes bæð*, 'gannet's bath'. Metaphoric and metonymic expressions, which congregate around certain familiar themes of Old English poetry, such as seafaring, warfare and weapons, are matched by groups of synonyms related to the same themes. Thus the words *beorn, scealc, freca, ȝuma, wiȝa, hæleþ, eorl, ȝar-berend, hyse*, and *rinc* may all be translated as 'warrior'. Groups of synonyms and ready compounding could function together to suggest fresh compounds; thus the unparalleled *wælfeld*, 'slaughter-field, battle field', in *Brunanburh* must have been suggested by one of the seventy or so other compounds with the same first element, probably by its synonym, *wælstōw*. In poetry, compounds are often formed for connotational rather than denotational effect; thus compounds with *morȝen*, 'morning', and with *ceald*, 'cold', tend to carry connotations of doom only loosely connected with their everyday meanings (Salmon 1959), and both *eald*, 'old', and *ær*, 'before', may have strongly approbatory associations, so that *ærȝōd* (literally, 'before good') may be translated 'excellent' (Stanley 1955). Both groups of synonyms and lexical creativity were encouraged by the nature of the verse, which consisted of two half-lines (a and b) connected by an alliterative pattern.

Frequently, the meaning of a word or phrase in the first pair of half-lines would be summed up in variant wording by a half of the succeeding line. Both the existence of a stock of synonyms commencing with different letters, and the possibility of creating new ones by compounding and derivation are obviously of great convenience to this feature of the discourse structure of Old English verse.

> Ðā þær Byrhtnoð onȝan   beornas trymian,
> rād and rædde,   rincum tæhte.

> Then Byrhtnoth began to draw up the warriors there, rode about and instructed, directed the warriors.

Approximately 30,000 lines of verse are still extant, but this quantity is greatly exceeded by extant prose. This includes legal and administrative texts such as charters, wills, writs and codes of law, religious writings such as sermons and devotional works – both translated from the Latin and original – histories and annals, and works intended to be of a practical instructional nature in secular as well as religious matters. The excerpts included in this collection can give no more than a taste of the richness which survives.

1

DIALECT TEXTS

These three texts are included in order to give more advanced students the opportunity to investigate something of the regional variety of the language preserved in Old English sources. They are also illustrative of the origins of later linguistic developments. The Lindisfarne Gospel gloss in particular demonstrates inflectional changes associated with Middle English already in progress; the Vespasian Psalter gloss and the brief Kentish document demonstrate continuity within dialects, showing affinities in the first case with the language of the Middle English *Ancrene Wisse*, and in the second with south-eastern Middle English texts, notably the *Ayenbite of Inwit*, and in this book, with the Kentish Sermon (Excerpt 12).

Dictionaries were uncommon in an age when books had to be copied by hand, and English–Latin dictionaries of any size were not available until the fifteenth century. Consequently, readers tended to ease the demands made upon their linguistic competence by inserting the English equivalents above the Latin words of the text. This practice is called 'glossing' (< Lat. *glosa*; cf. *OED gloze*), a word whose semantic development is instructive. In the following excerpts, for convenience, the relative positions of Latin texts and Anglo-Saxon glosses have been reversed.

A   The Vespasian Psalter gloss

The Vespasian Psalter (British Library MS Cotton Vespasian A. I) contains the psalms in a Latin version (known as the Roman version) which preceded Jerome's Vulgate Bible, nine canticles and three hymns, as well as prayers and some liturgical material. It is a luxury work produced on good-quality vellum with considerable richness of decoration. Whoever ordered its production intended it for the altar or cathedral treasury rather than the library, but exact details of its origin are unknown. Its modern history begins with a reference by Matthew Parker in 1566 and its acquisition by Sir Robert Cotton in 1599. Beyond this, there has been some scholarly controversy, but an early fifteenth-century account of its treasures by a monk of the abbey of St Augustine's, Canterbury, contains the description of a book alleged to have been brought by St Augustine, which has been identified as the Vespasian Psalter. The current consensus is that the Latin manuscript was produced in Canterbury in the first half of the eighth century. At some time in the ninth century, when Mercia held sway in England, an English interlinear gloss was added to the Latin text of the original, not apparently by a local man but by someone who had received training in a Mercian scriptorium, and so wrote consistently in a Mercian dialect. Parallels with the language of the ME *Ancrene Wisse* are taken to suggest a West Mercian origin.

Excerpt (i) is the apocryphal Psalm 151, added in the MS as an afterthought to the original total; excerpt (ii) is one of the nine canticles.

These excerpts share with the Lindisfarne Gospel gloss many features common to Anglian texts, for example: the failure of breaking before *l*-groups (*befalden, swalwan, alle*); smoothing of diphthongs before sounds written *c, g* or *h*, either alone or with *r* or *l* intervening (*betwih, smēʒu, ēʒan*); the writing of the *i*-mutation of *ō* as *ōē* (*foedde*) and -*ad* rather than -*od* in the past participles of Weak Class 2 verbs (*welʒelīcad, gehefeldad*). Some features, however, are more characteristic of Mercian alone, for example: forms lacking diphthongisation by preceding palatal consonants (*scēp, ʒēra*), and above all the Mercian 'second fronting' of short *æ* to *e* and short *a* to *æ* (the preceding two and *wes, seʒde, cweð, daeʒa*).

(i)

Pusillus eram inter frater meos et adolescentior
Lȳtel ic wes betwih brōður mīne ond iu[n]ʒra

in domo patris mei pascebam oves patris mei manus meae
in hūse feadur mīnes ic fōēdde scēp feadur mīnes. Honda mīne

fecerunt organum; digiti mei aptaverunt psalterium et
dydun orʒanan; finʒras mīne wysctun hearpan. Ond

quis adnuntiavit Domino meo? ipse Dominus, ipse omnium
hwelc seʒde Dryhtne mīnum? Hē Dryhten, hē allra

exaudivit me; ipse misit angelum suum, et tulit me de ovibus

5 ᵹehērde mec; hē sende enᵹel his, ond nōm mec of scēpum

patris mei et unxit me in misericordia unctionis

feadur mīnes, ond smirede mec mildheartnisse smirenisse

suae fratres mei boni et magni, et non fuit beneplacitum in

his brōður mīne ᵹōde ond micle, ond ne wes welᵹelīcad in

eis Domino. exivi obviam alienigenae, et

him Dryhtne. Ic ūtēode onᵹeᵹn fremðes cynnes men, ond

maledixit me in simulacris suis; ego autem

werᵹcweodelade mec in herᵹum heara; ic sōðlīce

evaginato ab eo ipsius gladio amputavi caput ejus,

10 ᵹebroᵹdnum from him his āᵹnum sweorde ic ācearf hēafud his

et abstuli obprobrium de filiis Israhel.

ond onweᵹ āfirde edwīt of bearnum Israēla.

(ii)

Ego dixi in dimedio dierum meorum: vadam ad portas

Ic cweð in midum daeᵹa mīnra: ic fearu tō ᵹete

inferi quaesivi residuum annorum meorum; dixi: non videbo

helle. Ic sōhte lāfe ᵹēra mīnra; ic cweð: ic ne ᵹesīo

Dominum Deum in terra viventium non aspiciam hominem ultra

Dryhten ᵹod in eorðan lifᵹendra. Ne ᵹelōciu ic mon māē

et habitatorem quievit generatio mea; ablata est, et

15 ond eardiend. ᵹestilde cnēoris mīn; wilāēded is, ond

convoluta est a me quasi tabernaculum pastorum praecisa

befalden is from mē swē swē ᵹeteld heorda. Forcorfen

est velut a texente vita mea; dum adhuc

is swē swē from ðǣm weofendan līf mīn; mit te nū ᵹēt

ordirer succidit me de mane usque ad vesperam finies

ᵹehefeldad ācearf mec. Of marne oð ēfen ᵹeendas

me; a vespere usque ad mane quasi leo sic contrivit

mec; from ēfenne oð marᵹen swē swē lēa swē forðrǣste

omnia ossa mea; de mane usque ad vesperam finies me sicut

20 all bān mīn; of marne ot ēfen ᵹeendas mec. Swē swē

pullus hirundinis sic clamabo; meditabor ut columba

brid swalwan swē ic cleopiu; ic smēᵹu swē swē culfre.

adtenuati sunt oculi mei aspicientes in excelso Domine, vim
ȝeðynnade sind ēȝan mīn ȝelōcende in heanis. Dryhten, nēd

patior; responde pro me, quid dicam aut quid
ic ðrōwiu ondsweora fore mē hwet ic cweðe oððe hwet

respondebit mihi quod ipse fecerim recogitabo omnes annos
ondsweorað mē ðæt ic seo[l]fa dōa. Ic ðencu all ȝēr

meos in amaritudine animae meae. Domine, si sic vivitur,
25   mīn in bitternisse sāwle mīnre. Dryhten, ȝif swē bið lifd,

aut in talibus vita spiritus mei, corripies me, et
oððe in weolerum līf ȝāstes mīnes, ȝeðrēas mec, ond

vivicabis me. ecce in pace amaritudo mea amarissima;
ȝelīffestes me. Sehðe, in sibbe bitternis mīn sīe bittreste;

tu autem eruisti animam meam, ut non perirem et
ðū sōðlīce ȝeneredes sāwle mīne, ðet ic ne forwurde. Ond

projectisti post tergum tuum omnia peccata mea, quia
āwurpe on bec ðinne alle synne mīne, forðon

non infernus confitebitur tibi, neque mors laudabit te.
30   nāles hel ondetteð ðē, ne dēað hereð ðec.

non expectabunt qui descendunt in lacum veritatem tuam;
Ne bīdað ðā ofdūne steoȝun in sēað sōðfestnisse ðīne;

vivens vivens ipse confitebitur tibi, sicut et ego hodie.
lifȝende, lifȝende hē onddetteð ðē, swē ond ic tō deȝe.

pater filiis notam faciet veritatem tuam. Domine salvos
Feder bearnum cūðe dōð sōðfestnisse ðīne. Dryhten, hāle

nos fac; et psalmus nostros cantabimus cunctis diebus vitae
ūs dōa; ond salmas ūre wē sinȝað allum deȝum līfes

nostrae in domo Domini.
35   ūres in hūse Dryhtnes.

Notes

6   **smirede mec** 'anointed me'   The verb (WS *smierwan*) exhibits the
lack of breaking characteristic of Anglian texts (also *āfirde* in line 11).
The pronoun form (WS *mē*) is characteristically Anglian and archaic, but
is found in WS verse and inscriptions such as that on the Alfred Jewel,
which reads 'Ælfred mec hēht ȝewyrcan'.

9   **werȝcweodelade** 'cursed' (WS *wearȝcwedolian*)   Anglian dialectal
features are evident in almost every syllable. *Werȝ-*, like *herȝum* in the

same line, shows Anglian smoothing of the diphthong *ea*. The preterite formed with *-ad* rather than *-od* is characteristic of Anglian Weak Class 2 Verbs. The form *cweodel* has a diphthong derived from the back mutation of *e* by an earlier back vowel in the second syllable. Back mutation of *e* occurred in West Saxon only when labial or lateral consonants intervened. The asterisk before the WS form cited indicates that it is a reconstructed form which has not actually been recorded in texts.

heara (WS *hiera*)   A form created by analogy with the second-fronted, then back-mutated, demonstrative form *þeara*, also found in the Vespasian Psalter. Compare the *ha* forms of the plural pronoun in the *Ancrene Wisse*.

12   **dæȝa** (WS *daȝa*)   Second fronting of short *æ* to *e* and of short *a* to *æ* is a phenomenon peculiar among the Anglian dialects to the language of the Vespasian Psalter gloss. It is called 'second' by counting the similar development of Germanic short *a* to OE short *æ* as the first example of such fronting. It did not take place before *l*. Other examples are: *cweð* (12); *hwet* (23); *bec* (29). The forms *ȝete* (WS *ȝeate*) and *ȝēr* (WS *ȝēar*, lines 12, 13) are derived from the second fronting of an *æ* surviving as *æ* rather than *ea* by the lack of diphthongisation by the preceding palatal *g*, which is characteristic of the Mercian dialect.

14   **ȝelōciu ic**   The first-person present tense form of the Weak Class 2 verb *ȝelōcian*. The *-u* inflexional ending is characteristic of earlier Anglian texts.

21   **ic cleopiu**   A back-mutated form with the Anglian *-u* ending. Notice the use of the present tense to render the Latin future, as also *ic ðencu* (24) and *hereð* (30).

34   **deȝum**   The expected form would be *dæȝum*, with second fronting of the *a* restored before back vowels in all dialects. This form must be an analogical development from the regular singular *deȝ*.

B   The Lindisfarne Gospel gloss

With the possible exception of the Bewcastle Cross, the Lindisfarne Gospels (BL Cotton Nero D. IV) are the most imposing physical monument of pre-Conquest Northumbrian culture. A tenth-century note on folio 259 records that the book was written by Eadfrith, bishop of Lindisfarne from 698 to 721. Since the monastery of Lindisfarne had been founded by Aidan, a member of the Celtic Church, the manuscript shows many points of contact with the Irish artistic tradition. In its decoration and writing it closely resembles the Irish Book of Kells, but there are also similarities in effect between its carpet-like decoration and the Anglo-Saxon garnet and gold jewellery from Sutton Hoo.

The monastery on Lindisfarne was vulnerable to attack from the sea, and in 875 the monks were forced to desert their home under the pressure of Danish raids. They carried with them the relics of St Cuthbert, and their famous Gospels. From 883 until their settlement in Durham in 995 the Lindisfarne community lived in Chester-le-Street, a few miles away, and it was probably here that Aldred, one of their number, inserted an interlinear English gloss above the Latin text. This gloss furnishes one of the most important sources extant for the study of the Northumbrian dialect of Old English.

This late Northumbrian text already exhibits significant divergence in its inflexional system from the more familiar WS forms. Loss of final -*n* is common in verb infinitives (*efneȝlǣda, sealla, dōa*) (see Early Middle English, p. 66) and Weak adjectives (*seista*), and the second-person-singular and third-person-singular and plural of present-tense verbs is frequently written -*es* or -*as* (*stondes ȝē; ðū efnes; hēa ȝebiddas; hē wōenas*). Other characteristically Northumbrian features are: <a> written before *r* where WS has <ea> (*arð*); confusion of *ea* and *eo* (*feolo, ȝeade*); frequent use of -*o* to represent a final unstressed vowel (*oðero, idlo, willo*); and the writing of <oe> where WS had *e* by *i*-mutation of *o* (*fōerde, cuoeð, ȝedōēmendo*) and between *w* and *r* (*woercmenn*).

(i)

Simile est enim regnum caelorum homini patrifamilias
ȝelīc is forðon rīc heofna ðǣm menn fador hīerodes

qui exiit primo mane conducere operarios in
sē ðe fōerde ǣrist *vel* ār in merne efneȝlǣda ðā woercmenn in

vineam suam. Conventione autem facta cum
wīnȝeard his. ȝesomnunȝ uutetlice ȝewearð mið ðǣm

operariis ex denario diurno misit
wyrcendum *vel* woercmonnum of penninȝ dæȝhuæmlīce, sende

eos in vineam. Et egressus circa horam tertiam vidit alios
5   his in wīnȝeard. And ȝefōerde ymb tīd ðȳ ðirdda ȝesæh ōðero

stantes in foro otiosus. Et illis dixit:
standende in sprēc *vel* in ðinȝstōw idlo. And ðǣm cueð:

Ite et vos in vineam et quod iustum fuerit dabo vobis.
ȝāað and ȝīe in wīnȝeard and þætte reht bið ic selo īuh.

Ille autem abierunt. Iterum autem exiit circa sextam
Ðā uutetlice ӡeēodon. Eftsōna sōðlīce ӡeēode ymb ðā seista

et nonam horam et fecit similiter. Circa undecimam vero
and nōn tīd and dyde ӡelīc. Ymb ðā ellefta ēc

exiit et invenit alios stantes et dicit illis: Quid
10 ӡeēade and ӡemōette ōðero stondende and cuoeð him: Hwæt

hic statis tota die otiosi. Dicunt ei: Quia nemo
hēr stondes ӡē allen dæӡe idlo. Cuōedun him: forðon næniӡ

nos conduxit. Dicit illis: Ite et vos in vineam.
monn ūsiӡ efne ӡelæde. Cuoeð him: Ӡāað and ӡīe in wīnӡeard.

Cum sero autem factum esset dicit
Mið ðȳ efern *vel* ic sædi uutetlice ӡeworden wēre cuoeð

dominus vineae procuratori suo: Voca operarios et
hlāfard ðære wīnӡearde ӡirōefæ his: Cēiӡ ðā wercmenn and

redde illis mercedem incipiens a novissimis usque ad
15 ӡeld him meard onӡann from ðæm lætmēstum wið ðæm

primos. Cum venissent ergo qui circa undecimam
forðmēstum. Mið ðȳ ӡecuōmun uutetlice ðā ðe ymb ðā ællefta

horam venerant acceperunt singulos denarios. Venientes
tīd ӡecuōmon onfenӡon suindriӡo penninӡas. Cymende

autem et primi arbitrati sunt quod plus essent
uutetlice and forðmēsto ӡedōēmendo wēron þæt forðor wēron

accepturi acceperunt autem et ipsi singulos
onfenӡendo onfenӡon uutetlice *vel* ēc and ðā ilco syndriӡe

denarios et accipientes murmurabant
20 penninӡas and mið ðȳ ӡefenӡon hīa huæstredon *vel* deӡlice

adversus patremfamilias dicentes: Hi novissimi
yfle sprēcon wið ðæm hīorodes cuoðendo: ðās hlætmēsto

una hora fecerunt et pares
ān tīd *vel* huīl dydon *vel* worohton and ðū efnes *vel* ӡelīco

illos nobis fecisti qui portavimus pondus
ðā ūs ðū dydest wē ðā ðe bēron hefeӡnise *vel* byrðen

diei et aestus. At ille respondens uni eorum
ðæs ðæӡes and hæto *vel* byrn. Sōð hē onduearde ānum hiora

dixit: Amice non facio tibi injuriam
25 cueð: Lā frēond *vel* lā mēӡ ne dōm ic ðē laæðo *vel*

nonne ex denario convenisti mecum. tolle quod
baeliȝniso āhne for penniȝ ðū cuōme mec mið. Nim þætte

tuum est et vade volo autem et huic
ðīn is and ȝāa *vel* ȝeonȝ. Ic willo uutetlice and ðissum

novissimo dare sicut et tibi. aut non licet mihi quod
hlætmēsto sealla swā and ðē; *vel* ne is rehtlīc mē þæt

volo facere an oculus tuus nequam est quia ego bonus
ic willo dōa *vel* ēȝo ðin wōhȝfull is forðon ic ȝōd

sum. Sic erunt novissimi primi et primi
am. Suǣ bīðon ðā hlætmēsto forðmēst and ðā forðmēst

novissimi. multi sunt enim vocati pauci autem electi.
hlætmēst. Moniȝe sint forðon ȝecēiȝdo lythwon uutetlice ȝecoren

(ii)

Orantes autem nolite
Hēa ȝebiddas *vel* ðon ȝīe ȝebiddas uutetlice nalles ȝē

multum loqui sicut ethnici faciunt putant
feolo *vel* moniȝful ȝesprēca suǣ esuico dōas; hē wōenas

enim quod in multiloquio suo exaudiantur.
forðon ðā ðe in moniȝfald sprēc his bīðon ȝehēred.

Nolite ergo assimilari eis scit enim Pater vester
Nallas ȝē ðonne wosa ȝelīc him wāt forðon fader īurre

quibus opus sit vobis ante quam petatis eum.
of ðǣm ðearf sīe *vel* is īuh ǣr ðon ȝīe bidde hine.

Sic ergo vos orabitis:
Suē ðonne īuih ȝīe bidde:

Pater noster qui es in caelis
fader ūsær ðū arð *vel* ðū bist in heofnum *vel* in

sanctificetur nomen tuum. Adveniat regnum tuum.
heofnas, sīe ȝehālȝad noma ðīn. Tōcȳmeð rīc ðīn.

Fiat voluntas tua sicut in caelo et in terra. Panem
Sīe willo ðīn suǣ is in heofne and in eorðo. Hlāf

nostrum super substantiale da nobis hodie. Et demitte
ūserne ofer pīstlic sel ūs todæȝ, and forȝef

nobis debita nostra sicut nos dimittimus debitoribus
ūs scylda ūsra, suǣ uōe forȝefon scyldȝum

nostris. Et ne inducas nos in temtationem. Sed libera nos a malo.
ūsum. And ne inlǣd ūsih in costunȝe, ah ȝefrīȝ ūsich from yfle.

si enim dimiseritis hominibus peccarta eorum
ȝif forðon ȝīe forȝēafas monnum synna hiara,

dimittet et vobis Pater vester caelestis delicata vestra.
45 forȝefes and oc īuh fader īuer heofonlic synna īuerra.

Si autem non dimiseritis hominibus nec Pater
ȝif sōðlice ȝīe nalles forȝeafa monnum, ne fader

vester dimittet peccata vestra.
īuerre forȝefes synna īuerre.

Notes

2 **in merne** (WS *in morȝne*) This late form exhibits *i*- mutation of *o* and simplification of the following consonant group.

5 **ȝesǣh** (WS *ȝesēah*) An example of Anglian smoothing.

6 **sprēc** (WS *sprǣc*) WS *ǣ*[1] is represented in Anglian texts by *e*.
 in ðinȝstow Final *-e* is omitted in this dative form.

7 **þætte** A contracted form of the relative *þæt þe*.
 ic selo The present tense form is used to render a Latin future, as is usual in OE.

11 **allen dæȝe** (WS *eallum dæȝe*) The Northumbrian spelling suggests uncertainty in the form of the inflection.

14 **hlāfard ðǣre wīnȝearde ȝirōefǣ his** This phrase is a good example of the inflectional confusion already apparent in tenth-century Northumbrian. A WS version would read *hlāford ðæs wīnȝeardes ȝerēfan his*, 'the lord of the vineyard to his reeve'. Here *wīnȝeard* is a Strong and *ȝerēfa* a Weak masculine noun. In this text, *wīnȝeard* seems to be considered Strong feminine, and *ȝerēfa*, having lost its final *-n*, is treated as though it were also a Strong noun. Final *-æ* is found in inflections in early Northumbrian texts, but here probably represents orthographical confusion between *æ* and *e*.

20 **hīa** Northumbrian form of the WS *hīe*, 'they'. As also *hēa* (32).

34 **bīðon** (WS *beōð – bið* sing.) The Northumbrian plural is evidently formed by analogy with the plural *sindon* of the verb *wesan*.

35 **wosa** (WS *wesan*) This form, with back mutation by *a* and rounding after *w*, is characteristically Northumbrian.

38 **ūsær** (WS *ūre*) The Northumbrian form is restricted to verse in WS. Other characteristically Northumbrian personal pronoun forms are *ūsih/ūsich* (43/43) and *īuh* (7). The form *mec* (26) is used more widely in Anglian texts, but is restricted to verse in WS.

in heofnum *vel* **in heofnas**   The glossator offers a choice of dative or accusative forms to render the Latin ablative.

45   **oc**   The use of *oc*, apparently without the sense 'but', and simply as an additive conjunction, is extremely rare in OE and may imply the influence of Scandinavian *ok*.

C A Kentish Charter

The kingdom of Kent was distinct from the rest of England in customs, laws, and settlement history, and was probably distinct also in dialect, but lost its political independence early, falling successively under the control of Mercian and then West Saxon overlords. Canterbury, as the premier see, was most directly affected, and documents from Canterbury often exhibit dialectal influence from these external sources. The number of documents with an arguably unmixed Kentish dialect is rather restricted within the Old English period. The excerpt below has been chosen because it illustrates fairly profusely, and at an early date, some of the features which south-eastern Middle English texts associate with Kent. By the tenth century, as the result of local sound changes, the vowel inventory of Kentish had been reduced to a system with only two front vowels: *i*, and *e*. This is illustrated here by the representation of WS *ǣ*² by *ē* (*ðēm*, *ēlce*) and of short WS *æ* by *e* (*dei*, *et*, *hwet*, *hebbe*, *elmesse*, *ðet*). There is evidence, too, of the raising of the first element and unrounding of the second element of the diphthongs *ēo*, *eo* (here spelt <ia> in *bebīade*, *sīa*, *fiah*), which results in later Old Kentish in the merger of the long diphthongs *īo* and *ēo* as *īo*, and the short diphthongs *io* and *eo* as *eo*. Note that, unlike the Vespasian Psalter, *æ* before *l*-groups is here subject to breaking: *eald*, *healde*, *ealra*.

Although loosely described as a charter, the following document, extant in BL MS Cotton Augustus ii. 52, is rather a list of rents bestowed upon the monastery of Christ Church, Canterbury. It dates from the middle of the ninth century.

Ðis sindan ȝeðinȝa Ealhburȝe and Ēadwealdes et ðēm lande et Burnan, hwet man ēlce ȝēre ob ðēm lande tō Crīstes cirican ðēm hīwum āȝiaban scel, for Ealhburȝe and for Ealdred and fore Ēadweald and Ealawynne: xl ambra mealtes and xl and cc hlāba,

5   i wēȝe cēsa, i wēȝe speces, i eald hrīðer, iiii weðras, x ȝōes, xx

henfuȝla, iiii fōðra weada. And ic Ealhburȝ bebīade Ēadwealde
mīnem mēȝe an ȝodes naman and an ealra his hāliȝra ðet hē ðis
wel healde his dei and siððan forð bebēode his erbum tō healdenne
ðā hwīle ðe hit crīsten sē.

And suelc mon sē ðet lond hebbe ēȝhwylce Sunnandeȝe xx
ȝesuflra hlāfa to ðāre cirican for Ealdredes sāule and for Eahlburȝe.

Ðis is sīa elmesse ðe Ealhhere bebēad Ealawynne his dōēhter et
Ðenȝleshām, et iii sulunȝum: ēlce ȝēre c peninȝa tō Crīstes cirican
ðēm hīȝum. And suelc man sē ðisses landes brūce, āȝebe ðis fiah
an ȝodes ȝewitnesse and an ealra his hāliȝra, and suilc man suē hit
āwēȝe, ðonne sē hit on his sāwale, nas on ðes ðe hit dōn hēt.

Notes

2   **ob** 'from' (WS *of*).   <b> spellings where <f> would be more familiar
are not infrequent in early OE. Their early phonetic significance is uncertain, perhaps representing the voiced allophone [v], but possibly instead
a bilabial pronunciation. Here, and in other later Kentish documentary
material, they represent the survival of archaic spelling practice (*āȝīaban*;
hlāba, beside *hlāfa*; *erbum*).

3   **scel** 'shall' (WS *sceal*).   This form represents the Kentish raising of *æ*
to *e*. The *æ* had not been diphthongised because Kentish did not experience the diphthongisation by the preceding palatal consonant *sc* which is
found in West Saxon and Northumbrian.

5   **ȝōēs** 'geese' (WS *ȝēs*).   The *i*-mutation of *o*, *ō* has not yet been fully
unrounded to *ē* (also *dōēhter*).

6   **weada** 'of wood'.   Apparently an inverted spelling for *io*. (Campbell
1969: §297)

8   **dei** 'day' (WS *dæȝ*).   Compare *Sunnandeȝe*. Probably evidence of the
vocalisation of ȝ to produce a new diphthong *ei*. As also *hiȝum* and *hiwum*,
producing the new diphthong *iu*. These diphthongisation processes were
completed in early Middle English.

9   **sē** 'may be' (WS *sīe*).   An extremely rare form. The usual form of the
singular present subjunctive of *bēon* in Kentish is *sīo* or *sēo*.

2

ALFRED'S PREFACE TO THE

PASTORAL CARE

King Alfred the Great succeeded to the throne of Wessex at a time of acute danger from Danish invasion, but by a combination of military tactics and diplomacy related in the *Anglo-Saxon Chronicle* and Asser's *Life of Alfred*, he succeeded in making his kingdom sufficiently secure to devote time during his last decade to his own education and that of his people. He himself learned to read at the age of thirty-eight, and, with the aid of scholars assembled from both home and abroad, he sought to make available in English those Latin texts which he judged to be of greatest educational advantage. Six major Latin works were translated into English in the course of this educational initiative, including Bede's *Ecclesiastical History of the English People* and Boethius's *Consolation of Philosophy*, later translated also by Chaucer and Queen Elizabeth I.

The *Cura Pastoralis* of Gregory the Great, a work of guidance for holders of ecclesiastical office, was one of those books which King Alfred judged it 'most necessary' for the clergy of his kingdom to know. It had the additional attraction that its author had been the pope who had, in 597, sent St Augustine to bring Christianity to England. At the beginning of his translation Alfred placed a prefatory letter in which he explains the circumstances in which his decision was made and canvasses the collaboration of the reader in his educational plans. There is general agreement that this preface represents Alfred's own composition.

The translation of the *Pastoral Care* was produced in multiple copies for distribution to the various dioceses, and survives today in half a dozen manuscripts, two of which date from the king's lifetime. The excerpt is based on the better preserved of these, Bodleian Library Hatton 20, a manuscript which Alfred sent to his old friend Bishop Wærferð of Worcester. That it remained in Worcester after the Anglo-Saxon period is proved by the early thirteenth-century glosses, largely in Latin, added by a Worcester

Plate 1 *Cura Pastoralis* (Bodleian Library MS Hatton 20, fol. 1v)

scribe whose work is recognisable by his characteristically tremulous hand-writing. The manuscript was introduced to scholarship by Joscelyn and Parker in the late sixteenth century.

This excerpt represents the West Saxon language of the last decade of the ninth century: Early West Saxon of the kind found also in the Parker

MS of the *Anglo-Saxon Chronicle* from its beginning until the entry for 924. The most striking indicator of the early state of the language in this text is its use of <io> alongside <eo> spellings and its full and correct use of grammatical inflexions.

The facsimile illustrates the opening page of the text, with the direction to Worcester written in insular half-uncials at the head. Half-uncials are a display script derived on the Continent from the uncial script (cf. Latin *uncia*, 'an inch') favoured for legal and schoolbooks. The main text is a rather untidy Hiberno-Saxon script, whose character set, although based on the Latin alphabet, has been adapted for use in England. Note the use of long *s*, and of long *r* and long *f*, as well as the rune 'wynn' for *w* in *Wærferð*. The Irish Latin form of *g* <ȝ> (yogh) is used and the derivation of <ð> 'eth' from insular *d* is apparent. The digraph *æ* is also used. Capitalisation is not used for punctuation purposes except for capital short *s* forms to commence clauses. Nevertheless, a fairly complex punctuation system marks three degrees of pause between clauses. There are no abbreviations except for the use of the Tironian sign for 'and', and an acute accent is sometimes used (especially over the vowel in *on*) perhaps to indicate that the pronunciation should receive some degree of stress. In line 4, the form *woruld* originally lacked its *d*, and was marked for correction by a triangle of three dots. The word *furðum* in lines 16 and 18 has the Latin gloss *etiam* added in the tremulous hand of the thirteenth-century Worcester annotator.

> Ælfred kyninȝ hāteð ȝrētan Wærferð biscep his wordum luflīce
> ond frēondlīce; ond ðē cȳðan hāte ðæt mē cōm swīðe oft on ȝemynd,
> hwelce wiotan iū wæron ȝiond Anȝelcynn, ǣȝðer ȝe ȝodcundra
> hāda ȝe woruldcundra; ond hū ȝesæliȝlica tīda ðā wæron ȝiond
> Anȝelcynn; ond hū ðā kyninȝas ðe ðone onwald hæfdon ðæs folces
> 5   ȝode ond his ærendwrecum hīersumedon; ond hīe ǣȝðer ȝe hiora
> sibbe ȝe hiora siodu ȝe hiora onweald innanbordes ȝehīoldon,
> ond ēac ūt hiora ēðel rȳmdon; ond hū him ðā spēow ǣȝðer ȝe mid
> wīȝe ȝe mid wīsdome; ond ēac ðā ȝodcundan hādas, hū ȝiorne
> 10   hīe wæron ǣȝðer ȝe ymb lāre ȝe ymb liornunȝa, ȝe ymb ealle ðā
> ðīowotdōmas ðe hīe ȝode dōn scoldon; ond hū man ūtanbordes
> wīsdōm ond lāre hieder on lond sōhte; ond hū wē hīe nū sceoldon
> ūte beȝietan, ȝif wē hīe habban sceoldon. Swǣ clæne hīo wæs
> oðfeallenu on Anȝelcynne ðæt swīðe fēawa wæron behionan
> 15   Humbre ðe hiora ðēninȝa cūðen understondan on Enȝlisc oððe

King Alfred sends in cordial and amicable terms greeting to his
bishop Wærferð; and I cause you to know that it often comes into
my mind what learned men there once were throughout England,
both religious and laymen; and how blessed times there were then
throughout England; and how the kings who had rule over the
people obeyed God and his messengers; and how they maintained
both their peace, morality and control within, and also expanded
their realm externally; and how they were successful then in both
war and counsel; and also the religious orders, how zealous they
were in both teaching and learning, and concerning all the services
that they had to render to God; and how from abroad people came
here into this land seeking wisdom and instruction, and how we
now have to get them from abroad, if we must have them. So completely was learning fallen away in England that there were very
few on this side of the Humber who could understand their divine

furðum ān ærendʒewrit of Lǣdene on Enʒlisc āreccean; ond ic
wēne ðætte nōht moniʒe beʒiondan Humbre nǣren. Swǣ fēawa
hiora wǣron ðæt ic furðum ānne ānlēpne ne mæʒ ʒeðencean be
sūðan Temese ðā ðā ic tō rīce fēnʒ. ʒode ælmihteʒum sīe ðonc
ðætte wē nū æniʒne onstal habbað lārēowa. Ond for ðon ic ðē
bebīode ðæt ðū dō swǣ ic ʒelīefe ðæt ðū wille, ðæt ðū ðē ðissa
woruldðinʒa tō ðǣm ʒeǣmetiʒe, swǣ ðū oftost mæʒe, ðæt ðū ðone
wīsdōm ðe ðē ʒod sealde ðǣr ðǣr ðū hiene befæstan mæʒe, befǣste.
ʒeðenc hwelc wītu ūs ðā becōmon for ðisse worulde, ðā ðā wē hit
nōhwæðer ne selfe ne lufodon, ne ēac ōðrum monnum ne lēfdon;
ðone naman ænne wē lufodon ðætte wē Crīstne wǣren, ond swīðe
fēawa ðā ðēawas.

Ðā ic ðā ðis eall ʒemunde, ðā ʒemunde ic ēac hū ic ʒeseah, ǣr
ðǣm ðe hit eall forherʒod wǣre ond forbærned, hū ðā ciricean
ʒiond eall Anʒelcynn stōdon māðma ond bōca ʒefylda, ond ēac
micel menʒeo ʒodes ðīowa; ond ðā swīðe lȳtle fiorme ðāra bōca
wiston, for ðǣm ðe hīe hiora nānwuht onziotan ne meahton for
ðǣm ðe hīe nǣron on hiora āʒen ʒeðīode āwritene. Swelce hīe
cwǣden: 'Ure ieldran, ðā ðe ðās stōwa ǣr hīoldon, hīe lufodon
wīsdōm, ond ðurh ðone hīe beʒēaton welan ond ūs lǣfdon.
Hēr mon mæʒ ʒīet ʒesīon hiora swæð, ac wē him ne cunnon æfter
spyriʒean. Ond for ðǣm wē habbað nū ǣʒðer forlǣten ʒe ðone
welan ʒe ðone wīsdōm, for ðǣm ðe wē noldon tō ðǣm spore mid
ūre mōde onlūtan'.

Ðā ic ðā ðis eall ʒemunde, ðā wundrade ic swīðe swīðe ðāra
ʒōdena wiotena ðe ʒiū wǣron ʒiond Anʒelcynn, ond ðā bēc ealla
be fullan ʒeliornod hæfdon, ðæt hīe hiora ðā nænne dǣl noldon
on hiora āʒen ʒeðīode wendan. Ac ic ðā sōna eft mē selfum
andwyrde, ond cwæð: 'Hīe ne wēndon ðætte ǣfre menn sceolden
swǣ reccelēase weorðan ond sīo lār swǣ oðfeallan: for ðǣre
wilnunʒa hīe hit forlēton, ond woldon ðæt hēr ðȳ māra wīsdōm
on londe wǣre ðȳ wē mā ʒeðēoda cūðon'.

Ðā ʒemunde ic hū sīo ǣ wæs ǣrest on Ebriscʒeðīode funden,
ond eft, ðā hīe Crēacas ʒeliornodon, ðā wendon hīe hīe on heora
āʒen ʒeðīode ealle, ond ēac ealle ōðre bēc. Ond eft Lǣdenware swǣ
same, siððan hīe hīe ʒeliornodon, hīe hīe wendon ealla ðurh wīse
wealhstodas on hiora āʒen ʒeðīode. Ond ēac ealla ōðra Crīstna
ðīoda sumne dǣl hiora on hiora āʒen ʒeðīode wendon. Forðȳ
mē ðyncð betre, ʒif īow swǣ ðyncð, ðæt wē ēac sume bēc, ðā ðe
nīedbeðearfosta sīen eallum monnum tō wiotonne, ðæt wē ðā on

services in English or translate even a letter from Latin into English; and I think that there were not many beyond the Humber. There were so few of them that I cannot think of even a single one south of the Thames when I succeeded to the kingdom. Thanks be to almighty God that we now have any supply of teachers. And therefore I command that you do as I believe you wish, that you disengage yourself as often as you can from worldly affairs to the end that you apply the wisdom that God gave you wherever you can apply it. Think what punishments then came upon us on account of this world, when we neither loved it [wisdom] for itself nor passed it on to other men; we loved alone the name that we were Christians, and very few [of us loved] the practices.

When I remembered all this, then I remembered too how I saw, before it was all ravaged and burned, how the churches throughout the whole of England were full of books and of treasures, and also a great host of God's servants; but they had very little benefit from the books because they could not understand anything of them because they were not written in their own language. It is as if they had said 'Our forefathers who had these places before us loved wisdom, and through it they acquired riches and bequeathed them to us. Their track may still be seen here, but we do not know how to follow it. And so now we have relinquished both the wealth and the wisdom, because we did not wish to bend with our mind to that trail.'

When I remembered all this then I wondered very greatly at the good scholars who were once throughout England, and who had entirely learned all those books, that they had not wished to translate any part of them into their own language. But then I soon answered myself and said: 'They did not believe that ever men should be so careless and teaching fall away so: they neglected it deliberately, intending that there should be the more wisdom in the land the more languages that we knew.'

Then I remembered how the Law was first found in the Hebrew language, and afterwards, when the Greeks learned it, they turned it all into their own language, and also all the other books. And similarly the Romans, after they had learned them, turned them all through skilled translators into their own tongue. And also all other Christian people have changed some part of them into their own language. Therefore it seems to me better, if it seems so to you, that we also turn some books – those that may be most necessary for all

ðæt ȝeðīode wenden ðe wē ealle ȝecnāwan mæȝen, ond ȝedōn,
swæ wē swīðe ēaðe maȝon mid ȝodes fultume, ȝif wē ðā stilnesse
habbað, ðætte eall sīo ȝioȝuð ðe nū is on Anȝelcynne frīora monna,
ðāra ðe ða spēda hæbben ðæt hīe ðǣm befēolan mæȝen, sīen tō
60   liornunȝa oðfæste, ðā hwīle ðe hīe tō nānre ōðerre note ne mæȝen,
oð ðone first ðe hīe wel cunnen Enȝlisc ȝewrit ārǣdan. Lǣre mon
siððan furður on Lǣdenȝeðīode ðā ðe mon furðor lǣren wille ond
tō hīerran hāde dōn wille.

Ðā ic ðā ȝemunde hū sīo lār Lǣdenȝeðīodes ǣr ðissum
65   āfeallen wæs ȝiond Anȝelcynn, ond ðēah moniȝe cūðon Enȝlisc
ȝewrit ārǣdan, ðā onȝan ic onȝemanȝ ōðrum mislicum ond
maniȝ fealdum bisȝum ðisses kynerīces ðā bōc wendan on Enȝlisc
ðe is ȝenemned on Lǣden *Pastoralis*, ond on Enȝlisc 'Hierdebōc',
hwīlum word be worde, hwīlum andȝit of andȝiete, swæ swæ ic
70   hīe ȝeliornode æt Pleȝmunde mīnum ærcebiscepe, ond æt Assere
mīnum biscepe, ond æt ȝrimbolde mīnum mæsseprīoste, ond æt
Iōhanne mīnum mæsseprēoste. Siððan ic hīe ðā ȝeliornod hæfde,
swæ swæ ic hīe forstōd, ond swæ ic hīe andȝitfullīcost āreccean
meahte, ic hīe on Enȝlisc āwende; ond tō ælcum biscepstōle on
75   mīnum rīce wille āne onsendan; ond on ælcre bið ān æstel, sē bið
on fifteȝum mancessa. Ond ic bebīode on ȝodes naman ðæt nān
mon ðone æstel from ðǣre bēc ne dō, ne ðā bōc from ðǣm mynstre:
uncūð hū lonȝe ðǣr swæ ȝelǣrede biscepas sīen, swæ swæ nū, ȝode
ðonc, welhwǣr siendon. Forðȳ ic wolde ðætte hīe ealneȝ æt ðǣre
80   stōwe wǣren, būton se biscep hīe mid him habban wille, oððe hīo
hwǣr tō lǣne sīe, oððe hwā ōðre bī wrīte.

Notes

1–2   **hāteð ȝrētan Wærferð biscep . . . ond ðē cȳðan hāte** 'commands Bishop
Wærferð to be greeted and I order you to be informed'   This greetings
formula is close to that found in contemporary writs.

11–12   **man . . . sōhte** 'people . . . sought'   *Man* is frequently used in OE as an
indefinite pronoun, and may often be translated 'they' or rendered by a
passive construction.

17   **nǣren**   A contracted negative form of the subjunctive (*ne* + *wǣren*).
The subjunctive is required by the implicit hypothesis in the verb *wēnan*.
Cf. *cwǣden* (33) and *sceolden* (43).

22–23   **ðone wīsdōm . . . hiene**   The noun *wīsdōm* is masculine, and therefore
requires the masculine accusative *hiene*. In line 24, however, natural gender
asserts itself, and the neuter accusative *hit* refers to *wīsdōm*.

men to know – into that language which we all may understand, and cause, as we very easily may with God's help [and] if we have peace, that all the free-born young people that are now in England, among those who have the means to apply themselves, should be set to learning, as long as they are competent for no other employment, until they know well how to read English writing. Let a man afterwards learn deeper in the Latin language when he desires to learn more and to achieve a higher office.

When I remembered how before this the teaching of the Latin language had so fallen away throughout England, although many knew how to read English writing, then, among the other various and manifold concerns of this kingdom, I began to translate into English the book which is called *Pastoralis* in Latin, and in English 'Shepherd-book', at times word for word, at times sense for sense, as I learned it from Plegmund my archbishop, and from Asser my bishop and from Grimbold my priest, and from John my priest. After I had learned it, and as I understood it, and most meaningfully might interpret it, I turned it into English; and I intend to send one to each diocese in my kingdom; and in each will be a pointer which will be worth fifty mancuses. And I command in God's name that no man should take the pointer from the book, nor the book from the monastery – [it is] unknown how long there may be such learned bishops as now, thanks to God, there are everywhere. Therefore I have desired that they always remain at that place, unless the bishop wishes to have them with him, or it [the book] is on loan somewhere, or someone is making a copy of it.

24	**hwelc wītu us ða becōmon** 'what punishments then came upon us' The reference is probably to the Scandinavian invasions. Medieval commentators habitually regard national misfortune as divine retribution.
29	**eall forherȝod . . . ond forbærned** The *for-* prefix, which is etymologically related to Latin *per-*, carries an implication of intensification and often of ruination. Compare its use in the excerpt from the *Peterborough Chronicle*.
46–47	**ðȳ māra wīsdōm . . . ðȳ wē mā** This correlative construction employing the instrumental case of the definite article is quite common. Literally 'by that much more wisdom . . . by that much we knew more about languages'.
54–61	The construction of this sentence is somewhat tortuous, involving many embedded and dependent clauses. Its structure can be best indicated by a table.

FORÐȲ   mē ðyncð [ʒif īow swǣ ðyncð]
          ðæt wē ēac sume bēc [ðā ðe niedbeðearfosta . . .]
          ðæt wē ðā on ðæt ʒeðīode wenden. . . . .
OND ʒedōn [swǣ wē swīðe ēaðe maʒon . . .]
          ðætte eall sīo ʒioʒuð [ðara ðe ðā spēda . . .]
              sīen tō liornunʒa oðfæste
              ðā hwīle ðe. . . .
              oð ðone first. . . .

Note the quasi-causative use of *ʒedōn* and the use of inflected forms of the demonstrative pronoun as a clause connective: *frīora manna . . . ðāra ðe.*

70–72   **Pleʒmunde . . . Assere . . . ʒrimbolde . . . Iohanne**   All are scholars whom Alfred attracted to Wessex to aid in his work of cultural reconstruction. Plegmund was of Mercian origin and became Archbishop of Canterbury in 890; Asser was a Welshman who wrote a Latin biography of Alfred; Grimbold came from France; John was from Saxony and became abbot of Athelney, Somerset.

77   **æstel**   The word has been derived from Latin *hastula*, 'little spear', and is thought on the evidence of glosses to mean a pointer to be used in reading. Its value is great. Fifty mancuses was the legal value of fifty oxen or three hundred sheep. It has been suggested that the 'Alfred Jewel', discovered at Athelney but now in the Ashmolean Museum, Oxford, once adorned an *æstel*. The word *mancus* is a rare Arabic borrowing into OE.

3

CÆDMON

The account of how a cow-herd received poetic skills through divine intervention is given in Bede's *Historia Ecclesiastica*, where Bede asserts that Cædmon was the first to write religious poetry in English, and quotes the sense of this first poem 'but not the order of the words', since this cannot be rendered in Latin. Many manuscripts, however, quote the English version of what has become known as Cædmon's Hymn. The verbal ordering to which Bede referred is worth noticing, for it is generally characteristic of Old English verse style. The line is divided syntactically and metrically into two halves, linked by alliteration. There is no rhyme. Within the structure of the line, a sense of balance arises from the two half-lines, and the subject matter unfolds in a partially repetitive way. Semantically related words and phrases are balanced against one another, creating the characteristic effect of parallelism of sense and structure with variation in expression. This results in a solemn and portentous manner appropriate to the subject matter.

Both Bede (673–735) and Cædmon were Northumbrians. The former spent his entire life after the age of seven in the monastery at Jarrow on Tyne, but achieved scholarly eminence throughout Western Europe. Cædmon's biography is unknown, but he was attached as a lay brother to the monastery of Abbess Hild in Whitby, so that the miraculous events described in the excerpt must have taken place during her abbacy, that is, between 657 and 680.

As a scholar, Bede wrote exclusively in Latin, and the earliest texts of his *Ecclesiastical History* are Latin ones. The version of Cædmon's Hymn given in the earliest Latin manuscript (CUL MS Kk. 5. 16) is written in the Northumbrian dialect and dates from a very few years after Bede's death. It reads as follows.

Nu scylun herʒan   hefænricæs uard
metudæs maecti   end his modʒidanc
uerc uuldurfadur   sue he uundra ʒihuaes
eci dryctin   or astelidæ
he aerist scop   aelda barnum
heben til hrofe   haleʒ scepen
tha middunʒeard   moncynnæs uard
eci dryctin   æfter tiadæ
firum foldu   frea allmectiʒ

The version in the excerpt below differs considerably from this, both because it is much later and because it is written in West Saxon rather than the original Northumbrian. Bede's work, like Gregory's *Pastoral Care*, was one of those selected for translation into English as part of King Alfred's educational initiatives at the close of the ninth century. The work was in fact done by Mercian translators employed by the king, but in the manuscript upon which the following text is based (Bodleian Library MS Tanner 10) considerable West Saxonisation has taken place. Nevertheless, the pairing of near synonyms (*ʒemǣred ond ʒeweorðad; halette ond ʒrett*) and some Anglian forms – *-ad(e)* preterite and past participle inflections; *nēten* (66); *ʒehwerfde* (67); *wreoton* (69) *ʒēmde* (80) – may still testify to their work.

In ðeosse abbudissan mynstre wæs sum brōðor syndriʒlīce mid
ʒodcundre ʒife ʒemǣred ond ʒeweorðad, for þon hē ʒewunade
ʒerisenlice lēoð wyrcan, þā ðe tō æfæstnisse ond tō ārfæstnisse
belumpen, swā ðætte, swā hwæt swā hē of ʒodcundum stafum
5   þurh bōceras ʒeleornode, þæt hē æfter medmiclum fæce in
scopʒereorde mid þā mæstan swētnisse ond inbryrdnisse ʒeʒlænʒde
ond in Enʒliscʒereorde wel ʒeworht forþbrōhte. Ond for his
lēoþsonʒum moniʒra monna mōd oft tō worulde forhoʒdnisse ond
tō ʒeþēodnisse þæs heofonlican līfes onbærnde wæron. Ond ēac
10   swelce moniʒe ōðre æfter him in Onʒelþēode onʒunnon æfæste
lēoð wyrcan; ac næniʒ hwæðre him þæt ʒelīce dōn meahte, for þon
hē nales from monnum ne þurh mon ʒelǣred wæs, þæt hē þone
lēoðcræft leornade, ac hē wæs ʒodcundlice ʒefultumed ond þurh
ʒodes ʒife þone sonʒcræft onfēnʒ. Ond hē for ðon næfre nōht
15   lēasunʒe ne īdles lēoþes wyrcan meahte, ac efne þā ān þā ðe tō
æfæstnesse belumpon, ond his þā æfestan tunʒan ʒedafenode sinʒan.

In this abbess's monastery was a certain brother outstandingly honoured and made famous by divine grace, because he was accustomed to compose suitable songs such as pertained to religion and piety, so that whatever he learned of religious literature from scholars, after a short space of time, he brought that forth well wrought in the English tongue and in poetic language adorned with the greatest sweetness and inspiration. And through his songs the spirits of many men were often kindled with contempt for the world and desire for association with the heavenly life. And also many like him among the English nation afterwards began to compose religious poetry; but none could do it like him, because he was not instructed by a man nor through men so that he learned that poetic skill, but he was divinely aided and through the grace of God received the power of poetry. And therefore he could never make a fictional or unprofitable poem, but those alone which pertained to religion, and which it befitted that pious tongue of his to sing.

Wæs hē se mon in weoruldhāde ȝeseted oð þā tīde þe hē wæs
ȝelȳfdre ylde, ond hē næfre næniȝ lēoð ȝeleornade. Ond hē for þon
oft in ȝebēorscipe, þonne þǣr wæs blisse intinȝa ȝedēmed, þæt hēo
ealle sceolden þurh endebyrdnesse be hearpan sinȝan, þonne hē
ȝeseah þā hearpan him nēalēcan, þonne ārās hē for scome from
þǣm symble ond hām ēode tō his hūse. Þā hē þæt þā sumre tide
dyde, þæt hē forlēt þæt hūs þæs ȝebēorscipes ond ūt wæs ȝonȝende
tō nēata scipene, þāra heord him wæs þǣre neahte beboden, þā hē
ðā þǣr in ȝelimplīcre tīde his leomu on reste ȝesette ond onslēpte,
þā stōd him sum mon æt þurh swefn ond hine hālette ond ȝrētte
ond hine be his noman nemnde: 'Cedmon, sinȝ mē hwæthwuȝu.'
Þā ondswarede hē ond cwæð: 'Ne con ic nōht sinȝan; ond ic for
þon of þeossum ȝebēorscipe ūtēode, ond hider ȝewāt, for þon ic
nāht sinȝan ne cūðe. 'Eft hē cwæð, se ðe mid hine sprecende wæs:
'Hwæðre þū meaht mē sinȝan.' Þā cwæð hē: 'Hwæt sceal ic sinȝan?'
Cwæð hē: 'Sinȝ mē frumsceaft.' Þā hē ðā þās andsware onfēnȝ, þā
onȝon hē sōna sinȝan in herenesse ȝodes Scyppendes þā fers ond
þā word þe hē næfre ȝehȳrde; þāra endebyrdnes þis is:

Nū wē sculon heriȝean   heofonrīces Weard,
Meotodes meahte   ond his mōdȝeþanc,
weorc Wuldorfæder,   swā hē wundra ȝehwæs,
ēce Drihten,   ōr onstealde.
Hē ǣrest sceōp   eorðan bearnum
heofon tō hrōfe,   hāliȝ Scyppend.
Þā middanȝeard   monncynnes Weard,
ēce Drihten,   æfter tēode
firum foldan,   Frēa ælmihtiȝ.

Þā ārās hē from þǣm slǣpe, ond eal þā þe hē slǣpende sonȝ
fæste in ȝemynde hæfde, ond þǣm wordum sōna moniȝ word in
þæt ilce ȝemet ȝode wyrðes sonȝes tōȝeþēodde. Þā cōm hē on
morȝenne tō þǣm tūnȝerēfan, þe his ealdormon wæs; sæȝde him
hwylce ȝife hē onfēnȝ. Ond hē hine sōna tō þǣre abbudissan
ȝelǣdde ond hire þā cȳðde ond sæȝde. Þā heht hēo ȝesomnian
ealle þā ȝelǣredestan men ond þā leorneras, ond him ondweardum
hēt secȝan þæt swefn ond þæt lēoð sinȝan, þæt ealra heora dōme
ȝecoren wǣre, hwæt oððe hwonon þæt cuman wǣre. Þā wæs him
eallum ȝeseȝen, swā swā hit wæs, þæt him wǣre from Drihtne
sylfum heofonlic ȝifu forȝifen. Þā rehton hēo him ond sæȝdon

He was, this man, settled in the worldly estate until the time when he was of advanced age, and he had never learned any poetry. And because of that, often at a party, when there was considered to be an occasion for celebration, so that they all in order had to sing to the harp, whenever he saw the harp draw near him, he got up in embarrassment from the feast and went home to his house. When he did that on one particular occasion, left the house with the party and went out to the cattle shed (whose care was entrusted to him that night) and at the appointed time laid down his limbs in rest and fell asleep, then there stood by him a certain man in a dream and he hailed him and greeted him and called him by his name: 'Cedmon, sing me something.' And he answered and said: 'I don't know how to sing; and that's why I went out from this party, and came away here, because I didn't know how to sing.' Again, he who was speaking with him said: 'Nevertheless you can sing for me.' Then he said: 'What have I to sing?' He said 'Sing to me about the creation.' When he had received this reply, he began to sing at once lines and words in praise of God the Creator which he had never heard before; their order is this:

> Now we have to praise the guardian of the heavenly kingdom, the power and the conception of the creator, the deeds of the father of glory, as he, the eternal lord, established the beginning of every wonder. He, the holy creator, first shaped heaven as a roof for men on earth. Then mankind's guardian, almighty and eternal lord, afterwards adorned the fields for men.

Then he arose from that sleep and all those things that he had sung in his sleep he had fixed in memory, and quickly he added to those words many words in the same metre of song dear to God. Then in the morning he came to the estate overseer, who was his superior; he told him what a gift he had received. And he immediately led him to the abbess and told and revealed those things to her. Then she commanded all the most learned men and scholars to be gathered and ordered him to tell the dream and sing the verse before them, so that it might be discerned by the opinion of all of them, what that gift was and where it had come from. Then it was apparent to them all, just as was indeed the case, that the heavenly gift had been bestowed on him by the Lord himself. Then they told

55   sum hāliʒ spell ond ʒodcundre lāre word; bebudon him þā, ʒif hē
meahte, þæt hē in swinsunʒe lēoþsonʒes þæt ʒehwyrfde. Þā hē ðā
hæfde þā wīsan onfonʒne, þā ēode hē hām tō his hūse, and cwōm
eft on morʒenne, ond þȳ betstan lēoðe ʒeʒlenʒed him āsonʒ ond
āʒeaf þæt him beboden wæs.

60   Þā onʒan sēo abbudisse clyppan ond lufiʒean þā ʒodes ʒife in
þǣm men; ond hēo hine þā monade ond lǣrde þæt hē woruldhād
ānforlēte ond munuchād onfēnʒe; ond hē þæt wel þafode. Ond
hēo hine in þæt mynster onfēnʒ mid his ʒōdum, ond hine ʒeþēodde
tō ʒesomnunʒe þāra ʒodes þēowa, ond heht hine lǣran þæt ʒetæl
65   þæs hālʒan stæres ond spelles. Ond hē eal þā hē in ʒehȳrnesse
ʒeleornian meahte mid hine ʒemyndʒade, ond swā swā clǣne nēten
eodorcende in þæt swēteste lēoð ʒehwerfde. Ond his sonʒ on his
lēoð wǣron swā wynsumu tō ʒehȳranne þætte þā seolfan his
lārēowas æt his muðe wreoton ond leornodon. Sonʒ hē ǣrest be
70   middanʒeardes ʒesceape ond bī fruman moncynnes ond eal þæt
stǣr ʒenesis (þæt is sēo ǣreste Moyses booc); ond eft bī ūtʒonʒe
Israhēla folces of Æʒypta londe ond bī inʒonʒe þæs ʒehātlandes
ond bī ōðrum moneʒum spellum þæs hālʒan ʒewrites canōnes
bōca, ond bī Crīstes menniscnesse ond bī his þrōwunʒe ond bī his
75   ūpāstīʒnesse in heofonas ond bī þæs Hālʒan ʒāstes cyme ond þāra
apostola lāre; ond eft bī þǣm dæʒe þæs tōweardan dōmes ond bī
fyrhtu þæs tintreʒlican wiites ond bī swētnesse þæs heofonlecan
rīces hē moniʒ lēoð ʒeworhte. Ond swelce ēac ōðer moniʒ be þǣm
ʒodcundan fremsumnessum ond dōmum hē ʒeworhte. In eallum
80   þǣm hē ʒeornlīce ʒēmde þæt hē men ātuʒe from synna lufan ond
māndǣda, ond tō lufan ond tō ʒeornfulnesse āwehte ʒōdra dǣda;
for þon hē wæs se mon swīþe æfæst ond reʒollecum þēodscipum
ēaðmōdlīce underþēoded. Ond wið þǣm þā ðe in ōðre wīsan dōn
woldon, hē wæs mid welme micelre ellenwōdnisse onbærned; ond
85   hē for ðon fæʒre ænde his līf betȳnde ond ʒeendade.

    For þon þā ðǣre tīde nēalǣcte his ʒewitenesse ond forðfōre,
þā wæs hē, fēowrtȳnum daʒum ǣr, þæt hē wæs līchomlicre
untrymnesse þrycced ond hefʒad, hwǣðre tō þon ʒemetlīce þæt hē
ealle þā tid meahte ʒe sprecan ʒe ʒonʒan. Wæs þǣr in nēaweste
90   untrumra monna hūs, in þǣm heora þēaw wæs þæt hēo þā
untrumran ond þā ðe æt forðfōre wǣron inlǣdan sceoldon, ond
him þǣr ætsomne þeʒnian, Þā bæd hē his þeʒn on ǣfenne þǣre
neahte þe hē of worulde ʒonʒende wæs þæt hē in þǣm hūse him
stōwe ʒeʒearwode þæt hē ʒerestan meahte. Þā wundrode se þeʒn

and recounted to him a holy story and words of religious teaching; they instructed him then, if he could, that he should turn it into the harmony of poetry. When he had received it in that manner, he went home to his house, and came back in the morning, and sang to them, giving back what had been dictated to him adorned with the finest poetry.

Then the abbess embraced and esteemed the grace of God in the man; and she admonished him and advised him that he should give up the secular world and take up the monastic life; and he readily consented to that. And she received him into the monastery with his goods, and affiliated him to the congregation of the servants of God, and instructed him to learn the narrative of the holy history and message. And he assimilated all those things which he could learn by hearing, and just like a clean beast chewing its cud, turned them into the sweetest song. And his song and his poetry were so appealing to hear that his teachers themselves learned and wrote from his mouth. He sang first about the creation of the world and the origin of mankind and all the history of Genesis (that is the first book of Moses); and after about the exodus of the Israelites from the land of Egypt and their entrance into the promised land, and about many other stories from the text of the canonical books, and about Christ's incarnation and his passion and about his ascension into heaven and about the advent of the Holy Ghost and the teaching of the apostles; and after that about the day of approaching judgement and about the horror of excruciating punishment; and he made many poems about the sweetness of the heavenly kingdom. And he made many others like them about divine graciousness and justice. In them all he zealously took heed to draw men away from the love of sins and evil deeds, and awakened them to love and desire for good deeds; because the man was very pious and humbly committed to monastic discipline. And he was incensed with the fervour of great anger against those who wished to act in any other way; and therefore he closed and ended his life in a becoming way.

So when the time of his departure and death drew near, he was for fourteen days before oppressed and burdened by physical infirmity, yet so moderately that all the time he could both speak and walk about. There was in the vicinity an infirmary, in which it was their custom to put the sick and those that were on the point of death, and look after them all together. Then on the evening of the night that he was to depart the world he told his attendant to

95   for hwon hē ðæs bǣde, for þon him þūhte þæt his forðfōr swā
nēah ne wǣre; dyde hwæðre swā swā hē cwæð ond bibēad. Ond
mid þȳ hē ðā þǣr on reste ēode, ond hē ȝefēonde mōde sumu þinȝ
mid him sprecende ætȝædere ond ȝlēowiende wæs, þe þǣr ǣr inne
wǣron, þā wæs ofer middeneaht þæt hē fræȝn hwæðer hēo ǣniȝ

100   hūsl inne hæfdon. Þā ondswarodon hēo ond cwǣdon: 'Hwylc þærf
is ðē hūsles? Ne þīnre forþfōre swā nēah is, nū þū þus rōtlīce ond
þus ȝlædlīce tō ūs sprecende eart.' Cwæð hē eft: 'Berað mē hūsl tō.'
Þā hē hit þā on honda hæfde, þā fræȝn hē hwæþer hēo ealle smolt
mōd ond būton eallum incan blīðe tō him hæfdon. Þā ondswaredon

105   hȳ ealle ond cwǣdon þæt hēo nǣniȝne incan tō him wiston, ac hēo
ealle him swīðe blīðemōde wǣron; ond hēo wrixendlīce hine bǣdon
þæt hē him eallum blīðe wǣre. Þā ondswarade hē ond cwæð:
'Mīne brōðor, mīne þā lēofan, ic eom swīðe blīðemōd tō ēow ond
tō eallum ȝodes monnum.' Ond swā wæs hine ȝetrymmende mid

110   þȳ heofonlecan weȝneste ond him ōðres līfes inȝonȝ ȝeȝearwode.
Þā ȝȳt hē fræȝn, hū nēah þǣre tīde wǣre þætte þā brōðor ārīsan
scolden ond ȝodes lof rǣran ond heora ūhtsonȝ sinȝan. Þā
ondswaredon hēo: 'Nis hit feor tō þon.' Cwæð hē: 'Teala: wuton
wē wel þǣre tide bīdan.' Ond þā him ȝebæd ond hine ȝeseȝnode

115   mid Crīstes rōdetācne, ond his hēafod onhylde tō þām bolstre, ond
medmicel fæc onslēpte, ond swā mid stilnesse his līf ȝeendade.
Ond swā wæs ȝeworden þætte swā swā hē hlūttre mōde ond bilwitre
ond smyltre wilsumnesse Drihtne þēode, þæt hē ēac swylce swā
smylte dēaðe middanȝeard wæs forlǣtende, ond tō his ȝesihðe

120   becwōm. Ond sēo tunȝe, þe swā moniȝ hālwende word in þæs
Scyppendes lof ȝesette, hē ðā swelce ēac þā ȳtmæstan word in his
herenisse, hine seolfne seȝniende ond his ȝāst in his honda
bebēodende, betȳnde. Ēac swelce þæt is ȝeseȝen þæt hē wǣre ȝewis
his seolfes forfōre, of þǣm wē nū secȝan hȳrdon.

Notes

8   **lēoþsonȝum . . . (lēoðcræft . . . sonȝcræft)**   The words *lēoð* and *sonȝ*
are used interchangeably. No distinction is made between poetry and song.
The first of these words is therefore tautologous, and probably compounded
for decorative purposes.

12   **from monnum ne þurh mon**   OE *from* has an agentive significance.
The translators also exploited the ambiguity of OE *mon*, in its senses
respectively of 'man' and 'mankind'. Thus, he was not taught by men nor

prepare a place for him in the infirmary so that he may rest. Then the attendant marvelled why he told him this because it seemed to him that his death was not so near; nevertheless he did as he said and instructed. And then he went there to his resting place, and rejoicing in spirit, he was chatting and joking somewhat together with those who were already in there. It was past midnight when he asked whether they had any Eucharist inside. Then they answered him and said: 'What need have you for Eucharist? Your passing is not so near, now you are speaking to us so cheerily and merrily.' He said again: 'Bring the Eucharist to me.' When he had it in his hands, he asked whether they all had a tranquil and friendly spirit without any rancour towards him. Then they all answered and said that they felt no rancour towards him, but they were all very well disposed to him; and they in turn bade him that he should be well disposed to them all. Then he answered and said: 'My brothers, my dear friends, I am well disposed to you and to all God's men.' And so he was strengthened by the heavenly viaticum [Eucharist administered to the dying] and prepared for entry into the next life. But still he asked how close to the hour it was when the brothers should arise and raise up praise to God, singing their matins. Then they answered: 'It is not long till then.' He said: 'Well, let us await that hour.' And then he prayed and crossed himself with the sign of Christ's cross, and lowered his head to the pillow, and slept for a little while, and so in tranquillity he ended his life. And so it came about that in just as pure and innocent a spirit and serene devotion as he had served God, so with a similarly tranquil death he was relinquishing the world, and came into his sight. And that tongue, that had set so many salutary words in praise of the Creator, then ended in the same way with final words in his praise, as he crossed himself and commended his spirit into his hands. So also it is apparent from what we have just heard tell that he was aware of his own departure.

through the agency of mankind. The phrase *þurh mon* is thus parallel and in contrast with *þurh ჳodes ჳife* in the following *ac*-clause.

14–15 **næfre nōht lēasunჳe** Double negation is normal in OE. However, the accumulation of heavy negators – *he nales . . . ne* (12); *næfre næniჳ lēoð* (18) – and the front shifting of *ne* – *ne con ic nōht sinჳan* (28) – may be taken to be emphatic.

15 **þā ān þā ðe** Literally, 'those alone those that'.

19   **ȝebēorscipe**   The base of this derived form is *bēor*, 'beer'; the prefix *ȝe-* has a collectivising meaning; and the suffix *-scipe* forms abstract from concrete nouns.

23   **wæs ȝonȝende** *egressus esset*   The expanded form, consisting of the verb 'to be' and the present participle, is particularly common in this excerpt (cf. 30, 93, 98, 102). It usually translates the Latin imperfect or imperfect subjunctive, but in 93 renders a construction with the future participle *erat exiturus*.

26   **þā stōd him sum mon æt**   Literally, 'then stood to him a certain man by'. The idiom exhibits the usual Subject–Verb inversion after an adverbial (*þā*) and the preposition occurs as usual at the end of the group.

27   **Cedmon**   The more familiar spelling *Cædmon* is a West Saxonisation of this, the original Northumbrian form of the name.

44   **eal þā þe hē slæpende sonȝ**   The demonstrative *þā* must be interpreted as neuter plural, 'those things'. *Slæpende* is the present participle functioning as qualifier of *hē*.

64   **heht**   The older, poetic and Anglian form (used also on the Alfred Jewel inscription) of the preterite, *hēt*, of the verb *hātan*.

86   **forðfōre**   Literally 'journey forth', but so common a euphemism in OE that it is best translated as 'death' or 'passing'.

122–23 **hine seolfne seȝniende ond his ȝāst in his honda bebēodende, betynde**   Imitates the Latin *signando sese et spiritum suum in manus commendando, clauderet*. Old English may simply use the accusative personal pronoun to form reflexive constructions (*hine ȝeseȝnode*, 114), but the pronoun may also be supported by the adjective *seolf*, 'same'.

4

A HOMILY OF ÆLFRIC

Ælfric (*c.* 955–*c.* 1010) is one of a handful of Anglo-Saxon authors whose name is known to us. He was a priest and a monk who lived all his life in Wessex and was influenced by the monastic and intellectual revival presided over by Æthelwold and St Dunstan. After teaching in the monastic school in Winchester, he proceeded to the monastery at Cerne Abbas, Dorset, where his Catholic Homilies were written between about 986 and 992. In 1005 he became abbot of the new monastery at Eynsham in Oxfordshire. His purpose in writing the Homilies, he explains, is to make the essential teachings of the Church available in simple terms to those incapable of understanding Latin. About two-thirds of Ælfric's collection are, like this excerpt, homilies in the stricter sense of the word: that is, sermon discourses in which a scriptural narrative is followed by a spiritual or moral interpretation of the text. Here, after relating the scriptural account of the workers in the vineyard, Ælfric states his authority for making a traditional equation between the vineyard and the kingdom of heaven, going on from there to a more detailed allegorical and moral interpretation of the narrative.

As Alfred noted in his Preface to the translation of *Cura Pastoralis* (Excerpt 2), monastic culture had sadly declined since the great days of Bede's Northumbria. But Ælfric lived in a time of reconstruction, for which Alfred's military and cultural efforts and Æthelstan's victory at Brunanburh (Excerpt 6) had provided the foundation. Wessex had gained dominance and imposed some unity upon England, and with the support of King Edgar, Archbishop Dunstan and Bishops Oswald and Æthelwold worked to reconstitute monastic life, modelling their practices on those of northern France. Æthelwold, to whose school Ælfric belonged, had a particular interest in literacy, and his Winchester school developed certain characteristic verbal choices which are exemplified in Ælfric's writings. More significantly, a relatively consistent way of writing West Saxon was developed, which, through its adoption by royal clerks, became used beyond the West Saxon dialect area by others writing in English. This excerpt is written in this standard West Saxon, which is the language of most extant Old English literature.

Drihten sǣde þis biʒspel his leorninʒcnihtum, ðus cweðende: *Simile est regnum celorum homini patrifamilias, qui exiit primo mane conducere operarios; et reliqua.* Se Hǣland cwæð þæt heofenan rīce wǣre ʒelīc sumum hīredes ealdre, sē ðe fērde on ǣrnemeriʒen, and wolde hȳrian wyrhtan intō his wīnʒearde. Þā ʒewearð þām hlāforde
5   and ðām hȳriʒmannum wið ānum peninʒe, and hī ēodon intō ðām wīnʒearde. Eft, ymbe undern dæʒes, ēode þæs wīnʒeardes hlāford ūt, and ʒemētte ōðre hȳrmenn standende ȳdele on ðǣre strǣt; and hē cwæð him tō: 'ʒāð intō mīnum wīnʒearde, and ic sylle ēow þæt riht bið.' Hī ðā ēodon tō his weorce be ðām behāte.
10 Ymbe midne dæʒ and nōntīde ēode se hīredes ealdor ūt, and dyde hand swā ʒelīce. Æt nēxtan, twā tīda ofer nōne ēode se hlāford and ʒemētte mā wyrhtan standan, and him tō cwæð 'Hwī stande ʒē hēr ealne dæʒ ǣmtiʒe?' Hī andwyrdon: 'For ðan þe ūs nān mann ne hȳrde.' Se hlāford cwæð: 'ʒāð into mīnum wīnʒearde.' Witodlīce
15 on ǣfnunʒe cwæð se hlāford tō his wīcnere 'Clypa ðās wyrhtan and āʒyld him heora mēde. Fōh on ðām endenēxtan, oð þæt þū cume tō ðām fyrmestan.' Þā cōmon ðā endenēxtan þe on ǣfnunʒe wǣron ʒehȳrede, and heora ǣlc underfēnʒ ǣnne peninʒ. Hwæt, ðā fyrmestan þe on ǣrnemeriʒen cōmon wēndon þā þæt hī māran
20 mēde onfōn sceoldon. Ðā underfēnʒon hī ǣnlīpiʒe peneʒas, swā swā ðā ōðre. Þā onʒunnon hī tō ceoriʒenne onʒēan hīredes ealdor and cwǣdon: 'Ðās endenēxtan menn worhton āne tīde, and þū dydest hī ūs ʒelīce æt ðǣre hȳre, wē ðe bǣron byrðene ðises dæʒes and hǣtan.' Þā andwyrde se hlāford and cwæð tō hēora ānum:
25 'Þū frēond, ne dō ic ðē nænne tēonan. Hū lā, ne ʒewearð unc tō ānum peninʒe? Nim þæt ðīn is and ʒā ðē forð. Ic wille sōðlīce syllan þisum latestan swā micel swā ðē. Hū ne mōt ic dōn þæt ic wylle? Oððe ðīn ēaʒe is yfel, for ðan ðe ic eom ʒōod?' Þus wǣron
30 þā latestan fyrmeste and þā fyrmestan endenēxte. Fela sind ʒecīʒede and fēawa ʒecorene.

The Lord told this parable, saying thus to his disciples: *Simile est regnum celorum homini patrifamilias qui exiit primo mane conducere operarios et reliqua.* The Saviour said that the kingdom of heaven was like a certain master of a household who went in the early morning and wished to hire labourers into his vineyard. Then the lord and the hired men settled on one penny, and they went into the vineyard. About the third hour of the day the owner of the vineyard went out again and met some other labourers standing unemployed in the street, and he said to them: 'Go into my vineyard, and I will give you what is just.' They then went to his work according to that promise. Around midday and the ninth hour the master of the household went out and made similar bargains. Next, two hours after the ninth hour, the master went out and met more workmen standing and said to them: 'Why are you standing here all day unoccupied?' They replied: 'Because no one hired us.' The master said: 'Go into my vineyard.'

Truly, in the evening the master said to his steward: 'Call those workmen and pay them their wages; begin from the last until you come to the first.' Then the last ones who were hired in the evening came, and each of them received one penny. Well, the first ones who came in the early morning expected then that they should receive a greater reward. When they received a single penny just like the others, they began to complain against the master of the household, and said: 'Those last men worked for one hour and you treated them like us in payment, we who bore the burden and heat of this day.' Then the lord replied and said to one of them: 'Friend, I do you no injury; look, did we not agree between us on one penny? Take what is yours and go. I truly intend to give to this last as much as to you. What, may I not do what I wish? Or are you resentful because I am generous?' Thus were the last first, and the first last. Many are called and few chosen.

ʒrēʒōrius se trahtnere cwæð þæt þis ʒodspel hæfð lanʒne tiʒe on his trahtnunʒe, ðā hē wile mid sceortre race befōn, þæt hit tō hefiʒtȳme ne ðince þām heorcniʒendum.

35 Mīne ʒebrōðra, ʒelōme ic ēow sǣde þæt heofonan rīce ʒetācnað þās andwerdan ʒelaðunʒe, for ðan þe rihtwīsra manna ʒeʒaderunʒ is ʒecweden heofenan rīce. So hīredes ealdor is ūre Scyppend, sē ðe ʒewylt ðā ðe hē ʒesceōp, and his ʒecorenan on þisum middanearde ʒeāʒnað, swā swā hlāford his hīred on his healle. He hæfð þone

40 wīnʒeard ʒewislīce ealle ðā ʒelēaffullan ʒelaðunʒe, swā swā se wīteʒa cwæð Isaias: 'Sōðlīce ʒodes wīnʒeard is Israhēla hīwrǣden.' Mid þām naman is ʒeswutelod eal ʒodes folc. Be ðām wīnʒeard cwæð Drihten tō Iūdēiscre ðēode: 'Ic secʒe ēow, þæt ʒodes rīce bið ēow ætbrōden, and bið forʒyfen ðǣre ðēode þe his wæstmas wyrcað.'

45 Þes wīnʒeard sprytte ʒodes ʒecorenan, fram ðām rihtwīsan Ābel oð ðām endenēxtan hālʒan ðe on ende þyssere worulde ācenned bið, swilce hē swā fela wīnbōʒa ʒetȳddrode. Witodlīce ðæs hīredes ealdor ʒehȳrde wyrhtan intō his wīnʒearde on ærnemeriʒen, eft on undern, and on midne dæʒ, on nōntīde, and on ðǣre endlyftan tīde; for

50 ðan þe hē fram frymðe middaneardes oð his ʒeendunʒe ne āblинð tō āsendenne bydelas and lārēowas tō lǣrenne his folc, þæt hī symle þā misweaxendan bōʒas of āscrēadian, þæt ðā tōweardan ðēonde bēon. Witodlīce ʒif se wīnʒeard næfð þone ymbhwyrft, and ne bið on riht ʒescrēadod, ne bið hē wæstmbǣre, ac forhraðe āwildað.

55 Swā ēac ʒodes folc, būton ðā lārēowas scrēadian symle ðā leahtras þurh heora lāre āweʒ, ne bið þæt lǣwede folc wæstmbǣre on ʒōdum weorcum.

Notes

1   **his leorninʒcnihtum** 'his disciples'   The word *cniht* in OE means 'servant' or 'boy'. This compound and the word *ʒelaðunʒ* (36), meaning the Church as congregation, are considered to represent verbal choices characteristic of the Winchester school.

7–8   **ēode þæs wīnʒēardes hlāford ūt**   Note the tendency of the preposition to appear at the end of the clause separated from its associated verb. Like modern German, Old English has some verbs with separable prefixes: *ūt-ʒān* occurs as well as *ʒān . . . ūt*.

9–10   **ic sylle**   The present tense is normally used in OE for future reference.

11–12   **dyde hand**   The idiom refers to the custom of striking hands on a bargain.

Gregory the commentator said in his commentary that this gospel has a long significance which he will relate with a short account, so that it may not seem too burdensome to those hearing it. My brothers, repeatedly I have told you that the kingdom of heaven represents this present congregation, because a gathering of righteous people is called the kingdom of heaven. The master of the household is our Creator, he who has power over those whom he created, and claims his chosen on this earth just as a lord his retinue in his hall. He owns the vineyard; that is, the whole congregation of the faithful, just as the prophet Isaiah said: 'Truly God's vineyard is the tribe of the Israelites.' By that name is indicated all God's people. Concerning the vineyard, God spoke to the Jewish people: I tell you that the kingdom of God shall be snatched away from you and be granted to that people which labours for its increase.

This vineyard grows with God's elect from the righteous Abel until the last saints who will be born at the end of this world. Just as he propagated so many vine-shoots, certainly the master of the house hired labourers into his vineyard in the early morning. Again at the third hour, and at midday, the ninth hour, and at the final hour, because he from the beginning of the world until its end does not cease from sending preachers and instructors to teach his people, so that they may continuously prune out the badly growing shoots so that the future ones may be thriving. Indeed, if the vineyard does not have that cultivation, and is not properly pruned, it is not productive, but very quickly goes wild. So, too, God's people without instructors continuously to prune away sins through their teaching. An ignorant population is not productive in good works.

13	**Hwī stande ӡē** The form with final -*e* replaces the usual plural inflexion, -*að*, when the subject pronoun immediately follows the verb.
20–21	**hi māran mēde onfōn sceoldon** The usage here admirably illustrates the sense of inevitability, rather than simple futurity, borne by OE *sculan*.
26–27	**ne ӡewearð unc to ānum peninӡe** Literally, 'did it not agree (happen) to us two for one penny'. The construction is impersonal, but the use of the dual form *unc* serves to emphasise the contract.
38	**ӡewylt** This form of *ӡewieldeð* exhibits the syncope of inflexional -*e*- and the subsequent assimilation of stem and inflexional consonant which is typical of WS. Anglian preserves the ending -*eð*.

his ȝecorenan   The past participle, *ȝe-coren*, of *cēosan*, 'to choose' (which is a kind of verbal adjective), is converted to a Weak noun and used substantivally.

51   **bydelas and lāreōwas**   Ælfric goes on to explain that these are, in the different ages, the patriarchs (which he renders *hēahfæderas*), the prophets, and apostles.

56   **wæstmbǣre**   A transparent compound, meaning literally 'fruit-bearing'.

5

ÆLFRIC'S COSMOLOGY

This excerpt contains the account of creation given in Ælfric's *De Temporibus Anni*, a work completed around 993 when he was at Cerne Abbas, and which survives in eight manuscripts. The earliest, CUL MS Gg. 3. 28, on which the present text is based, is nearly contemporary with the work's composition. The major sources used are the scriptural account given in Genesis and two Latin works of Bede, *De temporum ratione* and *De natura rerum*. Knowledge of cosmology was introductory to an understanding of astronomy, and this was of importance in medieval monasteries since the computation of the calendar was based upon it, which in turn made possible the certain identification of religious feast days. Characteristically, Ælfric appends an allegorical and moral interpretation to the natural science he recounts. This piece of scientific writing illustrates quite well some of the features of Ælfric's earlier prose style: a simple and non-Latinate vocabulary, phrasal repetition and sequences, and phrases syntactically and semantically balanced and contrasted. Balance may depend on a simple opposition of semantics within a similar structural pattern (*on dæȝ bufon eorðan and on niht under ðysse eorðan*); or semantic opposition within a formal correlative syntactic structure (*Ælc ðinȝ swā hit ðē fyrr bið swā hit ðā læsse ðincð*); or the semantic opposition may be constructed around the alliteration of a common word-pair (*Sēo is weaxende þurh ācennedum cildum and wāniȝende þurh fordfārendum*). Ælfric's artistry, in keeping with his concern to write in the simple style which he thought appropriate for instruction, seeks to be unobtrusive. His work is none the less constructed with considerable skill (Godden 1992).

As explained in the previous excerpt, Ælfric's training in Winchester ensured that he wrote in standard West Saxon, which is the language of this excerpt also. Note the third-person-singular present-tense verbs *scinð* (20), *onlīht* (45), *oferswīð* (45), and *ārīst* (51). All exhibit the syncope of inflexional

-e- characteristic of WS and later Kentish OE. In the latter two there is also assimilation to the consonantal sound of the stem. The sequence of sound changes in the development of *onlīht* was: *onlīhteð* > *onlīhtð* > *onlīhtt* > *onlīht*.

On ðām ðriddan dæʒe ʒesceōp se ælmihtiʒa ʒod sǣ and eorðan and ealle eorðlīce spryttinʒa. Ðās ðrȳ daʒas wǣron būton sunnan and mōnan and steorran and eallum tīdum ʒelīcere wǣʒan mid lēohte and þēostrum aðenede. On ðām fēorðan dæʒe ʒesceōp ʒod
5　twā miccle lēoht, þæt is sunne and mōna, and betǣhte þæt māre lēoht þæt is sēo sunne tō ðām dæʒe and þæt lǣsse lēoht þæt is se mōna tō ðǣre nihte. On ðām ylcan dæʒe hē ʒeworhte ealle steorran and tīda ʒesette. On ðām fiftan dæʒe hē ʒesceōp eal wyrmcynn and ðā micclan hwalas and eal fisccynn on mislicum and meniʒfealdum
10　hīwum. On ðām sixtan dæʒe hē ʒesceōp eal dēorcynn and ealle nȳtenu þe on fēower fōtum ʒāð and þā twēʒen men Adam and Ēuan. On ðām seofoðan dæʒe hē ʒeendode his weorc and sēo wucu wæs ðā aʒān.
　　Nū is ælc dæʒ on ðysum middanearde of ðǣre sunnan līhtinʒe.
15　Sōðlice sēo sunne ʒǣð be ʒodes dihte betwux heofenan and eorðan, on dæʒ bufon eorðan and on niht under ðysse eorðan, eal swā feorr adūne on nihtlicere tīde under þǣre eorðan swā hēo on dæʒ bufon ūpāstīhð. Ǣfre hēo bið yrnende ymbe ðās eorðan and eal swā lēohte scīnð under ðǣre eorðan on nihtlicere tīde swā swā hēo
20　on dæʒ dēð bufon ūrum hēafdum. On ðā healfe ðe hēo scinð þǣr bið dæʒ and on ðā healfe ðe hēo ne scīnð ðǣr bið niht. Ǣfre bið on sumere sīdan þǣre eorðan dæʒ and ǣfre on sumere sīdan niht. Ðæt lēoht ðe wē hātað dæʒerēd cymð of ðǣre sunnan þonne hēo ūpweard bið and hēo ðonne tōdrǣfð þā nihtlican ðēostru ðurh
25　hire micclan lēohte. Eal swā ðicce is sēo heofen mid steorrum āfylled on dæʒ swā on niht ac hī nabbað nāne līhtinʒe for ðǣre sunnan andwerdnysse. Wē hātað ǣnne dæʒ fram sunnan ūpʒanʒe oð ǣfen ac swā ðēah on bōcum is ʒeteald tō ānum dæʒe fram ðǣre sunnan ūpʒanʒe oð þæt hēo eft becume þǣr hēo ǣr ūppstāh: on ðām fæce
30　sind ʒetealde fēower and twenti tīda. Sēo sunne is swiðe micel – eal swā brād hēo is þæs ðe bēc secʒað swā eal eorðan ymbhwyrft – ac hēo ðincð ūs swiðe unbrād forðan ðe hēo is swiðe feor fram ūrum ʒesihðum. Ælc ðinʒ swā hit ðē fyrr bið swā hit ðē lǣsse ðincð. Wē maʒon hwæðere tōcnāwan be hire lēoman þæt hēo unlȳtel is. Swā

On the third day the Almighty God created sea and earth and all the vegetation in the world. Those three days were lacking sun and moon and stars, and all times were overspread in equal measure by light and dark. On the fourth day God created two great lights, that is the sun and the moon, and assigned the greater light, that is the sun, to the day and the lesser light, that is the moon, to the night. In the same day he made all the stars and established the seasons. On the fifth day he created the race of creeping things and the great whales and the race of fish in many and various forms. On the sixth day he created all kinds of animals and all beasts that walk on four feet, and the two humans Adam and Eve. On the seventh day he completed his task and the week was then past.

Now, each day in this world results from the sun's light. Indeed, by God's arrangement, the sun moves between the heaven and earth: during the day above the earth and by night beneath this earth, just as far down below the earth at night-time as it ascends above during the day. Constantly it is running around this earth, and shines just as brightly beneath the earth at night-time as it does during the day above our heads. On that side where it shines there is day, and on that side where it does not shine there is night. Always there is on one particular side of the earth day, and always on the other side night. The light which we call dawn comes from the sun rising, and it then drives away the night-time darkness with its great light. The sky is just as thickly filled with stars in the day-time as at night, but they have no brightness because of the sun's presence. From sunrise until evening we call one day; however in books it is reckoned as one day from the sun's rising until it comes again [to that point] where it earlier arose: in that space of time are counted twenty-four hours. The sun is very large – as books say, it is just as wide as the entire circumference of the earth – but it seems very small to us because it is very distant from our sight. The further anything is the smaller it seems. We may discern however that it is large on account of its great light. As soon as it rises, it shines alike over the whole earth and covers equally the entire breadth of the earth.

35 hraðe swā hēo ūpāstīhð hēo scīnð ʒeond ealle eorðan ʒelīce and
ealre eorðan brādnysse endemes oferwrīhð. Ēac swilce ðā steorran
ðe ūs lȳtle ðincað sind swīðe brāde ac for ðām micclum fæce þe
ūs betwēonan is hī sind ʒeðūhte ūrum ʒesihðum swīðe ʒehwæde.
Hī ne mihton swā ðēah nān lēoht tō eorðan āsendan fram ðære
40 hēalican heofenan ʒif hī swā ʒehwæde wæron swā swā ūrum ēaʒum
ðincð. Sōðlice se mōna and ealle steorran underfōð lēoht of ðære
micclan sunnan and heora nān næfð nænne lēoman būton of ðære
sunnan lēoman; and ðēah ðe sēo sunne under eorðan on nihtlīcere
tīde scīne þēah āstīhð hire lēoht on sumere sīdan þære eorðan þe
45 ðā steorran bufon ūs onlīht and ðonne hēo ūpaʒæð hēo oferswīð
ealra ðæra steorrena and ēac þæs mōnan lēoht mid hire ormætan
lēohte.
Sēo sunne ʒetācnað ūrne hælend Crīst, se ðe is rihtwīsnysse
sunne swā swā se wīteʒa cwæð: *Timentibus autem nomen domini*
50 *orietur sol iustitie et sanitas in pennis eius* 'Ðām mannum þe him
ondrædað ʒodes naman ðām ārīst rihtwīsnysse sunne and hælð
is on hire fiðerum.' Se mōna ðe weaxð and wānað ʒetācnað
þās andwerdan ʒelaðunʒe ðe wē on sind. Sēo is weaxende þurh
ācennedum cildum and wāniʒende þurh fordfarendum. Þā beorhtan
55 steorran ʒetācniað ðā ʒelēaffullan on ʒodes ʒelaðunʒe ðe on ʒoddre
drohtnunʒe scīnað. Crīst sōðlice onlīht hī ealle þurh his ʒife swā
swā se ʒodspellere Iohannes cwæð: *Erat lux uera que inluminat*
omnem hominem uenientem in hunc mundum 'Ðæt sōðe lēoht cōm
þe onlīht ælcne mannan cumendne to ðisum middanearde.' Næfð
60 ūre nān nān lēoht æniʒre ʒodnysse būton of Crīstes ʒife. Se ðe is
sōðre rihtwīsnysse sunne ʒehāten.

Notes

5 **twā miccle lēoht, þæt is sunne and mōna** The phrase *þæt is* con-
cords with neither *lēoht* (as it does by chance in lines 6–7) nor *sunne* or
mōna. It is rather an independent explanatory clause equivalent to Latin
videlicet or *scilicet*. *Þæt* is used cataphorically and uninflected (Mitchell
1985: §323–7, §2136).

8–9 **wyrmcynn . . . hwalas . . . fisccynn** We have here an attempt at scientific classification of types of creatures, and it is probably more than
coincidental that the word *cynn* is both etymologically connected with,
and has the sense of, Latin *genus*, which had already been used in such
contexts by Latin authors. More widely in OE usage *wyrm* may include
many types of worm, snake and insect. *Hwæl* is used of walruses as well as

Similarly, the stars which seem small to us are very broad, but because of the great space that is between us, they seem very small to our sight. But they could not thus send any light from their exalted heaven if they were as small as they appear to our eyes. Truly the moon and all stars receive light from the great sun and none of them has any brightness except from the sun's brightness, and although the sun may shine beneath the earth at night-time yet its light goes to one side of the earth and lights the stars above us; and when it comes up it overwhelms the light of all the stars and of the moon with its intense brightness.

The sun symbolises our saviour Christ, he who is the sun of righteousness, as the prophet says: *Timentibus autem nomen domini orietur sol iustitiae sanitas in pennis eius*, 'To those men who fear God's name shall arise the sun of righteousness and healing is in his wings.' The moon which waxes and wanes signifies this present congregation which we are in. It is growing through children born and dwindling through deaths. The bright stars signify the faithful in God's congregation who shine in virtuous living. Christ truly illuminates them all through his grace just as the evangelist John says: *Erat lux vera que inluminat omnem hominem venientem in hunc mundum*, 'The true light came that enlightens each man coming into this world.' None of us has the light of any goodness except by God's grace. He that is called the sun of true righteousness.

whales, and in *Physiologus*, the whale is classed as a fish. Seals may even be considered *fisccynn*.

10–11   **dēorcynn . . . nȳtenu**   The apparent distinction between wild and domesticated animals suggested by Bede's Latin is not made in wider OE usage, where *nȳten* is used of a badger, and both explicitly tame reindeer and a wild panther are referred to as *dēor*.

11–12   **þā twēʒen men Adam and Ēuan**   The concept of *man* as the name of a species is sufficiently distinct from its reference to the male to permit what sounds in modern English an extraordinary statement.

19   **lēohte 'lightly'**   Adverbs are readily formed from nouns by the addition of *-e* to the stem.

24   **tōdrǣfð**   The prefix *tō-* is etymologically related to the word *two*, and carries the force of separation or splitting. In combination with some agentive verbs it therefore acts as an intensifier.

28–30   **ðēah on bōcum is ʒeteald . . . fēower and twenti tīda**   *Byhrtferð's Manual* refers to the period from sun-up to sun-down as the *ceorlisc*, 'ordinary' day. The twenty-four-hour day is described in Bede's Latin as the 'artificial day' (*dies artificialis*) However, Chaucer, 'Man of Law's Tale', 2, and 'Squire's Tale', 116, regards the artificial day as from sunrise to sunset, and the natural day is twenty-four hours.

32   **hēo ðincð ūs swīðe unbrād**   An impersonal construction, 'it seems to us . . .'. The verb *ðyncan* is usually used impersonally, *ðencan* personally, i.e. meaning 'to think'. Note the passive construction (38).

33   **swā hit ðē fyrr bið swā hit ðē lǣsse ðincð**   The impersonal verb is here contained in a correlative construction using *swā . . . swā* and the repeated instrumental form of the demonstrative *ðē*.

52   **hire fiðerum**   *Hire* refers to *sunne*, which is feminine. *Fider* is used for both 'feather' and 'wing' in OE. The modern word *wing* is a Scandinavian borrowing.

59–60   **Næfð ūre nān nān lēoht**   Literally, 'None of us has no light.'

6

THE BATTLE OF BRUNANBURH

The *Anglo-Saxon Chronicle* in four different manuscripts contains as the entry for the year 937 a brief heroic poem, telling of a crushing defeat inflicted on a coalition of Picts and Scots, Strathclyde Welsh, and Norse Vikings by the West Saxons. The victory at Brunanburh was important in establishing national unity under West Saxon dominion, and contemporary awareness of this fact may lie behind the triumphalistic tone of the poem. Despite its historical importance, the site of the conflict has been forgotten. All that can be said with certainty is that Brunanburh was somewhere in northern England or southern Scotland, and that the flight of the Scandinavians to their ships indicates a site not far from the sea or some large estuary. Despite the opinion of the early twelfth-century chronicler Florence of Worcester that the Vikings approached the battlefield from the Humber, it is probable that the battle took place on the western side of the country.

The Battle of Brunanburh was written to commemorate the great deeds of Æthelstan and for an elite who would appreciate the expression of the heroic ideals of the past in a very correct and formal verse. The metre is very regular, and copious use is made of synonyms, compounds, and the parallelism and variation characteristic of correct OE verse. The technique has been seen as artificial, the conscious re-creation of standards developed in much earlier poetry. The poetic language is highly conventional, and more than twenty half-lines are recorded elsewhere. Nevertheless, a large number of compounds are unknown from other sources and may be original, *ealdorlanȝ, heaþolind, scipflota, hereflēma, bilȝesleht, wælfeld, hasupād, ȝārmittinȝ, ȝuðhafoc* among them. Variant readings in some manuscripts are of a kind which suggest that the scribe was unfamiliar with the phrasing of poetic language, and that it gave him difficulty. See the notes for some examples.

The text below, based on MS A of the *Anglo-Saxon Chronicle*, was written in Winchester about 955. It is predominantly in West Saxon but contains a number of words of an archaic or dialectal kind, apparently added by the poet to his composition for the sake of ornament. There are also a number of late inflexional forms: *-an* for *-on* (5, 23, 52, 53, 70, 71, 72, 73); *-an* for *-um* (6, 24); *-un* for *-um* (43). *-Un* for *-on* (10, 22, 27, 28, 47, 48) is probably the survival of an archaic and poetic spelling.

Hēr Æþelstān cyninȝ,   eorla dryhten,

beorna bēahȝifa,   and his brōþor ēac,

Ēadmund æþelinȝ,   ealdorlanȝne tīr

ȝeslōȝon æt sæcce   sweorda ecȝum

5   ymbe Brunanburh;   bordweal clufan,

hēowan heaþolinde   hamora lāfan,

afaran Ēadweardes;   swā him ȝeæþele wæs

from cnēomǣȝum,   þæt hī æt campe oft

wiþ lāþra ȝehwæne   land ealȝodon,

10   hord and hāmas.   Hettend crunȝun,

Sceotta lēoda   and scipflotan

fæȝe fēollan.   Feld dunnade

secȝa swāte,   siðþān sunne ūp

on morȝentīd,   mǣre tunȝol,

15   ȝlād ofer ȝrundas,   ȝodes condel beorht,

ēces Drihtnes,   oð sīo æþele ȝesceaft

sāh tō setle.   Þǣr læȝ secȝ mæniȝ

ȝārum āȝēted,   ȝuma norþerna

ofer scild scoten,   swilce Scittisc ēac

20   wēriȝ, wīȝes sæd.   Wesseaxe forð

ondlonȝne dæȝ   ēorodcistum

on lāst leȝdun   lāþum þēodum,

hēowan hereflēman   hindan þearle

mēcum mylenscearpan.   Myrce ne wyrndon

25   heardes hondpleȝan   hæleþa nānum

þǣra þe mid Anlāfe   ofer ēarȝebland

on lides bōsme   land ȝesōhtun

fæȝe tō ȝefeohte.   Fife læȝun

In this year King Æthelstan, the lord of warriors, giver of rings to men, and also his brother, Prince Eadmund, won eternal glory in battle with the edges of swords around Brunanburh; they, the sons of Eadweard, split the shield-wall, hacked the battle-shields with swords, as it was inborn in them from their ancestors that they should often in battle defend land, treasure and homes against every foe. The enemy perished, the men of the Scots and the sailors fell doomed. The field streamed with the blood of men, from when the sun in the morning, the glorious day-star, bright candle of God the eternal lord, glided up over the plains, until when that noble creation sank to rest. There lay many a warrior destroyed by spears, many a Northman shot above his shield, as also Scots exhausted, satiated with battle. Through the entire day the West Saxons pressed forward in troops on the track of the hostile people, hewed the fugitives cruelly from the rear with stone-sharpened blades. Neither did the Mercians refuse fierce hand-play to any of the heroes among those who with Anlaf, over the stirring sea in the bosom of the ship, had come to land, as doomed men to the fight. Five young kings lay on the battlefield, laid to rest by swords, and also likewise seven of Anlaf's earls, and countless of the Scottish and Viking army. There the chief of the Northmen, compelled by necessity, was driven to the prow of his ship with a scanty band; the king launched his ship on the water, departed on the tawny flood, and saved his life. So also there did the wise Constantine go north in flight to his home, the grey-headed warrior had no cause to rejoice in the company of kinsmen. He was deprived of kin and of friends killed on the field of battle, struck down in the strife, and he left his son in the place of slaughter, destroyed by wounds, young in battle.

on þām campstede   cyninӡas ӡiunӡe
30   sweordum āswefede,   swilce seofene ēac
eorlas Anlāfes,   unrīm heriӡes,
flotena and Sceotta.   Þǣr ӡeflēmed wearð
Norðmanna breӡu,   nēde ӡebēded
tō lides stefne   lītle weorode;
35   crēad cnear on flot,   cyninӡ ūt ӡewāt
on fealene flōd,   feorh ӡenerede.
Swilce þǣr ēac se frōda   mid flēame cōm
on his cȳþþe norð,   Costontinus,
hār hilderinӡ;   hrēman ne þorfte
40   mēcӡa ӡemanan: hē wæs his mǣӡa sceard,
frēonda befylled   on folcstede,
beslaӡen æt sæcce,   and his sunu forlēt
on wælstōwe wundun   forӡrunden,
ӡiunӡne æt ӡūðe.   Ӡelpan ne þorfte
45   beorn blandenfeax   bilӡeslehtes,
eald inwidda,   ne Anlāf þȳ mā;
mid heora herelāfum   hlehhan ne þorftun,
þæt hēo beaduweorca   beteran wurdun
on campstede,   cumbolӡehnāstes,
50   ӡārmittinӡe,   ӡumena ӡemōtes,
wǣpenӡewrixles,   þæs hī on wælfelda
wiþ Ēadweardes   afaran pleӡodan.
Ӡewitan him þā Norþmen   næӡledcnearrum,
drēoriӡ daraða lāf,   on Dinӡesmere,
55   ofer dēop wæter   Difelin sēcan,
eft Īra land,   ǣwiscmōde.
Swilce þā ӡebrōþer   bēӡen ætsamne,
cyninӡ and æþelinӡ,   cȳþþe sōhton,
Wesseaxena land,   wiӡes hrēmӡe.
60   Lētan him behindan   hrǣ bryttian
saluwiӡpādan,   þone sweartan hræfn,
hyrnednebban,   and þane hasupādan,
earn æftan hwīt,   ǣses brūcan
ӡrǣdiӡne ӡūðhafoc   and þæt ӡrǣӡe dēor,
65   wulf on wealde.   Ne wearð wæl māre
on þis ēiӡlande   ǣfre ӡīeta
folces ӡefylled   beforan þissum
sweordes ecӡum,   þæs þe ūs secӡað bēc,

The grey-haired warrior, the old dissembler, had no need to boast about the clash of swords; no more had Anlaf. With the remnants of their armies they need not laugh and say that they were better in warlike deeds on the battlefield, in the clash of standards, the meeting of spears, the encounter of men, the exchange of weapons, in which they competed on the field of slaughter against the sons of Eadweard. The Northmen, a sad remnant left by the javelins, departed humiliated in their nailed boats upon Dingesmere seeking Dublin, back to Ireland across the deep water. Likewise the brothers, both together, king and prince, made for home, the West Saxon land, exultant from battle. They left behind them to share the corpses the dark-coated one, the black, horny-beaked raven, and the dun-coated one, the white-tailed eagle, to enjoy the carrion, the greedy war-hawk, and that grey beast, the forest wolf. According to what books and old scholars tell us, there was never yet in this island before this time a greater slaughter of people killed by the edge of the sword since the Angles and Saxons, coming from the east across the broad ocean, landed here, and, proud war-smiths, they sought out Britain, overcame the Welsh, and eager for glory took possession of a homeland.

Notes

1   **Hēr**   Not strictly speaking a part of the poem, but the usual device for marking the place of an entry in the annals.

6   **hamora lāfan**   A poetic phrase referring to swords: 'the legacy (lit. leavings) of hammers'.

14–16   **mǣre tunȝol ... condel beorht ... sīo æþele ȝesceaft; ȝodes ... ēces Drihtnes**   Two interlocked strands of a common OE poetic device, semantic parallelism with variation in wording.

18   **āȝēted**   Along with *ȝeflēmed* (32), *nēde* (33), *hlehhan* (47) and *ēiȝlande* (66), this represents an Anglian form, where WS would have *ie/y* as the result of the *i*-mutation of *ea*.

24   **mēcum mylenscearpan**   This interesting phrase contains an Anglian form restricted in WS to verse, *mēce*, 'sword, blade', an otherwise unrecorded poetic compound *mylenscearp*, 'sharpened on a grindstone', and a confusion of the inflexional endings *-an/-um* characteristic of Late WS.

49   **cumbolȝehnāstes** 'clash of standards'   The word, which is unrecorded elsewhere, was not immediately understood by the copyist of A, who at first wrote the nonsensical *culbodgehnades*.

ealde ūðwitan,   siþþan ēastan hider
70 Enȝle and Seaxe   ūp becōman,
ofer brād brimu   Brytene sōhtan,
wlance wīȝsmiþas,   Wēalas ofercōman,
eorlas ārhwate,   eard beȝēatan.

53 **Norþmen næȝledcnearrum**   MS D (datable to about 1016) here reads *norðmen dæȝ ȝled on ȝarum*, which sounds like an attempt to make sense of matter dictated but not understood. The compound *næȝledcnearrum* is not recorded elsewhere, nor is the word *cnear* (35), which is used of Scandinavian ships and may be borrowed from that source; cf. Old Norse *knörr*, gen. *knarrar*.

7

THE BATTLE OF MALDON

In the year 991 the Essex militia commanded by their *ealdorman*, Byrhtnoth, confronted an invading force of Vikings near Maldon. The latter had landed on the island of Northey in the Blackwater estuary, which was joined to the mainland by a narrow causeway uncovered at low tide. In order to break the stalemate and commence battle, Byrhtnoth allowed the enemy to cross the causeway, an evidently risky tactic, but one which is not unparalleled in medieval warfare (Oman 1953). With hindsight, however, the poet sees that Byrhtnoth's decision cost him the victory and his life, yet he presents the facts in no spirit of disapproval.

The *Anglo-Saxon Chronicle* mentions the incident only briefly, but probably not more than a decade after the event a poem was composed which, in contrast to *Brunanburh*, which rejoices in military strength, sought to emphasise the traditional values of the loyalty and heroism of Byrhtnoth's retainers in defeat. A more reflective and idealistic work which values virtues more than might, *The Battle of Maldon* is metrically looser and less metaphorically ornamented than more formal Old English poetry, but uses considerable rhetorical skill in the composition of speeches. The poem employs much traditional diction: the synonym group *beorn, rinc, lēod, man, hæleð, wiʒa, ʒuma* for 'man, warrior', poetic compounds such as *ʒārrǣs*, 'spear-onslaught' (32), *ʒūðpleʒa*, 'battle-play' (61), and *wīhaʒa*, 'battle-hedge' (102), and fixed formulae such as *wordum mǣlan* (26). The compound *bricʒweard*, 'bridge-guard' (85), seems to have been the poet's own creation.

The only manuscript of the *Battle of Maldon* was destroyed in the Cotton fire of 1731, but a transcription had been made by David Casley, deputy keeper of the Cottonian collection, and it is upon this that all modern editions are based. The text is written in standard West Saxon, and its lateness is suggested by signs of spelling confusion in representing inflexions consisting of a vowel followed by a nasal consonant: *handon* (7), *folman* (21, 108), *lēodon* (23).

brocen wurde.
Hēt þā hyssa hwæne   hors forlǣten,
feor āfȳsan,   and forð ȝanȝan,
hicȝan tō handum   and tō hiȝe ȝōdum.

5   Þā þæt Offan mæȝ   ǣrest onfunde,
þæt se eorl nolde   yrhðo ȝeþolian,
hē lēt him þā of handon   lēofne flēoȝan
hafoc wið þæs holtes,   and tō þǣre hilde stōp;
be þām man mihte oncnāwan   þæt se cniht nolde

10   wācian æt þām wīȝe,   þā hē tō wǣpnum fēnȝ.
Ēac him wolde Ēadric   his ealdre ȝelǣstan,
frēan tō ȝefeohte,   onȝan þā forð beran
ȝār tō ȝūþe.   Hē hæfde ȝōd ȝeþanc
þā hwīle þe hē mid handum   healdan mihte

15   bord and brād swurd;   bēot hē ȝelǣste
þā hē ætforan his frēan   feohtan sceolde.
      Ðā þǣr Byrhtnōð onȝan   beornas trymian,
rād and rǣdde,   rincum tǣhte
hū hī sceoldon standan   and þone stede healdan,

20   and bæd þæt hyra randas   rihte hēoldon
fæste mid folman,   and ne forhtedon nā.
Þā hē hæfde þæt folc   fæȝere ȝetrymmed,
hē līhte þā mid lēodon   þǣr him lēofost wæs,
þǣr hē his heorðwerod   holdost wiste.

25   Þā stōd on stæðe,   stīðlīce clypode
wīcinȝa ār,   wordum mælde,
se on bēot ābēad   brimlīþendra
ǣrænde tō þām eorle,   þǣr hē on ōfre stōd:
'Mē sendon tō þē   sǣmen snelle,

30   hēton ðē secȝan   þæt þū mōst sendan raðe
bēaȝas wið ȝebeorȝe;   and ēow betere is
þæt ȝē þisne ȝārrǣs   mid ȝafole forȝyldon,
þon wē swā hearde   hilde dǣlon.
Ne þurfe wē ūs spillan,   ȝif ȝē spēdaþ tō þām;

35   wē willað wið þām ȝolde   ȝrið fæstnian.
Ȝyf þū þat ȝerǣdest,   þe hēr rīcost eart,
þæt þū þīne lēoda   lȳsan wille,
syllan sǣmannum   on hyra sylfra dōm
feoh wið frēode,   and niman frið æt ūs,

40   wē willaþ mid þām sceattum   ūs tō scype ȝanȝan,

. . . was broken. Then he ordered each of the young men to abandon his horse, drive it far away, and go forward concentrating on his strength and fighting spirit. As soon as Offa's kinsman discovered that the earl would not tolerate slackness he let his beloved hawk fly from his hands towards the wood, and stepped towards the battle. That way it might be understood that the boy did not intend to weaken in the fight when he took up weapons. In addition to him, Eadric too wished to serve his leader, his lord, in the fight; he then began to carry his spear forward into combat. He maintained a valiant spirit as long as he could hold his shield and broadsword with his hands; he fulfilled his proud boast when he had to fight before his lord.

Then Byrhtnoth began to draw up the warriors there, rode about and instructed them, directed how they had to stand and hold the position, and ordered that they should hold their round shields properly, firmly in their fists, and that they should have no fear. When he had suitably arranged the army, he dismounted among the men where it was most pleasing to him, where he knew his personal guard to be most loyal. Then a Viking messenger stood on the bank and loudly called, spoke in words; he arrogantly delivered the seafarers' message to the earl, where he stood on the shore: 'Bold seamen have sent me to you, ordered me to tell you that you may quickly send rings in exchange for security; and it is better for you that you buy off this onslaught with tribute than we should share such cruel battle. We need not destroy each other, if you are sufficiently wealthy; we are willing to establish a truce in exchange for the gold. If you who are most influential take the view that you wish to ransom your people, give to the seamen money for friendship at their own assessment, and accept peace from us; we intend to embark with the payment, go to sea, and keep the peace with you.'

Byrhtnoth spoke, raised his shield, brandished his slender spear, and spoke in words, angered and resolute, gave him an answer: 'Do you hear, seafarer, what this army says? They will give you spears as a tribute, the deadly spear-point and the ancient sword, equipment that will not avail you in battle. Messenger of the seamen, report back again, say to your people the much more unwelcome news that here stands with his troop a noble earl who will defend this country, Ethelred my lord's home, its people and its land. The heathen shall fall in the battle. It seems to me too shameful that

on flot fēran,   and ēow friþes healdan.'
    Byrhtnōð maþelode,   bord hafenode,
wand wācne æsc,   wordum mælde,
yrre and ānræd   āʒeaf him andsware:
45 'ʒehȳrst þū, sælida,   hwæt þis folc seʒeð?
Hī willað ēow tō ʒafole   ʒāras syllan,
ættrynne ord   and ealde swurd,
þā hereʒeatu   þe ēow æt hilde ne dēah.
Brimmanna boda,   ābēod eft onʒēan,
50 seʒe þīnum lēodum   miccle lāþre spell,
þæt hēr stynt unforcūð   eorl mid his werode,
þe wile ʒealʒean   ēþel þysne,
Æþelrēdes eard,   ealdres mīnes,
folc and foldan.   Feallan sceolon
55 hǣþene æt hilde.   Tō hēanlic mē þinceð
þæt ʒē mid ūrum sceattum   tō scype ʒanʒon
unbefohtene,   nū ʒē þus feor hider
on ūrne eard   in becōmon.
Ne sceole ʒē swā sōfte   sinc ʒeʒanʒan;
60 ūs sceal ord and ecʒ   ǣr ʒesēman,
ʒrim ʒūðpleʒa,   ǣr wē ʒofol syllon.'
    Hēt þā bord beran,   beornas ʒanʒan,
þæt hī on þām ēasteðe   ealle stōdon.
Ne mihte þǣr for wætere   werod tō þām ōðrum;
65 þǣr cōm flōwende   flōd æfter ebban,
lucon laʒustrēamas.   Tō lanʒ hit him þūhte,
hwænne hī tōʒædere   ʒāras bēron.
Hī þǣr Pantan strēam   mid prasse bestōdon,
Ēastseaxena ord   and se æschere.
70 Ne mihte hyra æniʒ   ōþrum derian,
būton hwā þurh flānes flyht   fyl ʒenāme.
Se flōd ūt ʒewāt;   þā flotan stōdon ʒearowe,
wīcinʒa fela,   wīʒes ʒeorne.
Hēt þā hæleða hlēo   healdan þā bricʒe
75 wiʒan wīʒheardne,   sē wæs hāten Wulfstān,
cāfne mid his cynne,   þæt wæs Cēolan sunu,
þe ðone forman man   mid his francan ofscēat
þe þǣr baldlīcost   on þā bricʒe stōp.
þǣr stōdon mid Wulfstāne   wiʒan unforhte,
80 Ælfere and Maccus,   mōdiʒe twēʒen,

with our money you should embark uncontested now you have
penetrated thus far into our homeland. Nor shall you so easily carry
off treasure: point and edge shall bring us together, grim war-play,
before we give tribute.' He then commanded the warriors to go
bearing shields so that they all stood on the river bank. Nor might
the warband get at the other because of the water; there high tide
came flowing after the ebb, the waters enclosed them. Too long it
seemed to them till they bore spears together. There they stood in
force alongside the river Blackwater, the East Saxon vanguard and
the ship army. Neither might any of them injure the other unless
someone through an arrow's flight received his death. The tide went
out; then the sailors stood ready, many Vikings eager for combat.
Then the protector of men ordered a battle-hardened warrior called
Wulfstan to hold the bridge; it was Ceola's son, brave like all his
people, who with his javelin killed the first man who most boldly
there stepped on to the bridge. There stood with Wulfstan unafraid
warriors, Ælfhere and Maccus – a valiant pair; those would not flee
at the ford, but they unflinchingly defended against the enemy
as long as they could handle weapons. When they realised and
clearly saw that they found fierce bridge-guards there, the wretched
strangers began to use cunning. They asked that they might have a
landing place to go over the ford, bringing foot-soldiers.

Then the earl, on account of his overconfidence, allowed too
much land to a more hateful people. Byrhthelm's son called across
the cold water (the warriors listened): 'Now room is made for you,
come quickly to us, warriors to the battle; God alone knows who
may control the battlefield.' The slaughterous wolves advanced (they
did not care about the water), the Viking band, west across the
Blackwater bore shields over the bright water, seamen bearing lime-
wood shields to land. There Byrhtnoth with his warriors stood
ready against the enemy. He ordered the battle-line to be formed
with shields and that the war-band hold firm against the enemy.
The fight was near, glory in battle. That time was come when there
doomed men should perish. There a shout was raised up, the ravens
circled, the eagle greedy for carrion; there was uproar on the ground.
Then they let fly from their hands file-hard spears, cruelly sharpened
javelins; bows were busy, shield received point.

þā noldon æt þām forda   flēam ȝewyrcan,
ac hī fæstlīce   wið ðā fȳnd weredon,
þā hwīle þe hī wǣpna   wealdan mōston.
Þā hī þæt onȝēaton   and ȝeorne ȝesāwon
85   þæt hī þǣr bricȝweardas   bitere fundon,
onȝunnon lyteȝian þā   lāðe ȝystas,
bǣdon þæt hī ūpȝanȝan   āȝan mōston,
ofer þone ford faran,   fēþan lǣdan.
        Ðā se eorl onȝan   for his ofermōde
90   ālȳfan landes tō fela   lāþere ðēode.
Onȝan ceallian þā   ofer cald wæter
Byrhtelmes bearn   (beornas ȝehlyston):
'Nū ēow is ȝerȳmed,   ȝāð ricene tō ūs,
ȝuman tō ȝūþe;   ȝod āna wāt
95   hwā þǣre wælstōwe   wealdan mōte.'
Wōdon þā wælwulfas   (for wætere ne murnon),
wīcinȝa werod,   west ofer Pantan,
ofer scīr wæter   scyldas wēȝon,
lidmen tō lande   linde bǣron.
100   Þǣr onȝēan ȝramum   ȝearowe stōdon
Byrhtnōð mid beornum;   hē mid bordum hēt
wyrcan þone wīhaȝan,   and þæt werod healdan
fæste wið fēondum.   Þā wæs feohte nēh,
tīr æt ȝetohte.   Wæs sēo tīd cumen
105   þæt þǣr fǣȝe men   feallan sceoldon.
Þǣr wearð hrēam āhafen,   hremmas wundon,
earn ǣses ȝeorn;   wæs on eorþan cyrm.
Hī lēton þā of folman   fēolhearde speru,
ȝrimme ȝeȝrundene   ȝāras flēoȝan;
110   boȝan wǣron bysiȝe,   bord ord onfēnȝ.

Notes

1   **brocen wurde**   The beginning of the poem is missing, but not many
lines can have been lost.

2–4   **hēt ... forlǣtan ... āfȳsan ... ȝanȝan ... hicȝan**   All are infinitives
dependent on *hēt*, the later preterite form of *hātan* (see Excerpt 3, line 64).

6   **se eorl**   In early verse this means 'man, warrior', but here is a title equivalent to *ealdorman*. Influence by Scandinavian *jarlr* has been suggested
(McKinnell 1975).

9   **oncnāwan**   The prefix *on-* has ingressive aspect – that is, it directs attention to the beginning, the bringing about, of the state denoted by the verbal base. Thus the verb *cnāwan* 'know' is made to mean 'recognise, become aware'.

    se cniht   The word is about to undergo important semantic changes. In OE it develops from 'boy, servant' to 'retainer'. The modern sense 'knight' appears after the Conquest in the twelfth century.

24   **heorðwerod**   Literally 'hearth-troop'. The compound implies those troops closest to the leader, the household retainers who shared his hall.

35–39   **ȝrið fæstnian . . . niman frið**   The word *grið* is a Scandinavian borrowing. The collocation with *frið* is a formula of legal origin found also in the *Ormulum*.

42   **Byrhtnōð maþelode**   A formulaic phrase for introducing a formal speech. Uses a verb restricted to verse (cf. *wordum mælde*). A similar formula is employed in the eighth-century south German epic, the *Hildebrandeslied*.

47   **ættrynne ord and ealde swurd**   The word *ættryne* literally means 'poisoned', but there is no evidence for the use of poisoned weapons in Anglo-Saxon England; therefore translate as 'deadly'. The connotations of *ealde*, 'old' are approving. Weapons and ornaments handed down from previous generations were greatly valued, since the pace of technological change was not such as to render them obsolete, and they were seen as having proved their worth.

52   **þe wile ȝealȝan**   The force of the verb *willan* is here clearly that of intention. Compare the sense of inevitability in *sceoldon* (105).

75–78   **se wæs hāten . . . þæt wæs Cēolan sunu . . . þe . . . þe**   A sequence of quasi-relative clauses. Note the use of the masculine form of the demonstrative followed by what is properly the neuter form (here used indefinitely without concord) and then the two uses of the relative particle *þe*.

89   **for his ofermōde**   The sense of this word is disputed. Although it can mean 'pride' in religious contexts, the implicit moral criticism of that interpretation seems inappropriate to the qualities of a heroic leader. Nevertheless, it is undeniable that the poet questions Byrhtnoth's judgement in the light of events by his words *landes tō fela*.

91   **Onȝan ceallian þā ofer cald wæter**   The phrase is paralleled in Scandinavian literature, and the suggestion that it is a literary formula is supported by the use of the Anglian form rather than the WS *ceald*. On the gloomy associations of the word in Old and Middle English literature, see Salmon 1959.

110   **bord ord onfēnȝ**   The use of the singular to describe an action envisaged to be repeated many times throughout the battlefield is a characteristic feature of OE (and also of ME alliterative) epic style.

EARLY MIDDLE ENGLISH

(1100–1300)

The beginnings of Middle English might plausibly be associated with the invasion of 1066, after which England found itself host to a second language, Norman French, alongside the English used by the majority. But to equate the beginning of Middle English with the Norman Conquest would be only partly true, and to understand why this is the case it is necessary to outline some of the major differences between the stages of the language which modern scholars have called Old and Middle English.

Changes in the progression from Old to Middle English are traceable at every level of analysis, not merely in the lexicon. Phonologically, Middle English is distinguished by a number of alterations in the quantity of stressed vowels, which changes the distribution of long and short vowels from that in Old English. Late in the Old English period, short vowels before certain consonant groups (*ld, rd, rl, rn, mb, nd,* and *ng*) were lengthened. Thus the Anglian words *cald* and *ald* (WS *ceald* and *eald*) developed a long *a*, which about 1200 was rounded to produce the modern forms *cold* and *old*. However, long vowels before two consonants other than these 'lengthening groups', and those in a position before a single consonant three syllables from the end of a word, were shortened. The noun *godspell,* 'gospel' (originally with the long vowel of *gōd*) and the verb *bletsian,* 'bless' (originally derived from the noun *blōd,* with a long root vowel) therefore developed short root vowels. This shortening was accompanied by the progressive monophthong-isation of the OE diphthongs spelt <ea> and <eo> and the emergence of new diphthongs through the vocalisation of the sequence front vowel + [j] in words like *way* and *lay* and vowel + [x] in words like *law, bow.* Two new diphthongs spelt <oi, oy> derived mostly from French borrowings such as *joie.* Short *œ* was lowered to *a* in all contexts. During the early thirteenth century, the stressed vowels underwent further changes in quantity when vowels in open syllables were lengthened (see Excerpt 9).

Equally importantly, the grammar of English underwent striking changes. Accelerating a process of case reduction which is already observable in the decline of dual number and instrumental case in earlier Old English, the inflexional system distinguishing case, gender and number in nouns and adjectives was greatly simplified. Vowels in unstressed inflexional endings ceased to be differentiated in pronunciation. The OE dative plural *-um* was already spelt <an> and <on>, indicating indistinct pronunciation, in Late West Saxon (see Excerpt 7), and the wealth of OE noun and adjective inflexions was gradually reduced to *-es*, *-en*, *-ene* and the ubiquitous *-e*. In the North the loss also of final *-n* produced a situation anticipating Modern English at a very early date (see Excerpt 1). As inflexions became less important in indicating the syntactical function of nouns, the role of prepositions increased, and word order became more fixed within clauses. The definite article was steadily reduced to the simple form *þe*, and the originally neuter form of the definite article *þæt* was increasingly used as an invariable relative pronoun. The thirteenth century witnesses the earliest shift of the interrogative pronouns *who* and *which* (OE *hwā*, *hwelc*) to relative use. Verbs were also affected, so that in both the South and the North the third person ceased to distinguish adequately between singular and plural (NorthOE *-es*; *-as* > NorthME *-es*; *-es* and WS *-eþ*; *-aþ* > SouthME *-eþ*; *-eþ*). The personal pronouns also became indistinct as the result of phonetic change, and new forms began to appear: *scœ*, 'she', is found first in the *Peterborough Chronicle* (1154), and *þeჳჳ*, 'they', is first recorded in the *Ormulum* (*c.* 1180) (see Excerpt 9).

This last is notable apart from its function in the grammar since it is a wordform borrowed from a Scandinavian language: Early Middle English is made distinct from Old English also by the relatively high number of recent foreign lexical borrowings. Many of these are, of course, from Norman French, but a substantial number, especially in the North and East, are from Danish and Norwegian. These are words borrowed into English from settlers in the Danelaw in the two hundred years preceding the Conquest, but, as a result of the cultural status of the West Saxon written standard, not recorded in writing until after the Norman Conquest, when the English language itself lost prestige by comparison with French. This incidental effect of the Norman Conquest is the final major differentiating feature between Old and Middle English which will find a place here. From being a language of high status, relatively standardised in written form by scribal training, English fell into lower esteem beneath both Latin and French as written languages. Lacking any centralised authority to legislate its writing in standard form, English began to be written individually by scribes in their own local dialects, employing the skills they had learned for rendering Latin and French. This brought about changes to the spelling system, so that in the course of the thirteenth century <æ> and <ð> gradually disappeared and <sc>, <c + front vowel> and <cȝ> came to be written <sh>, <ch> and <gg> respectively. Above all, Middle English emerged as a language of variety. The diversity of the spoken language, which in modern times has once again been hidden by a written standard, is ever present in written Middle English.

Clearly, the changes described above did not happen at once. They took place over many centuries and at a different pace in the various dialect areas. Generally speaking, inflexional loss was more rapid in the areas settled by Scandinavians, so that the South and South-West, which had remained under continuous West Saxon control, preserved the grammar of the Anglo-Saxon language longest. The following features are characteristic.

OE <y> is written <u> (western part only);

OE <eo> continued to be written as late as the fourteenth century in the West;

Initial [s] and [f] had been voiced, and were written <z> and <v> (compare modern *fox* and *vixen*);

-en plurals survive in nouns in considerable numbers;

Feminine and plural third person pronouns are still restricted to forms beginning with *h-* (*ha, he, heo*);

i-/y- survives as a prefix of the verbal past participle;

Weak Class 2 verbs are still distinguished from other Weak and Strong verbs by the presence of an *-i-* in the infinitive, the third-person-plural present tense, and the present participle (*luuien, luuie, luuiende/luuinde*).

In a few respects, however, the South diverged from earlier OE more markedly than the North. Thus the long *ā* of OE in words like *stān*, *hām* or *hlāford* was rounded to *o* in the South by 1200, but remained unchanged in the North. The plural dative inflexion *-um*, which had been reduced to a sound represented by the spellings *-an* and *-on* in late West Saxon, seems to have survived longer in the Danelaw, where it was preserved by identification with the same inflexion in Danish. Furthermore, the Old English of Kent had been distinct from that of Wessex, so that Middle English there still preserved the distinction by which:

> West Saxon <y> was written <e>;
> the reflex of West Saxon long *ēo* was written <ie> (from earlier *īo*).

Both of these spellings reflect changes which had taken place long before the Conquest. In the North, too, OE dialect divergences re-emerged in Middle English. In the tenth century, the Lindisfarne Gospel gloss already exhibits the loss of final *-n* in verb infinitives and provides evidence of third-person present-tense forms in *-es* and *-as* (see Excerpt 1B, p. 14). These latter both appear in Middle English as *-es*, the ancestor of the form of the modern third-person present singular. Two further distinguishing features of the northern dialect in Middle English are the present participle form ending in *-ande* and the spelling of OE <hw> and <cw> with <qu> or <quh>. The participle ending derives from the Scandinavian influence which was heavy upon this dialect, the spelling from the influence of French-trained scribes.

It is evident from this brief discussion – which can do no more than give an impression of the variety of Middle English – that the emergence of the language changes associated with the beginning of Middle English were only loosely connected with the Norman Conquest. In many cases, the dialect writing that the Conquest initiated simply revealed changes which had been in progress for centuries, or diversity which had already been part of pre-Conquest Old English. It revealed also the extent of lexical, syntactical and grammatical influence upon Old English which had come from the extensive Scandinavian settlement of the preceding two hundred years. Scandinavian influence was now apparent not only in hundreds of lexical borrowings, but also among grammatical words such as pronouns (*they*, *their*, *them* and probably *she*), prepositions (*til* and *fro*), derivational affixes (*um-*, *-leik*), and even the inflexional ending *-ande*. Yet, far-reaching as the influence of Scandinavian upon Old English was, it was not, any more than the Norman Conquest, the sole contributory factor in the emergence of Middle English. Rather, we should look to a coalition of contributing factors implicit within Old English, accelerated by contact with Scandinavian, and completed by the Norman Conquest. The major contribution of this last was to suppress standardised English before setting it free in infinite new variety, and subsequently enriching its vocabulary by copious loanwords and phrases.

8

THE *PETERBOROUGH CHRONICLE*

The *Peterborough Chronicle*, preserved in Bodleian Library MS Laud Misc. 636, is a descendant of the *Anglo-Saxon Chronicle*, instituted during the reign of King Alfred and maintained at various monastic sites throughout Anglo-Saxon England. In Peterborough, the compilation of the *Chronicle* survived the Conquest, and continued longer than elsewhere. In 1116 it was destroyed by fire but re-established by copying a version borrowed from a southern source. From 1121 to 1132 the renewed record was kept by a Peterborough monk, writing on six different occasions. His work is followed by a single continuous account in a different hand which covers the remaining years until 1154, when the *Chronicle* was discontinued.

The perspective of the Continuations differs from what went before, exhibiting the foreshortening effect of parochialism. Events around Peterborough loom larger than those of national importance, and the warmth of feeling that proximity generates contributes to greater vigour in the narrative. Personal experience and close acquaintance are drawn upon as testimony, and indignation enlivens rhetorical structures. In the excerpts given below, the accounts of the career of Henry d'Angély and of the anarchy of Stephen's reign are both highly coloured presentations of an affronted Peterborough viewpoint. It is as well to remember that in the annal for 1123 the annalist speaks with approval of Henry, but he changed his mind on further acquaintance. Although the atrocities described in the 1137 annal have general truth, the Peterborough area seems to have been particularly unfortunate in suffering the tyranny of Geoffrey de Mandeville, who fortified the abbey of Ramsey.

The language of the two Peterborough Continuations is distinct from that of the borrowed annals, since elements of the local language and features associated with Early Middle English supersede an essentially standard West Saxon original. This is very clear from the morphology. Already in the

First Continuation the simplification of inflexions is well advanced: in the definite article, accusative forms appear for dative (*tofor þone weofede*; *fram þa selua tune*), and among the nouns, plurals of whatever case frequently end in -*es* (*þurh his micele wrences*, 36–37). Weak nouns have adopted the -*es* plurals proper to Strong masculine nouns (*huntes*, 61; *bucces*, 64), and Weak Class 2 verbs are no longer distinguishable by their inflexional -*i*- from other weak verbs (*ðolen*, 45; *hunten*, 61). The characteristically northern and east Midland loss of the prefix has already occurred in past participles (*numen*, 17; *gifen*, 51). East Midland developments, as well as continuity from Anglian OE, are evident also in the spelling and phonology (see Notes). French borrowing is absent in the first excerpt, except as personal or place names, but a few words of probable Scandinavian origin are found (*oc, toc, baðe*).

A   First Continuation (1127)

Mcxxvii   Ðis gear heald se kyng Heanri his hird æt Cristesmæsse
on Windlesoure. Þær wæs se Scotte kyng Dauid and eall ða heaued,
læred and læuued, þet wæs on Engleland. And þær he let sweren
ercebiscopes and biscopes and abbotes and eorles and ealle þa ðeines
5   ða þær wæron his dohter Æðelic Englaland and Normandi to hande
æfter his dæi, þe ær wæs ðes Caseres wif of Sexlande; and sende
hire siððen to Normandi, and mid hire ferde hire broðer Rotbert
eorl of Gleucestre and Brian þes eorles sunu Alein Fergan, and lett
hire beweddan þes eorles sunu of Angeow, Gosfreið Martæl wæs
10   gehaten: hit ofþuhte naþema ealle frencisc and englisc, oc se kyng
hit dide for to hauene sibbe of se eorl of Angeow and for helpe to
hauene togænes his neue Willelm. Ðes ilces gæres on þone lententide
wæs se eorl Karle of Flandres ofslagen on ane circe þær he læi and
bæd hine to Gode tofor þone weofede amang þane messe fram his
15   agene manne. And se kyng of France brohte þone eorles sunu
Willelm of Normandi, and iæf hine þone eorldom, and þet landfolc
him wið toc. Þes ilce Willelm hæfde æror numen ðes eorles dohtor
of Angeow to wife, oc hi wæron siððen totweamde for sibreden:
þet wes eall ðurh þone kyng Heanri of Engleland. Siððen þa nam
20   he þes kynges wifes swuster of France to wife; and forþi iæf se kyng
him þone eorldom of Flandres.

Ðes ilce gæres he gæf þone abbotrice of Burch an abbot, Henri
wæs gehaten, of Peitowe, se hæfde his abbotrice Sancte Iohannis of
Angeli on hande. And ealle þa ærcebiscopes and biscopes seidon
25   þet hit wæs togeanes riht, and þet he ne mihte hafen twa abbotrices
on hande. Oc se ilce Heanri dide þone king to understandene þet
he hæfde læten his abbotrice for þet micele unsibbe þet wæs on þet
land, and þet he dide ðurh þes Papes ræd and leue of Rome and
ðurh þes abbotes of Clunni and þurh þæt he wæs legat of ðone
30   Romescott: oc hit ne wæs naðema eallswa, oc he wolde hauen baðe
on hande, and swa hafde swa lange swa Godes wille wæs. He wæs
on his clærchade biscop on Scesscuns; siððan warð he munec on
Clunni, and siððon prior on þone seolue minstre; and siððon he
wærð prior on Sauenni. Þaræftor, þurh þet he wæs ðes kynges mæi
35   of Engleland and þes eorles of Peitowe, þa geaf se eorl him þone
abbotrice of Sancte Iohannis minstre of Angeli. Siððon, þurh his
micele wrences, ða beiæt he þone ærcebiscoprice of Besencun, and
hæfde hit þa on hande þre dagas; þa forlæs he þet mid rihte, forþi

ẽ

1127   At Christmas in this year King Henry held his court in Windsor. King David of Scots was there and all the chief men, both learned and laymen, who were in England. And there he got the archbishops, bishops, abbots, earls and all the noblemen who were there to swear that his daughter, Æthelic, who had previously been the Emperor of Germany's wife, [should have] England and Normandy after his time; and afterwards he sent her to Normandy, and her brother Robert, Earl of Gloucester, and Brian, son of the earl Alein Fergan, travelled with her, and he had her married to the son of the Earl of Anjou, [who] was called Geoffrey Martel: all the French and English were never more affronted, but the king did it in order to have friendly relations with the Earl of Anjou and to get help against his nephew, William. In this same year during Lent, Charles, Earl of Flanders, was slain by his own men as he lay in church and prayed to God before the altar, during the mass. And the King of France brought the earl's son, William, from Normandy, and gave the earldom to him, and the people of that land accepted him. This same William had previously taken as wife the Earl of Anjou's daughter, but they were afterwards separated on grounds of consanguinity: that was all by the agency of King Henry of England. After that he took as a wife the sister of the king of France's wife; and that is why the king gave him the earldom of Flanders.

In this same year he gave the abbacy of Peterborough to an abbot from Poitou, called Henry, who possessed the abbacy of St Jean d'Angély. And all the archbishops and bishops said that it was improper, and that he could not possess two abbacies. But the same Henry gave the king to understand that he had given up his abbacy on account of the great unrest that was in that land, and that he did that by the advice and permission of the pope of Rome, and the abbot of Cluny, and because he was the agent of papal taxation: but it was not at all so, and he wished to possess both, and so he did as long as God's will allowed it. In his clerical career he was bishop in Soissons; afterwards he became a monk in Cluny, and after a prior in the same monastery; and afterwards he became prior at Souvigny. After that, because he was kinsman to the king of England and the Earl of Poitou, the earl then gave him the abbacy of the monastery of St Jean d'Angély. Afterwards, through his great cunning and trickery, he obtained the archbishopric of

þet he hit hæfde æror beieten mid unrihte. Siððon þa beiet he þone
biscoprice of Seintes, þet wæs fif mile fram his abbotrice; þet he
hæfde fulneah seoueniht on hande; þenon brohte se abbot him of
Clunni, swa swa he æror dide of Besencun. Þa beþohte he him þet
gif he mihte ben rotfest on Engleland þet he mihte habben eal his
wille. Besohte þa þone kyng and sæide him þet he wæs eald man
and forbroken man, and þet he ne mihte ðolen þa micele unrihte
and þa micele unsibbe ða wæron on here land, and iærnde þa þurh
him and ðurh ealle his freond namcuðlice þone abbotrice of Burhc.
And se kyng hit him iætte, forði þet he wæs his mæi and forþi þet
he wæs an hæfod ða að to swerene and witnesse to berene þær ða
eorles sunu of Normandi and þes eorles dohter of Angeow wæron
totwemde for sibreden. Þus earmlice wæs þone abbotrice gifen
betwix Cristesmesse and Candelmesse at Lundene. And swa he ferde
mid þe cyng to Wincestre. And þanon he come to Burch. And þær
he wunede eallriht swa drane doð on hiue: eall þet þa beon dragen
toward, swa frett þa drane and dragað fraward – swa dide he: eall
þet he mihte tacen, wiðinnen and wiðuten, of læred and of læwed,
swa he sende ouer sæ; and na god þær ne dide ne na god ðær ne
læuede. Ne þince man na sellice þet we soð seggen; for hit wæs ful
cuð ofer eall land þet swa radlice swa he þær com – þet wæs þes
Sunendæies þet man singað 'Exurge, quare obdormis, Domine?' – þa
son þæræfter þa sægon and herdon fela men feole huntes hunten.
Ða huntes wæron swarte and micele and ladlice, and here hundes
ealle swarte and bradegede and ladlice, and hi ridone on swarte
hors and swarte bucces. Þis wæs segon on þe selue derfald in þa
tune on Burch and on ealle þa wudes ða wæron fram þa selua
tune to Stanforde; and þa muneces herdon ða horn blawen þet hi
blewen on nihtes. Soðfæste men heom kepten on nihtes; sæidon,
þes þe heom þuhte, þet þær mihte wel ben abuton twenti oðer
þritti horn-blaweres. Þis wæs sægon and herd fram þet he þider
com eall þet lententid onan to Eastren. Þis was his ingang: of his
utgang ne cunne we iett noht seggon. God scawe fore!

Besançon, and had it for three days; then, justly, he relinquished that which he had previously unjustly obtained. Then he got the bishopric of Saintes, which was five miles from his abbacy; that he possessed for very nearly a week; the abbot of Cluny brought him from there, just as earlier he did from Besançon. Then he thought to himself that if he might take root in England that he could have all his own way. He implored the king and told him that he was an old and broken man and that he could not suffer the great injustice and disturbance that were in their land, and he desired through him and through all his important friends the abbacy of Peterborough. And the king obtained it for him, because he was his kinsman and because he was prominent in swearing the oath and bearing witness when the son of the Earl of Normandy and the Earl of Anjou's daughter were separated for consanguinity. Thus the abbey was wretchedly bestowed in London between Christmas and Candlemass. And so he went with the king to Winchester, and from there he came to Peterborough. There he lived just as the drone does in the hive: all that the bees bring in the drone devours and takes away – as he did: all that he could take, from inside and out, from clerks and common people, he sent across the sea; he contributed nothing and left nothing. Nor should any man think it marvellous that we state the truth; for it was well known throughout the land as soon as he came there – it was on the Sunday when 'Exurge [etc.]' is sung. Then immediately after many men saw and heard many hunters hunt. The hunters were dark and huge and ugly, and their hounds all dark and wide-eyed and ugly and they rode on dark horses and dark goats. This was seen in the same deer-park in the township of Peterborough and in all the woods from the same town to Stamford. And the monks heard the horns blown that they blew at night. Sensible men stayed in at night; they said, as it seemed to them, that there might well be about twenty or thirty hornblowers. This was seen and heard from [the time] that he came all that Lent up to Easter. This was his arrival: of his departure we cannot yet speak. May God provide!

Notes

1   **Ðis gear** 'this year'   Annals frequently begin with some version of this phrase, but in earlier entries the dative case is clearly indicated.

2   **heaued**   The spelling <u> of the voiced fricative consonant between vowels, normally spelt <f> in OE, is owing to French influence, cf. *hauene* (11), *læuede* (58), but also *hæfod* (49).

4   **ðeines**   The spelling (cf. OE *ðegn*) suggests the emergence of a new diphthong /ei/, as also in *seidon* (24), *dæi* (6) and *læi* (13).

5   **Æðelic**   Better known as Matilda. She had been married to the Emperor Henry V, who died in 1125.

8   **Alein Fergan**   Count of Brittany. *Brian* and *sunu* are in apposition. Although in apposition with *þes eorles*, the name *Alein Fergan* is not inflected.

11   **dide**   The <i> spelling in words where OE has <y> represents an unrounding of the OE vowel characteristic of the east Midlands in ME. Cf. *þince* (58).

12   **Willelm**   William Clito, son of Robert Curthose, Duke of Normandy.

14–15   **fram his agene manne** 'by his own men'   In OE *fram* takes the dative, whose plural was *mannum*. The dative form here is modelled on that of the singular of masculine nouns, but in correct OE *man* has a mutated dative singular, *men*. The writer's failure to understand this inflexional system is apparent.

20   **þes kynges . . . to wife**   The head of the noun phrase is *swuster*, which is preceded by two genitive modifiers in the OE manner, and succeeded by a dative qualifier. The phrase *to wife* is also a dative idiom meaning 'as a wife'. A dative -*e* is often used in such phrases, but may be omitted: *of Engleland* (19).

31   **swa Godes wille wæs**   This phrase suggests that the passage was written after Henry had ceased to hold St Jean d'Angély in 1131, but the closing words of the excerpt imply composition before his departure from England in 1132.

38   **þre dagas**   The monophthongisation of OE *ēo*, which is found at an early date in the east Midlands, is suggested by other spellings in this text: *ben* (43), *blewen* (67).

39   **beieten**   WS *begieten*. In WS the palatal consonant (written *g*) diphthongised the following *e*. The spelling here is descended from an Anglian antecedent.

59–60   **þes Sunendæies**   Sexagesima Sunday, 6 February 1127.

62   **Ða huntes**   The allusion is probably to the 'Wild Hunt', a legend of ghostly hunters riding on stormy nights led by the Devil. Analogous hunts are found in Celtic and in Scandinavian myth, where the leader is the god Odin.

63 **bradegede** 'broad-eyed' The form *egede* suggests an OE antecedent spelt *ēge* rather than WS *ēage*, the product of Anglian smoothing.

64 **derfald** WS *dēorfeald*. The spelling exemplifies both the east Midland monophthongisation of *ēo* and the failure of the breaking of *æ* before *l*-groups characteristic of Anglian OE. Cf., however, the spelling *eald* (44).

66 **herdon** WS *hīerdon*. The *i*-mutation of *ea* produced *īe* in West Saxon, but *e* in Anglian dialects.

B   Final Continuation (1154)

Mcxxxvii   Dis gære for þe king Stephne ofer sæ to Normandi, and
ther wes underfangen forþi ðat hi uuenden ðat he sculde ben alsuic
alse the eom wes, and for he hadde get his tresor; ac he todeld it
and scatered sotlice. Micel hadde Henri king gadered gold and
syluer, and na god ne dide me for his saule tharof.

Þa þe king Stephne to Englalande com, þa macod he his
gadering æt Oxeneford; and þar he nam þe biscop Roger of Serebyri,
and Alexander biscop of Lincol, and te canceler Roger, hise neues,
and dide ælle in prisun til hi iafen up here castles. Þa the suikes
undergæton ðat he milde man was, and softe and god, and na
iustise ne dide, þa diden hi alle wunder. Hi hadden him manred
maked and athes suoren, ac hi nan treuthe ne heolden. Alle he
wæron forsworen and here treothes forloren, for æuric rice man
his castles makede and agænes him heolden; and fylden þe land ful
of castles. Hi suencten suyðe þe uurecce men of þe land mid castel-
weorces. Þa þe castles uuaren maked, þa fylden hi mid deoules and
yuele men. Þa namen hi þa men þe hi wenden ðat ani god hefden,
bathe be nihtes and be dæies, carlmen and wimmen, and diden
heom in prisun, and pined heom efter gold and syluer untellendlice
pining: for ne uuæren næure nan martyrs swa pined alse hi wæron.
Me henged up bi the fet and smoked heom mid ful smoke. Me
henged bi the þumbes other bi the hefed, and hengen bryniges on
her fet. Me dide cnotted strenges abuton here hæued, and uurythen
it ðat it gæde to þe hærnes. Hi diden heom in quarterne þar nadres
and snakes and pades wæron inne, and drapen heom swa. Sume
hi diden in crucethur, ðat is, in an ceste þat was scort and nareu
and undep; and dide scærpe stanes þerinne, and þrengde þe man
þærinne ðat him bræcon alle þe limes. In mani of þe castles wæron
lof and grin: ðat wæron rachenteges ðat twa oþer thre men hadden
onoh to bæron onne. Þat was sua maced ðat is fæstned to an beom,
and diden an scærp iren abuton þa mannes throte and his hals, ðat
he ne myhte nowiderwardes, ne sitten ne lien ne slepen, oc bæron
al ðat iren. Mani þusen hi drapen mid hungær. I ne can ne I ne mai
tellen alle þe wunder ne alle þe pines ðat hi diden wrecce men
on þis land; and ðat lastede þa xix wintre wile Stephne was king,
and æure it was uuerse and uuerse. Hi læiden gæildes on the
tunes æure umwile, and clepeden it 'tenserie'. Þa þe uurecce men
ne hadden nammore to gyuen, þa ræueden hi and brendon alle the

ℰ

1137   In this year King Stephen went over the sea to Normandy; and was received there because they thought that he would be just like his uncle was, and because he still had his treasure; but he divided and scattered it foolishly. King Henry had gathered much gold and silver, and no good for his soul was done with it.

When King Stephen came to England, he held a parliament at Oxford, and there he took Roger, bishop of Salisbury, and Alexander, bishop of Lincoln, the chancellor Roger, his nephews, and imprisoned them until they surrendered their castles. When the traitors realised that he was a gentle man and soft and good and did not exact [harsh] justice, they all perpetrated atrocities. They had done him homage and sworn oaths, but they did not keep any faith. They were all perjured and their oaths abandoned, for every powerful man made his castles and held [them] against him; and filled the land full of castles. They greatly oppressed the poor men of the land with the building of castles; when the castles were made, they filled them with devils and wicked men. Then they took those people that they thought had any property, both by day and by night, men and women, and put them in prison and tortured them for their gold and silver with unspeakable torture; for never were martyrs tortured as they were. They were hung up by the feet and smoked with foul smoke. They were hung by the thumbs or by the head, and coats of mail hung on their feet. Knotted strings were placed around their head and were twisted until they went to the brain. They put them in a dungeon where there were adders and snakes and toads, and they killed them in that way. Some they put in a torture-box: that is, in a chest that was short, narrow and shallow. And they put sharp stones in it and pressed the man in there so that they broke all his limbs. In many of the castles there were headband and halter: those were chains such that two or three men had difficulty in carrying one. It was made thus, that is, fastened to a beam. And they put a sharp iron [blade] around the man's throat and neck, so that he could not [move] in any direction, nor sit, nor lie, nor sleep, but had to support all that iron. They killed many thousands by starvation. I do not know nor can I tell all the atrocities nor all the torments that they did to poor men in this land; and that lasted for the nineteen years that Stephen was king, and continuously it got worse and worse.

40   tunes, ðat wel þu myhtes faren al a dæis fare, sculdest thu neure
finden man in tune sittende, ne land tiled. Þa was corn dære, and
flec and cæse and butere, for nan ne wæs o þe land. Wrecce men
sturuen of hungær. Sume ieden on ælmes þe waren sum wile rice
men; sume flugen ut of lande. Wes næure gæt mare wreccehed
on land, ne næure hethen men werse ne diden þan hi diden. For
45   ouersithon ne forbaren hi nouther circe ne cyrceiærd, oc namen
al þe god ðat þarinne was, and brenden sythen þe cyrce and al
tegædere. Ne hi ne forbaren biscopes land ne abbotes ne preostes,
ac ræueden munekes and clerekes, and æuric man other þe
ouermyhte. Gif twa men oþer iii coman ridend to an tun, al
50   þe tunscipe flugæn for heom, wenden ðat hi wæron ræueres. Þe
biscopes and lered men heom cursede æure, oc was heom naht
þarof, for hi uueron al forcursæd and forsuoren and forloren.
War sæ me tilede, þe erthe ne bar nan corn, for þe land was al
fordon mid suilce dædes, and hi sæden openlice ðat Crist slep, and
55   his halechen. Suilc, and mare þanne we cunnen sæin, we þoleden
xix wintre for ure sinnes.

Notes

1   **þe king Stephne**   The word order of the title is not that of OE (*Ælfred cyning*), and although it may imitate Latin, the presence of the definite article suggests that it is modelled on Norman French. French loanwords include: *tresor, canceler, prisun, castles, iustise, tenserie.*

3   **get** 'yet, still'   Compare note to First Continuation (39).

5   **na god ne dide me**   An impersonal construction. *Me* is an unstressed form of *man*. For *dide* see First Continuation, note on line 11. Note here *king* (1); *sinnes* (56).

9   **dide ælle in prisun**   The phrase is perhaps modelled on French *faire en prison*. Cf. *iustise ne dide, faire justice* (11).
iafen up   Verbs with an immediately following prepositional element (phrasal verbs) emerged under Scandinavian influence. Cf. *him wið toc* (ON *taka við*), First Continuation (17).

11   **wunder** 'atrocities'   The noun is a neuter plural and therefore correctly endingless. Most nouns in the excerpt have the -*es* plural derived from the nominative and accusative plural of OE strong masculines. A weak plural is preserved in *halechen* (55).

13   **rice man**   Here probably derived from OE *rice*, 'powerful', but in line 42 the context suggests semantic association with French *riche.*

They imposed taxes on the villages again and again, and called it 'protection-money'. When the poor folk had no more to give, they robbed them and burned all the villages, so that you might well travel a whole day's journey and you would not find anyone settled in a village nor the land cultivated. Then corn was expensive, and meat, and cheese, and butter, for there was none in the country. Poor people died of starvation. Some survived on charity who were once rich men; some fled from the land. There was never more misery in the land, and neither did heathens do worse than they did; for too often they spared neither the church nor the churchyard, but they took everything of value that was inside and afterwards burned the church and everything together. Neither did they spare the bishops', abbots' or priests' land, but robbed monks and clerics, and every man robbed any other whom he could overpower. If two or three men came riding into a village, all the villagers fled because of them; they thought that they were robbers. The bishops and learned men continually cursed them, but that was nothing to them, for they were all excommunicated, perjured and damned. Wherever the earth was tilled, it bore no corn, for the land was all ruined by such deeds. And they said openly that Christ and his saints slept. Such, and more than we can say, we suffered for nineteen years for our sins.

18	**carlmen** ON *karlmenn*. There is substantial lexical influence from Scandinavian sources in the excerpt: *bathe, syluer* (OE form is *seolfor* giving ME *seluer*), *bryniges, hærnes, drapen, þrengde*. The prefix in *umwile* (37) is of Scandinavian origin.
26	**crucethur** 'torture-box' Probably derived from the Latin *cruciator*.
42	**sturuen of hungær** The verb still has the more general sense of OE *steorfan*, 'to die'.
48–49	**æuric man other þe ouermyhte** The verb is in the subjunctive, and its subject is the relative particle *þe*, dependent on *æuric man*. The direct object is *other*.

9

THE *ORMULUM*

The *Ormulum* is a collection of metrical homilies (sermons or religious discourses containing an illustrative story) based on gospel stories, each followed by an interpretation for 'your souls' need'. The twenty thousand lines of the extant text represent only a fraction of the initial plan, which may be considered merciful, since its author's literary skills are not of a high standard. Orderliness of presentation and zeal for instruction are his major characteristics: his verse is rigidly regular, and his faith in the rhetorical device of *inculcatio* (the repetition of an instructional point) is wearying. The essential interest of this text lies in its role as a linguistic witness, and here it is of first-rate importance.

The author gives his name as Orm in an opening address to his brother, Walter, a fellow Augustinian canon. The name is of Scandinavian origin, and research (Parkes 1983) suggests that the text may have been written in an area of relatively heavy Scandinavian settlement, at Bourne in Lincolnshire, the home at a later date of Robert Mannyng (see Excerpt 16). The composition can be dated on palaeographic evidence at about 1180.

The value of the *Ormulum* for linguistic analysis arises from the fact that it is written in the author's own hand, and is therefore free from copying errors, but it has particular significance through the author's personality and purpose. Unlike most medieval authors, Orm takes extreme pains to preserve the form as well as the content of his text. Regularity of metre is matched by remarkable consistency in spelling. Further details are given in the notes, but one peculiar aspect of this may be discussed here. First, a definition: an open syllable is one with the structure CV, and a closed syllable has the structure (C)VC (where V = vowel or diphthong, and C = consonant). In two-syllable words, like *faderr*, the medial consonant (*d*) begins the second syllable, so that the first syllable is open (CV-), and the second syllable closed (-CVC). Orm's spelling system takes account of

Plate 2   *Ormulum* (Bodleian Library MS Junius 1, fol. 70v) these syllable types. After a short vowel or diphthong in closed syllables, Orm doubles the final consonant (*þatt, wass, menn*), but in open syllables, the consonant beginning the next syllable is not doubled (*su-ne, fa-derr, ha-fenn*). Consequently, a single consonant in a closed syllable shows that the preceding vowel is long, and so the *Ormulum* contains valuable evidence about lengthening before consonant groups: *land*, 3; but *lanng* (6) is short. Moreover, a distinction in metrical distribution between OE short vowels in open syllables and the other possible combinations can be used to show that ME open syllable lengthening had not yet occurred in words like *faderr* and *sune*.

Orm was greatly concerned for his spelling system and in his Dedication begs any copyist neither to omit words nor harm the metre, and that:

> . . . he loke wel þatt he
> An bocstaff wríte twiȝȝess
> Eȝȝwhær þær itt uppo þiss boc
> Iss writenn o þatt wise.
> (*Dedication*, 103–6)

Otherwise, he says, English cannot be written correctly. The fallacy in this, in a land where English was spoken so variously, seems to have escaped him. There is, however, no evidence that anyone attempted to copy his work, and it survives only in Bodleian Library MS Junius I.

The facsimile illustrates Orm's awkward and unprofessional hand. His manuscript is written in two tall columns, but in order to ensure that the interpretation of his exemplary story begins at the head of the second column, he has been forced to write the close of the Bible story across two column-widths at the foot of the page, and to use uncharacteristic abbreviations in the formulaic phrase *Off ure sawle nede* (104). Although the letters *f* and superscript *r* have their Continental form, the descent of Orm's writing from Anglo-Saxon practice is evident in the use of <æ>, <þ>, <ȝ>, the rune <ρ> 'wynn' for *w*, and the insular forms of the letters *a*, *r*, and *s*. The special form of *g*, by which he denotes the stop [g] is clear in *godd*, and the digraph <ȝh> can be seen in *ȝho*. The type in which the *h* is written superscript, and which represents the velar fricative, occurs in *serrȝhen* (72). Doubling of consonants to indicate a preceding short vowel is accomplished in a variety of ways: by the use of superscripts, and by doubling the abbreviation marks for *n* or *m* as well as in the usual manner. Note, too, the special form of doubled <þ> in *kiþeþþ*.

For convenience of presentation, the text is printed here as though Orm wrote short lines of alternately eight and seven syllables, but the metre is better regarded as consisting of a fifteen-syllable line, rigidly divided by a caesura after the eighth syllable.

Secundum Lucam XV: Cum factus esset Ihesus
Christus annorum xii ascendentibus illis

Affterr þatt tatt te Laferrd Crist
Wass cumenn off Egyppte
Inntill þe land off Ḡalile,
Till Nazaraeþess chesstre,

5   Þæraffterr seȝȝþ þe ḡoddspell boc
Bilæf he þær well lannḡe
Wiþþ hise frend, tatt haffdenn himm
To ȝemenn annd to ḡætenn,
Wiþþ Marȝe þatt hiss moderr wass

10   Annd maȝȝdenn þwerrt űt clene,
Annd wiþþ Josæp þatt wass himm sett
To fedenn annd to fosstrenn.
Annd illke Lenntenn forenn þeȝȝ
Till Ȝerrsalæmess chesstre

15   Aȝȝ att te Passkemesstedaȝȝ,
Swa summ þe boc hemm tahhte,
To frellsenn þær þatt heȝhe tid
O þatt Judisskenn wise,
Forr þatt teȝȝ wærenn ḡode menn,

20   Annd ḡodess laȝhess heldenn.
Annd siþþenn, o þatt ȝer þatt Crist
Wass off twellf winnterr elde,
Þeȝȝ comenn in till Ȝerrsalæm
Att teȝȝre Passkemesse,

25   Annd heldenn þær þatt hallȝhe tid
O þatt Judissken wise.
Annd Jesu Crist wass þær wiþþ hemm,
Swa summ þe ḡoddspell kiþeþþ.
Annd affterr þatt te tid wass ḡan

30   Þeȝȝ wenndenn fra þe temmple
Annd ferrdenn towarrd Nazaræþ
An daȝȝess ḡanḡ till efenn,
Annd wenndenn þatt te Laferrd Crist
Wiþþ hemm þatt ḡate come,

35   Annd he wass þa bihinndenn hemm
Bilefedd att te temmple;
Annd tatt ne wisste nohht hiss kinn,

After the Lord Christ was come from Egypt into the land of Galilee, to the city of Nazareth, the Gospel says he remained there after that for a very long time with his friends who took care of him and protected him, with Mary who was his mother and a virgin utterly pure, and with Joseph who was appointed to support and nurture him. And each Lent they went to the city of Jerusalem, always at the festival of the Passover just as the book instructed them, to observe there that important feast in the Jewish manner, because they were good people and maintained God's laws. And afterwards, in that year that Christ was twelve years of age, they came to Jerusalem at their Passover and kept that holy festival in the Jewish manner. And Jesus was there with them, as the Gospel reveals. And after the festival was past, they went from the temple and journeyed towards Nazareth one day's march till evening, and [they] thought that the Lord Christ came that way with them; and he was left behind them at the temple; and his kinsfolk did not know that, but thought that he had come and they went on their way forward until it came to evening, and then they missed their child and it worried them, and they went and looked for him among relatives and acquaintances, and they found no trace of him because he was at the temple. And then they went back again to search for that dear child and came back to Jerusalem to look for him within. And they found him there on the third day in the temple among the group of Jews who were informed about the Bible. And there he sat questioning them about their book's teaching. And it seemed to all there who heard him a great marvel that he was so profound and so wise in answering and in asking. And Saint Mary came to him and spoke thus to him: 'Dear son, why did you treat us like this, causing us such trouble? The two of us have searched for you everywhere, both I and your father with grieving heart and heavy spirit. Why did you do this deed?' And then Jesus Christ said to them both thus: 'Why were you so concerned to seek me? Why did you grieve? Did you not know that I ought to advance my father's will? Nor that I ought to be concerned about his affairs?' And at that time they could not fully understand that speech; and he then went off with them and complied with their wishes, and came with them to Nazareth, as the Gospel makes clear. And he submitted

Acc wennde þatt he come,
Annd ȝedenn heore weȝȝe forþ
40 Till þatt itt comm till efenn,
Annd ta þeȝȝ misstenn þeȝȝre child,
Annd itt hemm offerrþuhhte,
Annd ȝedenn till, annd sohhtenn himm,
Bitwenenn sibbe annd cuþe,
45 Annd teȝȝ ne fundenn nohht off himm,
Forr he wass att te temmple.
Annd teȝȝ þa wenndenn efft onnȝæn
Þatt dere child to sekenn,
Annd comenn efft till ȝerrsalæm,
50 To sekenn himm þær binnenn.
Annd teȝȝ himm o þe þridde daȝȝ
Þær fundenn i þe temmple,
Bitwenenn þatt Judissken flocc
Þatt læredd wass o boke;
55 Annd tære he satt to fraȝȝnenn hemm
Off þeȝȝre bokess lare;
Annd alle þatt himm herrden þær,
Hemm þuhhte mikell wunnderr
Off þatt he wass full ȝæp annd wis
60 To swarenn annd to fraȝȝnenn.
Annd Sannte Marȝe comm till himm
Annd seȝȝde himm þuss wiþþ worde,
'Whi didesst tu, lef sune, þuss
Wiþþ uss, forr uss to swennkenn?
65 Witt hafenn sohht te widewhar
Icc annd ti faderr baþe
Wiþþ serrhfull herrte annd sariȝ mod,
Whi didesst tu þiss dede?'
Annd tanne seȝȝde Jesu Crist
70 Till baþe þuss wiþþ worde,
'Whatt wass ȝuw swa to sekenn me?
Whatt wass ȝuw swa to serrȝhen?
Ne wisste ȝe nohht tatt me birrþ
Min faderr will forþenn?
75 Ne þatt me birrþ beon hoȝhefull
Abutenn hise þingeʒss?'
Annd teȝȝ ne mihhtenn nohht tatt word

himself and bowed to them both through firm obedience, and remained with them until he was thirty years of age. And our lady Mary took all that she saw and heard of her son Jesus Christ, and concerning his divinity, and held it all in her thought, just as the Gospel makes known, and she laid it all together for ever in the treasure chest of her thought. And her son grew and thrived both in wisdom and in age, and he was beloved and dear to God and good people; and that was just, for he was God, and good in every way. Here, this way, this Gospel ends, and it behoves us to search through it to see what it teaches us about the needs of our soul.

Notes

2	**cumenn** As in the *Peterborough Chronicle*, written thirty years earlier and sixteen miles to the south, past participles no longer possess the OE prefix: *sett* (11); *ḡan* (29).
5	**seȝȝþ** The third-person-singular present tense ends in (*e*)*þ*. Orm uses <ȝ> for the palatal [j] and his own version of Carolingian *g* for the velar plosive [g].
7	**frend** The OE mutated plural was endingless; the form with *e* is of Anglian origin, since in that dialect *io* was not *i*-mutated (WS *frīend*) and developed to *ēo*. Orm's text provides striking evidence of the EM monophthongisation of *ēo* to *e*, since, to about line 13,000, he wrote <eo> but then changed his practice, writing <e> and systematically correcting his earlier work.
10	**þwerrt út** 'utterly' (ON *þvert + ut*) The passage contains ample evidence of the influence of Scandinavian languages: *till* (used in the sense of motion towards); the pronoun *þeȝȝ, þeȝȝre*; *ḡætenn* (8); *summ* (16); *laȝhess* (20); *aȝȝ* (15); *fra* (30); *ḡate* (34); *mikell* (58); *baþe* (70), etc. The use of the acute accents and the breve elsewhere can be explained in some cases by a desire to distinguish homographs, but in the case of monosyllables such as the examples in the excerpt, the accents may be intended to emphasise that the syllable is long, despite the expectations of Latin readers.
22	**winnterr** The usual noun plural in the *Ormulum* is *-es*, which is extended to OE neuters (*þinḡess*) and one mutated form (*bokess*), but a few common expressions have other endings or are without ending: *wiþþ worde* (62) and genitive plural *sawle* (104).
28	**kiþeþþ** OE *cyþan*. The *i*-spelling of OE *y* is characteristic of East Midland texts: *kinn* (37); *didesst* (68).
41	**þeȝȝ, þeȝȝre** Although not all are exemplified in the excerpt, the *Ormulum* is the earliest ME text to exhibit the modern, Scandinavian-derived set of third-person-plural pronouns. In unstressed positions within

ȝét ta wel unnderrstanndenn;
Annd he þa ȝede forþ wiþþ hemm
80 Annd dide hemm heore wille,
Annd comm wiþþ hemm till Nazaræþ,
Swa summ þe ḡoddspell kiþeþþ,
Annd till hemm baþe he lutte annd bæh
Þurrh soþfasst herrsummnesse,
85 Annd wass wiþþ hemm till þatt he wass
Off þrittiȝ winnterr elde.
Annd ure laffdiȝ Marȝe toc
All þatt ȝho sahh annd herrde
Off hire sune Jesu Crist,
90 Annd off hiss ḡoddcunndnesse,
Annd all ȝhőt held inn hire þohht,
Swa summ þe ḡoddspell kiþeþþ,
Annd leȝȝde itt all tosamenn aȝȝ
Inn hire þohhtess arrke.
95 Annd hire sune wex annd þraf
I wissdom annd in elde,
Annd he wass Ḡodd annd ḡode menn
Well swiþe lef annd dere;
Annd tatt wass rihht, forr he wass Ḡodd,
100 Annd ḡod onn alle wise.
Her endeþþ nu þiss ḡoddspell þuss
Annd uss birþ itt þurrhsekenn,
To lokenn whatt itt læreþþ uss
Off ure sawle nede.

the sentence, the OE *h*- forms are still used for the oblique cases: *heore*, *hemm* (80).

56   **lare**   The rounding of /aː/ to /ɔː/, which commenced in the South, is not found in this early text: *sariȝ* (67); *swa* (71).

60   **swarenn and fraȝȝnenn**   Weak Class 2 verbs no longer possess a distinct inflexional -*i*-. Indeed, the reduction of all inflexional vowels to an invariable -*e* is further advanced here than in the *Peterborough Chronicle*.

65   **Witt hafenn** 'We two have'   Dual number survives in the personal pronouns, in increasingly formulaic use, until the mid thirteenth century. The verb 'have' (OE *habbað*) here shows the analogical extension of the fricative from the second- and third-person-singular forms (*hæfst*, *hæfð*). The inflexional -*en* of the plural present is characteristic of East Midland ME, and is derived from the OE subjunctive. Comparison of the spelling

hafenn with that of the preterite *haffdenn* (7) is a good illustration of Orm's spelling consistency, in which the addition of the preterite suffix causes the first syllable to become closed, requiring a doubling of the consonant after the short *a*.

71   **Whatt wass ʒuw**   *Ʒuw* is dative, and the construction is an impersonal idiom, as also *me birrþ* (73).

88   **ʒho**   This form, together with the form *scæ* in the *Peterborough Chronicle* annal for 1140, is among the earliest evidence for the ancestor of the modern form *she*. The sequence of the graphs <ʒ> and <h> is used by Orm in two distinct ways, with distinct significance: with superscript *h*, <ʒʰ> represents the voiced velar fricative in words like *heʒhe* (17) and *laʒhess* (20); its voiceless equivalent Orm writes <hh> (*mihhtenn, sahh, nohht*). The graph <ʒh> is written with normal *h* only in the word *ʒho*. In view of Orm's phonetic care, this may imply that a unique sound is involved here, and this has been interpreted as the peripheral phoneme /ç/ (Vachek 1954).

sahh and herrde   The verb *sahh* exhibits Anglian smoothing of the long *ēa* diphthong which is preserved in WS. The form *herrde*, too, is Anglian, since the *i*-mutation of *ēa* which produced *hīerde* in WS resulted in *hērde* in Anglian areas.

91   **ʒhŏt**   An elision of *ʒho* and *itt*.

10

VICES AND VIRTUES

Having lost its opening pages, the text now called *Vices and Virtues* survives, without any indication of its author's title, only in British Library MS Stowe 34. Its content is an exchange between a soul, who confesses its sins, and allegorised Reason, who then expounds the virtues. The exchange is not conceived in a dramatic spirit, however, and no true dialogue develops. Rather, the work constantly shows traces of thematic compilation, both in minor stylistic choices (for example, the introductory formula *hier . . . cumþ*) and in the organisation of its material according to well-established schemata such as the five wits, the seven gifts of the Holy Ghost, the three Christian virtues, the four cardinal virtues, and the four daughters of God. Following such inherited schemata rather than developing his own theme sometimes leads the author into repetition. Although lacking some of the stylistic vigour and attractive humanity of the *Ancrene Wisse*, its near contemporary, *Vices and Virtues* is not without literary accomplishment, and as a representative of very early religious prose from the eastern half of England, it is an important witness.

Its origins are obscure. The Stowe manuscript may be dated on palaeographical grounds to about 1200, and is known to have belonged in the sixteenth century to William Fleetwood, Recorder of London. Nothing is known of the author of the work, but as a lettered man he is likely to have been associated with some religious order. He does not, however, direct his work towards a monastic audience, and indeed he refers to 'these monks' rather distantly as an example to his audience. Other statements suggest that, although associated with some order, he was not himself a monk (*Þa ðe bieð on religiun, hie bieð under scrifte, swa bihoueð us alswa*, 'those who are in religious orders, they are under the obligation of penance, as we ought also to be'). It is possible that the 'we' to whom he refers was a college of secular canons.

The London associations of the manuscript are largely borne out by the language in which it is written. It is copied by two scribes, the first of whom tended to preserve more fully the older spellings of his exemplar, but the evidence of both suggests an early text from the East Saxon area. Generally southern and early features are the well-preserved inflexional system, the use of prefixes to indicate the past participle, the preservation of final *n* in the infinitive, h-forms of the personal pronouns, and the distinct Weak Class 2 forms: *luuieð* (69) and *luuien* (85). More specific indications of a south-eastern origin are signs of rounding of OE *ā* at a very early date, <a> spellings for WS *ǣ* and the writing of the reflex of WS *y* as <e> and <u>: *euele* (4), *kenne* (16), *wurse* (14). Further details are given in the notes.

Of witte. Hier after cumþ an oðer Godes ʒiue þe is icleped *sciencia*, þat is, inʒehied oðer witt. Ðurh hire ðu miht witen alle craftes ðe on boche bieð ʒewriten. Hie ðe takð gode þeawes and god lif to leden, hu ðu scalt fram ðan euele buʒen and hu ðu scalt gode

5 werkes don. Ac hit bieð sume ðe bieð swiðe wise ihealden ðurh ðessere Godes ʒiue, and want hem seluen and iec sumen oðre te michele hearme, þat ðe Godd hem ʒaf for here michele gode. Herof sade ðe apostel: *Scientia inflat, karitas edificat.* He seið þat ðis scarpe iwitt swelð ðane mann ðe hes haueð wiðuten charite. On swilche

10 wise hie swelð ðat he latt wel of him seluen, and forhoweð oðre ðe swo ne cunnen; and on swilche wise he forliest ðat him betst scolde helpen, þat is, Godes luue and mannes. Forðan þat wite ðu te fulle soðe, ðanne ðu forliest mannes luue for ði modinesse, þe þingð ðat þu naust naht to wurðin ne te luuen ane wurse mann ðane ðu art,

15 oðer ðat he nis alswa wis alse ðu, oðer he nis na swa riche se ðu, oðer of swa heiʒe kenne swa ðu, oðer naht alswa wurðed mann swa ðu on ðare lease woreld; and for ðelliche þing hine forhowest and forlatst ðat tu ne wilt to him clepiʒen, ne to his niede him helpen. Fulʒewis ðu forliest hier rihtes Godes luue and his grace,

20 and nem ðis to forbisne. Bute ðu habbe Godes luue and alre manne, ðu ne miht don non god ðe æure Gode bie ʒecweme. Ðarof sade ðe apostele: 'Gif ic deale all ðat ic habbe for Godes luue, and ʒiet on-uuen ðan ʒiue mine likame to barnin alto duste for Godes luue, and ic hatie on-lepi mann, ðanne ne habbe ic naht kariteð, and

25 swa ic habbe all forloren. Nu seið sum mann: 'Scal ic luuiʒe ðane euele mann?' Hlest hwat se heiʒeste ðe seið: *Diliges proximum sicut te ipsum,* 'Luue ðine nexte alswa ðe seluen, hwat manne swo he æure bie.' Ne bie he næure swa swiðe forʒelt, æure he is ðin nexte after ʒekynde. Luue ða ʒekynde, and hate his euel. Ʒif ðu miht hit

30 bieten, biet hit alswo ðu woldest ðat me bette þin, ʒif ðu wære swo forʒilt also he, and þenc ðat ðe writt seið þat æure bie ðe mildce ouer ðe rihte dome. For ðelliche þinge maniʒe of ðe wel wise menn forlieseð Godes luue and his grace, forði ðat hie ne habbeð, ne reccheð to habben, here emcristenes luue, ac hopieð to here michele

35 wisdome, and ofte bieð beswikene. Wolden hie hlesten ðane hali apostel, swa hie ne ðorften. *Si quis uidetur inter nos sapiens esse, stultus fiat ut sit sapiens,* 'Ʒif ʒeure ani,' he seið, 'is ihealden for wis on ðare woreld, becume sott, and swa he mai bien wis.'

Ðe wise woreld-mann, he halt michel sothade ðat mann forlate,

40 for Godes luue, hus and ham, wif and child, and gold and seluer, and alle worldes wele, and becume swo michel wrecche also he ðe

Here, after this, comes another gift of God, which is called *scientia*, that is understanding or knowledge. Through it you may know all the skills that are written in books. It teaches you good behaviour and to lead a good life, how you ought to turn away from evil, and how you ought to do good deeds. But there are some who, through this gift of God, are considered very wise, but turn to great harm to themselves and also to some others that which God gave them for their great benefit. The apostle said this about it: *Scientia inflat, caritas aedificat.* He says that 'This keen understanding puffs up the man who has it without charity.' It puffs him up in such a way that he thinks well of himself, and despises others who are not so aware; and in this manner he loses what ought to help him best; that is the love of God and man. Therefore know the whole truth, when you relinquish men's love through your pride, it seems to you that you do not have to esteem or love any man inferior to yourself: either because he is not so wise as you, or he is not so rich as you, or from so noble a family as you, or not such a respected person as you in the deceptive world; and for such things you despise him, and neglect to call on him, nor help him in need. Certainly here you justly lose God's love and his grace, and take this as an example! Unless you have the love of God and of all men you can do no good deed that may ever be pleasing to God. The apostle said this: *Si distribuero omnes facultates meas, etc.*, 'If, for God's love, I share out all that I have, and yet further than that, give my body to be burned to dust for God's love, but I hate a single person, then I do not possess love, and so I have lost everything.' Now someone will say: 'Ought I to love the wicked man?' Listen to what the Most High tells you: *Diliges proximum sicut te ipsum*, 'Love your neighbour as yourself, whatever kind of man he may be.' Be he never so guilty, he is always your neighbour in nature. Love the shared nature, and hate his wickedness. If you might reprove it, reprove it as you would wish someone to reprove yours, if you were as guilty as he, and remember that Scripture says that mercy should always be above strict justice. On account of such things, many very wise men lose God's love and his grace, because they do not have, nor care to have, their fellow Christian's love, but put their trust in their great wisdom, and are often deceived. If they would [only] listen to the apostle, they would not stand in this need! *Si quis videtur inter vos sapiens esse, stultus fiat, ut sit sapiens*, 'If any of you,' he says, 'is considered wise in worldly things, let him become a fool, and thus he may be wise.'

naht ne hadde; seið ðat him is betere to sitten on his aʒen, and
ʒiuen almessen and herberʒin sæli menn, ðanne he scolde al ðat
laten, and libben bi oðre mannes almesse. Hleste we herof Cristes
45   aʒene dom, and swa we muʒen bien ðe sikerere of ðese iflite. Hit
seið on ða hali goddspelle þat an riche iungman cam to Crist be ðo
daiʒen ðe he hier lichamliche was wuniende, and seide: *Quid faciam,
domine, ut habeam vitam eternam?* 'Hlauerd,' cwað he, 'hwat mai ic
don ðat ic mihte hauen ðat eche lif?' Vre drihten him andswerede,
50   and seide: *Mandata nosti,* 'ʒecnoust þu Godes bebodes. Ne sleih,
ne ne stell, ne reaue, ne forliʒe ðe on hordomes, ne oðre Godes
forbodes ne tebrec.' 'A, hlaueerd,' cwað he, 'alle ðese bebodes ic
habbe ihealde fram childhade, swa ðat ic nabbe nan tebrocen.'
Ðe ʒiet him andswerede Crist: 'God man ðu art al swo he ðe non
55   heued-senne ne haueð idon.' *Si uis perfectus esse, vade et uende
omnia que habes, et cetera,* 'Gif ðu wilt,' he seide, bien ðurhut god
mann, 'ga and sell all ðat tu hafst, and ʒif hit Godes wrecchen, and
swa folʒe me.' Ðies ʒunge mann ʒiede awei sari. Hier we habbeð
ilierned ðat it is betere to læten all ðat te mann awh, mid gode
60   wille, þanne he abide allhwat deað hit him beneme, his unþankes.
Hlest nu hwat Crist sade be ða riche manne ðe ʒiede awei sari, and
his ræd nolde lesten: 'Ne mai na more,' cwað he, 'ðe riche mann
cumen in to heuene riche, ðanne mai ðe oluende cumen ðurh ðe
nædle eiʒen.' *Ve uobis diuitibus, qui habetis consolationem uestram,*
65   'Wa ʒeu,' cwað he, 'ʒie riche menn, ðe habbeð swa michele blisse
of ʒeuer michele richeise, þat ʒie Godd forʒeten and ʒeure saule
hæle!' For ði ne mai wexen non god sad of Godes wordes on ʒeure
herte molde, for ðan michele embeðanc ðe ʒie habbeð on ʒeure
michele wele, ðe ʒie michel ʒitsið, and luuieð, and likeð, and dradeð
70   to forliesen. Amang alle ðese embeðankes is ðe wrecche hierte swa
iheueʒed, þat non Godes word upp ne mai springen, ne of Godd
þenken, ne of his riche, ne of his saule hale. Ac gleues and skentinges,
and hundes and haueekes, and alle ðo þing ðe ʒeu hier gladien mai,
þat ʒe willen bliðeliche isien and ʒehieren; and all ðis ʒe mihten
75   hauen, ʒif ʒe Godd luueden mare ðanne all ðis ðe we embe hauen
ispeken. Maniʒe of ʒeu bien swiðe beswikene. Weneð ðat ʒe
luuen more Godd ðanne ʒe don ʒeure eihte; ac læt him seggen
ðat soðeste, ðe is mid rihte Soð icleped: *Vbi est tesaurus, ibi est
et cor tuum,* 'Ðar ðe ðin hord is, þær is þin herte,' he sæde. Ðar is
80   ðin herte ðarof ðe ðu mæst þenkst, and ðar is ðin mæste luue.
Vnderstand nu wel ðe seluen, and loke hwaðer ðu þenke more

The worldly wise man considers it great foolishness that, for God's love, a man should give up house and home, wife and child, and gold and silver, and all worldly prosperity, and become so much a poor man as he who had nothing; he says that it is better to stay put with his own things, and give charity and lodging to blessed men, than that he should leave all that, and live on other people's charity. Let us listen to Christ's own judgement on this, and thus we may be surer in this dispute. It says in the holy Gospel that a rich young man came to Christ in the days when he was dwelling incarnate here, and he said: *Quid faciam, Domine, ut habeam vitam aeternam?* 'Lord,' he said, 'what should I do so that I may have eternal life?' Our Lord answered him and said: *Mandata nosti*, 'You know God's commandments. Thou shalt not slay, nor steal, nor rob, nor commit adultery, nor break any other of God's commandments.' 'Ah, Lord,' he said, 'I have kept all these commandments from childhood, so that I have not broken any.' Then again Christ answered him: 'You are a good man to the extent that you have not committed any capital sin.' *Si vis perfectus esse, vade et vende omnia quae habes etc.*, 'If you wish,' he said, 'to be a thoroughly good man, go and sell all that you have and give it to God's poor people, and thus follow me.' This young man went away downcast. Here we have learned that it is better to give up all that one owns voluntarily than to wait until death takes it away against one's will. Listen now to what Christ said about the rich man who went away downcast, and would not heed his advice: 'The rich man,' said he, 'may no more come into the kingdom of heaven than may the camel come through the eye of a needle.' *Vae vobis divitibus, qui habetis consolationem vestram*, 'Woe to you,' he said, 'you rich men who get so much pleasure from your great wealth that you forget God and the well-being of your souls!' Therefore no good seed may grow in the soil of your heart for the great concern you have with your great wealth, that you covet so much, and love, and like, and dread to lose. Amid all these concerns the poor heart is made so heavy that no word of God may spring up, nor remembrance of God, nor of his kingdom, nor of the salvation of one's soul. But entertainment and amusement, and hounds and hawks, and all those things that may delight you here, which you eagerly desire to see and hear; and you could have all this, if you loved God more than all this that we have spoken about. Many of you are greatly deceived. You think that you love

of Godd ðe of ðin eihte, and wite ðu te soþe: hwarof ðu mare
þenkst, ðat tu luuest mare.

Walewa ðas siðes, þat ani mann ðat Godd hafð iȝiuen witt and
85   wisdom, scall luuien more ðe scaftes ðe Godd ȝescop ðanne he do
his sceppend, ðe him and alle þing ȝescop. Lieue saule, ic ðe warni
and ȝierne bidde ðat tu, mid ðessere Godes ȝiue ðe *scientia* hatte,
understande and lierne fastliche ða ȝekyndes of sennes, hwannen
and hwanne hie cumen, þat ðu muȝe bien war wið hem; and ðar
90   ðu art ðurh hem ȝewunded, ðat ðu cunne hes halen; and eft, of
ðese hali mihtes, ðat tu hes kunne wel ȝecnawen, and mid Godes
fultume wiðhealden.

Notes

1   **Hier**   In the manner of the *Anglo-Saxon Chronicle*, the author uses the
word to situate his treatment of a particular virtue in a sequence probably
imposed by his source. The spelling <ie> is problematic. It is the usual
spelling in this text for WS *ēo*, Kentish *īo*, the latter of which was spelt
<ie> in south-eastern Middle English. The scribe sometimes first writes
<eo> or <e>, then corrects to <ie>, suggesting that he is following a
spelling tradition not his own. Use here of <ie> for OE *ē* (also in *ȝie*, 65
and *bieten*, 30) and perhaps *ȝehieren* (74) is a natural confusion in a man
whose own language did not preserve a distinction between OE *ēo* and *ē*.

3   **takð**   The WS word *tæcan* has *ǣ²* (derived from the *i*-mutation of *ā*).
The <a> spelling of the WS *ǣ¹* and *ǣ²* was restricted to Essex and Middlesex. Elsewhere, spellings were <æ, e, ea>.

6   **want**   The Anglian form would have been *wended*, and the syncope
and assimilation of the inflexion suggests West Saxon. However, the spelling
<a> rather than <e> of the reflex of Germanic short *a* + *i*-mutation before
a nasal is found only in Essex and London.

8   **sade**   The loss of /j/ before a following *d* is characteristic of non-Anglian
areas, but Kentish has the form *sede*, since OE short *æ* appeared as *e* in
Kentish OE.

9   **hes**   Accusative form of the third-person pronoun. Plural in line 91;
possibly also plural here. The geographical distribution of this form is very
restricted and scattered: Gloucester, Essex, Middlesex, north Kent and
west Norfolk.

haueð   The unsyncopated form suggests an Anglian origin, but forms of
the third-person-singular present tense with the syncope and assimilation
associated with Saxon OE are common in the text, e.g. *latt* (10); *forliest* (11).
In line 39 *halt* exhibits syncope and assimilation, but the vowel suggests an
Anglian form in which breaking has not occurred before *l* + consonant.

God more than your possessions; but let him say what is most true, who is justly called Truth: *Ubi est thesaurus, ibi est et cor tuum*, 'Where your treasure is, there is your heart,' he said. Your heart is in that place you think of most, and there is your greatest love. Now, understand yourself well, and consider whether you think more about God than about your belongings; and know the truth: whatever you think about more, that you love more.

Alas for the ways of any man to whom God has given understanding and wisdom and who loves more greatly things that God has created than he does his creator, who made him and all things. Dear soul, I warn and earnestly entreat you that you, with this gift of God which is called *scientia*, understand and securely learn the natures of sins, whence and when they may come, so that you may be on your guard against them; and when you are wounded by them, that you may know how to cure them; and further, about these holy virtues, that you may know well how to recognise them, and with God's help keep them.

14	**wurse** In this word the reflex of OE *y* is *u* (normally a western feature, but found in London, Middlesex and Essex). It may also be *i/y: ȝekynde* (29), *forȝilt* (31) (East Midland); or, most commonly, *e: kenne* (16), *euele*, *hlest* (26), *forȝelt* (28) (south-eastern). Compare the *Proclamation of Henry III* (Excerpt 13).
19	**rihtes** 'by right' An adverbial may be formed from a noun in OE by the use of the genitive singular inflexion. The idiom continues into later ME. Cf. *his unþankes* (60).
20	**alre manne** 'of all men' Cf. OE *ealra manna*.
24	**kariteð** This form represents Anglo-Norman borrowing, perhaps surviving from an earlier version. The central French form, *charite* (9), is one of the earliest occurrences of this form in English.
29	**after ȝekynde** 'according to nature' Sinners share human nature with the just man, who must therefore feel compassion, while hating the associated sin.
30	**me bette þin** *Me* is an indefinite pronoun, *bette* a third-person subjunctive, and *þin* a disjunctive pronoun: 'one should reprove yours'.
33	**hie** The third-person pronouns all have the *h*-form of OE, but phonetic change has eroded the differences in pronunciation. Here *hie* means 'they'; in line 3 it means 'she'. The masculine singular has its traditional spelling, *he* (28). To appreciate the significance of these spellings, see note to line 1.

40   **hus and ham**   A traditional alliterative phrase in which OE long *ā* shows no sign of rounding (cf. *hali*, *aჳene*), but traces of rounding are evident in some spellings: *swo* beside *swa*, *more* beside *mare*, *non* (21) and *an* (1), and *na more* (62).

63   **heuene riche**   The word *heuene* is a genitive modifier of *riche*, 'kingdom'. Although derived from the genitive plural, *heofona*, the number significance is no longer important in this phrase. See also *nædle eiჳen* (64), *saule hæle* (66–67), *herte molde* (68). A handful of structures of this type (e.g. *herte rote*, *lady grace*) survive into late ME.

74–75   **all ðis ჳe mihten hauen**   The author suggests that no harm attaches to earthly possessions, so long as they are secondary to the love of God. For a more sophisticated statement of the Augustinian view that the love of earthly things may lead on to the love of God, see *Ancrene Wisse*.

11

THE *ANCRENE WISSE*

[handwritten: education from preist to 'nuns']

[handwritten: nuns]

The *Ancrene Wisse* or 'Guide of Anchorites' vies with the *Peterborough Chronicle* for the title of best-known Early Middle English text. Its importance both to the history of English prose and to the study of language development has often been stressed, but its familiarity is probably due more to the happy chance that such importance can here be found in a document with its own intrinsic appeal. The *Ancrene Wisse* is readable for pleasure and entertainment, for its author's insight and humanity, his wit and his unobtrusive mastery of the presentation of his discourse. His work achieved the distinction of translation into French and Latin, and was copied and adapted throughout the medieval period.

The title *Ancrene Wisse* is given on the first folio of Corpus Christi College, Cambridge MS 402, a text which, although not in the author's hand, is perhaps not much more than a decade later than the date of composition. This version, which is intended for the use of three noble sisters who have forsaken the world to live as recluses, is that normally referred to as *Ancrene Wisse*. Adaptations in other MSS for use by other communities have gained the name *Ancrene Riwle*. Although MS CCCC 402 can be dated at about 1230, nothing is known directly of its origin or the author of its contents. The manuscript was, however, associated with Wigmore Abbey, Herefordshire, by 1300. Evidence has been presented to place the origin of the work in Limebrook Priory, three miles south-west of Wigmore, and the authorship has been more speculatively credited to one Brian of Lingen (Dobson 1976).

The language of the *Ancrene Wisse* corresponds well with such an origin. Its strikingly consistent spelling system is largely shared with the 'Katherine Group' of texts in MS Bodley 34. Such consistency, involving several texts, implies regulation, and regulation is likely only through scribal training in a major centre. Thus, in the *Ancrene Wisse* we encounter an early and very local example of language standardisation. An instructive comparison might be made between the solutions sought to the problem of writing their local language by these western scribes and by Orm.

The language of the *Ancrene Wisse* is much more conservative than that of northern or eastern texts. OE spelling traditions are maintained (<þ> tends to be used initially and <ð> finally, and <ea> and <eo> are still written). Moreover, in its writing of short *æ* as <e>, *AW* continues the tradition of the Vespasian Psalter. Morphologically, the text is also relatively conservative: *-en* noun plurals are common, the forms of Weak Class 2 verbs are still distinct (*makieð*, 24; *luuien*, 18); past participles preserve their prefix (*ispillet*, 12; *icrunet*, 113); and personal pronouns have *h*-forms. Lexically, there are ample signs of the French influence which reflects the social milieu for which the work was composed, but there are also a few Scandinavian borrowings.

Seinte Pawel witneð þet alle uttre heardschipes, alle flesches pinsunges ant licomliche swinkes, al is ase nawt aʒeines luue, þe schireð ant brihteð þe heorte. *Exercitio corporis ad modicum ualet:*
pietas autem ualet ad omnia. Þet is, licomlich bisischipe is to lutel
5   wurð, ah swote ant schire heorte is god to alle þinges. *Si linguis*
hominum loquar et angelorum etc.; si tradidero corpus meum ita ut
ardeam etc.; si distribuero omnes facultates meas in cibos pauperum,
caritatem autem non habeam, nichil michi prodest. 'Þah ich cuðe,'
he seið, 'monne ledene ant englene, þah ich dude o mi bodi alle
10   pine ant passiun þet bodi mahte þolien, þah ich ʒeue poure al þet
ich hefde – ʒef ich nefde luue þerwið to Godd, ant to alle men in
him ant for him, al were ispillet.' For, as þe hali abbat Moyses
seide, al þet wa ant al þet heard þet we þolieþ o flesch, ant al þet
god þet we eauer doð, alle swucche þinges ne beoð nawt bute as
15   lomen to tilie wið þe heorte. ʒef þe axe ne kurue, ne spitelsteaf ne
dulue, ne þe sulh ne erede, hwa kepte ham to halden? Alswa as na
mon ne luueð lomen for hamseolf, ah deð for þe þinges þet me
wurcheð wið ham, alswa na flesches derf nis to luuien bute forþi
þet Godd te reaðere þiderward loki mid his grace, ant makeð þe
20   heorte schir ant of briht sihðe, þet nan ne mei habben wið
monglunge of unþeawes, ne wið eorðlich luue of worltliche þinges;
for þis mong woreð swa þe ehnen of þe heorte þet ha ne mei
cnawen Godd ne gleadien of his sihðe. Schir heorte, as Seint Bernard
seið, makieð twa þinges – þet tu, al þet tu dest, do hit oðer for luue

[handwritten: 1215 4th Lateran council, preists could preach in vernacular, mass still in latin]

[handwritten: hardships]

Saint Paul bears witness that all external privations, all mortification of the flesh and bodily labour are as nothing compared with love, which purifies and makes the heart bright. *Exercitio corporis ad modicum uale: pietas autem ualet ad omnia.* *[handwritten: (piety), (piety is worth everything)]* That is, bodily exertion counts for little, but a sweet and pure heart is good in all things. *Si linguis hominum loquar et angelorum etc.; si tradero corpus meum ita ut ardeam etc.; si distribuero omnes facultates meas in cibos pauperum, caritatem autem non habeam, nichil michi prodest.* 'Though I knew,' he said, 'the languages of men and of angels, though I inflicted on my body all the pain and suffering that the body might endure, though I gave to the poor all that I had – if I had not love along with it towards God, and towards all people in him and for him, all would be wasted.' For, as the holy abbot Moses said, all the misery and all the harshness that we endure in the flesh, and all the good that we ever do, all such things are as no more than tools with which to cultivate the heart. If the axe did not cut, nor the spade dig, nor the plough plough, who would care to own them? Just as no-one loves tools for themselves, but does so for the things that are achieved with them, so no suffering of the flesh is to be loved except because God more readily may look towards it with his grace, and it makes the heart pure and of clear sight, which none may have with a mixture of vices nor with the earthly love of worldly things; for this mixture troubles the eyes of the heart so that they may not know God nor rejoice in his sight. As

25   ane of Godd, oðer for oþres god ant for his biheue. Haue in al þet
      tu dest an of þes twa ententes, oðer ba togederes; for þe leatere
      falleð into þe earre. Haue eauer schir heorte þus, ant do al þet
      tu wult; haue wori heorte – al þe sit uuele. *Omnia munda mundis,*
      coinquinatis uero nichil est mundum. Apostolus. Item Augustinus:
30   *Habe caritatem, et fac quicquid uis, uoluntate uidelicet rationis.* Forþi,
      mine leoue sustren, ouer alle þing beoð bisie to habben schir heorte.
      Hwet is schir heorte? Ich hit habbe iseid ear: þet is, þet ȝe na þing
      ne wilnin ne ne luuien bute Godd ane, ant te ilke þinges, for Godd,
      þe helpeð ow toward him. For Godd, ich segge, luuien ham, ant
35   nawt for hamseoluen, as is mete, oðer clað, mon oðer wummon þe
      ȝe beoð of igodet. For, ase seið Seint Austin, ant spekeð þus to ure
      Lauerd: *Minus te amat qui preter te aliquid amat quod non propter*
      te amat. Þet is, 'Lauerd, leasse ha luuieð þe þe luuieð eawt bute þe,
      bute ha luuien hit for þe.' Schirnesse of heorte is Godes luue ane. I
40   þis is al þe strengðe of alle religiuns, þe ende of alle ordres. *Plenitudo*
      legis est dilectio. 'Luue fulleð þe lahe,' seið Seinte Pawel. *Quicquid*
      precipitur, in sola caritate solidatur. Alle Godes heastes, as Sein
      Gregoire seið, beoð i luue irotet. Luue ane schal beon ileid i Seinte
      Mihales weie. Þeo þe meast luuieð schulen beo meast iblisset, nawt
45   þeo þe leadeð heardest lif; for luue hit ouerweieð. Luue is heouene
      stiward, for hire muchele freolec. For heo ne edhalt naþing, ah
      ȝeueð al þet ha haueð, ant ec hireseoluen; elles ne kepte Godd nawt
      of þet hiren were.
          Godd haueð ofgan ure luue on alle cunne wise: he haueð muchel
50   idon us, ant mare bihaten. Muchel ȝeoue ofdraheð luue. Me al þe
      world he ȝef us in Adam, ure alde-feader; ant al þet is i þe world he
      weorp under ure fet – beastes ant fuheles – ear we weren forgulte.
      Omnia subiecisti sub pedibus eius, oues et boues uniuersas, insuper et
      pecora campi, volucres celi, et pisces maris qui perambulant semitas
55   *maris.* Ant ȝet al þet is, as is þruppe iseid, serueð þe gode to sawle
      biheue; ȝet te uuele seruið eorðe, sea, ant sunne. He dude ȝet mare
      – ȝef us nawt ane of his, ah dude al himseoluen. Se heh ȝeoue nes
      neauer iȝeuen to se lahe wrecches. *Apostolus: Cristus dilexit ecclesiam*
      et dedit semet ipsum pro ea. 'Crist,' seið Seinte Pawel, 'luuede swa
60   his leofmon þet he ȝef for hire þe pris of himseoluen. Neomeð nu
      gode ȝeme, mine leoue sustren, for hwi me ah him to luuien. Earst,
      as a mon þe woheð – as a king þet luuede a gentil poure leafdi
      of feorrene londe – he sende his sonden biuoren (þet weren þe
      patriarches ant te prophetes of þe Alde Testament) wið leattres

St Bernard says, two things make a pure heart: that you do all that you do either solely for the love of God, or for the good and advantage of another. In everything you do, have one of these purposes, or both together; for the latter is included in the former. If you always have a pure heart, thus, you may do all that you wish; have a disturbed heart and everything turns out badly. *Omnia munda mundis, coinquinatis uero nichil est mundum. Apostolus. Item Augustinus: Habe caritatem, et fac quicquid uis, uoluntate uidelicet rationis.*

Therefore, my dear sisters, above all things be diligent to have a pure heart. What is a pure heart? I have said it before: it is that you neither love nor desire anything except God alone, and those very things, for God's sake, that help you towards him. For God, I say, love them, and not for themselves, such as food, or clothing, or man or woman that you are benefited by. For, as St Augustine says, and speaks thus concerning our Lord: *Minus te amat qui preter te aliquid amat quod non propter te amat.* That is, 'Lord they love you less who love anything but you unless they love it for your sake.' Pureness of heart is simply the love of God. In this is the entire force of all sects, the purpose of all religious orders. *Plenitudo legis est dilectio.* 'Love fulfils the law,' says St Paul. *Quicquid precipitur, in sola caritate solidatur.* All God's commandments, as St Gregory says, are rooted in love. Love alone shall be laid in St Michael's balance. Those who love most greatly shall be most blessed, not those who lead the hardest life, for love outweighs it. Love is the steward of heaven, because of her great generosity. For she withholds nothing, but gives all that she has, and also her very self; otherwise God would not care for what was hers.

God has earned our love in all manner of ways: he has done much for us, and promised more. A great gift attracts love. But he gave us, or our ancestor Adam, the whole world; and he cast everything in the world beneath our feet – the animals and birds – before we were convicted of sin. *Omnia subiecisti sub pedibus eius, oues et boues uniuersas, insuper et pecora campi, uolucres celi, et pisces maris qui perambulant semitas maris.* And yet all that exists, as is said above, the good man uses for the benefit of his soul; yet the earth, sea and sun serve the evil man. He did yet more: gave us not only from his possessions, but gave himself entirely. So noble a gift was never given to such base wretches. *Apostolus: Christus dilexit ecclesiam et dedit semet ipsum pro ea.* Christ, says St Paul, so

65   isealet. On ende he com himseoluen, ant brohte þe Godspel as leattres i-openet, ant wrat wið his ahne blod saluz to his leofmon, luue-gretunge forte wohin hire wið ant hire luue wealden. Herto falleð a tale, a wrihe forbisne.

A leafdi wes mid hire fan biset al abuten, hire lond al destruet, 70   ant heo al poure, inwið an eorðene castel. A mihti kinges luue wes þah biturnd upon hire swa unimete swiðe þet he for wohlech sende hire his sonden, an efter oðer, ofte somet monie; sende hire beawbelez baðe feole ant feire, sucurs of liueneð, help of his hehe hird to halden hire castel. Heo underfeng al as on unrecheles, ant 75   swa wes heard-iheortet þet hire luue ne mahte he neauer beo þe neorre. Hwet wult tu mare? He com himseolf on ende; schawde hire his feire neb, as þe þe wes of alle men feherest to bihalden; spec se swiðe swoteliche, ant wordes se murie, þet ha mahten deade arearen to liue; wrahte feole wundres ant dude muchele meistries 80   biuoren hire ehsihðe; schawde hire his mihte; talde hire of his kinedom; bead to makien hire cwen of al þet he ahte.

Al þis ne heold nawt. Nes þis hoker wunder? For heo nes neauer wurðe forte beon his þuften. Ah swa, þurh his deboneirte, luue hefde ouercumen him þet he seide on ende: 'Dame, þu art iweorret, 85   ant þine van beoð se stronge þet tu ne maht nanesweis wiðute mi sucurs edfleon hare honden, þet ha ne don þe to scheome deað efter al þi weane. Ich chulle, for þe luue of þe, neome þet feht upo me ant arudde þe of ham þe þi deað secheð. Ich wat þah to soðe þet ich schal bituhen ham neomen deaðes wunde; ant ich hit 90   wulle heorteliche, forte ofgan þin heorte. Nu þenne b{i}seche ich þe, for þe luue þet ich cuðe þe, þet tu luuie me, lanhure efter þe ilke dede dead hwen þu naldest liues.' Þes king dude al þus: arudde hire of alle hire van, ant wes himseolf to wundre ituket and islein on ende, þurh miracle aras þah from deaðe to liue. Nere þeos ilke 95   leafdi of uueles cunnes kunde, ȝef ha ouer alle þing ne luuede him herefter?

Þes king is Iesu, Godes sune, þet al o þise wise wohede ure sawle þe deoflen hefden biset. Ant he, as noble wohere, efter monie messagers ant feole goddeden, com to pruuien his luue, ant schawde 100   þurh cnihtschipe þet he wes luuewurðe; as weren sumhwile cnihtes iwunet to donne; dude him i turneiment ant hefde for his leoues luue his scheld i feht as kene cniht on euche half iþurlet. His scheld þe wreah his goddhead wes his leoue licome þet wes ispread o rode – brad as scheld buuen in his istrahte earmes, nearow bineoðen as loved his love that he gave for her the price of himself. Now take good heed, my dear sisters, why he ought to be loved. First like a man who goes wooing – like a king who loved a noble lady from a distant land – he sent his messengers in advance (who were the patriarchs and prophets of the Old Testament) with private letters. At last he came himself, and brought the Gospel as open letters, and wrote with his own blood a salutation to his beloved, a love-greeting to woo her with and to possess her love. A tale belongs to this, an example with hidden meaning.

A lady was besieged all around by her enemies, her land laid waste, and she impoverished, within a castle of earth. The love of a great king was however directed towards her, so immeasurably greatly that he sent her in courtship his messengers, one after another, often many together; he sent her precious gifts both many and fine, help with provisions, and aid from his noble court to hold her castle. She received all [this] as one uncaring, and was so hard-hearted that he could never be the closer to her love. What more could you wish? At last he came himself, showed her his handsome face, he who was the fairest of all to look upon. He spoke so very sweetly, and in words so cheering that they might raise the dead to life. He performed many marvels and did great feats in her sight, showed her his power, told her about his kingdom, and offered to make her queen of all he possessed.

All this amounted to nothing. Was not this scorn a marvel? For she was never worthy to be his handmaiden. But, through his graciousness, love had so overcome him that in the end he said: 'Lady, you are attacked, and your foes are so strong that, without my help, you could in no way escape their hands, so that they should not put you to a shameful death after all your miseries. For your love, I will take the fight upon myself and rescue you from those who seek your death. However, I know for sure that I shall receive a mortal wound among them; and I cordially desire it in order to win your heart. Now I beseech you, for the love that I have revealed to you, that you may love me at least after that deed, when I am dead, when you would not when I was alive.' This king did it all: rescued her from all her enemies, and was himself atrociously ill-treated and slain in the end; however, by a miracle, he arose from death to life. Would not this same lady be of a very base nature if she did not love him above all things after that?

105   þe an fot (efter monies wene), set upo þe oðer. Þet þis scheld naueð
siden, is for bitacnunge þet his deciples, þe schulden stonden bi
him ant habben ibeon his siden, fluhen alle from him ant leafden
him as fremede, as þe Godspel seið: *Relicto eo omnes fugerunt*. Þis
scheld is iȝeuen us aȝein alle temptatiuns, as Ieremie witneð: *Dabis*
110   *scutum cordis laborem tuum*. Nawt ane þis scheld ne schilt us from
alle uueles, ah deð ȝet mare – cruneð us in heouene *scuto bone*
uoluntatis. 'Lauerd,' he seið, Dauið, 'wið þe scheld of þi gode wil þu
hauest us icrunet' – scheld, he seið, of god wil, for willes he þolede
al þet he þolede. *Ysaias: Oblatus est quia uoluit*.

Notes

9   **monne ledene ant englene** 'the language of men and angels'   This text
preserves genitives descended from both the *-a* genitive plural of the Strong
masculine nouns and the *-ena* genitive plural of Weak nouns. The rounding of short *a* before a nasal is found west of a line from Morecambe Bay,
following the Pennine chain to the Severn estuary.

12   **hali**   *Ancrene Wisse* does not exhibit the southern rounding of OE
long *ā*. By 1230, however, rounding had extended to Hereford, so this
spelling is to be taken as evidence of conservative spelling practice.

15   **lomen**   OE Weak nouns and Strong feminine nouns have plurals in
-en. Masculine and neuter nouns (and feminines ending in *-ung*) have *-es*
plurals.

18   **wurcheð**   OE *wyrcan*. The spelling <u> for WS *y* is found in western
areas: *lutel* (4), *dude* (9). It originates as an attempt by French-trained
scribes to write the OE sound [y], which coincided with the French sound
spelt <u>.

19   **loki**   Long-stemmed Weak Class 2 verbs lose final *-n* in the infinitive,
but retain their characteristic *-i-*.

22   **ha** 'they'   *Ancrene Wisse* possesses a complete system of plural third-
person pronouns with medial *a*, and also a nominative singular feminine,
ha. These forms are almost restricted to Gloucestershire, Worcestershire
and Herefordshire. A parallel with the genitive plural *hare* is found in the
OE of the Vespasian Psalter gloss, *heara*. The latter probably developed
analogically from the demonstrative *þeara* found in VP.

24   **makieð twa þinges**   The sense depends not on word order, but on
recognising that *makieð* has a plural inflexion in concord with the plural
þinges.

31   **leoue sustren**   In western areas the reflex of the OE diphthong *ēo*
continued to be written <eo> into the fourteenth century (cf. *South English Legendary*).

This king is Jesus, God's son, who in all these ways wooed our soul that devils had besieged. And, like a noble lover, after many messengers and generous deeds, he came to prove his love, and showed her by deeds of valour that he was worthy of love, as knights were once accustomed to do. He entered a tournament and, for his beloved's love, like a bold knight had his shield pierced on each side. His shield, which covered his deity, was his precious body that was spread out on the cross, broad like a shield above with his outstretched arms, narrow beneath like the one foot – according to the opinion of many – set upon the other. That this shield has no sides is to signify that his disciples, who should have stood by him and been its sides, all fled from him and left him like a stranger, as the Gospel says: *Relicto eo omnes fugerunt.* This shield is given to us against all temptations, as Jeremiah witnesses: *Dabis scutum cordis laborem tuum.* Not only does this shield shield us from all evils, but it does yet more: it crowns us in heaven *scuto bone uoluntatis.* 'Lord,' he says, David, 'with the shield of your good will you have crowned us' – shield, he says, of good will, because willingly he suffered all that he suffered. *Ysaias: Oblatus est quia uoluit.*

41	**lahe** One of a few Scandinavian borrowings in the piece. Most are of widespread use (*lahe*, 58; *baðe*, 73) but the abstract noun-forming suffix *-lec* in *freolec* (46) is worthy of special notice, as is the use of *þah* (9) in preference to OE-derived *þei*, the form common in the South. This Scandinavian influence can be explained by Danish settlement in Shropshire, Worcestershire and Herefordshire in the reign of Canute.
51	**alde-feader** Failure of breaking before *l*-groups and retraction to *a* suggests an Anglian OE antecedent.
64–65	**leattres isealet** Sealed letters are here contrasted with letters patent; both French phrases based upon earlier Latin ones. Letters patent were those documents containing royal Acts for which the letter served as confirmation, and was therefore intended to be accessible to all concerned. Sealed letters contain private communications. The word *saluz* (66) refers to the opening greeting of the letter. Compare Alfred's Preface to the *Cura Pastoralis* (Excerpt 2) or *Kyng Alisaunder* (Excerpt 15).
73	**beawbelez** This is the only known ME context of a word which in OF means a child's plaything.
85	**van** 'foes' The voicing of initial fricatives is a southern feature. *Ancrene Wisse* comes from close to its northern boundary.
87	**ich chulle** The southern form of the pronoun, spelt *ich*, with assimilation to a western form of the verb 'will'.

95   **of uueles cunnes kunde**   Literally 'of the nature of an evil race'. A sequence of genitive modifiers possible in Old English, but unidiomatic by the fourteenth century.

104–105   **brad as scheld . . . upo þe oðer**   A long kite-shaped shield seems to be envisaged, narrow at the base. The representation of the crucified Christ with one foot nailed over the other would have been a relatively recent iconographic development at the time *Ancrene Wisse* was composed.

12

A KENTISH SERMON:

THE MARRIAGE AT CANA

The following excerpt is taken from one of five sermons translated into English and included in MS Bodleian Laud Misc. 471 in the latter half of the thirteenth century. All five, and also Anglo-Norman and Latin examples in the same manuscript, are from originals composed between 1168 and 1175 by Maurice de Sully, Bishop of Paris, for use by the priests of his diocese. The popularity of Maurice's sermons in France is attested by the large number of surviving manuscripts; it is a popularity which must have derived in part from the simplicity in structural plan and language, which is evident also in English translation. Like the example given below, Maurice's sermons fall into three parts: the presentation in literal terms of a scriptural event, followed by an exposition of its allegorical and spiritual significance, the whole completed by the application of the teaching to everyday morality.

The translator is unknown, but by comparison with both the language of the OE Kentish glosses and that of the precisely localisable *Ayenbite of Inwit*, he must have been writing in Kent. By the standards of these other texts, however, the Kentish in this manuscript is not pure, so that the text may have been copied by a scribe from a more northerly location. Morphologically, the text shows characteristics of southern origin: a few nouns preserve *-en* plurals (*faten*, 13; *deden*, 34); archaic forms of the verb 'to have' persist (*habbeþ*, 23); the past participle still retains its prefix; *h*-forms of the pronouns are used; and the text still retains substantial traces of grammatical gender in its inflexions. Phonologically, the South-East is indicated by the spelling of the reflex of WS *y* as <e> (*bredale*, 3; *uuluelden*, 16) and of *ēo* as <ie>. In areas where the reflex of OE *y* and *ēo* were represented in this way, the spelling of WS *ǣ* as <e> (*ǣ*[1]: *deden*; *ǣ*[2]: *anhet*) may be taken to indicate Kentish, since more northerly texts with this combination include <a> spellings for *ǣ* (cf. *Vices and Virtues*). Finally, and most specifically

Kentish, is the spelling of OE *ēa* as \<ia\> (*beliaue*, 27, and with lengthened diphthong, *ihialde*, 24). The text does not, however, consistently represent WS short *æ* as \<e\>, nor *ēo* as \<ie\>.

Nuptie facte sunt in Chana Galilee, et erat mater Iesu ibi; vocatus est autem Iesus ad nuptias et discipuli eius. Þet holi godspel of today us telþ þet a bredale was imaked ine þo londe of Ierusalem, in ane cite þat was icleped Cane, in þa time þat Godes sune yede in erþe
5 flesliche. To þa bredale was ure Leuedi Seinte Marie, and ure Louerd Iesus Crist and hise deciples. So iuel auenture þet wyn failede at þise bredale; þo seide ure Leuedi Seinte Marie to here sune: 'Hi ne habbet no wyn.' And ure Louerd answerde and sede to hire: 'Wat belongeth hit to me oþer to þe, wyman?' Nu ne dorste hi namore
10 sigge, ure Lauedi; hac hye spac to þo serganz þet seruede of þo wyne, and hem seyde: 'Al þet he hot yu do, so doþ.'
   And ure Louerd clepede þe serganz and seyde to hem: 'Folvellet,' ha seyde, 'þos ydres (þet is to sigge, þos croos, oþer þos faten) of watere.' For þer were vi ydres of stone þet ware iclepede baþieres, wer
15 þo Gius hem wesse for clenesse and for religiun, ase þe custome was ine þo time. Þo serganz uuluelden þo faten of watere, and hasteliche was iwent into wyne, bie þo wille of ure Louerde. Þo seide ure Lord to þo serganz: 'Moveth togidere and bereth to Architriclin (þat was se þet ferst was iserued).' And also hedde idrunke of þise wyne þet
20 ure Louerd hedde imaked of þe watere (ha niste nocht þe miracle, ac þo serganz wel hit wiste þet hedde þet water ibrocht), þo seide Architriclin to þo bredgume: 'Oþer men, seyde he, 'doþ forþ þet beste wyn þet hi habbeþ ferst at here bredale; and þu hest ido þe contrarie, þet þu hest ihialde þet beste wyn wath nu!' Þis was þe
25 commencement of þo miracles of ure Louerde þet he made flesliche in erþe; and þo beleuede on him his deciples. I ne sigge nacht þet hi ne hedden þerbefore in him beliaue; ac fore þe miracle þet hi seghe was here beliaue þe more istrengþed.
   Nu ye habbeþ iherd þe miracle; nu ihereþ þe signefiance.
30 Þet water bitockned se euele Cristeneman. For also þet water is natureliche schald, and akelþ alle þo þet hit drinkeþ, so is se euele Cristeman chald of þo luue of Gode, for þo euele werkes þet hi doþ; ase so is lecherie, spusbreche, roberie, manslechtes, husberners, bakbiteres, and alle oþre euele deden, þurch wyche þinkes man
35 ofserueth þet fer of helle, ase Godes oghe mudh hit seid. And alle

The holy Gospel for today tells us that a marriage was arranged in the land of Jerusalem, in a city that was called Cana, in the time that God's son went on earth incarnate. Our Lady Saint Mary, and our Lord Jesus Christ and his disciples had all gone to the wedding. The chance so befell that the wine ran out at this wedding; then our Lady Saint Mary said to her son: 'They have no wine.' And our Lord answered and said to her: 'What concern is that of mine or yours, woman?' Now she dare say no more, our Lady; but she spoke to the servants who had served the wine, and said to them: 'All that he bids you to do, do it.'

And our Lord called the servants and said to them: 'Fill up', he said, 'those water-vessels (that is to say those water-pots, or those vats) with water.' For there were six stone vessels that were called 'bath-tubs', where the Jews washed themselves for purification and for religious purposes, as the custom was in that time. The servants filled up the vessels with water, and quickly it was turned into wine by the will of our Lord. Then our Lord said to the servants: 'Go together and carry them to the master of the feast (that was he who was served first).' And as soon as he had drunk some of this wine that our Lord had made from the water (he did not know of the miracle, but the servants knew it well who had brought the water), then the master of the feast said to the bridegroom: 'Other men,' he said, 'have the best wine that they have served first at their wedding, and you have done the reverse, in that you have kept the best wine until now!' This was the beginning of the miracles of our Lord that he performed here incarnate on earth; and then his disciples had faith in him. I do not say that they did not have faith in him before that, but because of the miracle that they saw their faith was more strengthened.

Now you have heard the miracle; now hear the meaning. That water signifies the bad Christian. For, as water is cold by nature, and cools all those who drink it, so is the bad Christian cold in the love of God, on account of the wicked deeds that they do: such as lechery, adultery, robbery, murders, arsonists, slanderers, and all other wicked deeds, through which things are deserved the fire þo signefied þet water, þet þurch yemere werkes oþer þurch yemer iwil liesed þo blisce of heuene. Þet wyn, þat is naturelliche hot ine himselue, and anhet alle þo þet hit drinked, betokned alle þo þet bied anheet of þe luue of ure Lorde.

40   Nu, lordinges, ure Lord God Almichti, þat hwylem in one stede and ine one time flesliche makede of watere wyn, yet ha deþ mani time maked of watere wyn gostliche, wanne þurch his grace maked of þo euele manne good man, of þe orgeilus umble, of þe lechur chaste, of þe niþinge large; and of alle oþre folies, so ha maket of

45   þo watere wyn. Þis his si signefiance of þe miracle. Nu loke euerich man toward himseluen yef he is win: þet is to siggen, yef he is anheet of þo luue of Gode; oþer yef he is water: þet is, yef þu art chold of Godes luue. Yef þu art euel man, besech ure Lorde þet he do ine þe his uertu, þet ha þe wende of euele into gode, and þet he

50   do þe do swiche werkes þet þu mote habbe þo blisce of heuene. *Quod uobis prestare dignetur.*

Notes

3   **londe**   Rounding of OE long *ā* is usual in this passage: *holi* (2), *stone* (14), *gostliche* (42), *one* (40) (but see also *ane* (3)). This form is probably derived from OE *land* by lengthening before *nd* followed by the southern rounding of long *ā* to *o*.

5   **flesliche**   The spellings <s> and <ss> (*wesse*) for [ʃ] are probably due to the influence of French scribal attempts to render unfamiliar English sounds, as also are <t> (*habbet*), <d> (*signified*), and <dh> (*mudh*), written to represent /θ/.

6   **iuel** 'befell'   This preterite form preserves a prefix, but also exhibits southern voicing of an initial fricative. This voicing is found south of a line roughly from the Thames estuary to north Worcestershire. See also *Folvellet* (12) – which also has south-eastern <e> for WS *y*.

8   **sede**   WS *sægde*. The loss of the palatal before *d* occurs in Kent and in Saxon areas, and is accompanied by lengthening of the vowel. The resulting *æ* generally develops to *e* in ME, except in Essex, where *a*-forms are found. See *Vices and Virtues* (Excerpt 10).

13   **ha**   The *a*-form of the masculine third-person-singular pronoun is found mostly in the same area as the initial voicing of fricatives mentioned above (note to line 6). Together they became associated in the Early Modern period with the speech of countryfolk, viewed from a London perspective.
        faten   With *deden* (34), exemplifies the southern use of *-en* noun plurals.

of hell, as God's own mouth put it. And the water signifies all those who through wretched deeds or wretched intent have failed to attain the bliss of heaven. The wine, which has the natural property of heat, and which heats all those who drink it, symbolises all those who are warmed by the love of our Lord. Now, lords, our Lord God Almighty, who once, while incarnate, at a particular place and time made wine from water, still he does it many times, makes wine of water spiritually, when through his grace he makes a good man from an evil man, the humble from the proud, the chaste from the lecher, the generous from the miser; and so from all other follies, he makes wine from water. This is the meaning of the miracle. Now let every man consider himself, whether he is wine, that is to say whether he is warmed by the love of God, or whether he is water, that is if you are cold in God's love. If you are a wicked man, beg our Lord that he may put in you his power, so that he may change you from evil to good, and that he may cause you to perform such actions that you may have the bliss of heaven.

24   **wath** 'until'   An unusual form, restricted to the language of the South-East.

30   **se euele Cristeneman**   The south-eastern *e* for WS *y* is frequent in the passage. A conservative – and therefore southern or western – form of ME is indicated by the preservation of different inflexional forms of the definite article. Cf. *þet water* (30), and the use of *þa/þe* for the plural.

31   **schald**   Also *chald* (32). The spelling of the initial consonant of these forms indicates palatalisation caused by a following *ea*, derived from breaking of *æ* before *ld* at an earlier stage. The antecedent of this form was therefore not Anglian. That the *a* has not been rounded to *o*, as is usual in this text, suggests that it was not lengthened, but see also *chold* (48).

43   **orgeilus**   Of the vices and virtues mentioned here, and the misdemeanours in line 33, a relatively limited number are indicated by words of French origin: *roberie, umble, lechur, chaste, large*. The persistence of OE words in this domain is evidence for the early date of the text. The word *niþinge* is an OE borrowing from Scandinavian.

13

A PROCLAMATION OF HENRY III
(1258)

Although the languages of all official business from the twelfth century until the early fifteenth century were Latin and French, two documents survive which give us a glimpse of the early use of English in this domain. The first is a brief charter of 1155 in which Henry II confirms the rights and privileges of the monastery of Christ Church, Canterbury, and whose linguistic forms are strikingly more conservative than the nearly contemporary Final Continuation of the *Peterborough Chronicle*. The second is the following excerpt, an open letter proclaiming the determination of King Henry III to uphold the terms of the agreement reached with the barons in the Provisions of Oxford.

The proclamation was issued in both French and English, the use of English perhaps being dictated by its political importance, since competence in English was seen as a distinguishing characteristic between the settled Anglo-Norman barony and the Continental French incomers favoured by the king. The English text survives in two manuscripts, one in the Public Records Office and the other among the city records now in the Bodleian Library, Oxford, and printed with facsimile and translation in O. Ogle, *Royal Letters Addressed to Oxford* (Oxford, 1892). As mentioned in the proclamation, copies were sent to each county in England, and the copy surviving in the Public Records Office, although designated as that for Huntingdonshire, may have been the exemplar upon which other copies were based. The text printed here is that of the Public Records Office version. The language of the proclamation is that of London in the mid thirteenth century, and exhibits many of the southern and linguistically conservative features which may be expected in a city which had originally been the capital of the East Saxons and had remained outside the direct influence of Scandinavian settlement. The diphthongs *ea* and *eo* are still written, and *æ* is written for both long and short vowels. Pronouns still have the OE *h*-forms and Weak

Class 2 verbs are still distinguishable from other weak verbs. Verbs also retain the prefix in the past participles, and the southern form of the present participle, *ilestinde* (9), is found. The third-person-plural present tense of the verb 'to have' preserves its earlier OE form *habbeþ* (6). The spelling <oa> is used freely to represent a sound developed from OE *ā* and for the long *ā* produced before late OE lengthening groups, *loande*, *foangen* (but see also *amanges*, 21).

The passage is of stylistic interest in that it represents the earliest English example of curial style, a ceremonious official style imitated from Latin and French and marked by the use of legal phrasing, both to ensure clarity of reference and to convey a sense of importance (Burnley 1986). Some features are marked in the notes.

Henri, þurȝ Godes fultume King on Engleneloande, Lhoauerd
on Yrloande, Duk on Normandi, on Aquitaine, and Eorl on
Aniow, send igretinge to alle hise holde, ilærde and ileawede, on
Huntendoneschire. Þæt witen ȝe wel alle þæt we willen and vnnen
þæt, þæt vre rædesmen alle, oþer þe moare dæl of heom, þæt beoþ
ichosen þurȝ us and þurȝ þæt loandes folk on vre kuneriche, habbeþ
idon and shullen don in þe worþnesse of Gode and on vre treowþe,
for þe freme of þe loande þurȝ þe besiȝte of þan toforeniseide
redesmen, beo stedefæst and ilestinde in alle þinge a buten ænde.
And we hoaten alle vre treowe, in þe treowþe þæt heo vs oȝen, þæt
heo stedefæstliche healden and swerien to healden and to werien
þo isetnesses þæt beon imakede and beon to makien, þurȝ þan
toforeniseide rædesmen, oþer þurȝ þe moare dæl of heom, alswo
alse hit is biforen iseid; and þæt æhc oþer helpe þæt for to done
bi þan ilche oþe aȝenes alle men riȝt for to done and to foangen.
And noan ne nime of loande ne of eȝte wherþurȝ þis besiȝte muȝe
beon ilet oþer iwersed on onie wise. And ȝif oni oþer onie cumen
her onȝenes, we willen and hoaten þæt alle vre treowe heom healden
deadliche ifoan. And for þæt we willen þæt þis beo stedefæst and
lestinde, we senden ȝew þis writ open, iseined wiþ vre seel, to
halden amanges ȝew ine hord. Witnesse vsseluen æt Lundene þane
eȝtetenþe day on þe monþe of Octobre, in þe two and fowertiȝþe
ȝeare of vre cruninge. And þis wes idon ætforen vre isworene
redesmen, Boneface Archebischop on Kanterburi, Walter of
Cantelow, Bischop on Wirechestre, Simon of Muntfort, Eorl of
Leirchestre, Richard of Clare, Eorl on Glowchestre and on Hurtford,
Roger Bigod, Eorl on Northfolke and Marescal on Engleneloande,
Perres of Sauueye, Willelm of Fort, Eorl on Aubemarle, Iohan of
Plesseiz, Eorl on Warewik, Iohan Geffrees sune, Perres of Muntfort,
Richard of Grey, Roger of Mortemer, Iames of Aldithele, and
ætforen oþre inoȝe.

And al on þo ilche worden is isend into æurihce oþre shcire
ouer al þære kuneriche on Engleneloande, and ek in-tel Irelonde.

Notes

1–4   **Henry ... Huntendoneschire**   The *salutatio* of the letter. Compare this,
and the connection to the following sentence through a subjunctive, with
Alfred's opening of his Preface to the *Pastoral Care*. Alfred does not continue in the plural with the 'royal' *we*.

Henry, through the grace of God King of England, Lord of Ireland, Duke of Normandy, of Aquitaine, and Earl of Anjou, sends greeting to all his loyal [subjects], clerical and lay, in Huntingdonshire. That you may all know well that we desire and are pleased that that which all our counsellors, or the greater part of them, who have been chosen by us and by the common people of our kingdom, have done and shall do to the glory of God and in loyalty to us, for the country's benefit through the provisions of the aforesaid counsellors, should be forever firm and enduring. And we order all our faithful [subjects] by the loyalty that they owe us, that they should steadfastly maintain, and swear to maintain and to defend those agreements that are made and may be made by the aforementioned counsellors, or by the greater part of them, as is before stated; and that each should help the other, by the same oath, to act towards all men so as to give and receive justice. And no one may seize land or property as a result of which this provision may be in any way hindered or impaired. And if any [person] or any [persons] oppose this, we desire and command that all our loyal [subjects] consider them deadly enemies. And because we wish that this should be firm and lasting, we send you this open writ, sealed with our seal, for you to keep with you in your archives. Witnessed by ourself in London on the eighteenth day of the month of October in the forty-second year of our reign. And this was done before our sworn counsellors, Boniface, Archbishop of Canterbury; Walter of Cantiloupe, Bishop of Worcester; Simon de Montfort, Earl of Leicester; Richard of Clare, Earl of Gloucester and of Hertfordshire; Roger Bigod, Earl of Northumberland and Marshal of England; Piers of Savoy; William of Fort, Earl of Albemarle; John of Plessis, Earl of Warwick; John, Geoffrey's son; Piers of Montfort; Richard of Grey; Roger of Mortimer; James of Aldithele, and before many others. And in exactly the same words [this writ] has been sent to every other county throughout the kingdom of England, and also into Ireland.

King   OE *y* is written <i>, but in *kuneriche* (6) is written <u>, and in *iwersed* (17), <e>. The three different spellings represent three different dialect areas, respectively the East Midlands, West Midlands and the South-East. London texts frequently have all three types.

5–6   **beoþ ichosen**   The form of the verb 'to be' is identical to that in OE; the past participle retains a phonetically reduced version of the prefix, but the verb (OE *gecoren*) has been remodelled on the infinitive form (*cēosan*).

8   **þan toforeniseide**   Devices to ensure clarity within chains of reference are part of the legal inheritance of curial style. Among these are repetition of words and phrases, as well as identifying phrases such as this and *alse hit is biforen iseid* (14).

9   **a buten ænde**   The significance of the spelling with *æ* is not certain, but the failure of Germanic short *a* to develop to *e* when *i*-mutated before *n* is characteristic of the Essex dialect. See *Vices and Virtues* and *Kyng Alisaunder*. The impressive-sounding phrase is characteristic of documents written in the curial style: *stedefæst and lestinde* (19–20). Note also the free use of synonymous pairs of words and phrases, and extended qualifications of statements.

10   **we hoaten**   First-person present indicative. In most of the present-tense plural forms of verbs, indicative forms are no longer distinct from subjunctives, as was the case in the East Midlands. Distinct forms are maintained in *habbeþ* (6) and *beoþ* (5).

15   **oþe**   Although the reflex of OE long *a* is usually distinguished from the reflex of OE *o* in spelling by the use of <oa> for the former, a few spellings suggest that in some words there may have been no distinction in pronunciation: *alswo* (13); *two* (22); *þo* (32).

32   **worden**   There are very few noun plurals in the passage. Although *-en* plurals are normally considered to be associated with the conservative South and West, this OE neuter word occurred very widely either endingless or with the *-en* inflexion for plural. *Þinge* (9) is an endingless OE neuter; *ifoan* (19) has the original Weak plural ending.

14

THE *SOUTH ENGLISH LEGENDARY*

The *South English Legendary* is the name given by modern scholars to a collection of saints' lives and associated material which was probably compiled in Worcester in the last quarter of the thirteenth century. It was extremely popular from the beginning, flourished in the fourteenth century, and continued to be copied throughout the medieval period. It is anonymous, and its history illustrates graphically the general truth that medieval English texts ceased to be the property of their author, becoming a common heritage adaptable to the purposes of any literate person. The earliest manuscripts contained about seventy lives, but this count had doubled by the end of the fifteenth century.

The excerpt printed here is part of a popular scientific treatise tacked on to the 'Legend of St Michael'. Reference to hell in the legend leads on to an account of the cosmos, meteorology, the human constitution in terms of its composition from the four elements – earth, water, air and fire – and closes with a description of procreation and psychology. The author acknowledges no sources for his eclectic account, and modern scholarship has discovered none; but there are some parallels with the *Secretum Secretorum*, and compare Ælfric's *De Temporibus Anni* (Excerpt 5) above. The version in Bodleian Library MS Laud Misc. 108, on which this excerpt is based, seems to have been produced in western Oxfordshire about 1300. A southern origin is indicated by the spelling of the reflex of OE *a* as <o>, and rounding is confirmed by the rhymes in lines 40–1, 74–5, 98–9. The South is further suggested by the use of -*ene* as a noun plural ending in *steorrene* (9) and *cloudene* (58), the *h*-forms of the personal pronouns, the preservation of the prefix in past participles, and the present participle form in -*inde* (79). The continued use of the spelling <eo>, and the writing of WS *y* as <u> suggest the West. WS *y* is represented by <uy> over a more restricted area, including Worcester, Warwick, Gloucester and west Oxfordshire. The spelling *guod* is found only in the South-East and in west Oxfordshire.

Þe Eorþe nis bote a luytel hurst aȝein þe riȝte heouene, iwis.
Heouene geth al aboute þe eorþe, euene it mot weyȝe;
Amidde riȝt heouene þe eorþe is ase þe streon amidde þe eyȝe.
Muche is þat on þanne more þane þat oþur, for þe leste steorre is
5   In heouene, ase þe bok us tellez, [more] þane al þe eorþe, iwis.
For ho-so were an heiȝ bi ane steorre, ȝif it so miȝte beo,
So luyte wolde þe eorþe þinche þat vnneþe he scholde it ouȝt iseo.
Þe heouene geth ene aboute, þoruȝ daiȝe and þoruȝ nyȝt;
Þe mone and þe steorrene with him heo berth, and þe sonne þat is
    so briȝt:
10   For þat is euene aboue þin heued riȝt atþe nones stounde,
Ounder þine fet euene it is at midniȝt onder þe grounde,
And cometh up ȝwane þe sonne arist, and [o]uer þe is at none;
Heo makez euene þus hire cours, and comez aboute wel sone.
Ase an appel þe eorþe is round, so þat eueremo
15   Half þe eorþe þe sonne bischineth, hov-so it euere go,
And noon it is binethen us, ȝwane it is here midniȝt;
Ase man may þe soþe iseo, ho-so hauez guod insiȝt:
Ase ȝif þov heolde ane clere candele biside an appel riȝt,
Euene half þe appel heo wolde ȝiuen hire lijȝt.

20   Eiȝte firmamenz þare beoth, swuche ase we iseoth.
Þe ouemeste is þe riȝtte heouene in ȝwan þe steorrene beoth
For Godes riche is þare aboue þat last withouten ende;
Þarto we beoth imaked – god leue us þudere iwende.
Þare bineoþe beoth seoue firmamenz, þat euerech of heom, iwis,
25   One steorre hath withoute mo, þat planete icleoped is.
Ichulle nemmen heore seoue names, and formest biguynne hext:
Saturnus is al aboue and Iupiter sethþe next,
Þanne Mars bineoþen him, and sethþe þe sonne is,
Venus sethþe, þe clere steorre, Mercurius þanne, iwis,
30   Þat wel selden is of us iseiȝe. Þe Mone is next þe grounde.
Þoruȝ gret wit of clergie heore names weren furst bifounde:
For euerech of þeos seouene mouwen gret wonder on eorþe do,
Boþe of wederes and of fruyt, ase heore power ȝif þareto.
And also man, ȝwane he is ibore onder heore power, iwis,
35   Schullen habbe diuers lijf, euere ase heore vertue is:
Some lechours, some glotones, and some of oþur manere.
And natheles a man of guod inwit of alle he may him skere:
For þe planetes ne doth non oþur but ȝiuez in mannes wille,

The earth is no more than a little spot compared with the true heaven. Heaven goes all around the earth, steadily it must move. The earth is in the middle of the true heaven like the pupil amid the eye. The one is much larger than the other, for as books tell us the least star in heaven is indeed bigger than the whole earth. For whoever were aloft beside a star (if that could happen) would think the earth to be so small that he should hardly see it at all. The heaven goes steadily round, by day and night, and carries the moon and stars with it, and the sun which is so bright, for what is exactly above your head at noontime, is directly beneath your feet, under the ground, at midnight, and comes up when the sun rises, and is above you at noon; it steadily makes its way thus, and quickly comes around. The earth is round like an apple, so that the sun continuously lights up half the earth, wherever it is, and it is noon beneath us when it is midnight here; a truth that anybody can see, who has good perception. It is as if you held a bright candle next to an apple; it would give light to exactly half the apple.

There are eight heavenly spheres. As we can see, the uppermost is the true heaven in which the stars are: for God's kingdom, which lasts without end is above it – we are created for it; God grant us to go there. Seven heavenly spheres are beneath, of which each one has only one star, that is called a planet. I shall name their seven names, beginning first from the highest. Saturn is above all, and Jupiter next, then Mars beneath it and afterwards the Sun, the bright star Venus after, then Mercury, that is very rarely seen by us. The Moon is nearest the ground. Their names were first discovered by great skill of learning, for each of those seven may work marvellous effects on earth both with regard to weather and fruit, as their particular virtues extend. And so, according to the force of the planet under which they are born, people have different lives: some lechers, some gluttons, and some have other characteristics. But nevertheless a man of good discrimination can purify himself, because the planets do no more than act upon man's will to be good or grosser, according to what their force extends, and gives him also the disposition to do this or that; but nevertheless there is still conscience, which each wise man may use, for nobody has such a disposition to be a lecher or villain in such a way that he cannot guard against it: but nevertheless, few do so.

The [distance] between heaven and earth is great, for one could travel forty miles and still a bit more every day and not come to the

To beon luþur oþur guod, ase heore uertue wole to tille,
40 And ʒiuen him also qualite to don so and so;
Ake nouʒt forþan after is inwit; ech wys man may do:
For swuch qualite no man ne hath to beon lechor oþur schrewe,
Þat he þarewith ne may him wite – ake natheles so doth fewe.

. . .

Muche is bitwene heouene and eorþe, for þe man þat miʒte go
45 Euereche daye fourty mile, and ʒeot sumdel mo,
He ne scholde nouʒt to hexte heouene, þat ʒe alday iseoth,
Comen in eiʒte þousende ʒer, þere as þe steorrene beoth;
And þei Adam, ore furste fader, hadde bigonne anon
Þo þat he was furst imad, and toward þe heouene igon,
50 And hadde eche daie fourti mile euene opriʒt igo,
He ne hadde nouʒt ʒeot to heuene icome bi a þousende mile and
mo.
Sikere ʒe beon I segge ʒeov soth ileue ho-so ileue –
Hov schulle we þat comiez so late after Adam and Eue?
Ake ʒwane a man is on eorþe ded, and his soule beo guod,
55 Heo nath with hire non heuinesse of flesche ne of blod:
ʒif heo is þanne withoute sunne, heo hath aungles cuynde,
And mai beo nouþe here and þer, ase quik ase mannes muynde.
For ase ʒe iseoth þe liʒtengue out of þe cloudene iwende,
Þat comieth of þat on half of þe world and also sone in þe oþur
ende,
60 Wel smartloker scheot ane mannes soule; ʒe, more þane swuche
seuene,
ʒif heo is oute of sunne, þene riʒte wei into heouene.
Ake wel sonere he may to helle come – þarefore it is isene
Þat wel mo to helle wendez. ʒe, ich drede swuche tene.

Bineoþe þe loweste heuene, þat þe mone is on ibrouʒt,
65 So beoth þe foure elemenz, of ʒwan we beoth iwrouʒt.
Next þe mone þat fuyr is hext – echone huy beoth rounde –
Þe eir is þanne next bineothe, and tillez riʒt to þe grounde,
Sethþe is watur, and sethþe þe eorþe – þeos beoth foure, iwis,
Of ʒwan man and eche quic þing forsoþe imaked is.
70 Ore louerd in echon of þis foure al dai scheweth is miʒte,
Ase ʒe mowe in þe stude of fuyre iseo a wonder siʒte,
Scheote as þei it a steorre were bi þe lofte an heiʒ,
Ake þe steorrene beoth feorre aboue, for þat is sumdel neiʒ.

highest heaven that you see every day, where the stars are, in eight
thousand years. And although our first father, Adam, had begun
straight away when he was first made, and walked towards heaven
forty miles a day directly upwards, he would not yet have come to
heaven, by a thousand miles or more. You may be certain I tell you
the truth, believe it who may – how shall we who come so late after
Adam and Eve? But when a man is dead on earth, and his soul is
good, it has with it no heaviness of flesh or blood; if it is then
without sin, it has the nature of an angel, and may be now here and
now there as quickly as human thought. For as you see the light fall
from the skies, that comes from one side of the world and as quickly
ends in the other, much quicker shoots a man's soul if he is free
from sin, yes, more than seven times as quickly, on the direct route
to heaven. But he may come to hell much quicker: therefore it is
apparent that far more go to hell – yes, I dread such suffering.

Beneath the lowest heaven, where the moon is lodged, are the
four elements from which we are formed. Next to the moon, fire
is the highest – each is spherical. Next below that is the air, which
extends right to the ground; after that is water, and then the earth.
These make four, I think, from which man and every living thing is
surely made. In each of these four, Our Lord daily shows his might,
as [for example] in the region of fire you may see a wondrous
sight: something like a star shoots through the air above; but the
stars are farther above, for that is fairly close. The sun can perform
great [feats] of strength and power here among us: it draws up the
essence from the water and from the earth too. In dry weather it
draws up from the earth a kind of dry exhalation, so that carried
by the heat of the sun, it goes up above the air, and when it comes
among the fire it begins to ignite and shoots forth all burning until
it is all burned up. Thus, such things are not seen except when
it is hot. Lightning also comes from this source, when it reaches
moisture; for that same dry exhalation, when it is drawn aloft by
previous heat, and there is a cloud nearby, at once as it is on fire,
it shoots through the cloud and while it is in the water, it makes
a very loud rumbling, as if a man took an iron ingot that was
glowing with fire and thrust it in water, it would rumble loudly,
so that it could be heard from afar. So that fire up aloft, that is
kindled near the cloud, rumbles loudly in the water as it passes
through; and that, indeed, is thunder, and certainly nothing else.
And when the fire shoots through it, that is lightning, and that

Þe sonne may here among us gret strencþe and miȝte do:
75 He drauth up þe kuynde of þe watere, and of the eorþe also;
He drauȝth up of þe eorþe in druye wedere as it were a druye breth,
So þat þoruȝ hete of þe sonne aboue þe eir it geth,
And ȝwane it comez among þe fuyre, sone it bigynnez forto tiende
And al berninde it scheot forth, þat hit beo ibarnd to ende.
80 Þarefore men ne iseoth no swuch þing bote it beo in hete.
Liȝtingue comez also þare-of ȝwane it comez to wete:
For al þat ilke druye breth þat is so idrawe an heiȝ,
Þoruȝ hete þat was bifore and a cloud þat þare was neiȝ,
Anon so it is afuyre; it scheot þoruȝ þe cloude,
85 And þe ȝwile it is in þe watere, it goþeleth swyþe loude:
Ase ȝif a man nome ane sclabbe of ire, þat glowynde were afuyre,
And pulte in watere; it wolde goþeli loude, þat men miȝten it feor ihuyre.
Also þat fuyr up an heiȝ þat bi þe cloude is itend,
Hit goþelez in þe watere loude as it þoruȝout iwent –
90 And þat is þe þondre, iwis, and siker non oþur þing;
And ȝwane þat fuyr scheot þoruȝout, þat is þe liȝting,
And þat scheot abrod þoru al þe world. Þat comez aftur þe dunte;
And natheles it þinchez bifore, for it ne may nouȝwere atstunte.
Ȝif here were an heiȝ stepel and a man aboue sete,
95 And men iseiȝen him smiten al an heiȝ guode duntes and grete,
Þou miȝtest him seo wel longue smite þe duntes with þine eiȝe
Are þov scholdest þene dunt iheore, ȝif he were ouȝt heiȝe –
For man mai iseo wel feor a þing anon so it is ido,
Ȝif þare nis noþing bitweone; ake man ne may nouȝt iheore so.

Notes

1   **hurst**   OE *hyrst*, 'a wooded hill or hillock'. Recorded very rarely in western ME, apparently meaning more generally 'a place'.

5   **tellez**   The third-person-singular present-tense inflexion in this text is normally -*eth*, with numerous examples with the syncopation of *e* and the subsequent assimilation characteristic of Saxon-derived forms of ME: *berth* (9), *arist* (12), *last* (22). The fairly frequent -*ez* forms are best interpreted as arising from spelling confusion.

9   **heo**   Apparently to be interpreted here as 'he', but in line 13 as 'she'.

12 **ȝwane**   The spelling <ȝw> for OE <hw> is restricted to west Oxfordshire.

shoots out through the whole world. That comes after the blow, but nevertheless seems to be before, because it may nowhere come to an end. If there were a high steeple and a man seated up above, and people could see him strike, as hard as he could, good, solid blows, you would see him strike the blows (with your eye) very long before you would hear the blow, if he were at all high: for one can see something from a long way off as soon as it is done, if there is nothing in between, but one cannot hear thus.

26   **Ichulle**   This contraction of *ich* and *wulle* is of predominantly southern and western forms of the pronoun and verb.

53   **comiez**   Also *comieth* (59). The plural inflection proper to Weak Class 2 verbs has been extended to this Strong verb. Unless the subject of *comieth* is *cloudene*, the potential distinction offered between singular and plural is not exploited.

55   **heo nath**   The contracted form of the negative particle *ne* and the verb 'to have' is commonest in much the same area as the spelling <uy>. See introductory notes.

68   **watur**   The spelling of unstressed vowels with <u> is predominantly a western characteristic.

79   **ibarnd**   The retention of the prefix is found broadly in the South, but the particular form of this verb, with an *-a-* spelling, is south-west Midland.

85   **goþeleth**   The word has no known etymology, and seems to be sound echoic. In line 87, the infinitive is formed as a Weak Class 2 infinitive.

86   **sclabbe**   The word *slab* seems to be technical in ME, used only of a flat mass of iron or steel. The etymology is obscure.

15

KYNG ALISAUNDER

Early Middle English romance should not be confused with the pastoral idylls of later periods any more than with popular modern love stories. Its ethos often has more in common with epic, and although the love between the hero and heroine forms an important thread of the plot in many romances, acts of military heroism, comradeship, repossession of lost domains, and the violent reassertion of justice are more significant themes. Like many early romances, *Kyng Alisaunder* is the adaptation of an Anglo-Norman original, in this case the *Romance of Alexander* by Thomas of Kent. It recounts the Greek hero's exploits and battles, but his love for Candace is no more important to the story than any other episode, and indeed corresponds to a decline in his fortunes shortly preceding his death. This is a narrative of wonders, politics, travel and action, which pauses only briefly to contemplate the deeper significance of the events portrayed.

Like the related romances, *Arthour and Merlin* and *Richard Coer de Lion* (and the less strikingly similar *Seven Sages of Rome*), *Kyng Alisaunder* seems to have been produced in the London area towards the end of the thirteenth century and, like them, was included in the famous Auchinleck MS, which was compiled in London in the first third of the fourteenth century. However, only fragments of the Auchinleck version remain, and the poem is nearly complete in two other manuscripts, Lincoln's Inn MS 150 and Bodleian Library MS Laud Misc. 622. The text here is from the latter, a manuscript produced in London in the third quarter of the fourteenth century.

The excerpt contains a scene not unlike that in Shakespeare's *Henry V*, in which a young and inexperienced leader is taunted for his lack of maturity by a more established antagonist. The latter's message is presented as a letter and is marked by stylistic features characteristic of the *ars dictamen* (the art of formal composition of documents and letters in prose) as well as some of the technical language of clerks trained in the art. Linguistically the text belongs to a period in which the London language is showing a tendency towards standardisation: that is, several documents, written by different scribes, employ a similar range of written forms, not all directly derived from the native London language. This incipient standard, known as Type II standard (Samuels 1972: 165–70), is marked by the use of forms imported as the result of immigration from East Anglia and the south-east Midlands. As may be expected from a translated text, and especially one whose author lays explicit claim to literary sophistication, French borrowings – and even French phrases – are also common.

Herd ȝee habbeþ, ich wil reherce,
Hou þe messagers comen from Perce
For trowage and Philippe ennoyed –
Hou Alisaunder it hem wiþseide.

5   Now atte first þe messagers
Beeþ ycome to her empirers.
Hij saluen Darrye her lorde,
And siggen hym þis worde:
'Lorde, we weren in þi message

10   Jn Grece after trewage,
Ac it is wiþseid in al þing,
Of a ȝonge kniȝth þat þinkeþ be kyng.
Worþes þee non while he may lyue;
Oiþer þou most it al forȝyue,

15   Oiþer, he þee sent to sigge,
Dereynen it wiþ swerdes egge.
Darrie startleþ for þise tydynges,
And makeþ anguisshous þretynges.
He takeþ wiþ hym many a duk

20   Þat bileueþ on Belsabuk,
And gooþ myd hym to on orchard
And parlement hij haldeþ hard.
Jch ȝou telle, litel, jwys,
Of Alisaunder he heldeþ prys,

25   And [by] hire aldre radd and want
A lettre [to] hym is ysant,
By riche dukes þrittene.
Bouȝ hi baren of olyue grene.
Þe duk þere was of Ermynye.

30   Of Esclaueyne, and of Sulye,
Of Pyncenarde, and of Mede.
Þoo of Nynyue, good at nede,
Þe duk of Japhes and Taberye,
Þe duk of Fryse, and of Hungrye,

35   Þe duk of Moreb, and Calebyne,
And þe duk of Palestyne;
Þai comen alle, honde in honde,
Toforne Alisaundre in Tyre londe,
Vche wiþ bouȝ of olyue,

40   Þat was tokne of pays and of l[o]ue,

You have heard, I will repeat, how the messengers came from
Persia for tribute and disturbed Philip; how Alexander denied it
to them. Now as soon as possible the messengers are come to their
emperor. They greet their lord, Darius, and tell him these words:
'Lord, we were on your errand seeking tribute in Greece, but it
was utterly denied to us by a young knight who aspires to be
king. There will be none for you while he may live. He sent to say
to you that either you must forgo it all or claim it with the edge of
the sword.' Darius is agitated by this news and utters threats from
his dread. He takes with him many a duke who puts faith in
Beelzebub, and goes with them to an orchard and they hold earnest
council. I tell you they set little store by Alexander, and through
the consensus and design of them all a letter is sent to him with
thirteen rich dukes. They bear a bough of green olive. The duke
of Armenia was there, of Esclaveyne, and of Syria, of Thrace, and
of Media. Then of Nineveh, good in a tight corner, the duke of
Jaffa and Taberia, the duke of Phrygia, and of Hungary, the duke
of Moreb and Calebyne, and the duke of Palestine; they all came
hand in hand before Alexander in the land of Tyre, each with an
olive branch, that was a sign of peace and accord, and they took
him three things, sent to him by Darius as a present: a fine whip
and top, a purse full of gold, and a letter in a friendly manner,
whose content was this:

'Darius, king of all kings, who has the gods as his ancestors,
for his nearest related cousins are Jupiter and Apollo, rulers of all
[lit. untaught and educated] who are in this world, sends greeting
without esteem to a treacherous young robber. Alexander, you crazy
fool, your doomed blood is courting disaster! You have withheld
my tribute and committed an outrage against me – burned my
towns, slain my men. You deserve to be drawn. However, you have
no worth; I blame it all on your young blood. Therefore I have
sent you a whip and top as a present, and a little purse with gold,
because you are young. Go home and play with them, I advise
you, young lad! Otherwise I shall have you belaboured and beaten
by a few fellows and afterwards skinned alive, and all your people
wretchedly put to death. Do you think you are my equal? No,
indeed, wretched vagabond! I have more knights to make war than
there are stars in the sky, and more strong-boned men than pebbles
in the sea. Flee now quickly, so that you may not be found, or you
shall be hunted with hounds.'

And token hym þat Darrye hym sent
Þre þinges to present:
A scourge and a toppe of nobleys,
And ful of golde an haum[u]deys,
45   And a lettre, par amoure,
Of whiche swiche was þe tenure:
'Darrye, kyng of alle kynges,
Þe godes þat he haueþ to eldringes,
For his nexte by-syb cosyn
50   Beeþ Jubiter and Appolyn,
Gouernoures of lewed and lered
Þat beeþ in þis middellerd,
Sendeþ gretyng wiþouten amoure
To a ȝonge fals robboure.
55   Alisaunder, þou conion wood,
Jn þe spilleþ þi faye blood.
Þou hast wiþholde my trowage,
And ydon me more outrage –
Brent myne tounes, myne men yslawe.
60   Þou art worþi to ben ydrawe.
Nere-þe-lees, þou canst no good;
Jch wyte it al þi ȝonge blood.
Þere-fore Ich habbe þee ysent
A top and scourge to present,
65   And wiþ golde a litel punge,
For þou hast ȝeres ȝonge.
Wende þou hom þerewiþ and pleye,
Jch þee rede, ȝonge boye!
Oiþer Ich þee shal doo bete and dynge
70   Wiþ a fewe gadelynge,
And afterwardes quyk þee flen,
And alle þi folk wiþ sorouȝ slen.
Wenestou to be my pere?
Nay, jwys, wrecche pautenere!
75   Jch haue moo kniȝttes to werren
Þan ben in þe walken sterren,
And moo men wiþ stronge bones
Þan ben jn þe cee grauel-stones
Fleiȝe now swiþe, þat þou ne be yfounde,
80   Oiþer men þee shulle dryue wiþ hounde.'

This was the letter that Darius sent to Alexander as a present; but you shall hear how Alexander made it turn out differently. Alexander sees very well that his knights are disconcerted. He laughs and swears by the sun that he has won Media and Persia, 'Because this whip must signify that I shall win dominion over Darius, and also chastise him and his, the greatest and the least. Also the top, which is round, no doubt signifies that the world, which is round, shall be mine. And by the purse is meant that I shall receive tribute from old and young. Tell Darius this same tale, and that I do not wish to come to agreement with him except by the sword and spear's point.' These messengers hear his speech, and go home by hill and dale. Alexander swiftly disposes of his business with Tyre. He has wrongdoers put to death, and dispenses law and order to the others. (If the governmental law derived from the great lords, Darius is their lord and king.) Alexander established his steward there and went briskly towards Darius.

Notes

6   **empirers**   The final *-s*, which enables the rhyme with *messagers*, is preserved from the French nominative case of masculine nouns.

7   **Hij saluen**   The *-en* plural present inflexion is indicative of the East Midlands, but this text also contains the more southerly *-eþ* plural, sometimes in archaic forms like *habbeþ* (1). The third-person-plural pronoun is very variable: *he* (24), *þai* (37). This variety is typical of the Type II London standard.

8   **þis worde**   The rhyme confirms that the original had some noun plurals in *-e(n)*. In this case the *-e* plural has been adopted by an OE neuter. See also *sterren* (76), *hounde* (80).

13   **worþes þee**   An impersonal construction with an unexpressed subject. That the *-es* inflexion occurred in the original is proved by the rhyme *nedes–spedes* (105–6). The *-es* inflexion for the third-person-singular present tense is generally considered a northern form, but is found in London in the Type II language, where it derives from East Anglian immigration. It still occurs rarely in Chaucer MSS. The more usual inflexion in *Kyng Alisaunder* is *-eþ*.

25   **radd and want**   The spelling <a> of the reflex of WS $\bar{æ}^1$ in *radd* is characteristic of a small area including Essex, London and Middlesex. The rhyme *laste–chaste* (91–92) confirms an *a* pronunciation for $\bar{æ}^2$ also. The Essex–London association is further emphasised by the spelling <an> rhyming on the i-mutation of Germanic short *a* before a nasal in *ysant*. But compare lines 41–2, 63–4, 81–2.

Þis was þe wrytt þad Darrye sent
To Alisaunder to present,
Ac of Alisaunder ȝee shullen here
Hou he it tourned in oþere manere.
85   Alisaunder wel wele seeþ
Þat his kniȝttes dismaied beeþ.
He leiȝeþ and swereþ by þe sonne
Mede and Perce he haþ ywonne,
'Forþi þis scourge shal signifye
90   Þat J shal wynne þe maistrye
Of Darrye, and also chaste
Hym and hise, þe more and þe laste.
Þe top þat is rounde aboute
Signifieþ also, saunz doute,
95   ðat þe werlde þat rounde is
Shal be myne also, j-wys.
And bitokneþ by þe punge
Þat ich shal of elde and ȝonge
Of þis midlerde tol afonge.
100   Siggeþ Darrye þis ilk songe,
And þat ich nylle myd hym acorde,
Bot wiþ swerd and speres oorde.'
Þise messageres hereþ þis tale,
And wendeþ hom, by doune and dale.
105   Alisaunder alle hise nedes
Aȝeins Tyre swiþe spedes.
Þe mysdoers he dooþ ben yslawe,
And to þe oþere he ȝiueþ lawȝe
(Ȝif lawȝe were of þe grete lordynges
110   Js Darrye her lorde and kyng).
Alisaunder sett þere his baillyf.
To Darrie ward he went blijf . . .

46   **tenure**   The word is a semi-technical one, used by scribes recording documents to refer to the essential content of what they were entering into the record. The extensive French influence observable in *Kyng Alisaunder* stems not only from its status as a translation, or from the cultural pretensions of its author, but also from a milieu in which most scribes were employed in administrative work conducted exclusively in either French or Latin.

47–54   **Darrye . . . robboure**   The letter follows prescribed practice, beginning with a salutation formula placing the name of the more important correspondent before that of the lesser. Their inequality is here ludicrously emphasised by the choice of titles.

59   **Brent**   The past participle appears without a prefix, but more commonly is of the southern type with a prefix, and loss of final -*n* in Strong verbs.

68   **ȝonge boye**   The word *boye* is a social slight, an insult like the accusation of falseness. In early ME, *boye* had no necessary implication of age, and rather alleged low birth or employment as a servant (Diensberg 1985).

85–86   **seeþ . . . beeþ**   The rhyme would not be possible in the East Midlands, where third-person singular and plural inflexions were distinct.

LATER MIDDLE ENGLISH

(1300–1500)

The period from 1300 to 1500 includes most of the better-known works of English medieval literature: *Piers Plowman, Sir Gawain and the Green Knight*, the craft guild and some morality plays, Malory's *Morte d'Arthur*, and the works of Chaucer (*c.* 1343–1400) and his followers. It saw the extension of English to many spheres of life previously dominated by French and the accompanying enrichment of the lexicon from French sources, the rapid expansion of the education of laymen in Latin, the beginnings of more extensive popular literacy (further encouraged by the introduction of printing in 1476), and the emergence of more standardised forms of the written language. Throughout the period, however, texts continued to be copied by scribes, and English remained a language marked by great dialectal variety. In the south and the west, throughout the fourteenth century, the inflexional grammar of the language retained substantial traces of the Old English distinction between Weak (*-en*) and Strong (*-es*) noun plurals, the prefixed past participles of verbs, and the *h*-forms of the third-person pronouns. In the north and east, noun plurals mostly ended in *-es*, the prefixes of participles had been lost in the twelfth century, and the new *th*-forms and *she* were rapidly replacing the earlier ones. Although it should not be assumed that Chaucer's language is in any sense 'typical' Middle English, the language of London in the first decades of the fifteenth century is preserved in good Chaucer manuscripts, and is a useful point of orientation.

Nouns were no longer inflected for gender, and for case only in the singular of the genitive (possessive), where the *-es* inflexion is derived from the Strong Masculine nouns of Old English, and leaves us the 'apostrophe *s*' in the English of today. The majority of noun plurals are in *-es*; the handful of *-en* plurals are mostly familiar from modern English, but *toon*, 'toes' and *eyen*, 'eyes' are also found. Mutation plurals, such as *gees*, 'geese' and *men* are the same as those in modern English. The definite article is now usually the invariable *the*, but with the occasional appearance of a plural form, *tho* (from OE *þā*).

Personal pronouns have completely lost the Dual number, but still retain a relatively complex inflexional system. Set out in imitation of an Old English paradigm, it would look like this:

	First Person		*Second Person*	
Nom.	I, ich (ik)	we	þow	ye
Acc.	me	us	þe(e)	yow
Gen.	my(n)	our(e)	þy(n)	your(e)
Dat.	me	us	þe(e)	yow

Apart from the Scandinavian borrowing *ik* (cf. 'The Reeve's Tale', Excerpt 18A), first- and second-person pronouns are the direct phonological descendants of Old English. However, it should be noted that in more sophisticated circles French custom has influenced the use of the second-person pronouns, in that the plural has developed a special number-free usage. It is possible to address a single individual either by the singular or plural form of the pronoun. This new contrast has sociolinguistic implications similar to the choice of *tu* or *vous* in modern French or *du* or *Sie* in German.

	Third Person			
	Masculine	*Feminine*	*Neuter*	*Plural*
Nom.	he	she	it	þey
Acc.	hym	hir(e)	it	hem
Gen.	his	hir(e)	his	hir(e)
Dat.	hym	hir(e)	it	hem

The third-person forms also exhibit Scandinavian influence (*she, they*), but an equally significant development is the syncretism ('merger') of the dative and accusative cases. This process had already occurred in Old English in the first- and second-person pronouns, and it was also the path by which nouns had lost their case distinction. Among nouns, it was followed by the further syncretism of the nominative and accusative case forms. It may be noted that the -es genitive plural of nouns probably derived not from the nominative, but from the extension of the genitive singular -es of masculine nouns to the plural in phrases like *heuenes king* (*sing.* from OE *heofones*) and *heuene king* (plur. from OE *heofona*) where the genitive's role as modifier is more important than the distinction of number (Bennett and Smithers 1968).

Verbal inflexions in Chaucer's language diverge from those of West Saxon Old English in an unpredictable way, and this can be demonstrated in the present tense of the verbs 'to stand' and 'to be':

I stande	I am
þow standest	þow art
he stant, standeþ	he is
þey standen	þey ben (ar)

The third person of the verb 'to stand' has forms which are dialectally significant: *standeþ* corresponds to the unsyncopated -*eþ* inflexion of Anglian dialects, whereas the form *stant* corresponds to the syncopated and assimilated form of West Saxon. The verb 'to be' now takes its singular from the OE verb *wesan*, but its usual plural is from *bēon*. Thus, both verbs have plural forms which do not correspond to the expected developments from Old English. The phonetic reduction of inflexional vowels at the end of the Old English period eroded the contrast between third-person singular and plural inflexions, making it difficult to distinguish singular and plural expressions.

Northumbrian	Mercian	West Saxon
-es > -es	-eþ > -eþ	-(e)þ > -(e)þ
-as > -es	-aþ > -eþ	-aþ > -eþ

A contrast was restored in the East Midlands by the adoption in the plural of the -*en* plural from the subjunctive. Since phonetic changes had also disrupted the distinction between singular and plural among the OE *h*-forms of the third-person pronoun, it is possible to see the adoption of the pronouns *she* and *they* as part of the same regulatory mechanism restoring a clear distinction of number in the ME clause. The system of the modern verb is modelled on that of the East Midlands, but the form of the third-person singular is that of the North.

By Chaucer's time, a new form of the present participle had arisen, *standyng* (OE *standende*), and his language permitted a variety of forms of the past participle: *standen* (which is the form associated with the East Midlands) and *y-stande* (which is the prefixed form found in the South; OE *ʒestanden*). The infinitive, *standen*, may now be marked with *to* or *for to*, and may be found with or without the final *-n*.

Finally, it should be noted that Chaucer, Hoccleve, and a few other authors from a similar location and background, employ a careful distinction in the inflexions of monosyllabic adjectives whose stem ended in a consonant. This corresponds in part to the Old English distinction between Weak and Strong adjectives. In the syntactic contexts where Old English would have had a Weak (definite) form of the adjective, good Chaucer manuscripts write a final *-e*. This final *-e* is also written in the plural, Weak or Strong. Final *-e*, the last remnant of Old English inflexion, was puzzling to most scribes by the second decade of the fifteenth century, and they used it in traditional spellings, to mark a long root vowel, or simply as random decoration.

The continuing role of French in England is described in the excerpt from Bokenham's translation of Higden's *Polychronicon* (Excerpt 21). On the one hand it was the language associated with gentle birth and refinement of accomplishments, and on the other it suggested participation in the world of affairs. In the royal court and some major aristocratic houses, literature in French, which had begun in the opening decades of the twelfth century, continued to be written until the middle of the fourteenth. In the worlds of education, law and administration, French was an official language of instruction, pleading and record until the fifteenth century. In the later fourteenth century, however, it was kept active in these roles with some difficulty, and the formulaic Anglo-French of documents differs markedly from the colloquial mother tongue of everyday life across the Channel.

Although legal records continued to employ Anglo-French into the reign of Henry VIII, in most other spheres, documents written in English outnumber those in French after about 1430. Nevertheless, in 1450 instruction in French was still thought to be a valuable qualification for a successful career in commerce, and schools existed to teach it for this purpose.

The relative prestige of French was dependent on the varieties used in England. Initially, and for some generations after the Conquest, French could be learned within the households of the settlers, or through family contact with lands in Normandy. Hence the earlier kind of French used was based on the dialect of Normandy. But even before the loss of Norman lands in 1204, this linguistic connection was lost for all but the highest aristocracy, and from the middle of the thirteenth century the dominant influence on French in England was from the Ile de France. This change is apparent in the dialectal forms of borrowed words, where central French *charité* and *garde* replace earlier Norman French *carité* and *warde*. As French declined further in the fourteenth century, proficiency in native, artificially learned and largely written Anglo-French begins to be scorned by comparison with the fluency of speakers of fashionable Continental French. With the decline of French as a technical written medium in the early decades of the fifteenth century, many borrowings of technical words were made into written English.

Although the Early Middle English period had witnessed various individual (cf. Orm) and corporate (cf. *Ancrene Wisse*) attempts to write local dialects consistently, none of these was adopted very widely. The Later Middle English period saw the emergence of spelling systems which achieved much more general use. Chancery English, which begins to be written from about 1415, is the form of London English employed by scribes in the early fifteenth-century Chancery, which was situated in the street now known as Chancery Lane. The wider adoption of this spelling system during the century was partly the result of its status as an official language, partly from the volume of documents written in it, and partly from the acceptability of the dialectal mixture from which it was composed.

Unlike the earliest London English, Chancery English (like Chaucer's before it) was not predominantly southern in its dialect forms. Rather, as the beneficiary of spellings developed in preceding London standards, it had a markedly central and east Midland character. Immigration of literate men into London from further north had gradually altered the type of English written in the capital. In Chancery English the third-person present tense of the verb is still *-eth* in the singular, but *-e(n)* or endingless in the plural; the *h*-forms of the third-person-plural pronoun are still found in oblique cases, but the *th*-forms (first noted in the *Ormulum* with the spelling <þ>) are in the majority, and *they/thay* is the exclusive form of the nominative. The present participle of the verb now ends in *yng/ing*. The normal Chancery spellings of large numbers of words – many of a technical Franco-Latin derivation – are those which eventually became the standard forms. Although the spellings Caxton uses are not always exactly equivalent to those of Chancery documents, both he and later printers are influenced by the Chancery standard, and so helped to establish it as the basis of modern English spelling.

The fifteenth century is notable as the first great era in which the founding of grammar schools was viewed as a meritorious act among the wealthy and influential. During the century many grammar schools were founded, and although universities existed in Britain only in Oxford, Cambridge, St Andrews and Glasgow, the proportion of young men who attended them was relatively high, so that proficiency in Latin was more widespread among the lay population than ever before. Familiarity with Latin among a potential audience contributed to the development of later fifteenth-century prose and poetry. An interest in verbal composition is already evident among writers of Chaucer's time, and John Lydgate and later fifteenth-century authors are progressively more affected by the rhetorical ideas emerging from the Italian Renaissance. They are increasingly eager to exhibit their learning and adorn their verses with words culled from Latin or Franco-Latin sources. In prose, too, Franco-Latin influences are evident. Administrative prose based ultimately on Latin but adapted in French became noticeably more lexically ornate in the last two decades of the fourteenth century, and this tendency is echoed by English administrative prose after about 1420 (Excerpt 19). Lydgate's prose work, the *Serpent of Divisioun* (1422), imitates the administrative prose in both lexical elaboration and some aspects of syntax; and this prose style, which is paralleled by contemporary developments in France, reaches its extreme in the Middle English period in the work of Skelton (see Excerpt 24), but the pursuit of

Latinity as the model for English continued to flourish throughout the Early Modern period.

If the fifteenth century saw the appearance of numbers of Latin-derived multisyllabic words, some of which have become part of the vocabulary of Modern English, it also witnessed important syntactical and phonological developments. During the earlier fifteenth century, the system of long vowels in Middle English commenced a series of interconnected changes which radically affected the pronunciation of standard English, distancing it from the vowel systems of Continental languages. These can best be represented diagrammatically:

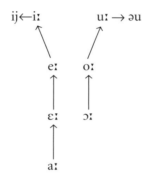

Middle English in the fourteenth century possessed the seven pure long vowels shown in the diagram, but by 1500 the highest vowels, front and back, had been diphthongised, and /eː/ and /oː/ had been raised to take their places. During the sixteenth century the remaining long vowels, /ɛː/, /ɔː/ and /aː/, were in turn raised so as to occupy the places vacated above them by the raising of the original fourteenth-century vowels. Although known traditionally as 'the Great Vowel Shift', and interpreted phonologically, recent scholarship has increasingly questioned the assumption that it was unique and unitary, pointing to different developments in different dialects (Johnston 1992, Smith 1996) and to the continuity of a series of raisings of long vowels extending over some hundreds of years and perhaps motivated by phonetic rather than phonological factors (Jones 1989).

Syntactical developments emerging in the later Middle English period include an increase in the use of periphrastic forms of the verb phrase, for example the emergence of the *do* periphrasis (see next section), and the emergence of the use of *who* as a relative pronoun, at first only in the oblique form, *whom*. By the end of the period, too, the order of an unmarked positive declarative clause was settled in the modern SVO (SPC) structure. Double negation became much rarer during the late fourteenth century with the disappearance of the particle *ne*.

16

ROBERT MANNYNG'S *CHRONICLE*
OF ENGLAND

Robert Mannyng is the author of two extant works, his better-known penitential handbook *Handlyng Synne*, which he translated from the Anglo-Norman *Manuel des Pechiez*, and the largely ignored *Chronicle* which he says he made 'not for þe lerid bot for þe lewid' – those who could understand neither Latin or French nor over-elaborate English composition. Although directed to a popular audience, the *Chronicle* is a close translation from earlier French sources: its first half is heavily dependent on Wace's *Brut*, and its second half is based on Peter of Langtoft's *Chronicle*. The first half therefore deals with the legendary history of Britain until the death of Cadwallader in 689, and the second with what Mannyng punningly called 'English geste', the deeds (stories) of later English history.

What is known of Mannyng's life must be gleaned from references in his works. He came from Bourne in south Lincolnshire (as the author of the *Ormulum* also seems to have done), and was in Cambridge, perhaps in the Gilbertine house of St Edmund's Hall, in 1300. By 1303 he was a canon in the Gilbertine priory of Sempringham near Bourne, where he translated *Handlyng Synne*, and in 1327 he was a chaplain in Lincoln. He mentions also spending some time in Sixhills priory, seventeen miles to the north-west of Lincoln, where he worked on his *Chronicle*, completing it on Friday, 25 May 1338.

The *Chronicle* exists in whole or in part in five extant MSS, the earliest of which is Lambeth Palace 131, the basis of the text below. This manuscript is dated *c.* 1350 but is not the author's holograph, and indeed Mannyng's statement that his work was 'written' by a fellow Gilbertine, one Robert of Malton, should be sufficient warning not to expect a work in pure Lincolnshire dialect. Morphologically, northern influence is apparent in the inflexion of the third-person-singular present tense of verbs in -*es* (the ancestor of the modern form), and northern or north-east Midland in the widespread loss of *-n* in infinitives and from the East Midland form of the third-person-plural present tense (*gynne*, 2), personal pronoun forms with þ- and the feminine, *sche*, and the scarcity of prefixes in past participles. The vocabulary has a number of Scandinavian borrowings – *þey* (2), *lowe* (3), *take* (29), *reyse* (43), *saught* (74) – but their quality is very different from those in the *Ormulum*, since they represent much more widely used vocabulary, and French influence is much more evident.

De ingratitudine filiarum, et planctu patris eorum, Leyr

Now gynnes Leyr to myslyke;
'Sone,' he seyde, 'þey gynne me swyke;
Fro myn aboue y am put lowe,
And ȝit scha[l] more wyþynne a þrowe.
5 Myn oþer doughter wyl y proue,
Þey scheo be wroþ to my behoue.'
And dight hym wyþ his apparaille
To wende in to Cornewaille.
He dwelt nought fullyk a ȝer,
10 Þat þey ne made hym gret daunger,
And lessede his knyghtes and oþer men:
Of þritty þey abated ten,
And ȝit of twenty abated fyue.
Þen wold Leyr han ben of lyue:
15 'Alas!' he seyde, 'y hider cam!
Fro wycke vntil wors y nam!'
To Gonorille agayn he ȝede,
He wend sche wold heue mended his nede,
Haue gyuen hym als scheo hadde byforn,
20 Sche swor by god þat hure leet be born
Þat scheo ne wolde, day ne nyght,
Halde bot hym and a knyght.

Lamentacio Regis Leyr

Þenne bygan Leyr to sorewe,
And ment his mone euen and morwe;
25 Þe grete richesse he hadde byforn,
Al was aweye and ylorn:

Of the ingratitude of daughters, and the lament of their father, Lear

Now Lear begins to be displeased and said, 'They soon begin
to betray me; from my high estate, I am humiliated, and will be
further so within a short time. I will try my other daughter, even
though she may be opposed to my welfare.' And he prepared
himself to go with his trappings to Cornwall. He remained there
for less than a full year before they became grudging towards him,
and reduced his knights and other men: from thirty they deducted
ten, and from twenty deducted a further five. Then Lear wished to
be dead. 'Alas!' he said, 'that I came here; after bad I got worse.' He
went back to Goneril; he thought she would be ready to improve
his plight, allow him what she had before. She swore by God who
caused her to be born that, day or night, she would not maintain
any more than him and a single knight. Then Lear began to mourn,
and evening and morning he complained. The great wealth he had
had before was all lost and gone: 'I have been alive too long, that
ever I should see this day! People can take an example from me
and a warning about relations from my case. I had wealth; now
I have none. My counsel and support is gone. Lady Fortune, you
are changeable; you are never steady for a day. No one can trust
in you: you turn him down who before was high; that man who is
down you raise up. There is no one who does not lament in your
presence. But where you look fondly, he is honoured as a king; and
whoever you turn your look away from is immediately cast down
in misery and woe. You will raise up the ill-natured and put the
good-natured in distress. When you are displeased with a king or
earl, you lamentably dash away their wealth. When I had possessions
and plenty of money, then I found friends who gathered round
me; now poverty is thrust upon me so that I have lost all sight of
them. Those whose love and loyalty should rightfully belong to me

'To longe alyue haue y be,
Þat euere schold y þys day se!
Ensample of me men may take,
30   And warnyng of sibbe for my sake.
Y hadde richesse, now haue y non;
My wyt and al myn help ys gon.
Lady Fortune, þou art chaungable!
O day art þou neuere stable!
35   No man may of þe affye:
Þou turnes hym doun þat er was heye;
Þat now ys doun, vpward þou turnes;
Wyþ þe nys non þat he ne mournes;
Bot þere þou gyuest þy loue-lokyng,
40   He ys worschiped als a kyng;
And whom þou turnest þy lokyng fro,
Sone ys he doune yn sorewe and wo.
Þe vnkynde þu wilt vp reyse,
Þe kynde þu puttest to meseyse.
45   Wyþ kyng and erl, when þe myslikes,
Þer welþe awey to wo þu strykes.
When y had god and welþe ynow,
Þen fond y frende þat to me drow;
Now pouerte ys put me byforn,
50   Þat al þer sight fro me ys lorn.
Þer loue schold lange to me þrow ryght,
Þat schewe me of loue semblaunt ne syght.
Dame Fortune, þy louely lok
And þy gode wille fro me þu tok
55   When y blamed my doughter ȝyng,
And gaf no kepe til hure kennyng
Þat seyde me soþ apertely:
Als y had, so was y worthy,
And also mykel scheo loued me.
60   Scheo seide bettere þan y couþ se;
Hure word noþyng y ne vnde[r]stod,
But mad me wroþ. Y couþe no god;
Y parceyued nought what was hure tent,
Bot now fele y wel what scheo ment;
65   Y fele hit wel þe soþe hit endes.
Whyder may y now to seke my frendes?

show me no semblance of it. Lady Fortune, you took away from me your loving glance and good wishes when I condemned my young daughter, and took no notice of the teaching of she who openly told me the truth: I was worthy according to what I possessed, and just so much she loved me. She spoke better than I could see; I did not understand her words at all, but got angry. It was foolish of me; I did not see what she intended, but now I well understand what she meant; I understand well that it sums up the truth. Where may I go now to look for friends? If I approach her for any benefit, she is not to be blamed even though she should disown me, for I denied her my land, gave her nothing and did not provide for her. Nevertheless, I will seek her out. I always found her virtuous and forgiving. She has taught me wisdom, and wisdom shall make her be reconciled with me. If I cannot bring her to that, she can do no worse than the others. I will now put to the test something that she said: she would love me as her father; and according to what she said, I shall test her good-nature and kindness.'

Notes

7   **hym** 'himself'   The pronoun is the usual reflexive form in ME. The *himself* type is developed in emphatic contexts.

14   **han**   This contracted form of the infinitive (*habben* > *haven* > *han*) is a widespread northern and Midland type.

17   **agayn**   The spelling of this word with <g> and <ay> rather than <ȝ> is predominantly a Midland one.

20   **leet be born** 'caused to be born'   The causative *leten* is widespread in ME.

22   **Halde**   An Anglian OE antecedent is suggested by the failure of breaking before an *l*-group. A northerly origin is suggested by the fact that the long *a* produced by the lengthening group *ld* has not subsequently been rounded. This excerpt shows rounding in some spellings (*longe*, 27) but not in others (*lange*, 51).

24   **his mone**   Lear's complaint is translated quite closely from its source in Wace's AN *Brut*, but behind that lies the complaint of Boethius to Fortune in *De Consolatione Philosophiae*. The work of this fifth-century author, which has been translated into English from King Alfred's time onwards, became the model for such laments, and their expression became formulaic. Compare this with Chaucer's translation of Boethius, Bk II and his use of similar material in the *Book of the Duchess*, 598ff. The passage contains some French vocabulary strongly associated with its theme, *chaungable*, *stable*, *Dame Fortune*, as well as a characteristic use of antithesis.

3yf y seke hure for any frame,
Þey sche me weyue scheo nys to blame,
For y defended hure my lond,
70   Ne nought hure gaf, ne hure ne fond.
Natheles, hure wol y seke;
Y fond hure euere god and meke.
Wisdam sche has me ytaught;
Wysdam schal make hure wiþ me saught.
75   3yf y may nought bryng hure þerto,
Wors þan þe oþere may sche nought do.
Scheo seyde a þyng y scha[l] now proue:
Als hure fader scheo wolde me loue;
And als scheo seyde, proue schal y
80   Hire kyndnesse and hure curtesy.'

37–8   **turnes . . . mournes**   The rhyme (cf. 45–46) confirms that the original
had an -*es* inflexion in both the second- and third-person singular of the
present tense. Although the latter extended south to London in the late
fourteenth century, the rhyme is more consistent with the north Midland
origin of the poem.

50   **þer** 'their'   Although oblique forms of the third-person-plural pronoun
are found in south Lincolnshire as early as 1180 in the *Ormulum*, they
are used in the London language of Chaucer only as an indication of a
character's northern origin in the 'Reeve's Tale'.

59–60   **me . . . se**   The rhyme on *me* confirms the evidence of spelling that OE
ēo has been monophthongised, an East Midland development.

62   **couþe no god**   This idiom, literally 'did not know any good', means
something like 'I was slow or ignorant', and often carries with it implicit
condemnation of social behaviour or lack of awareness.

17

THE *PEARL*

The *Pearl* is one of four works, all with moral and religious themes, which exist in a single manuscript, British Library MS Cotton Nero A. x, and are generally considered to be by the same author. Of these, *Patience* and *Cleanness* are adaptations of scriptural narratives, *Sir Gawain and the Green Knight* is set in the Arthurian past, and *Pearl* is a dream vision in which the author relates his own experience: the vision of a lady (apparently his recently deceased daughter, now in heaven) who instructs him on the doctrine of grace and redemption. All four poems are written in the alliterative metre which flourished in the North and West from the mid fourteenth until the end of the fifteenth century.

The manuscript is not in the hand of its author, but was written not far from his place of origin, and not long after the work's composition. Modern scholarly opinion dates the manuscript at the end of the fourteenth century and identifies its place of origin as an area in the north-west Midlands close to the borders of south-east Lancashire, east Cheshire, north-east Staffordshire and north-west Derbyshire.

Linguistically, *Pearl* exhibits many features proper to its north-west Midland origin. The northern spelling <qu> is used for OE <hw> (19). OE *ā* is written both <a> and <o>, and is proved by rhymes to have had both the northern unrounded and southern rounded pronunciations (85, 87, 89 and 118, 120). The third-person-plural present tense of the verb is written *-en* (*stonden*, 53) and also *-eȝ* (*bydeȝ*, 15). The former is characteristic of the East Midlands, the latter a variant spelling of the northern *-es*. The present participle ending is the Scandinavian-derived *-ande*, and Scandinavian influence is strong in the lexis also: *keste* (6), *glent* (10), *bolleȝ* (16), *blo* (23), *wyngeȝ* (33), *bonkeȝ* (50), *sterneȝ* (55). Indeed, Scandinavian borrowings occur at a rate of about three per stanza. Several are unobtrusive grammatical words: *fro* (1), *þay* (20), *ay* (41), *þaȝ* (74), *gayn* (78); and in the case of *syluer* (17) the Scandinavian form has been used in preference to the native *seluer*. The lexical richness of the excerpt is especially notable since French and Latin borrowings are also very dense here, and there are several words, too, of uncertain (*byg*, 42) or possibly Middle Dutch (*trylle*, 18; *schore*, 47) origin.

>   Fro spot my spyryt þer sprang in space;
>   My body on balke þer bod in sweuen.
>   My goste is gon in Godeʒ grace
>   In auenture þer meruayleʒ meuen.
> 5   I ne wyste in þis worlde quere þat hit wace,
>   Bot I knew me keste þer klyfeʒ cleuen;
>   Towarde a foreste I bere þe face,
>   Where rych rokkeʒ wer to dyscreuen.
>   Þe lyʒt of hem myʒt no mon leuen,
> 10 Þe glemande glory þat of hem glent;
>   For wern neuer webbeʒ þat wyʒeʒ weuen
>   Of half so dere adubbemente.
>
>   Dubbed wern alle þo downeʒ sydeʒ
>   Wyth crystal klyffeʒ so cler of kynde.
> 15 Holtewodeʒ bryʒt aboute hem bydeʒ
>   Of bolleʒ as blwe as ble of Ynde;
>   As bornyst syluer þe lef on slydeʒ,
>   Þat þike con trylle on vch a tynde.
>   Quen glem of glodeʒ agaynʒ hem glydeʒ,
> 20 Wyth schymeryng schene ful schrylle þay schynde.
>   Þe grauayl þat on grounde con grynde
>   Wern precious perleʒ of oryente:
>   Þe sunnebemeʒ bot blo and blynde
>   In respecte of þat adubbement.
>
> 25 The adubbemente of þo downeʒ dere
>   Garten my goste al greffe forʒete.
>   So frech flauoreʒ of fryteʒ were,
>   As fode hit con me fayre refete.
>   Fowleʒ þer flowen in fryth in fere,
> 30 Of flaumbande hweʒ, boþe smale and grete;
>   Bot sytole-stryng and gyternere
>   Her reken myrþe moʒt not retrete;

My spirit sprang up from that place; my body remained asleep on the mound. Through God's grace my spirit went on a marvellous voyage where wonders exist. I do not know where in this world it was, but I knew I was set down where cliffs cleave [the sky]; and I turned my face towards a forest, where splendid rocks were to be seen. No one could believe their light, the resplendent glory that shone from them; for never were fabrics woven by man of half so splendid decoration. Those hillsides were all adorned with crystal cliffs of such a brilliant nature. Bright woodlands are set around them, with trunks as blue as indigo; like burnished silver the leaves slide and quivered together, thick on every branch. When the light from clear patches of sky falls on them, they shone quite dazzlingly with a gleaming brightness. The pebbles that crunched on the ground were precious Eastern pearls. Sunbeams were dull and dim compared to that splendour. The splendour of the rich hills made my spirit forget all grief, and so refreshing were the fragrances from the fruits, that I was restored as well as if I had eaten food. Birds flew there together in the wood, both large and small, and of flaming colours. But neither citole-string nor a player on the giterne could reproduce their happy music. For when those birds beat their wings, they sang in sweet harmony. You could not have such delightful entertainment as to hear and see their splendour. Thus all adorned in a noble fashion was that wood where fortune has transported me. No one who can speak is worthy to describe its glory. I kept walking forward in pleasure; no slope so rough that it might hinder me. The further I went into the wood, the fairer grew the meadow, the shrubs, the scented herbs, the pear trees; and the hedgerows, the edges of the streams, and the splendid water meadows with steep banks like pure gold thread. I came to a stream that ran swiftly past its banks. Lord, its splendour was rich! The adornments of those precious depths were pleasant banks of bright beryl. Swirling sweetly, the water swept along, flowing directly with a murmuring sound. In the bed there stood bright stones that glowed and gleamed like a beam of light through glass, like

For quen þose bryddeȝ her wyngeȝ bete,
Þay songen wyth a swete asent.
35   So gracios gle couþe no mon gete
As here and se her adubbement.

So al watȝ dubbet on dere asyse
Þat fryth þer fortwne forth me fereȝ.
Þe derþe þerof for to deuyse
40   Nis no wyȝ worþé þat tonge bereȝ
I welke ay forth in wely wyse;
No bonk so byg þat did me dereȝ.
Þe fyrre in þe fryth, þe feier con ryse
Þe playn, þe plontteȝ, þe spyse, þe pereȝ;
45   And raweȝ and randeȝ and rych reuereȝ,
As fyldor fyn her bonkes brent.
I wan to a water by schore þat schereȝ –
Lorde, dere watȝ hit adubbement!

The dubbemente of þo derworth depe
50   Wern bonkeȝ bene of beryl bryȝt.
Swangeande swete þe water con swepe,
Wyth a rownande rourde raykande aryȝt.
In þe founce þer stonden stoneȝ stepe,
As glente þurȝ glas þat glowed and glyȝt,
55   As stremande sterneȝ, quen stroþe-men slepe,
Staren in welkyn in wynter nyȝt;
For vche a pobbel in pole þer pyȝt
Watȝ emerad, saffer, oþer gemme gente,
Þat alle þe loȝe lemed of lyȝt,
60   So dere watȝ hit adubbement.

. . .

The dubbement dere of doun and daleȝ,
Of wod and water and wlonk playneȝ,
Bylde in me blys, abated my baleȝ,
Fordidden my stresse, dystryed my payneȝ.
65   Doun after a strem þat dryȝly haleȝ
I bowed in blys, bredful my brayneȝ;
Þe fyrre I folȝed þose floty valeȝ,

the streaming stars that shine in the sky on a winter's night when the men of this earth are sleeping. For every pebble set there in the pool was an emerald, a sapphire, or other precious stone, so that all the pool gleamed with light, so glorious was its embellishment.

The precious embellishment of hill and valleys, wood and water and noble meadows inspired joy in me, reduced my misery, undid my distress, and ended my sufferings. Down beside a stream that ceaselessly flows I made my way joyfully, my mind brimful; the further I followed those well-watered valleys the stronger joy stirs my heart. Just as fortune acts whenever she puts anyone to the test, whether she bestows delight or sorrow, the man to whom she sends her will chances to have ever more and more. There was more joy of that kind than I could tell even though I had leisure, for an earthly heart would not be sufficient for the tenth part of those happy joys; therefore I thought that Paradise was over opposite those broad banks. I thought the water was an artificial conduit joining pleasure gardens made by the side of pools. Beyond the stream, by hill or valley, I thought the walled city would be situated. But the water was deep, and I dare not wade, and continuously I longed more and more. More and more, and still much more, I desired to see beyond the brook, for if it were beautiful where I was, the far side was much more lovely. I halted and stared about me; I tried hard to find a ford, but the further I walked along the bank, indeed the more dangers there were. And I kept thinking that I should not shrink from danger where there were so many precious delights. Then a new matter came to my attention that stirred my mind more and more. A greater wonder overwhelmed my reason: I saw beyond that fair flood a gleaming crystal cliff; many a noble ray sprang from it. At its foot there sat a child, a courtly and gentle maiden; her mantle was glistening white. I knew her well, I had seen her before. Like shining gold cut [into gold thread], so shone that beautiful [maiden] beneath the cliff. I looked long at her there, and the longer I looked the more I knew her. The more I examined her fair face, when I had perceived her exquisite form, such heartening splendour slipped into me as rarely was accustomed to happen before that. Desire urged me to call her, but amazement gave my heart a stunning blow. I saw her in such a surprising place, such a blow might well make my heart stunned. Then she raises up her fair forehead, her face white as polished ivory: that pierced my heart in stunned bewilderment, and ever longer, more and more.

Þe more strenghþe of ioye myn herte strayneȝ.
As fortune fares þer as ho frayneȝ,
70   Wheþer solace ho sende oþer elleȝ sore,
Þe wyȝ to wham her wylle ho wayneȝ
Hytteȝ to haue ay more and more.

More of wele watȝ in þat wyse
Þen I cowþe telle þaȝ I tom hade,
75   For vrþely herte myȝt not suffyse
To þe tenþe dole of þo gladneȝ glade:
Forþy I þoȝt þat Paradyse
Watȝ þer ouer gayn þo bonkeȝ brade.
I hoped þe water were a deuyse
80   Bytwene myrþeȝ by mereȝ made;
Byȝonde þe broke, by slente oþer slade,
I hoped þat mote merked wore.
Bot þe water watȝ depe, I dorst not wade,
And euer me longed ay more and more.

85   More and more, and ȝet wel mare,
Me lyste to se þe broke byȝonde;
For if hit watȝ fayr þer I con fare,
Wel loueloker watȝ þe fyrre londe.
Abowte me con I stote and stare;
90   To fynde a forþe faste con I fonde.
Bot woþeȝ mo iwysse þer ware,
Þe fyrre I stalked by þe stronde.
And euer me þoȝt I schulde not wonde
For wo þer weleȝ so wynne wore.
95   Þenne nwe note me com on honde
Þat meued my mynde ay more and more.

More meruayle con my dom adaunt:
I seȝ byȝonde þat myry mere
A crystal clyffe ful relusaunt;
100   Mony ryal ray con fro hit rere.
At þe fote þerof þer sete a faunt,
A mayden of menske, ful debonere;
Blysnande whyt watȝ hyr bleaunt.
I knew hyr wel, I hade sen hyr ere.

Notes

5	**wace** The very unusual spelling emphasises the rhymes with *space* and *grace*. The normal spelling in this text is *watʒ*.
18	**con trylle** The auxiliary *con* has a function equivalent to that of *gan* in Chaucer's language, supplying a metrical variant for the simple preterite, and facilitating the positioning of an infinitive in rhyme (see line 21). The rounding of short *a* before a nasal consonant is characteristic of an area west of a line extending from Morecambe Bay via the Pennine chain to the Severn valley. See also *mon* (9), *plontteʒ* (44). The spelling <vch> is also western, but does not occur commonly north of the Mersey.
25	**þo** This text retains a distinct plural form of the definite article.
26	**garten** This causal auxiliary is essentially an East Midland and northern form.
31	**sytole . . . gyternere** The citole is an instrument related to the zither; the giterne is a guitar-like instrument.
33	**wyngeʒ** The word was borrowed from Scandinavian, and replaced OE *feðer* in this sense. Two forms existed in ME: the present one, derived from Old Danish or Swedish, and *wenges*, derived from Old Norwegian.
34	**Þay** Although the Scandinavian-derived form of the third-person-plural pronoun is used in the nominative, the OE *h*-forms are used in oblique cases, as in Chaucer: *her* (33), *hem* (19).
35	**gete** Derived from Scandinavian *geta*. The OE root *-gietan* occurs only in compounds. First recorded in the *Ormulum*, *gete* quickly develops a very wide range of senses. Idiomatic uses with a following preposition (*get out*, *get in*) are frequent at the end of the fourteenth century.
46	**fyldor fyn** 'pure gold thread' Like the word *debonere* (102), this represents the reinterpretation of a French phrase as a single word: *fil d'or*, 'golden thread'; cf. *de bon aire*, 'of good breeding'.
48	**hit** The genitive singular of the third-person pronoun. With the loss of grammatical gender, ME pronouns were redistributed to indicate the sex of the referent; the old neuter forms were used to indicate non-animate referents. In the genitive, no distinction was made between genitive masculine and neuter (both were *his*), but the new functions demanded a distinction and various remedies emerged before *its* was widely adopted for non-animate reference in the later sixteenth century. *Hit* is first recorded, as a possessive, in this manuscript.
58	**gemme** This word had been borrowed from Latin during the pre-OE period, giving OE *gimm*. Its form here is that of Latin or French, suggesting re-formation or renewed borrowing from one of these languages.
69	**fares . . . ho frayneʒ** The inflexion of the third-person-singular present tense as *-es* is predominantly northern and north Midland. This text renders it occasionally as <es> but more commonly as <eʒ>, where ʒ is the scribe's

105   As glysnande golde þat man con schere,
       So schon þat schene an-vnder shore.
       On lenghe I loked to hyr þere;
       Þe lenger, I knew hyr more and more.

       The more I frayste hyr fayre face,
110   Her fygure fyn quen I had fonte,
       Suche gladande glory con to me glace
       As lyttel byfore þerto watȝ wonte.
       To calle hyr lyste con me enchace,
       Bot baysment gef myn hert a brunt.
115   I seȝ hyr in so strange a place,
       Such a burre myȝt make myn herte blunt.
       Þenne vereȝ ho vp her fayre frount,
       Hyr vysayge whyt as playn yuore:
       Þat stonge myn hert ful stray atount,
120   And euer þe lenger, þe more and more.

       form for <z>. The use of the <z> word ending derives from French spell-
       ing practice, and here suggests voiced pronunciation. The form ho, 'she',
       is developed by rounding from an earlier hā (see the excerpt from the
       Ancrene Wisse) and is a distinctively West Midland form.
101   **faunt** 'child'   This is an aphetic form of French *enfant*. Aphetic forms
       (forms in which an initial unstressed syllable is omitted) are common
       in this excerpt: *dubbet* (< F *aduber*), *stresse* (< F *destresse*), *strayneȝ* (< F
       estreindre), *baysment* (< F *abaissement*).

18

GEOFFREY CHAUCER

Geoffrey Chaucer (?1343–1400), the outstanding poet of the English Middle Ages, was born and raised in London, the son of a family who were of East Anglian origin but who had been established in London merchant society for two generations. Chaucer himself was perhaps educated at a London school, but certainly as a page in the household of the Countess of Ulster. He proceeded to a career in royal service and held the posts of Controller of Customs in the Port of London and later Clerk of the King's Works. He was married to the daughter of a French-speaking knight who had been part of the entourage of Queen Philippa, wife of Edward III. Thus, in his employment, in his social contacts, and perhaps also at home, he was in everyday contact both with the most elevated secular cultural and social values, and with the French language. His works may have been written in part for the nobles of the royal court, but are more arguably for the interest and entertainment of a group of talented officials who, like himself, were attached to the court.

From what is known of his life we should expect Chaucer's language to be a slightly conservative and more carefully selected version of the language of other London texts of his time, embellished perhaps by French and Latin borrowing derived from his experience and reading. This is essentially the case, but such a statement hides its wider variety. An assessment of Chaucer's language is complicated by the fact that almost all manuscripts containing his work date from after his death. In the rapidly changing linguistic conditions of late medieval London, this means that they need not precisely represent his own usage.

The examples given below are from two different manuscripts: the excerpt from 'The Reeve's Tale' is from the Hengwrt MS (National Library of Wales, MS Peniarth 392), written in London about 1403, that from *Troilus and Criseyde* is from Corpus Christi College, Cambridge MS 61, also written

wt of thise blake wawes for to saylle
O wynde o wynde the weder gynneth clere
for in this see the bote hath swych traylle
Of my connyng that vnneth I it stere
This see clepe I the tempestous matere
Of disespir that Troilus was Inne
But now of hope the kalendes bygynne

O lady myn that called art Cleo
Thow be my speed fro this forth and my muse
To ryme wel this boke til I haue do
ne nedeth here noon othere art to vse
for whi to euery louere I me excuse
That of no sentement I this endite
But out of latyn in my tonge it write

Wherfore I nyl haue neither thank ne blame
Of al this werk but prey yow mekely
Disblameth me if any word be lame
for as myn auctor seyde so sey I
Ek though I speke of loue vnfelyngly
No wondre is for it no thyng of newe is
A blynde man kan nat Iuggen wel in hewis

Ye knowe ek that in forme of speche is chaunge
With Inne a thousand yeer and wordes tho
That hadden pris now wonder nyce and straunge
vs thenketh hem and yet thei spake hem so
And spedde as wel in loue as men now do
Ek forto wynnen loue in sondry ages
In sondry londes sondry ben vsages

And forth if it happe in any wyse
That here be any louere in this place
That herkneth as the storie wel deuise
How Troilus com to his lady grace
And thenketh so nold I nat loue purchace
Or wondreth on his speche or his doynge
I noot but it is me no wondrynge

Plate 3   Chaucer, *Troilus and Criseyde* (Corpus Christi College, Cambridge MS 61, fol. 27r) in London within two decades of Chaucer's death. The facsimile shows the opening of Book II in the Corpus manuscript, and illustrates the luxurious nature of this text. It is written in an elaborated form of the *textura* hand and shows evidence of careful planning by a skilled professional copyist who has taken great care in presenting a text of solid and uniform appearance. His ruling lines can clearly be seen. There is no punctuation, but use is made of capitalisation both to mark the beginning of the Book itself and to introduce each verse line. The stanza structure is meticulously preserved. The expense incurred by the decorative nature of the script was matched in the original plan by a scheme of illustration for which many spaces have been left in the text. Taken together with the high quality of the vellum, this testifies to the growing stature of Chaucer's work among those who might be expected to be able to afford such a splendid production.

Some general points to note about Chaucer's language are its East Midland character (deriving from East Midland immigration into London and evident in the use of predominantly *-es* noun plurals, *-en* third-person-plural present-tense verbal inflexion, loss of the prefix in past participles, nominative personal pronoun *they*) but also traces of earlier south-eastern forms (some *-en* noun plurals, assimilated third-person present-tense singulars – see notes *RT* 70, *TC* 36 – use of the prefix in some past participles, and all oblique forms of personal pronouns remain *h*-forms).

A 'The Reeve's Tale'

Thanne were ther yonge, poure scolers two
That dwelten in the halle of which I seye.
Testyf they were and lusty for to pleye: *headstrong*
And oonly for hir myrthe and reuerye   *amusement*
5   Vpon the wardeyn bisily they crye   *earnestly*
To yeue hem leue but a litel stounde   *space of time*
To go to mille and seen hir corn ygrounde.
And hardily they dorste leye hir nekke   *certainly, bet their life*
The millere sholde noght stelen hem half a pekke
10 Of corn by sleighte ne by force hem reue.   *cunning, rob*
And atte laste the wardeyn yaf hem leue.
Iohn highte that oon and Aleyn highte that oother.   *was called*
Of oon town were they born that highte Strother,
Fer in the north, I kan noght telle where.
15 This Aleyn maketh redy al his gere
And on an hors the sak he caste anon.
Forth gooth Aleyn the clerk and also Iohn
With good swerd and with bokeler by his syde.   *round shield*
Iohn knew the wey hym neded no gyde.
20 And at the mille the sak adoun he layth.
    Aleyn spak first: 'Al hayl, Symkyn, in fayth.
How fares thy faire doghter and thy wyf?'
    'Aleyn welcome,' quod Symkyn, 'by my lyf,
And Iohn also. How now, what do ye here?'
25   'By god,' quod Iohn, 'Symond, nede has na peere.   *equal*
Hym bihoues serue hymself that has na swayn   *must, servant*
Or ellis he is a fool, as clerkes sayn.
Oure maunciple, I hope he wol be deed,   *think*
Swa werkes ay the wanges in his heed.   *so ache, eye-teeth*
30 And therfore is I come and eek Alayn
To grynde oure corn and carie it heem agayn.   *home*
I pray yow speed vs heythen what ye may'.   *away from here*
    'It shal be doon,' quod Symkyn, 'by my fay.   *faith*
What wol ye doon whil that it is in hande?'
35   'By god, right by the hoper wol I stande,'
Quod Iohn, 'and se how the corn gas in.   *goes*
Yet saw I neuere by my fader kyn
How that the hoper wagges til and fra.'

Aleyn answerde: 'Iohn, wiltow swa?
40   Thanne wol I be byneth, by my crown,
And se how that the mele falles down
Into the trogh. That sal be my desport.
For, Iohn, in faith I may been of youre sort:
I is as ille a millere as ar ye.'
45   This millere smyled of hir nycetee   *silliness*
And thoghte: 'Al this nys doon but for a wyle.   *only for a trick*
They wene that no man may hem bigile.   *believe*
But by my thrift yet shal I blere hir iye
For al the sleighte in hir phislophye.   *learning*
50   The moore queynte crekys that they make,   *subtle tricks*
The moore wol I stele whan I take.
In stede of flour yet wol I yeue hem bren.
The grettest clerkes been noght the wisest men,
As whilom to the wolf thus spak the mare.   *once*
55   Of al hir art counte I noght a tare.'   *weed*
Out of the dore he gooth ful pryuely
Whan that he saugh his tyme softely.
He looketh vp and doun til he hath founde
The clerkes hors ther as it stood ybounde
60   Bihynde the mille vnder a leefsel.   *arbour*
And to the hors he gooth hym faire and wel;
He strepeth of the bridel right-anon.
And whan the hors was laus, he gynneth gon
Toward the fen ther wilde mares renne,
65   And forth with 'wehe' thurgh thikke and thenne.
This millere gooth ayein. No word he seyde,
But dooth his note and with the clerkes pleyde   *job*
Til that hir corn was faire and wel ygrounde.
And whan the mele was sakked and ybounde,
70   This Iohn gooth out and fynt his hors away
And gan to crye 'Harrow and weilaway,   *alas*
Oure hors is lost. Alayn, for goddes banes
Step on thy feet. Com of, man, al atanes.   *at once*
Allas oure wardeyn has his palfrey lorn.'
75   This Alayn al forgat bothe mele and corn;
Al was out of his mynde his housbondrye.
'What, whilk wey is he gane?' he gan to crye.
The wyf cam lepyng inward with a ren.

80
She seyde: 'Allas youre hors gooth to the fen
With wilde mares as faste as he may go.
Vnthank come on his hand that boond hym so   *bad luck*
And he that bettre sholde haue knyt the reyne.'
    'Allas,' quod Iohn, 'Aleyn, for Cristes peyne
Lay doun thy swerd and I wol myn alswa.

85
I is ful wight, god waat, as is a ra.   *swift as a roe deer*
By god hert he sal nat scape vs bathe.
Why ne had thow pit the capil in the lathe?   *horse, barn*
Il-hail, by god. Alayn, thow is a fonne.'   *bad luck, fool*
    This sely clerkes haan ful faste yronne

90
Toward the fen, bothe Alayn and eek Iohn.
And whan the millere seigh that they were gon,
He half a busshel of hir flour hath take
And bad his wyf go knede it in a cake.
He seyde: 'I trowe the clerkes were aferd.

95
Yet kan a millere maken a clerkes berd   *make a fool of a clerk*
For al his art. Ye, lat hem goon hir weye.
Lo wher he gooth. Ye, lat the children pleye.
They gete hym noght so lightly by my croun.'
    Thise sely clerkes rennen vp and doun

100
With 'Keep, keep; stand, stand; iossa, warderere.   *down! behind!*
Ga whistle thow and I sal kepe hym heere.'
But shortly, til that it was verray nyght
They koude noght, thogh they dide al hir myght,
Hir capyl cacche, he ran alwey so faste,   *horse*

105
Til in a dych they caughte hym at the laste.
Wery and weet as beest is in the reyn
Comth sely Iohn and with hym comth Aleyn.   *poor*
'Allas,' quod Iohn 'the day that I was born,
Now ar we dryuen til hethyng and til scorn.   *contempt*

110
Oure corn is stole. Men wil vs foolis calle,
Bothe the wardeyn and oure felawes alle,
And namely the millere weilawey.'   *especially, alas*

B   Troilus and Criseyde, Prologue to Book II

Owt of thise blake wawes forto saylle,
O wynde, O wynde, the weder gynneth clere,   *begin*
For in this see the boot hath swych trauaylle

Of my connyng that vnneth I it steere: *understanding*

5 This see clepe I the tempestous matere   *call*

Of disespeir that Troilus was inne –

But now of hope the kalendes bygynne.   *early days*

O lady myn, that called art Cleo, –

Thow be my speed fro this forth, and my muse,   *help*

10 To ryme wel this book til I haue do;

Me nedeth here noon othere art to vse.

For-whi to euery louere I me excuse

That of no sentement I this endite,   *feeling, compose*

But out of Latyn in my tonge it write.

15 Wherfore I nyl haue neither thank ne blame

Of al this werk, but prey ʒow mekely,

Disomblameth me if any word be lame,

For as myn auctour seyde, so sey I;

Ek though I speeke of loue vnfelyngly,

20 No wondre is, for it no thyng of newe is:

A blynd man kan nat iuggen wel in hewis.   *colours*

ʒe knowe ek that in fourme of speche is chaunge

With-inne a thousand ʒeer, and wordes tho   *then*

That hadden pris now wonder nyce and straunge   *value, foolish*

25 Us thenketh hem, and ʒet thei spake hem so,

And spedde as wel in loue as men now do,

Ek forto wynnen loue in sondry ages,

In sondry londes, sondry ben vsages.   *customs*

And forthi if it happe in any wyse,   *way*

30 That here be any louere in this place

That herkneth, as the storie wol deuise,   *relate*

How Troilus com to his lady grace,   *favour*

And thenketh, 'so nold I nat loue purchace',   *obtain*

Or wondreth on his speche or his doynge,   *actions*

35 I noot, but it is me no wonderynge.   *I do not know*

For euery wight which that to Rome wente   *goes*

Halt nat o path or alwey o manere;

Ek in som lond were al the game shente   *ruined*

40
If that they ferde in loue as men don here,   *behaved*
As thus, in opyn doyng or in chere,   *manner*
In visityng in forme or seyde hire sawes;   *formal, speeches*
For-thi men seyn, ecche contree hath hise lawes.

45
Ek scarsly ben ther in this place thre
That haue in loue seide like and don in al,
For to thi purpos this may liken the,   *may please*
And the right nought, ȝet al is seide, or schal;
Ek som men graue in tree, som in ston wal,   *carve in wood*
As it bitit; but syn I haue bigonne,
Myn auctour shal I folwen if I konne.

Explicit prohemium secundi libri   *The proem of the second book is complete*

Incipit liber secundus   *The second book begins*

50
In May, that moder is of monthes glade,
That fresshe floures blew and white and rede
Ben quike agayn, that wynter dede made,   *alive*
And ful of bawme is fletyng euery mede;   *perfume, meadow*
Whan Phebus doth his bryght bemes sprede
55
Right in the white Bole, it so bitidde,   *Taurus*
As I shal synge, on Mayes day the thrydde,

That Pandarus, for al his wise speche,
Felt ek his parte of loues shotes keene,   *share*
That koude he neuere so wel of louyng preche,
60
It made his hewe a-day ful ofte greene;
So shop it that hym fil that day a teene   *happened, reversal*
In loue, for which in wo to bedde he wente,
And made er it was day ful many a wente.   *turning*

The swalowe Proigne with a sorowful lay
65
Whan morwen com gan make hire waymentyng   *lament*
Whi she forshapen was, and euere lay   *transformed*
Pandare a-bedde half in a slomberyng,
Til she so neigh hym made hire cheteryng,
How Tireux gan forth hire suster take,
70
That with the noyse of hire he gan awake,

And gan to calle, and dresse hym vp to ryse,   *prepare*
Remembryng hym his erand was to doone
From Troilus, and ek his grete emprise,   *undertaking*
And caste and knewe in good plite was the moone   *took omens*
75 To doon viage, and took his way ful soone   *journey*
Unto his Neces palays ther biside;
Now Ianus, god of entree, thow hym gyde!

Notes

The Reeve's Tale

3   **for to pleye**   The various forms of infinitive possible in Chaucer's language (with and without final -*n*, and with *to* or *for to*) are an important
metrical resource (cf. 6).

4   **reuerye**   Closely related in sense to *revelrye* but an independent development from French *resverie*.

5   **they crye**   The East Midland type of third-person-plural present tense
occurs in Chaucer both with and without final -*n*. Both rhyme (as here
and 26–7) and metre may depend on the choice (99).

7   **ygrounde**   The southern form of the Strong verb past participle with
prefix and lacking final -*n* is required by the metre and the rhyme (cf. 58–
9 and 89–90).

19   **hym neded**   An impersonal construction. *Hym* is originally a dative
form.

21   **Aleyn spak**   Throughout, these northern students speak in dialectal
forms distinct from Chaucer's ordinary language. The imitation of a dialect
distinct from that of the author and the scribe is rare in ME. The word
hayl (from a Scandinavian source) is a northern greeting. Other words
of northern distribution found in the students' speech include: *wanges,
heythen, ille, hethyng, fonne.*

22   **fares**   The use of the -*es* inflexion of third-person singular (*bihoues,
wagges*, etc.) and plural (*fares, werkes*, etc.) of the present tense is characteristically northern.

26   **na**   The OE form *nā* remains unrounded in the language of the students; see also *swa, gas, banes, atanes, waat, ra*, etc.

28   **hope**   The sense 'think, expect' is a northern one.

31   **heem**   It might be expected that the form would have been the
unrounded OE form *ham*. But this form is derived from Scandinavian
heimr.

38   **til and fra**   A northern version of the expression, closer in form to its
Scandinavian origin (*til ok fra*) than southern equivalents.

42   **sal**   The normal spelling in Chaucer MSS is *shal* or *schal.* Spellings like this are recorded from Kent, but were common in the North.

44   **I is ... ar ye**   The concord of *I* with *is* is simply outlandish, and an exaggeration of northern barbarism. The form *ar* rather than the more common Chaucerian *ben* is consistent with northern origin but found also in London.

48   **blere hir iye** 'blear their eye'   A fairly common idiom. Cf. Modern English *pull the wool over their eyes.*

49   **phislophye**   Perhaps a deliberately barbarous form used by a scorner of learning, but possibly simply a scribal error.

53   **grettest clerkes**, etc.   The proverb is derived from an Æsopian fable in which a wolf is tricked into reading the price of a foal supposedly written on the mare's hoof. Despite his literacy, he pays the price of rashness.

55   **not a tare**   One of numerous Chaucerian expressions of worthlessness. They include reference to beans, haws, leeks, rushes, vetch, herbs, motes, mites and rake handles.

70   **fynt** 'finds'   The form exhibits the syncope and assimilation characteristic of dialects descended from Saxon OE – here the earlier London language. Forms with *-eth* are, however, common in Chaucer.

72   **goddes banes**   Swearing by parts of God's body was very common at the end of the fourteenth century and is condemned in both 'The Pardoner's Prologue' and 'The Parson's Tale'.

77   **whilk**   The Scandinavian-influenced northern equivalent of more usual Chaucerian *which.* This form is recorded widely north of a line from the Mersey to the Wash.

86   **god hert** 'God's heart'   Genitive modifiers frequently have reduced forms of the genitive inflexion and are not necessarily northern, but the omission of <e> in the spellings may be intended to suggest northern loss of final *-e.*

87   **pit**   The East Midland and northern form of the verb 'put'.

89   **haan**   Usually spelt <han>. This is a north-east Midland form of the plural present tense, contracted from *haven.*

95   **berd**   The idiom 'to make someone's beard' means 'to make a fool of someone'.

97   **he gooth**   This phrase must refer to the horse, since in Chaucer's language these forms are singular.

104   **capyl**   This word is used by Chaucer only for working horses and in lower-life settings. In northern England it was more widely used.

Troilus and Criseyde

2   **gynneth**   This is originally the plural form of the imperative. Chaucerian imperatives to a single addressee show considerable variation, ending in *-e, -eth* or Ø.

3–4   **boot ... Of my connyng**   The complexity of the syntax is here resolved by the dependence of the phrase on Dante's *la navicella del mio ingegno*. Translate: 'begin to clear away the stormy weather, because the boat of my understanding has such trouble in this sea that I can hardly steer it'.

11   **me nedeth**   An impersonal construction, with no subject expressed.

13–14   **endite ... write**   The contrast between *write* and *endite* is here made quite strongly. The former means simply to write down (here from translation); the latter to compose from one's own resources (sometimes without the necessity of writing).

15   **nyl**   A contraction of the negative *ne* and *wyl*. The verb still carries the sense 'wish'.

17   **disomblameth**   Most MSS read *desblameth*, which more closely matches the French form from which the borrowing has been made, *desblasmer*. The *dis-* spelling of the prefix represents Latin influence, which gains ground in the fifteenth century. The *-om-* may be inspired by the elevated stylistic associations of the *-en-* prefix (usually spelt before *b*) which was productive in the later fourteenth and fifteenth centuries and common in technical and elevated language. The fact that it is unmetrical suggests scribal elevation of the language.

19   **though**   The earlier London form of this word was *þei3*. This Chaucerian form is of Scandinavian origin, and forms part of the East Midland influence on the London language which is also evident in the use of the pronoun *they*.

21   **hewis**   The rhyme on *is* suggests that Chaucer's language possessed a raised variant of the plural inflexion.

22   **fourme of speche**   This phrase does not refer to the forms of language as understood in modern linguistic theory. Chaucer is commenting not on linguistic change but on social change: the formulation of polite and acceptable utterance. The words *pris* and *nyce and straunge*, which indicate social and behavioural judgements, confirm this.

32   **lady grace**   The genitive modifier, derived from an OE weak feminine, is endingless in this formulaic phrase.

36   **wente**   This is apparently the present tense of the verb *wenden*, and exhibits syncope and assimilation common in earlier London (cf. *halt* in the next line, *bitit*, 48, and its preterite form, 55). The final *-e* is therefore unpronounced, and a scribal addition. During the fifteenth century, scribes, who could no longer understand the logic governing the occurrence of final *-e* in words where it was no longer pronounced, tended to overcompensate, adding *-e* randomly to words where it had never been pronounced. An example in this passage, which jeopardises the metre, is *plite* (74).

42   **hise lawes**   Note that no distinct inanimate form of the third-person pronoun has yet emerged in London English. The development of *its* does not take place until the later sixteenth century.

45   **this may liken the**   An impersonal construction with *this* as subject and the dative form of the personal pronoun. The rhyme with *thre* demonstrates the East Midland development of OE *eo* to *e*.

52   **Ben**   The East Midland form of the plural present tense, derived from the OE subjunctive form.

65   **gan make**   This is often, as here, a periphrastic form of the preterite, supplying an extra syllable required by the metre, and facilitating a rhyme (as in lines 69–70). In some instances the auxiliary may retain the sense 'began'.

72   **to doone**   As in OE, the inflected form of the infinitive is sometimes used when the sense is passive, i.e. 'to be done'.

19

A LETTER FROM THE CORPORATION
OF LONDON TO HENRY V (1417)

Chaucer's Host refers in the Clerk's Prologue (line 18) to 'heigh style', which he says is used when people write to kings. He contrasts it with plain style, and protests that it is difficult to understand. The letter below, which provokes some sympathy with his complaint, is the earliest of a series addressed by the Mayor and Aldermen of the City of London to King Henry V when he was campaigning in France. Its original is preserved in the Public Record Office in Guildhall Letter-book I, f. ccix.

The language of the letter is representative of other London documents of the time (Chambers and Daunt 1931), and is therefore significant in the development of Standard English (Samuels 1963), but it is included here as much because it is the representative of a particular epistolary and administrative style. This style could indeed be termed 'high style', but is better described as 'curial style': that is, a style associated with the court as the centre of power and government (Burnley 1986). Its origins are in the Latin of the papal *curia*, but it was adapted into Anglo-French, and became by the second half of the fourteenth century the accepted mode in which formal letters were exchanged between powerful magnates.

Paradoxically, the origins of this style are in a desire for clarity. This is achieved by very explicit devices of cohesion: wordforms are repeated, and further specified by deictic modifiers like *the (fore)seide* and *the which*. Expressions may be disambiguated by pairing near synonyms: *excellent and noble, drynk and infusion, sequestred and exiled*. Very extensive use is made of adjectival and adverbial modifiers. Clauses reflect familiar Latin structures, such as passives and ablative absolutes, and are often linked by the use of a present participle. By the late fourteenth century, however, clarity of content had taken second place to the ceremonious effect which could be achieved, and letters written in this style are intended to impress more than to inform. They honour social relationships: reinforcing the elevated status of a respected addressee, but also proclaiming the sophisticated skills of their author. To these ends, the syntactic and cohesive outline of the curial style is elaborated by the lavish use of Latinate lexical borrowing, and the long sentences and phrasal and lexical pairings become rhetorical in effect: *subiectif reuerence and servisable lowenesse, high excellence and excellent highnesse.*

In England, these developments took place first in Anglo-French, and although Excerpt 13 already contains a few early traces of curial style, the letter quoted below is among the earliest fully-developed examples in English. Elsewhere in English, the further development of the style can be traced in the florid prologues and epilogues of fifteenth-century literary authors, and the fascination with learned Latin and Franco-Latin lexical borrowing is fulfilled in the aureate style pioneered by Lydgate, and represented in the work of authors such as Skelton (Excerpt 24).

       Of alle erthely princes our most dred souereigne liege lord and noblest kyng, we, youre simple officers, mair and aldermen of youre trewe Citee of London, with exhibicion of alle maner subiectif reuerence and servisable lowenesse that may be hadde in dede,

5   or in mynde conceyued, recommende vs vnto your most noble and hye magnificence and excellent power, bisechyng the heuenly kyng of his noble grace and pitee that he so wold illumine and extende vpon the trone of your kyngly mageste the radyouse bemys of hys bounteuous grace, that the begunnen spede, by hys

10   benigne suffraunce and help yn your chiualiruse persoune fixed and affermed, mowe so be continued forth, and determined so to his plesaunce, your worship, and alle your reumys proffyt, that we and alle your other lieges to the desired presence of your most noble and graciouse persone, fro which grete distance of place

15   long tyme hath priued vs, the sonner myght approche and visuelly perceyue, to singuler confort and special joye of vs alle; makyng protestacion, our most dred soueraigne liege lord and noblest kyng, that be this feruent desire wiche we han to the bodyly sight of your most excellent and noble persone, our entente is noght to move

20   you fro no thing of your hye worship, ne to no thyng that myght be perille to your lond, that ye haue put in obbeissaunce.

       Our most dred soueraign liege lord & noblest kynge, for-as-moche as we trust verryly that the kyngly desyre of your inspired excellence deliteth to here of the welfare of your forsayd Cite, which

25   your noble and soueraign grace with innumerable prerogatifs &
liberalle fraunchises hath euer visited and endowed, like it vn-to
your kyngly mageste to vnderstonde that euer syn the tyme of your
last departyng it hath stonde, yit doth, and euer shal, by the help
of oure Lord almyghty, in as gret pees and tranquillite as euer
30   ded Cite in absence of his most soueraign and excellent lord.
And for-as-moch, most dred souerein liege lord and noblest kyng,
as the hertly desire of your forsayd Cite ys, as who seith, with an
heuenly drynk and infusion so oftetymes gladed and refresshid as it
hereth the soueraigne helth and prosperite of your most graciouse
35   & noble persoune, therfor we, mekely bowyng our hertes to-for
the clernesse of your kyngly mageste, biseche your high excellence
and excellent highnesse that it lyke, of the roted gentillesse and
gronded grace in your nobley, so to visyte vs in assertenyng of your
souueragn helth and prosperite, as it is seyd before, that we, in
40   defaute of such visitacion languisse not as men from so hie a grace
sequestred and exiled.

    Our most dred soueraign liege lord and noblest kyng, we, your
symple officers, specially beseche vnto alle the holy company of
heuenly knyghthode, assembled in the hie blisse wher-as is eternal
45   ioye and non euynesse, so be-shyne the noble knyghthode in your
cronicable excellence aporeued, that ye mowe in this world vpon vs
and alle your other lieges with report of wordly victory longe regne
and endure; and after, whan your graciouse erthely persoune from
your inward spirit ys dessolued, that ye mowe be brought tofor the
50   throne of the hye kynge, and ther with heuenly Ierarchies in eternal
glorie perpetuelly duelle and abyde.

    Wryten at your forsayd Cite of London, the xxe day of
Decembre. Your humble lieges and simple officers, Richard Merlawe,
Mair, and aldermen of your Cite of London.

Notes

1   **Of alle erthely princes . . .**   The opening words of the letter are the
salutatio or greeting formula, in which contemporary epistolary manuals
stated that the name of the more important addressee should precede that
of the writer.

5   **recommende vs vnto . . .**   The *commendatio* of the letter, in which the
writer seeks the good will of the addressee. It is here extended to extraordinary lengths, occupying a first sentence more than twenty lines long.
The gist of the sentence is that the senders commend themselves to the

king, at the same time *bisechyng* God to bring his campaign to a successful conclusion so that they can welcome him again, but at the same time *makyng protestacion* that they have no wish to recall him against his will. Note how the formality of this letter precludes any direct address, preferring abstract phrasing to refer to the addressee. The ceremoniousness is heightened by the weight given to nominal phrases by extensive pre- and post-modification, and by pairing of both words and phrases.

3–4   **exhibicion of alle maner subiectif reuerence** 'demonstration of all the respect proper for subjects'   The words *exhibicion* and *subiectif* are first recorded here, as are *radyouse* (8) and *visuelly* (15). Much of the lexis has been borrowed into English within the previous fifty years, often from technical contexts or in the works of learned authors like Wyclif and Trevisa; among these recent borrowings are: *extende, determined, feruent, inspired, prerogatifs, liberalle, endowed, infusion, assertenyng, sequestred, dessolued* and *ierarchies*.

7   **illumine**   The form of the word is a Latin one, contrasting with the French borrowing *enlumine* used by Chaucer. Other forms modelled on Latin include *inspired, innumerable* and *infusion*.

22   **Our most dred soueraign liege . . .**   The beginning of the *narratio* of the letter, which would normally contain whatever message was to be delivered. Once again the message is brief, but its expression is long. It simply states that the city is peaceful and requests news of the king's health and success. The phrase repeated in line 42 marks the beginning of the *petitio*, in which a request would normally be put to the addressee. Here the petition is to God on Henry's behalf.

26–27   **like it vn-to your kyngly mageste** 'may it please your royal majesty' The subjunctive mood of an impersonal construction, as also line 36.

28   **hath stonde, yit doth, and euer shal.**   Characteristic of curial documents are expressions which seek to assert the timelessness or the lack of exceptions to the claims being made.

47   **wordly** 'worldly'   Not an error, but a dialectal form common in East Anglia.

20

THE STUDY OF THE VERNACULAR
IN MEDIEVAL ENGLAND

Awareness of vernacular languages as the legitimate object of study emerged slowly from the shadow of Latin. Although Ælfric's *Colloquy* had been translated into Old English, the grammar it presented was that of Latin. Late thirteenth- and early fourteenth-century Anglo-French vocabularies such as that of Walter of Bibbesworth served the practical purpose of teaching French to native English speakers. French, indeed, was the route by which earlier medieval Englishmen arrived at a knowledge of Latin. But by the beginning of the fifteenth century a larger lay public and more widespread ignorance of French led to the increased production of basic educational texts in English. Generally, however, these continued to summarise Latin learning, or to instruct in the basics of the Latin language. English was not itself the target of scholarly interest, but might be incidentally analysed as the by-product of some other purpose. The two passages below offer examples of this. The Preface to a Wycliffite Biblical Concordance arises from the focus given to the study of English by the Wycliffite project of biblical translation. Passage B is part of an account of the basic curriculum of the medieval university, but has peculiar descriptive features which may be drawn from the individual introspection of a speaker of English.

A   The Preface to a Wycliffite Biblical Concordance

Two translations of the New Testament into English were made in the last quarter of the fourteenth century – the first a very literal rendering of the Vulgate, and the second, or Later Version, much more idiomatic in style. Collectively they are referred to as the Wycliffite Bible, since the stimulus for such translation derived from the doctrines of John Wyclif (c. 1330–84). It is no longer thought that Wyclif himself had a hand in the work, and although the names of Nicholas Hereford, John Purvey and John Trevisa have all been associated with it, scholarly consensus about the translators is still lacking. The important point is that at this period there existed a number of scholars, centred upon Oxford, who saw value in producing a Bible in English and were prepared to devote time and effort to the study of the problems raised by such a project. The Later Version (1395) is preceded by a preface which discusses some of the problems of translation with a degree of linguistic sophistication. The text reproduced here belongs to this milieu.

British Library MS Royal 17. B. 1 is an early fifteenth-century concordance based largely on the Early Version of the Wycliffite Bible but making use also of the Later Version. It commences with a preface which explains its compiler's methodology and the difficulties which he encountered in imposing a usable alphabetical order upon a language whose spellings could be so variable. Guidance is offered to the potential user, and this is followed by more than 1200 separate entries for individual words. The purpose of such a concordance was not primarily the study of language but as a tool for preachers, who could bring together distinct but verbally echoic parts of biblical text, which may then be combined into the theme of a sermon. Nevertheless, this preface provides an unusual insight into how an educated late-medieval Englishman viewed his language as a medium of communication. Its interest lies in its patiently analytic statements, strongly contrasting with the evaluative nature of most near-contemporary linguistic commentary.

The language of the piece has been identified as that of north-east Bedfordshire or extreme south Huntingdonshire, but such precision may be misleading since most of the forms would be equally at home anywhere in the south-central Midlands. The language is very similar to that of other Wycliffite writings and is of a type which has been recognised as an early quasi-standard language. The forms *miche* and *ony* are characteristic of this 'Wycliffite' or central Midland standard, but *suche*, *self* and *stede* (rather than *sich*, *silf* and *stide*) are more generally dispersed forms.

> Mannes mynde, þat is oft robbid of þe tresour of kunnyng bi þe
> enemye of science, þat is forȝetyng, is greetly releeued bi tablis
> maad bi lettre aftir þe ordre of þe A B C. *Ensaumple*: if a man haue
> mynde oonly of oo word or two of sum long text of þe Newe Lawe
> 5 and haþ forȝetyn al þe remenaunt, or ellis if he can seie bi herte
> such an hool text but he haþ forȝeten in what stede it is writen, þis

concordaunce wole lede him bi þe fewe wordis þat ben cofrid in his mynde vnto þe ful text, and shewe him in what book and in what chapitre he shal fynde þo textis which him list to haue.

10 Þis concordaunce sueþ not oonly þe ordre of þe A B C in þe firste lettris of wordis, but also in þe secounde, in þe þridde, in þe fourþe and so forþ; wherfore *Aaron* stondiþ bifore *Abba*, for þe secounde lettre of *Aaron*, which is *a*, stondiþ in þe A B C bifore *b*, which is þe secounde lettre of *Abba*. And *Abba* stondiþ bifore *Abel*,

15 for þe þridde lettre of *Abba*, þat is *b*, stondiþ in the A B C bifore þe þridde lettre of *Abel*, which is *e*. Þus *conferme* stondiþ bifore *confounde*, bi cause þe fifþe lettre of þis word *conferme* stondiþ in the A B C bifore þe fifþe lettre of *confounde*, þat is *o*; for in þe firste foure lettris of þese two, whiche ben *c*, *o*, *n*, and *f*, in no þing þei

20 discorden. Wherfore, if þou fynde ony word in þis werk þat is not set in þis forme, vnkunnyng or neglygence of þe writere is in cause, and liʒtly, bi oon þat can, may it be amendid. If it seme to ony creature þat cotaciouns of summe textis be not spoken off in wordis þere þei shulde be expressid, if þei be duly plauntid yn, so myche is

25 þe bettir, so þat þei be – not set inordinatly – aftir þe maner of þis drawyng.

Whanne a text conteyneþ two wordis and þou can not wel perceyue in wheþer of þo wordis þou shuldist seeke it, þou shalt fynde it quotid in oon of hem at þe leeste and sumtyme in boþe.

30 As, if þee list fynde þis text: *Womman, lo þi sone*; if þou fynde it not in S in þis word *sone*, þou shalt fynde it in V in þis word *womman*. If þou fynde not þis text: *Tribulacioun worchip pacience* in P in þis terme *pacience*, þou shalt fynde it in T in þis word *tribulacioun*; and þus of oþire lijk tixtis.

35 In Englisch as in Latyn ben wordis synonemus, þat is to seie manie wordis bitokenynge oo þing, as *kirke* and *chirche*, *accesse* and *nyʒcomynge*, *clepe* and *calle*, *ʒyue* and *gyue*, *ʒift* and *gift*, *bigyle* and *disceyue* and *defraude*. And sumtyme suche wordis varyen or diuersen al oonly in oo lettre, as *flax* and *flex*, *invie* and *envie*, *lomb*

40 and *lamb*. And oþorwhile haþ þat oon a lettre more þan þat oother, as *epistle* and *pistle*. Now it may be so þat in sum Newe Lawe is writen in sum text þis word *kirke* and in þe same text and in a noþir book is writen þis word *chirche*, and þus of oþire wordis bifore rehersid, and of manye mo lyk hem. If þou þanne seke a text

45 in ony of suche synonemus, and if þou fynde it not in oon of hem, loke in a noþir of hem; ʒhe, loke in alle suche synonemus, þouʒ

þer be þre or mo of hem, til þou fynde þe text wiþ which þe liste
mete. Remissioun is ofte maad in þis concordaunce fro such a
synoneme til a noþir. Sumtyme þe formere remittiþ to þe lattere
50   and sumtyme þe lattere remittiþ to þe formere.

Sumtyme þe same word and þe self þat is writen of sum man
in oo manere is writen of a noþir man in anoþir manere. As wher
summe writen þese wordis *thyng* and *theef* with *th*, oþire vsen to
writen þoo same wordis with þis figure þ. Wherfore alle þe wordis
55   of þis concordaunce of which the firste carecte is þis figure þ
bigynnen in þis table with *th* and in T þei stonden aftir here ordre
axiþ. Summe writen *gh* in summe wordis, whiche wordis ben writen
of summe oþire with a yogh þat is figured þus ȝ – as sum man
writeþ þus þese termes: *doughter, thought*, where a noþir writeþ
60   hem þus: *douȝter, thouȝt*. But for as miche as þe carect yogh, þat
is to seie ȝ, is figurid lijk a zed, þerfore alle þe wordis of þis table
þat biginnen wiþ þat carect ben set in Zed, which is the last lettre of
þe A B C. Also sum man writeþ sum word wiþ an *h*, which saame
word anoþer man writiþ wiþouten an *h*; as is of þe Englisch word
65   which þis Latyn word *heres* signyfieþ, which terme summe writen
with *h* þus, *here*, and summe þus, *eir*, wiþouten *h*.

Þese diuerse maneris of writyng ben to be considerid in þis
concordaunce. For perchaunce, aftir my manere of writyng, sum
word stondiþ in sum place, which same word aftir þi maner of
70   writyng shulde stonde in anoþer place. If it plese to ony man to
write þis concordaunce and him þenkiþ þat summe wordis ben not
set in ordre aftir his conseit and his manere of writyng, it is not
hard if he take keep wiþ good avisement in his owne writyng to sette
such wordis in such an ordre as his owne conseit acordiþ to.

75   In Englisch also as in Latyn ben wordis equiuouse, þat is whanne
oon word haþ manye significaciouns or bitokenyngis: as þis word
kynde bitokeneþ 'nature', and also such a man clepen we *kynde*
which is a free-hertid man and þat gladly wole rewarde what þat
men don for hym. An instrument wherwiþ we hewen clepen we an
80   *axe*, and I *axe* God mercy of synnes þat I haue don. Suche wordis
in þis concordaunce ben maad knowen bi sum word addid to hem
wherby it may be wist whanne þei ben taken in oon significacioun
and whanne in a noþir. Textis in whiche ben wordis of plural
noumbre ben quotid in þe wordis of singuler noumbre. A word
85   is singuler noumbre þat bitokneþ but oo þing, as *womman, man,
foot*; a word of plurel noumbre bitokneþ mo þingis þan oon, as

men, wymmen, feet. Loke þanne þe textis in whiche ben þese termes
men, wymmen, feet in her synguleris: *man, womman, foot.* Loke
also suche wordis *wakyng, wepyng, fadirheed, wickidnesse,* in wordis

90 þat þei comen of – as *wakyng* in *wake, wepyng* in *wepe, fadirheed* in
fadir and *wickidnesse* in *wickid,* and þus of oþire lyk hem – but if it
be so þat boþe þe wordis of whiche oþire wordis comen and also
þe wordis þat comen of hem ben expresly sett out in þis table as
cheef wordis of þis concordaunce, as is of þese wordis: *seruaunt,*

95 *serue,* and *seruyce,* for ech of þese þree is expressid bi hemself. And
þus it is of oþire wordis: *kyng* and *kyngdom* and of sum oþire, as
þou may conceyue liȝtly in þis table if þou take good heede.
    Where a chapiter spekiþ miche of a mater, þanne is sumtyme
shortly quotyd þe sentence and not þe wordis as in þis word *bischop*

100 is quotyd how – þe firste pistle to Tymothe, þe þridde *cap.,* and
Titum þe firste *cap.* – ben specified þe condiciouns of a bischop. And
in this word *charite* is quotyd how, in þe firste pistle to Corintheis,
þrittenþe *cap.,* Poul spekiþ of þe condicions of charite. Whanne þe
cheef wordis of þis concordaunce ben þe firste wordis of þe firste

105 textis þat ben qyotyd in hem, þanne ben þo wordis not rehersyd
aȝen in þe same firste textis, forwhi þei ben parties of þe same firste
textis as þou may persyue liȝtli in þese termes: *absent, abstene,*
Acaie, accepcioun, and in manye oþir. And whanne suche cheef
wordis ben not be firste wordis of suche firste textis, þanne stonden

110 þei absolutely and ben sett by hemself oon, to shewe redyly where
þo textis þat suen whiche perteynen to such wordis may be liȝtly
founden, as þou mai se in þese wordis: *Aaron, Abba, Abel,* and
in many mo. Þe cheef wordis of þis concordaunce I clepe alle þo
wordis þat goen bi lettre aftir þe ordre of þe A B C in þis present

115 table.
    If ony fruyt come of þis concordaunce, to God be onour and
doynge of þankyngis now and euere. Amen.

Notes

10 **Þis concordaunce sueþ . . . þe ordre of þe A B C**   Reference works in
alphabetical order are today the norm, but medieval glossaries were frequently arranged in order of topics and themes. Alphabetical ordering is
often very approximate before the seventeenth century.

22 **oon þat can** 'one who knows how'   The verb is still being used as a full
lexical verb, as in OE.

22–23   **ony creature**   The use of the word *creature as* an indefinite pronoun ('one, person') is common in Wycliffite writings but is also more widely spread in later medieval pious texts.

25–26   **so þat . . . drawyng**   The word *drawyng* may refer to a missing diagram but could have the sense 'arrangement'. In either case, this would be the earliest occurrence of such a sense. The manuscript reading is 'so þat þei be not set in ordinatly'. Good sense requires either the deletion of *not* or the understanding of *but* before *aftir*.

28   **wheþer** 'which [of two]'   The OE sense, etymologically related to *other*.

31   **þou shalt finde it in V**   The letter <V> is normally used for initial <U>, and <U> is considered equivalent to <W>. In fact only one page from thirty-one pages of <W> entries in the concordance is headed with <V>.

35   **wordis synonemus**   From the modern point of view, many of these 'synonyms' are mere dialectal variants of the same word: *kirke* and *chirche*; *gyue* and *ȝyue*; *gift* and *ȝift*; *lamb* and *lomb*; *flax* and *flex* are respectively northerly and southerly dialect forms, and *invie* represents Latin influence on spelling practice. The author is unconcerned with etymology, however, concentrating rather on synchronic practicalities.

60–61   **þe carect yogh . . . lijk a zed** 'the symbol "yogh"'   The word *carect* is used for written symbols which do not part of the normal Latin alphabet (sometimes magical symbols). The Irish Latin form of <g>, *yogh*, is confused in ME with the final -z written by French-influenced scribes to represent /z/ and /s/ (see Excerpt 17). Although the two symbols had different origins and represented a quite distinct range of sounds, the compiler classes them together purely on their similarity of form in the written language.

75   **wordes equiuouse** 'ambiguous'   Not previously recorded. Formed by adding the French derivative suffix *-ous* to Latin *equivoc*. The compiler does not make a distinction parallel to that between homonyms (words with identical form but different senses and different histories) and polysemous words (wordforms in which historical development has produced multiple significance in a single historical form).

78   **free-hertid** 'generous-hearted'   Compounds such as this, consisting of an adjective and a denominalised verb past participle, are a fourteenth-century development, but the type is more fully productive in the sixteenth century.

94   **cheef wordis**   *Cheef* is to be understood in its French sense – thus 'head words'.

99   **sentence** 'import, content'   In ME the word *sentence* refers primarily to meaning or content of an utterance rather than its formal structure. The grammatical conception of a sentence is often denoted by the word *resoun* in late fourteenth-century technical contexts.

110   **absolutly** 'in isolation'   Used in the technical grammatical sense of a
        word standing outside the syntactical relations of text.

116   **fruyt** 'benefit'   The word *fruyt* (Lat. *fructus*) is commonly used as a
        figure of the benefit to be derived from any literary activity. Cf. Chaucer's
        use of the terms *fruyt* and *chaf.*

B   A Fifteenth-Century Text on Phonetics

Trinity College, Cambridge MS R. 14. 52 is a compendium of medical
and astrological treatises, but also contains a brief account of the Seven
Liberal Arts (Grammar, Logic, Rhetoric, Arithmetic, Music, Astronomy and
Geometry). Its account of Grammar, however, merely mentions the parts
of speech and prosody, and confines itself to the lowest level of medieval
grammatical analysis, sounds and letters. As is usual with medieval treat-
ments of this topic, it makes no rigorous distinction between the written
and the spoken languages, regarding letters (*littera*, *lettres*) as the primary
unit of analysis, with associated sound (*vox*, *voice*) and shape (*figura*, *figure*)
related to it. The author's attempts at articulatory description are compromised both by the desire to find an iconic relationship between sound
and letter-shape, and by the assumption that a Latin phonemic inventory
is valid for a text in English. English phonemes such as /v/, /j/, /tʃ/, /dʒ/,
/θ/ and /ð/, as well as the significance of the spelling <gh>, are overlooked.
A rather unconvincing attempt is made to distinguish the articulation of
<k>, <q> and <c>. The explanation of the nasal consonant /n/ notes the
diversion of the airstream through the nasal cavity, but misunderstands the
mechanism involved. However, some of the articulatory descriptions, such
as those for the letters <d>, <t>, <l>, <r> and <s>, are more successful.
The *tremelyng* of *r* (37) seems to imply a trilled pronunciation such as is
found among some modern speakers of Scots.

   The manuscript can be dated around 1475, and is the work of a scribe
who also copied the poetry of Chaucer, Hoccleve and Lydgate (Mooney
1993). He is associated with the London book trade of the time, but the
content of the manuscript may connect it with the arts course in Oxford.
Dialectal forms in the passage (*to-guyder*) may also reflect this background,
but also a connection with the Wycliffite spelling tradition (*silf*, *theym*, and
the unstressed *-i-* in inflexions).

Gramer

First, the office of Gramer is to enforme our soule with vndirstondyng and, with due writyng and thynges vndirstondyng, duely to pronounce with congruyte as it is declared in the iiij parties of Gramer. For the first part that is cald Ortographie informyth
5   in rect and congrue writynge, and it is taught of Prescian in his more volume, from the bigynnyng vnto that part wher he saith a letter is þe last part of mannes voice. But for more cliere knowlache of þis part, we shuln vndirstonde the nature of our lettris, and firste of the v vowels, the whiche han divers placis and dyvers
10   maners of their generacioun. The placis, as Remygius saith, bien v: the lunges, the throte, the palate, the teeth, and the lippis; the maner of generacioun is in this forme, for generaly whan any substancial voice is caused, sumtyme of openyng is more in the mowth outward than withyn toward the lunges, and than it is like a triangle
15   whos foote is in the mowth and the poynt in the throte. And this is þe generacioun of the first letter 'A', and therfor it is in figure like a triangle. Or ellis it is contrarie wise, and than is 'V' caused, and his figure is turned and hath contrarie situacioun. Somtyme the throte is opened equaly on every part, and so is 'I' caused,
20   and therfor it hath a rect and egal figure. The generacioun of 'O' is in rounde openyng of the mowth, so that the tunge and the lippis bowe theym silf in their myddis; but 'e' is gendrid in the inward of the throte and the mowth, so that the mowth drawith to roundenesse more than the throte, and therfor his figure is half
25   cercle like a bowe with a part of a strynge in the over ende. And for bicause that the place of the complete generacioun of the letter *a* is bifore the place of *e*, the place of *e* bifore *i*, and *i* bifore *o*, and the generacion of *o* is bifore the generacioun of *v*, therfor thiese vowels be so ordeyned: *a e i o v*.
30   Furthermore the consonauntis bien divided, for sum be semyvowels and sum mutis. A semy vowell hath the sowne of a vowel bifore, but a mvte afterward. The semy vowels bien vj, and thei bien gendred thurgh touchyng of the tung to on of the palatis of the mowth. And if it touche the over palate, with streyneng out
35   of the tunge so that the pointe of the tunge towchith the palat, so is *l* causid; but if þe tunge be more bowed, and in maner with a tremelyng folowyng afterward, than is *r* gendred. And if the tung be in party streyned right and in part bowid, so that the sowne

40

goth nat oute completely bi the mowth but bi the nosethrillis, so is *n* caused. And if the tunge touche the lower palate twies, so is *x*. And if it touche but oones with an hissyng sowne, than is *s* gendred, for the sides of the tunge bien joyned to the sides of the palate. And if it touche the outward part with coniunccioun of the inward part of the lippis, so is *m* caused.

45

But the mvtis han iij placis of their generacioun: the lippis with both rowes of the teeth. If it be thurgh touchyng of the lippis, so that the nether smyte vpon the over lippe, so is *ff*; and if this touchyng be more outward, so is *b*; or ellis al without the mowth, and so is *p*. And if the tunge touche the over egge of the teeth, so is

50

d caused; or ellis it touchith the same place more withoute neere the teeth and than is *t* gendred. But if the tung touche the lower egge of the teeth with grete openyng of þe mowth, so is *k*, or with litel openyng, and than is *q*; or ellis it is in a meane bitwixt both, and so is *c*. And if the midpoynt of the tunge touche the nether

55

teeth, with a maner liftyng vp of the after part and depressioun of the part bi fore of the tung, so is *g*. And for bi cause that a smoth place and holl moist and hote is a goode place for sowne, therfor the consonauntis that bien gendred in suche placis bien cald semy vowels, for they sowne wele; but the place of teeth ne is nat playne

60

ne hote but cald, for thei bien made of erthly grosse matier. Also þe place of the outward part of the lippis is cold, for it is withoute the mowth in the aire; therfor the consonauntis that bien gendred in thiese placis bien cald mvtis, for their fieble sown *& cetera*.

Gramer also enformeth mannes soule with triewe vndirstandyng

65

of euery part of reasoun bi hym silf bi the secunde part that is cald Ethymologye, gyven and taught of Precian in thend of the grete volume. We bien also informed bi gramer in congruite and construccioun of partis of reason to-guyder bi the third part that is cald Diasintastik, gevyn of Prescian in the lasse booke. Also gramer

70

enformyth a mannes soule with a grete and a due pronunciacioun bi the fourth part cald Prosodie.

Notes

2

with . . . thynges vndirstondyng   The syntax is ambiguous, but is based on the Latin ablative absolute construction. The function of grammar is to bestow understanding, but also the ability to write and speak properly. *Congruyte* implies grammatical concord, but also euphony in pronunciation and harmony in sense.

5   **Prescian**   Priscian (sixth century AD) was the author of the advanced grammar of Latin most widely used throughout the Middle Ages. His *more volume* is probably the anglicisation of the Latin *Priscianus maior*, which refers to the final sixteen books of his *Institutiones grammaticae*. His chapter on letters begins: *Litera est pars minima vocis* . . . 'The letter is the smallest part of speech'. Compare: *a letter is þe last part of mannes voice*, 'a letter is the smallest part of human speech'. However, the author's recollections of the content of Priscian do not correspond very well to surviving texts, since these do not commence with Orthography.

10   **Remygius**   Ælius Donatus's *Ars grammatica minor* (fourth century AD) was the most popular basic Latin grammar of the Middle Ages, known familiarly as *Donet*. It was the subject of a Commentary by Remigius of Auxerre (841–908). Compare his *placis* with the points of articulation used in modern articulatory description: lips, teeth, alveolar ridge, hard palate, soft palate, uvula.

16–17   **figure like a triangle**   The attempt to find an articulatory motivation for letter shapes depends on Latin capitals for the letters *a, u, i* and *o*, but reverts to a miniscule letter form to explain *e*. The alphabetical order of the vowels is related to their supposed degree of frontness, but this does not correspond to the view of modern phoneticians.

47   **nether smyte vpon the over lippe**   The articulation of *f* which is described here seems to be a bilabial one, as distinct from the labio-dental articulation of modern English.

49   **the over egge of the teeth** 'the upper limit of the teeth'   Apparently the root of the teeth, or alveolar ridge.

60   **erthly grosse matier**   The author explains the difference between semi-vowels and mutes in terms of the characteristics of their places of articulation, understood in terms of the theory of the four elements, earth, air, fire and water. Moisture and heat are associated with the easy propagation of sound, so that the semi-vowels are consonants produced deeper in the vocal tract, whereas mutes are consonants produced more superficially.

65   **euery part of reasoun bi hym silf** 'every individual part of speech'   The word *reasoun* is that commonly used by grammarians to denote the form of a sentence. The word *sentence* is reserved for the content of an utterance. The author makes a distinction here between chapters which deal with grammatical forms in isolation under the title *Ethymologye*, and those dealing with grammatical constructions, under the heading *Diasintastik*. *Prosodie* deals with oral delivery. It is probable that the phrase *the lasse book* refers to the so-called *Priscianus minor*, a name given to the final two chapters of the *Institutiones grammaticae*.

21

OSBERN BOKENHAM'S

MAPPULA ANGLIAE

Osbern Bokenham (1393–?1447) was from a family associated with Old Buckenham, Norfolk, but spent most of his life as an Augustinian friar in the convent of Stoke Clare near the Suffolk–Essex border. In earlier life, however, he spent five years in Venice, and subsequently visited Rome and other parts of Italy on pilgrimage, where he gathered material for his best-known work, a collection of the lives of twelve women saints. In his 'Life of St Agnes' he tells us that he will write simply according to 'þe language of Suthfolk speche'. BL MS Harley 4011, which contains Bokenham's *Mappula Angliae*, was copied by two scribes near the middle of the fifteenth century, and is located by the *Linguistic Atlas of Late Mediaeval English* in Suffolk.

Bokenham confirmed his authorship of the *Mappula* by an acrostic by which the first letter in each chapter serves to spell out his name. His work, he says, is an adaptation of Ranulph Higden's Latin *Polychronicon* (*c.* 1327), and the passage on the diversity of the English people and their language printed here has become well known to students of the history of English from an earlier translation of it made in about 1385 by John Trevisa. Bokenham's version dates from about 1440 and differs in some respects from that of Trevisa. His distrust of the Scots is evident, and they are identified as the foreigners who have contributed to the mangling of English. His conception of linguistic change as corruption emerges more clearly and is more firmly related to Latin concepts of purity and barbarism.

Linguistically Bokenham's work is also influenced by Latin literacy, and the mannerism of fifteenth-century learned prose is already apparent in Latinate sentence constructions, the use of learned forms (*rurales, oryentalis, collaterall, artyke*) carried over from the Latin original, and word-pairs (*commodious and . . . profitable, congrese and conflicte*). Some of this vocabulary is not good Latin but is ostentatiously derived from that source and thus regarded as elevated. Despite Bokenham's statement about his Suffolk dialect, this excerpt shows no forms restricted to the East Anglian area: it is rather the combination of certain forms which testifies to East Anglian origin (*hit, here, syche, yche, byn, han(e), schuln*, 86, *yovyn*, 115). Most of the forms in this passage could, however, be found widely in the southern and eastern half of the Midlands at this period.

As towchynge þe firste parte of þis chapiture, hit is to been vndirstondyn that, as mony dyuerys peeples as hit haþe dwellers, so many hit haþe dyuersites of toungis and languagis. Nerþelees they been not all pure, but sum ben mixte and medlid on sundry
5 wysys. Scottis and Walsshmen, þe which ben the Brytouns propirly, as peeple moste ynpermyxt and leste medlyd with oþer, kepyn moste puerly hire firste propir speche or language. Nerþelees Scottys, of grete famulearyte and commvnycacyoun with þe Pyctis, sumwhat hane drawyn an medyllynge in hur toungis. The Flemmynges,
10 þe which as hit is seide beforn, dwellyn yn þe weste marche of Walis, hane left here rude barbarye and spekyn more Saxoonly or Englysshly. Angli, all be hit þat from the firste begynnynge, after þe thre dyuersytees of peeplis of Germayne þe whiche they comyn of, hadyn thre dyuersites of sowndyngis yn hure language and yn
15 þe thre dyuerys places, as Sowþe, Norþe, and Mydlonde, yet of commyxtioun dyuers, firste Danys and sethe with Normannys, they haue corrupte her first natif toungis and vsyn now I ne wot what straunge and pilgryms blaberyng and cheteryng, noþyng acordynge onto here firste speche.
20   And þis corrupcioun of Englysshe men yn þer modre tounge, begunne as I seyde with famylyar commixtion of Danys firste and of Normannys aftir, toke grete augmentacioun and encrees aftir þe commyng of William conquerour by two thyngis. The firste was: by decre and ordynaunce of þe seide William conquerour children
25 in gramer-scolis ageyns þe consuetude and þe custom of all oþer nacyons, here owne modre tonge lafte and forsakyn, lernyd here Donet on Frenssh and to construyn yn Frenssh and to maken here Latyns on þe same wyse. The secounde cause was þat by þe same decre lordis sonys and all nobyll and worthy mennys children were
30 fyrste set to lyrnyn and speken Frenssh, or þan þey cowde spekyn Ynglyssh, and þat all wrytyngis and endentyngis and all maner plees and contrauercyes in courtis of the lawe, and all maner reknyngis and countis yn howsoolde schulle be doon yn the same. And þis

35

seeynge, þe rurales, þat þey myghte semyn þe more worschipfull and
honorable and þe redyliere comyn to þe famyliarite of þe worthy and
þe grete, leftyn hure modre tounge and labouryd to kunne spekyn
Frenssh; and thus by processe of tyme barbariȝid thei in bothyn
and spokyn neythyr good Frenssh nor good Englyssh.

40

45

50

55

60

65

And yet yn þe Saxoyne or Englyssh tounge, þe whiche is
remaynyd but in a fewe vplondyssh peeple, be oryentalis, þat is
to sayne þe Est-ynglyssh men with be men of be west acordyn
more yn soundynge and spekynge, as men þat ben vndir oone
lyneal climat of hevene, þan don þe northen [with þe sowthern]
men. Also the Meerces, þe which byn clepid mydlonde ynglyssh,
as collaterall parteners of bothyn extremytes, bettir vndirstondyn
þe collaterall tounges, bothe the artyke, þe which is þe Northe, and
þe antartyke, þe which is þe Sowthe, þan þe two extremal toungis
vndirstondyn hemself togedir or þan eyþer vndyrstondith other.
For, as William pontyficis seith *libro tertio*, the norþehumbirlonde
pepelis tonge, specially yn Yorke, stradelith soo brode and so
vnsavorly is wyde, þat be sowtherne peple vnnethe can vndirstondyn
hit. And þat is, as he supposith, for oone of þe two causis, þat [is]
or for þe nygheness onto the Scottis or for þe grete distaunce of
kyngis of þe londe from þo marchis; the whiche byn more wone to
be conuersaunte yn þe sowþe place of Ynglond þan yn þe norþe,
for comynly þey drawe not norþe-warde butt yn strong hand, or
ageyns the Scottis or for to reforme and redresse ryot and mysrewle
of the same countre. The cause why þat kyngis be more expectant
and abydynge yn the sowþe þan in the norþe, may well be þus:
for þere, þat is to say by sowþe, þe erbe is more plentyvous,
and þe peple more copious, þe cytees and townys more worþi and
honorable, and þe portis or the hauenys more commodious and
more profitable . . . Þe peple of be sowþe place is more quyete yn
þemself and more softe þan is þe norþe place peple, þe which is
euermore inquiete, more mevable and more cruell. The mydlonde
peple is betwix þe norþyn and þe sowþirne, as is a participle beetwix
nowne and verbe, þat is to sey hit is a partyner with bothyn.

70

Also, quod he, þe Ynglysshe peeple amonge all oþur nacyouns
is syngulerly yevyn to gloteny and dronkynship, and moste
sumpteous and wastefull yn mete and drynke and cloþus. This vyce
hit is supposid þat þis londe drowh firste of Hardeknut the Dane,
þe whiche was þe firste kynge yn þis londe þat commaundid messe
of mete to be sette on his tablee at sowpeer. This peeple, quod he,

75 is delyvyr and swyfte boþe on foote and allso on horsbacke, apt and promte to all maner kynde of armys, and yn euery congresse and conflicte yn batylle is commynly wone, lesse þen tresoun or fraude and gyle goo vndir, to haue þe ouyr honde and þe victorye. Thes peeple – and principally of þe norþe place – is wondur coryous and besy to knowyn and to tellyn tydyngis and noveltees and merveylles
80 syche as þey hane herde or seyen, prompt to sekyn oþur cuntres, seldoun ryche yn hure propir soyle, more happe in ferre and foreyn cuntrees þan yn hure owne cuntree, and kunne bettur purchasyn new þyngis owtewarde þen kepyn here owne hereditable þyngis at hoom; for þe which cause þey lyghtly wyllyn be disperbylde yn to
85 straunge cuntrees. This peeple is also apt and redy to euery dede and manhode; and aforne þat þey schuln ought doo, inportune þey byn and fulle hardy, but aftir þe dede bettir avysid and more avesy; and therfore þey lyghtly willyn forsake þat þey hane begunne. And for þis cause hit is þat pope Eugenye seide Ynglyssh peeple to been
90 apte and able to euery thynge what so euyr they wolde, and worþi to be preferryd beforn all othur peeplys, ne were þe lyghtnesse of hur hertis and the hasty changeablenesse of hur wylle; and lyke as Hannybal seyde Romaynes myght nevir been ouyrcomyn but yn hure owne cuntre, ryght so þe Englyssh peeple, quod he, the whiche
95 yn straunge and foreyn countrees been ynvyncible, in hur owne seetes ben moste esy to ouercomyn. This peple sone lothith and lakkith hur owne þyngis and prey[sy]th and commendyth oþur mennys þyngis, vnnethe ony tyme content with þe degre of hure owne estate, and suche þyngis as longithe to oþur men þey gladly
100 wyllyn transfyguryn yn hemself. For a yeman wyll takyn vpon hym þat longith to a squyeer, a squyeer that longith to a knyght, a knyght that longith to an erle, and an erle þat longith to a duke, a duke þat longyþe to a kynge. And this þey serclyn abowten euery kynde and þey byn yn no kynde, but þey attamyn and assayen
105 euery ordir and þey byn yn non ordyr. For yn hur apporte of araye they byn dysgysid as treiectours or mynstrals. In commynycacioun and talkyng þey byn Cicerones, þat is to say as eloquent and as gay yn speche as was þat grete rethoryan Marcus Tullius Cicero . . . And vniversaly in all Englyssh men so moche is growyn and customyd
110 þe variable and þe vnstable chaunge of cloþingis and þe monyfolde dyuersitees of aray, þat yche of hem as now-adayes semyth for to been newtur gendur, þat is to say of yche oþer nacyoun þen of his owne. Of þe which thynge prophecied onys an holy recluse or an

115

120

anchorite þe tyme of kynge Egilredus, as seiþ Henricus *libro* 6,
seying on þis wyse: for as moche as Ynglyssh men been yovyn to
prodicioun, to drounkynshipe, and to neclygence of goddis howse,
they schull be thries conquerid and born downe and put vndir:
firste, quod he, by Danys, the secounde tyme by Normaundus, and
þe þryde tyme by Scottis, whom they haue yn leste reputacioun;
and yn so moche schall than þe worlde be variant and vnstabull
þat þe variaunce and þe vnstablenes of mennys hertis and soulys
schall mone be notid and markyd by þe monyfolde variaunce and
dyuersitees of mennys cloþis.

Notes

6   **ynpermyxt** 'unmingled'   The earliest recorded use of a rare word,
        adopted from the Latin original, *impermixti*.

7   **propir**   The word has the Latin sense 'own, characteristic'.

9   **Flemmynges**   Repeated Flemish settlements were made in southern
        Pembrokeshire during the course of the twelfth century, commencing in
        1105. These were encouraged by successive English kings as a means of
        controlling the native Welsh.

18   **pilgryms** 'foreign, outlandish' (Latin text *peregrinos*)   This sense of the
        word is otherwise recorded only in the Wycliffite translation of the Bible.
        Blaberyng and *cheteryng* are relatively common fourteenth-century words
        of onomatopoeic formation.

24   **decre and ordynaunce**   The document to which Bokenham refers
        was in fact a fourteenth-century forgery, but this does not invalidate the
        sociolinguistic significance of his observations about usage. In his transla-
        tion, Trevisa notes that the teaching of Latin through English had been
        introduced in Oxford by John of Cornwall in 1349. *Donet* refers to the
        fourth-century grammar of Aelius Donatus, the most widely used intro-
        ductory Latin grammar in medieval schools.

26   **here owne modre tonge . . . forsakyn**   The syntax parallels the Latin
        ablative absolute construction (*derelicto proprio vulgari*). See also line 34
        (*And þis seeynge . . .*), which contains the type of construction exemplified
        by the author of the Preface to the Later Version of the Wycliffite Bible as
        an unidiomatic English rendering of the ablative absolute (Latin text *Quibus
        profecto . . .*).

37   **barbariȝid**   This is the earliest recorded use of the word in English in
        its technical Latin sense; that is, the introduction of words and phrasing of
        foreign origin into a 'pure' language, resulting in the *corrupcioun* of the
        original. See also line 11, a related but somewhat different sense, with an
        implied value judgement. Bokenham's use is independent of his original.

43   **lyneal climat** (*climate lineati*)   The technical sense of *climat*, 'belt under the same latitude', appears in the fourteenth century. The adjective *lyneal* serves to disambiguate the technical term. Adjectives with the Franco-Latin suffix -*al* (cf. *collaterall*, 45; *extremal*, 47) become much more common in the fifteenth century. Although *lyneal* and *collaterall* have counterparts in classical Latin, *extremal* is a medieval learned formation.

54   **the whiche**   This form of connective, modelled on French *liquels*, is frequent in technical and administrative prose from the fourteenth century onwards. Its purpose was that of text cohesion, and it was thus often followed by a noun repeating an earlier reference. Here the omission of the noun and the distant remove from its reference (*kyngis*) mean that it does not function effectively as a cohesive device and is best regarded as a mannerism connected with the author's aspiration to learned style.

54–55   **wone to be conuersaunte** 'accustomed to be habitually living'   The sense is once more close to that of the Latin, *converso*, but the word does not occur in the Latin text.

62   **commodious** 'convenient' (Latin text *accommodatiores*)   Bokenham's form is from Medieval Latin *commodiosus*.

70   **sumpteous** 'lavish, extravagant' (Latin text *sumptuosa*)   The first recorded use of this Franco-Latin borrowing in this sense.

75–76   **congresse and conflicte**   These Franco-Latin borrowings, both with the sense 'hostile encounter', are used earlier than Bokenham only in the ME translation of Vegetius's technical work on the art of war. The Latin text supplies only *congressus*.

83   **hereditable** 'able to be inherited, inherited' (Latin text *haereditaria*)   The earliest recorded use in English of the Franco-Latin legal term.

106   **treiectours** 'jugglers'   The borrowing took place from French before 1300, and the usual form is *tregetour*. The form here partially restores a supposed Latin form *trans-iactor*. A similar creation of an erroneous Latin form is seen in the development of the familiar *adventure* from earlier French *aventure*.

112   **newtur gendur** 'neuter gender, no clear type'   Bokenham enjoys grammatical comparisons, and in discussing Midlanders (65) he says that they share some of the qualities of both Northerners and Southerners, as a participle (a verbal adjective) shares the qualities of a verb and an adjective, but it is not certain that the allusion here is grammatical. Rather, he is using the vocabulary of Aristotelian classification to emphasise the variety and disorder of the English people.

22

A PASTON LETTER

The letter printed here was sent, probably from Norwich, by Margaret Paston to her husband John, who was on business in London. The date is about 19 May 1448. It is a particularly lively example from a series of family and business letters which commences in 1425 and spans four generations.

John Paston belonged to a family in the ascendant. They originated in the village of Paston, eight miles south of Cromer in Norfolk, and by the seventeenth century had risen to be one of the most important families in East Anglia. John's father, William (1378–1444), had been sent to school and founded the family fortunes by a career in the law. John himself (1421–66) was educated at Cambridge and the Inner Temple before entering his father's profession. He added to his inheritance by his marriage in about 1440 to Margaret Mautby, through whom he secured more land in Norfolk and Suffolk, and he was forced by lengthy absences in London to leave its administration in her extremely capable hands.

She is not, however, the writer of this letter. She was not literate so she dictated it to a clerk, James Gresham, who came from Holt in north Norfolk and had been a trusted employee of her father-in-law. The postscript, however, is in a different hand, employing a different orthographic system with far more marked East Anglian peculiarities (see notes). Nothing is known of this clerk except that Margaret employed him more than any other.

Ryght worshipfull husbond, I recomaund me to yow, and prey yow to wete þat on Friday last passed before noon, þe parson of Oxened beyng at messe in our parossh chirche, euyn atte leuacioun of þe sakeryng, Jamys Gloys hadde ben in þe tovne and come homward by Wymondams gate. And Wymondam stod in his gate and John Norwode his man stod by hym, and Thomas Hawys his othir man

stod in þe strete by þe canell side. And Jamys Gloys come with his
hatte on his hede betwen bothe his men, as he was wont of custome
to do. And whanne Gloys was ayenst Wymondham, he seid þus,
'Couere thy heed!' And Gloys seid ageyn, 'So I shall for the.' And
whanne Gloys was forther passed by þe space of iij or iiij strede,
Wymondham drew owt his dagger and seid, 'Shalt þow so, knave?'
And þerwith Gloys turned hym and drewe owt his dagger and
defendet hym, fleyng into my moderis place; and Wymondham
and his man Hawys kest stonys and dreve Gloys into my moderis
place. And Hawys folwyd into my moderis place and kest a ston as
meche as a forthyng lof into þe halle after Gloys; and þan ran owt
of þe place ageyn. And Gloys folwyd owt and stod withowt þe gate,
and þanne Wymondham called Gloys thef and seid he shuld dye,
and Gloys seid he lyed and called hym charl, and bad hym come
hymself or ell þe best man he hadde, and Gloys wold answere hym
on for on. And þanne Haweys ran into Wymondhams place and
feched a spere and a swerd, and toke his maister his swerd. And
with þe noise of þis asaut and affray my modir and I come owt of
þe chirche from þe sakeryng; and I bad Gloys go in to my moderis
place ageyn, and so he dede. And thanne Wymondham called my
moder and me strong hores, and seid þe Pastons and alle her kyn
were [charls of Gy]myngham [and w]e seid he lyed, knave and
charl as he was. And he had meche large langage, as ye shall knowe
herafter by mowthe.

After non my modir and I yede to þe Priour of Norwich and
told hym al þis cas, and þe Priour sent for Wymondham and
þerwhyle we yede hom ageyn and Pagraue come with vs hom.
And whil Wymondham was with þe Priour, and we were at hom
in our places, Gloys stod in þe strete at my moderis gate and Hawys
aspyed hym þere as he stod on þe Lady Hastyngis chambre. Anon
he come doun with a tohand swerd and assauted ageyn þe seid
Gloys and Thomas my moderis man, and lete flye a strok at Thomas
with þe sword and rippled his hand with his sword. And as for
þe latter assaut þe parson of Oxened sygh it and wole avowe it.
And moche more thyng was do, as Gloys can tell yow by mouthe.
And for þe perilx of þat myght happe by þese premysses and þe
circumstances þerof to be eschewed, by þ'aduyse of my modir and
oþer I send yow Gloys to attend upon yow for a seson, for ease
of myn owen hert; for in good feyth I wolde not for xl li. haue
suyche anoþer trouble.

As touchyng my Lady Morlé, she seith þat she atte hire wille
wol haue þe benyfyce of hire obligacion, for hir counseyll telleth
hir, as she seith, þat it is forfayt. And she wole not haue the relif til
50   she hath your homage, etc.

The Lord Moleyns man gaderyth up þe rent at Gresham a gret
pace, and Jamys Gresham shall telle yow more pleynly þerof at his
comyng.

Nomore at þis tyme, but Almyghty God haue yow in his kepyng.
55   Wretyn in hast on Trynyté Sunday at euyn.

Yours, MARGARET PASTON

As touchyng Roger Foke, Gloys shall telle yow all, etc. Qwhan
Wymdham seyd þat Jamys xuld dy I seyd to hym þat I soposyd þat
he xuld repent hym jf he schlow hym or dede to hym any bodyly
60   harm; and he seyd nay, he xuld never repent hym ner have a ferdyng
wurth of harm þow he kelyd ȝw and hym bothe. And I seyd ȝys,
and he sclow þe lest chylde þat longyth to ȝwr kechyn, and jf he
dede he were lyke, I sopose, to dy for hym. It js told me þat he xall
kom to London jn hast. I pray ȝw be ware hw ȝe walkyn jf he be
65   þere, for he js ful cursyd-hertyd and lwmysch. I wot wel he wyl not
set vpon ȝw manly, but I beleve he wyl styrt vpon ȝw or on sum of
ȝwr men leke a thef. I pray ȝw hertyly þat ȝe late not Jamys kom
hom aȝen in non wyse tyl ȝe kom home, for myn hertys ese; for be
my trwth I wold not þat he were hurt, ner non man þat longyth to
70   ȝw jn ȝwr absens for xx pwnd. And in gode feyth he js sore hatyd
both of Wymdam and sum of hys men, and of oþer þat Wymdam
tellyth to hys tale as hym lyst, for þer as Wymdam tellyth hys tale
he makyth hem belevyn þat Jamys js gylty and he no þyng gylty.

I pray ȝw hertyly here masse and oþer servys þat ȝe arn bwn to
75   here wyth a devwt hert, and I hope veryly þat ȝe xal spede ryth wele
in all ȝwr materys, be grase of God. Trust veryly in God and leve
hym and serve hym, and he wyl not deseve ȝw. Of all oþer materys
I xall sent ȝw wurd jn hast.

Notes

1   **Ryght worshipfull husbond**   The letter begins with a formal *salutatio*
or address followed by a *commendatio* and a formula *prey yow to wete* to
introduce the substance or *narratio* of the letter. Cf. Alfred's Preface to the
Pastoral Care, and the letter in Excerpt 19.

3–4   **atte leuacioun of þe sakeryng** 'elevation of the host'   The moment in the mass when the priest officiating raises the consecrated elements before the congregation. The form *atte* is a contraction of *at þe*.

4   **Jamys Gloys**   The Paston family chaplain, and frequently also the clerk who wrote Margaret Paston's letters.

9   **ayeynst Wymondham**   The sense is 'opposite' or 'face to face with'. Wymondham was a gentleman from Felbrigg near Cromer. His words 'protect your head!' are to be interpreted as a threat to which Gloys replies with a calculated insult, since fifteenth-century politeness required a hat to be removed at meeting in token of respect. According to Caxton (*Knight of the Tower*, ed. M. Y. Offord, EETS SS 2 (1971), pp. 24–5) this gesture was observed also by women.

20   **charl**   Like *thef*, *knave* and *stronge hore*, the accusation of being a 'churl' was a frequent insult in the fourteenth and fifteenth centuries. Such abusive language was frequently the cause of legal action and fines being imposed. In fourteenth-century texts, including Chaucer, the Scandinavian-derived form *carl* is used as an insult. The OE-derived form *cherle* is more often used as the description of a social estate. The form here is probably a blend, since the spellings representing the late ME change from *er* to *ar* are not found in other work by Gresham. The textual emendation which identifies the status of the Pastons in Gimmingham is the suggestion of C. M. Barron (1972).

36   **Lady Hastyngis**   Wymondham's wife.

46   **suyche**   This form of the word 'such' is predominantly a west Norfolk one. Gresham's language is not strongly dialectal. Most of the forms he uses were widespread in the south-east Midlands, but against this background there occur a number of less distinctively East Anglian forms: *wete*, 'know', *meche*, 'much', *folwyd* (in which the vowel between *l* and *w* has been elided), *wretyn*.

47   **As touchyng**   A favourite connective in clerkly and administrative writing, as also is the use of the cohesive *þe seid* (37). These suggest some freedom of composition within Margaret's dictation. But the coherence of the letter is not dependent on the curial style, since here clauses are connected by a succession of simple additive conjunctions which obscure the more complex causal and temporal connections (contrast Skelton's dedication of his translation of Diodorus Siculus).

57   **Qwhan**   This northern spelling of 'when' is more or less restricted, south of the Wash, to East Anglia, although occurring sporadically elsewhere. The spellings <xuld> and <xal> are, however, very markedly East Anglian and occur nowhere else. Other, less distinctively East Anglian forms in this postscript are: *schlow/sclow*, *kechyn*, *dede*, *leke*, *hem*, *arn*.

65   **lwmysch** 'contentious'   *MED* (s.v. *loumish*) records the word only from the East Anglian *Promptorium Parvulorum*.

23

MALORY, 'THE GIANT OF ST MICHAEL'S MOUNT'

On 31 July 1485 England's first printer, William Caxton, published a volume of the adventures of King Arthur, which he called (borrowing the title of the final book) *Le Morte Darthur*. In Caxton's text, the author identifies himself as 'syr Thomas Maleore, knyght', asks for his readers' prayers, and fixes the completion of his task during the year following 4 March 1469. Until 1934, when a manuscript was discovered at Winchester College, Caxton's print was all that was known of Malory's work. The discovery of the manuscript initiated a major reassessment, since not only did it demonstrate that Caxton had made significant changes to his copy, but it provided further details of its author which Caxton had suppressed, notably that the work had been finished in prison.

Attempts to identify this prisoner-knight have been beset by controversy, but the most generally-accepted candidate is an individual from Newbold Revell, Warwickshire, who died on 12 March 1471. His reconstructed career is strikingly eccentric, encompassing origins in an established local family, status as a landowner, service as an MP, and accusations of a list of crimes ranging from rape and attempted murder to cattle-raiding and extortion. He spent numerous periods in prison, making two successful escapes, and it is conjectured that the completion of his Arthurian compilation took place during his imprisonment as a result of unsuccessful political manoeuvring.

Caxton represented Malory's work as translated from French, which suited the prejudices of his intended audience, but this is only partly true, since Book V, from which these excerpts are taken, is in fact an adaptation of the north Midland ME alliterative *Morte Arthur*. Many of the alliterative phrases and some of the characteristic lexical items of the original remain. The contrast with Caxton is striking: alliterative patterns are discarded; unfamiliar words are replaced by more generally used ones; French-derived

of the foure elementꝭ it shuld be taken for the lasse noble/ꝫ
of thees seuen colours are dyfferenced all manere of armes
penoncelles and baners by dyuerse deuyses taken by hault-
nesse fro the tyme ryght auncyent/

¶ Explicit

¶Thus endeth this boke whiche xppyne of ppse made ꝫ drewe out of the boke named Vegecius de re militari ꝫ out of
tharbre of bataylles wyth many other thynges sett in to the
same requisite to werre ꝫ batailles whiche boke beyng in frē-
sshe was delyuered to me Willm Caxton by the most crysten
kynge ꝫ redoubted prynce my naturel ꝫ souerayn lord kyng
henry the/VIJ/ kyng of englond ꝫ of fraūce in his palais of
westmestre the/xxiij/day of Januyere the/iiij/yere of his regne ꝫ desired ꝫ wylled me to translate this said boke ꝫ reduce
it in to our english ꝫ natural tonge/ꝫ to put it in enprynte
to thende that euery gentylman born to armes ꝫ all manere
men of werre captayns/souldiours/vptayllers ꝫ all other
shold haue knowlege how they ought to behaue theym in the
fayttes of warre ꝫ of bataylles/and so delyuered me the said
book thêne my lord therle of Oxenford awaytig on his said
grace/whiche volume conteynyng four bokes/J receyued of
his said grace ꝫ accordig to his desire whiche to me J repute
a comandemêt/ꝫ verili glad to obeye/ꝫ after the litpl conyng
that god hath lente me J haue endeuoyrd me to the vtterest
of my power to fulfylle ꝫ accōplisshe his desire ꝫ comaunde-
ment/as wel to reduce it in to englysshe/as to put it in enprī-
te/to thende that it may come to the sight ꝫ knowlege of euery gentylman ꝫ man of warre/ꝫ for certayn in myn oppiny-
on it is as necessary a boke ꝫ as requysite/as ony may be for
euery estate hye ꝫ lowe that entende to the fayttes of werre

Plate 4 Caxton, *The Fayt of Arms and of Chyvalrye* (fols. 141r & 141v)

Whether it be in Bataylles sieges/rescowse/& all other fayttes
subtyltees & remedyes for meschieues/Whiche translacyon
was finysshed the/viij/ day of Juyll the sayd yere & enpryn
ted the/xiiij/ day of Juyll next folowyng & ful fynysshyd/ the~
ne syth I haue obeyed his most dredeful comaudement/I hum
bly byseche his most excellent & bounteuous hyeues to pardo~
ne me of this symple & rude translacion Where in be no cury
ous ne gaye termes of rethoryk/But I hope to almighti god
that it shal be entendyble & vnderstanden to euery man/& al
so that it shal not moche varye in sentence fro the coppy recey
ued of my said souerayn lord/And Where as I haue erryd
or made defaulte I beseche them that fynde suche to correcte it
& so doyng I shal praye for them/& yf ther be ony thig ther
in to his plasir/I am glad & thinke my labour wel enplo~
yed for to haue the name to be one of the litel seruantes to the
hiest & most cristen kyng & prince of the World/Whom I by
seche almyghty god to preserue/kepe/& contynue in his noble
& most redoubted enterpryses as wel in bretayn/flaudres &
other placis that he may haue victorie honour/& renomee to
his perpetual glorye/For I haue not herd ne redde that ony
prynce hath subdued his subgettis with lasse hurte & c̄ and
also holpen his neighbours & frendis out of this londe/In
Whyche hye enterprises I byseche almyghty god that he may
remayne alleway vyctoryous/And dayly encrease fro ver
tu to vertue & fro better to better to his laude & honour in this
present lyf/that after thys short & transitorye lyf/he may at~
teyne to euerlastyng lyf in heuen/ Whiche god gaunte to
hym and to alle his lyege peple   AMEN/

Per Caxton

lexical items are preferred; there is considerable condensation, turning the dramatic impact of the original into smooth narration. This contrast has recently been given sharper focus by the discovery of ink marks from printer's type in the Winchester manuscript, which prove that it must have been in Caxton's workshop throughout the 1480s.

As well as aspects of lexical style, Caxton also altered the grammatical forms of the original: the north Midland forms of the third-person singular in *-ys* and *-is* are replaced by the more southerly form in *-eth* and northern present participles in *-ande* are replaced by the more general *-ynge*.

Caxton had spent many years as a merchant in Bruges, and he imported the new technology of moveable type from sources in Belgium and Germany. Its manufacturers naturally attempted to imitate the writing practices of the skilled copyists who had hitherto been the producers of all books. The facsimile of the epilogue of the *Faytes of Armes* (published 14 July 1489) is set in Caxton's Type 6, a Flemish *bâtarde* type, which he preferred for the production of books of courtly entertainment and instruction. It emulates a prestigious Flemish style of handwriting of the period. The insular letters, ʒ and þ, are no longer used, but ligatures common in scribal practice are still found: the crossed *ll* and *th*, *he*, *ho*, *be*, *bo* and *re* among others. Long *s* is used initially and medially, but Continental *s* is used finally. Abbreviation marks, especially where a vowel is followed by a nasal, are common, and the Christian Chi-Rho symbol is used in rendering Christine de Pizan's name. Spellings follow scribal practice in showing the elision of the vowel of the definite article before a word beginning with a vowel: *therle*, *tharbre*. Apostrophes are not yet used in English. Punctuation is rather haphazard. The virgule (/) marks off the items in a list and sets off numerals from the text, as well as certain clauses. Capitalisation is used for proper nouns.

A   The Winchester text

Than the kynge yode up to the creste of the cragge, and than he comforted hymself with the colde wynde; and than he yode forth by two welle-stremys, and there he fyndys two fyres flamand full hyghe. And at that one fyre he founde a carefull wydow wryngande hire handys, syttande on a grave that was new marked. Than Arthure salued hir and she hym agayne, and asked hir why she sate sorowyng. 'Alas,' she seyde, 'carefull knyght! Thou carpys over lowde! Yon

is a werlow woll destroy us bothe. I holde the unhappy. What
doste thou on this mountayne? Thoughe here were suche fyffty, ye
were to feyble for to macche hym all at onys. Whereto berys thou
armoure? Hit may the lytyll avayle, for he nedys none other wepyn
but his bare fyste. Here is a douches dede, the fayryst that lyved; he
hath murthered that mylde withoute ony mercy; he forced hir by
fylth of hymself, and so aftir slytte hir unto the navyll.'

'Dame,' seyde the kynge, 'I com fro the noble conquerrour,
sir Arthure, for to trete with the tirraunte for his lyege peple.'

'Fy on suche tretyse,' she seyde than, 'for he settys nought
by the kynge nother by no man ellys. But and thou have brought
Arthurs wyff dame Gwenyvere he woll be more blyther of hir than
thou haddyste geffyn hym halfendele Fraunce. And but yf thou
have brought hir prese hym nat to nyghe. Loke what he hath done
unto fyftene kynges: he hath made hym a coote full of precious
stonys, and the bordoures thereof is the berdis of fyftene kynges,
and they were of the grettyst blood that dured on erthe. Othir
farme had he none of fyftene realmys. This presente was sente hym
to this laste Crystemasse; they sente hym in faythe for savyng of
their peple. And for Arthurs wyffe he lodgys hym here, for he hath
more tresoure than ever had Arthure or ony of his elders. And now
thou shalt fynde hym at souper with syx knave chyldirne, and there
he hath made pykyll and powder with many precious wynes, and
three fayre maydens that turnys the broche that bydis to go to his
bed, for they three shall be dede within four oures or the fylth is
fulfylled that his fleyshe askys.'

'Well,' seyde Arthure, 'I woll fulfylle my message for alle your
grym wordis.'

'Than fare thou to yondir fyre that flamys so hyghe, and there
thou shalt fynde hym sykerly for sothe.'

Than he paste forth to the creste of the hylle and syghe where
he sate at his soupere alone gnawyng on a lymme of large man, and
there he beekys his brode lendys by the bryght fyre and brekelys
hym semys. And three damesels turned three brochis, and thereon
was twelve chyldir but late borne, and they were broched in maner
lyke birdis. Whan the kynge behylde that syght his herte was nyghe
bledyng for sorow. Than he haylesed hym with angirfull wordys:

'Now He that all weldys geff the sorow, theeff, there thou syttes!
For thou art the fowlyste freyke that ever was fourmed, and fendly
thou fedyst the, the devill have thy soule! And by what cause, thou

carle, hast thou kylled thes Crysten chyldern? Thou haste made many
martyrs by mourtheryng of this londis. Therefore thou shalt have thy

50   mede thorow Mychael that owyth this mounte. And also, why haste
thou slayne this fayre douches? Therefore dresse the, doggys son, for
thou shalt dye this day thorow the dynte of my hondis.'

Than the gloton gloored and grevid full foule. He had teeth
lyke a grayhounde, he was the foulyst wyghte that ever man sye,

55   and there was never suche one fourmed on erthe, for there was
never devil in helle more horryblyer made: for he was fro the hede
to the foote fyve fadom longe and large. And therewith sturdely he
sterte uppon his leggis and caughte a clubbe in his honde all of
clene iron. Than he swappis at the kynge with that kyd wepyn. He

60   cruysshed downe with the club the coronal doune to the cold erthe.
The kynge coverede hym with his shylde and rechis a boxe evyn
infourmede in the myddis of his forehede, that the slypped blade
unto the brayne rechis. Yet he shappis at sir Arthure, but the kynge
shuntys a lytyll and rechis hym a dynte hyghe uppon the haunche,

65   and there he swappis his genytrottys in sondir.

Than he rored and brayed and yet angurly he strykes, and fayled
of sir Arthure and the erthe hittis, that he kutte into the swarffe a
large swerde-length and more. Than the kynge sterte up unto hym
and raught hym a buffette and kut his baly in sundir, that oute wente

70   the gore, that the grasse and the grounde all foule was begone.

Than he kaste away the clubbe and caughte the kynge in his
armys and handeled the kynge so harde that he crusshed his rybbes.
Than the balefull maydyns wronge hir hondis and kneled on the
grounde and to Cryste called for helpe and comforte of Arthur.

75   With that the warlow wrath Arthure undir, and so they waltyrde
and tumbylde over the craggis and busshys, and eythir cleyght other
full faste in their armys. And other whyles Arthure was aboven
and other whyle undir, and so weltryng and walowynge they rolled
doune the hylle, and they never leffte tyll they fylle thereas the floode

80   marked. But ever in the walterynge Arthure smyttes and hittis hym
with a short dagger up to the hyltys, and in his fallynge there braste
of the gyauntes rybbys three evyn at onys.

And by fortune they felle thereas the two knyghtes aboode
with theire horsis. Whan sir Kay saw the kynge and the gyaunt so

85   icleyght togyder,

'Alas,' sayd sir Kay, 'we ar forfete for ever! Yondir is our lorde
overfallen with a fende.'

'Hit is nat so,' seyde the kynge, 'but helpe me, sir Kay, for this corseynte have I clegged oute of the yondir clowys.'

90 'In fayth,' seyde sir Bedwere, 'this is a foule carle,' and caughte the corseynte oute of the kynges armys and there he seyde, 'I have mykyll wondir, and Mychael be of suche a makyng, that ever God wolde suffir hym to abyde in hevyn. And if seyntis be suche that servys Jesu, I woll never seke for none, be the fayth of my body!'

95 The kynge than lough at Bedwers wordis and seyde,

'This seynte have I sought nyghe unto my grete daunger. But stryke of his hede and sette hit on a trouncheoune of a speare, and geff hit to thy servaunte that is swyffte-horsed, and bere hit unto sir Howell that is in harde bondis, and bydde hym be mery, for

100 his enemy is destroyed.' And aftir in Barflete lette brace hit on a barbycan, that all the comyns of this contrey may hit beholde.

B   Caxton's text

And soo he ascended vp in to that hylle tyl he came to a grete fyre, and there he fonde a careful wydowe wryngynge her handes and makyng grete sorowe syttynge by a graue newe made. And thenne

105 kynge Arthur salewed her and demaunded of her wherfore she made suche lamentacion. To whome she ansuerd and sayd.

'Syre knyghte, speke softe for yonder is a deuyll. Yf he here the speke he wylle come and destroye the. I holde the vnhappy. What dost thow here in this mountayne? For yf ye were suche fyfty as ye

110 be ye were not able to make resystence ageynst this deuyll. Here lyeth a duchesse deede, the whiche was the fayrest of alle the world, wyf to syre Howel, duc of Bretayne. He hath murthred her in forcynge her and hath slytte her vnto the nauyl.'

'Dame,' sayd the kynge, 'I come fro the noble conqueroure

115 kynge Arthur for to treate with that tyraunt for his lyege peple.'

'Fy on suche treatys,' sayd she, 'he setteth not by the kynge ne by no man els. But and yf thou haue broughte Arthurs wyf dame Gweneuer he shalle be gladder than thow haddest gyuen to hym half Fraunce. Beware! Approche hym not to nygh, for he

120 hath vaynquysshed xv kynges and hath maade hym a cote ful of precious stones enbrowdred with theyre berdes, which they sente hym to haue his loue for sauacion of theyr peple at this laste Crystemasse. And yf thow wylt speke with hym at yonder grete fyre at souper.'

125   'Wel,' sayd Arthur, 'I wyll accomplysshe my message for al your
ferdful wordes.' And wente forth by the creast of that hylle and
sawe where he satte atte souper gnawynge on a lymme of a man,
bekynge his brode lymmes by the fyre, and bercheles, and thre fayr
damoysels tornynge thre broches wheron were broched twelue yonge
130   children, late borne, lyke yonge byrdes.

Whanne kynge Arthur beheld that pyteous sy3te he had grete
compassion on them, so that his hert bledde for sorowe; and hayled
hym, sayeng in this wyse:

'He that alle the world weldeth gyue the shorte lyf and shame-
135   ful dethe! And the deuyl haue thy soule! Why hast thow murthred
this duchesse? Therfor aryse and dresse the, thow gloton, for this
day shall thou dye of my hand.'

Thenne the gloton anone starte vp and tooke a grete clubbe in
his hand and smote at the kynge that his coronal fylle to the erthe.
140   And the kynge hytte hym ageyn that he carf his bely and cutte
of his genytours that his guttes and his entraylles fylle doune to
the ground. Thenne the gyaunt threwe awey his clubbe and caught
the kynge in his armes that crusshyd his rybbes. Thenne the thre
maydens knelyd doune and callyd to Cryst for helpe and comforte
145   of Arthur. And thenne Arthur weltred and wrong that he was
other whyle vnder and another tyme aboue. And so weltryng and
walowynge they rolled doune the hylle tyl they came to the see
marke, and euer as they soo weltred Arthur smote hym with his
daggar. And it fortuned they came to the place where as the two
150   knyghtes were and kept Arthurs hors. Thenne when they sawe the
kynge fast in the gyaunts armes they came and losed hym.

And thenne the kynge commaunded syr Kaye to smyte of the
gyaunts hede and to sette it vpon a truncheon of a spere and bere
it to syre Howel and telle hym that his enemy was slayne, 'and after
155   late this hede be bounden to a barbycan that alle the peple may see
and behold hit'.

Notes

7   **Thou carpys** 'you speak' (from OSc *karpa*)   Second-person singular
forms with *-ys* and *-is* inflexions belong to the north Midlands and the
North (elsewhere *-est*). The verb *carpen* is common in (but not restricted
to) alliterative verse.

8   **werlow** 'devil' (from OE *wærloga*, cf. *warlock*)   Commoner in northern ME and in alliterative verse.

unhappy 'unfortunate' (OSc *happ*).

13   **that mylde**   The class shift (conversion) of adjectives to fulfil nominal functions is common in alliterative verse.

19   **more blyther**   Double comparatives of this kind arise in Early Middle English. The modern rules, by which monosyllabic adjectives show comparison by the use of an inflexion (except in special stylistic choices), developed in the seventeenth century.

29   **knave chyldirne** 'boy children'   The OE *cild* had both an endingless neuter plural and the nominative plural form *cilderu*. From the latter, with the centralisation of the final vowel, alternative forms developed: *childer* (with loss of final *-e*) and *childeren* (with the adoption of the Weak noun plural inflexion). The above form, like the modern standard one, therefore represents a historically double plural.

31   **that turnys**   Present-tense plural inflexions in *-ys* or *-is* are most frequent to the north of an approximate line from the Mersey to the Wash.

40–41   **brekelys hym semys** 'he seems to be without breeches'   The impersonal is grammatically unusual and may have arisen from confusion about the nature of the construction. Ordinarily the dative pronoun (*hym*, *me*, etc.) would refer to the person experiencing the appearance of something. Here it acts as subject of the verb. Impersonal constructions continued to be formed in the Early ME period, but had ceased to be productive in the fifteenth century.

44   **angirfull wordys** 'hostile words' (cf. OSc *angr* and Lat. *angor*)   The insults used (*theeff* and *carl* especially) were frequent in the fourteenth and fifteenth centuries (see Excerpt 22).

46   **freyke** 'creature'   Derived from the OE poetic word *freca*, 'warrior, hero'. It is most frequent in (although not restricted to) alliterative verse.

54   **sye** 'saw'   This is essentially a south Midland form, occurring most frequently south of the Wash.

60   **colde erthe**   For the poetic use of the adjective *colde* with its associations with fatality and death, see Excerpt 7.

73   **balefull**   Cf. *carefull* (4). According to *OED*, *baleful* was essentially a poetic word before the nineteenth century. Subjective reference, where the sense is 'full of pain or suffering', is almost restricted to consciously literary contexts, and is extremely rare after the sixteenth century.

85   **icleyght** 'clasped'   Past participle of *clechen*. See also *clegged* (89), 'seized, captured' (presumably from an unrecorded OE *clēcen*).

86   **ar**   This endingless form is recorded mostly in a belt bounded by a line from Morecambe Bay to the Humber in the North, and from the Mersey to the Wash in the South, but occurs also in London.

89   **corseynte** 'relic' (OF *cors saint*, 'holy body (of a saint)')   St Michael's Mount was a place of pilgrimage.

        clowys 'rocky bluffs' (OE *clōh*)   Like its modern form, *clough*, the word has a northerly distribution.

104   **makyng grete sorowe**   Caxton makes considerable use of verbal phrases modelled on French constructions with *faire* or *avoir*. See also *made . . . lamentacion* (106), *make resystence* (110), *had . . . compassion* (131–32).

111   **the whiche**   This connective is characteristic of bureaucratic English in the early fifteenth century, where its use is modelled on that of French *liquels*. It occurs already in Chaucer, and becomes very frequent among fifteenth-century writers. Note also the use of *to whome* in line 106, well separated from its antecedent. Both these connective devices have their ultimate origins in administrative Latin.

122   **haue his loue . . .**   This awkward construction again betrays the nature of the administrative prose that Caxton took as his model. The word *loue* is used with diplomatic significance only. Note also Caxton's selection of an abstract nominal phrase in preference to the more obvious verbal one.

131–32   **that pyteous syȝte . . . compassion**   Caxton's addition is a cliché of the kind of courtly narrative into which he is transforming Malory's work.

149   **fortuned**   The verb was used in the late fourteenth century to mean 'predestine'. In the fifteenth century it seems to have been adopted, often in legal and administrative language, as a more dignified alternative to *fallen* or *happen*.

24

JOHN SKELTON, TRANSLATION OF

THE *BIBLIOTHECA HISTORICA*

OF DIODORUS SICULUS

S kelton's translation of Diodorus Siculus, made from the Latin version of Poggio, is included as an extreme example of aureation in prose. The description of style as 'aureate' originated early in the fifteenth century with John Lydgate, who used it of his own stylistic aspirations in verse. It implies a careful consciousness in verbal choice based on rhetorical ideals, and more particularly a choice which will lend to the discourse both euphony in sound and dignity through the associations of the words selected. This generally results in the employment of vocabulary and sentence constructions with strong Latin associations. The second sentence here is of lengthy periodic structure, participular clauses are frequent, and the Latin ablative absolute construction can be seen to underlie lines 33–34, 42 and 44. The practice – though not the theory – of aureation is already evident in the bureaucratic and administrative English of some early fifteenth-century letters (see Excerpt 19), and lexical elaboration increases throughout the century. By Skelton's time the practice was a fully conscious and deliberate literary technique expressed in lexical doublets, and heavy modification and qualification. Looking back in his poem *Phyllyp Sparowe* to the time of Chaucer, Skelton found his English attractively simple and clear; but the praise is ambiguous, also implying some lack of distinction. In his own translation of Diodorus Siculus, Skelton was concerned to draw attention to himself as a learned practitioner in the artifice of rhetoric.

Details of Skelton's early life are lacking, although his family probably came from Yorkshire, and he himself was born in the early 1460s. He is best known for his vigorous and often polemical English verse, but three universities (Oxford, Louvain and Cambridge) between 1488 and 1493 honoured his skills in Latin rhetoric, and his translation of Diodorus Siculus is praised by Caxton in his prologue to *Eneydos* (1490). By 1488 he had joined the royal household, later becoming tutor to Prince Henry, and in 1496 he was described by Erasmus as the 'light and glory' of English letters. Although his career was not without reversals, he was closely associated with the court and acted as a kind of 'poet laureate' to Henry VIII, producing a poem to celebrate the Scottish defeat at Flodden in 1513. He died on 21 June 1529.

The precise date at which Skelton translated Diodorus Siculus is unknown, but the text survives in a single manuscript (Corpus Christi College, Cambridge 357) whose paper was probably manufactured in 1486–87.

For the difficulte of the processe, it briefly can not be expowned what the pagans, other-wise called paynyms, supposed of their goddis, and what they were that first gaaue enformacion to haue theyr goddes in reuerence and worshipp, and what oppynyon they hadde
5   of their inmortalite. But, as touchynge those thynges whiche vnto thistorye apperteyne, so as they may be more open and manyfeste vnto theym that shall it here and rede, distributynge theym in-to certayn chapitres so as that nothynge notable of memory shal be lefte behynde and not recounted, takynge our pryncyple of those
10   yeris and seasons passed of olde, as moche as maybe done in maters so remotyue, we shal wryte of mannes generacion and of alle the thynges whiche were doon in auncyente dayes by alle the world enuyron. By the iudicial oppynyon of clerkis and noble connynge men whiche brought vnto remembraunce the nature of thynges
15   and mater historyous, it is said hou the first generacion of man was by two maner wayes: somme iudged that the world was without begynnynge and incorruptyble, and that mankynde was without orygynal; somme estemyd how the world had a bygynnynge and that it was corruptible, and how men had the begynnynge of theyr
20   generacion by chaunce.
For they had this opynyon that from the first premordial of thynges, heuen and erthe had one ideal inmyxte with their nature; of whens, by distyncte bodyes to-gydre, this world toke this maner of ordre as we see. The aier for his parte toke his contynuel motyf;
25   the fyre for his parte by reson of his lightnes atteyned vnto supreme regyons of the ayer. Of the same consideracion, the sonne and the sterris toke their courses for theyr parte. And that mater engrosed

that was slymy and pounderous by commyxtion of humours, by
resons of his grosenes compacte, stode stylle and in his place
30 remayned. The see hou it was of moysture qualyfyed. The erthe
hou it was cloddy and clayye by qualitees endurate, and so euermore
remayneth soddy and softe. This erthe, whan it was first condensyd
and somwhat enthycked with the sonnes radyant hete, his superficyal
or vppermost parte by force of hete enbolned in many placis, ther
35 were many humours coagulate in whiche were exorted putryfactions
couerd ouer wyth a frotthy rayne as we see in fennys, plasshes, and
stondynge waters whan the feruencye of the ayer sodenly chauffeth
the cold ground. Whan it is soo that ony engendrure is made in
thyngis of moisture by hete therto annexed, and where-as by nyghte
40 the ayer [that] extendith enuyron mynystrith moisture, whiche
humour by dayetyme thurgh hete of the sonne is engrossyd, thenne
at the laste tho putrefactions vnto an hepe to-gyder ensommed, in
maner as it were the tyme of delyueraunce faste approchynge nygh,
and thoo frotthy raynes dissoluyd, they brynge forth formes and
45 facions of alle maner thynge vegetal and sensible lyf. Of whome,
those thyngis whiche hadde more hete than other, for theyr parte
were made byrdys and flewe vpp in-to the supreme region of
the ayer; and those that contenyd in theym moste of the erthe,
they were made crepynge wormes and other lyuynge bestes. Those
50 that toke for theyr parte moisture naturall, were brought vnto the
elemente of theyr kynde and callyd by name fysshes of the water.
The erthe fro thens forth endreyed from day to day with thardaunt
hete of the sonne bemes, as wel as by the blastys of wynde, it lefte
alle engendrynge of more vegetal bestes of sensible lyf; but those
55 that alle-redy were engendryd, by commyxtion eche of other they
engendryd by procreacion other creatures.

This oppynyon had Euripules, Anoxagoras that philosopher's
discyple, that where-as the heuen and the erthe were first myxte
to-gydre by inperfection; after, they were separated. And thenne
60 they brought forth euery thynge after theyr nature, as trees, byrdes,
wylde bestes, and alle maner of kyndely thynge.

How-be-it vnto dyuerse persones the first generacion of the
erthe be incredible; yet, not-withstondynge, thynges whiche a dayes
be done inferre a trew testymonye of the premysses. Not fer fro
65 Thebas of the contrey of Egipte, after that the grete deluge of the
flode of Nylus was ceased, the feruente hete of the sonne chafynge
the wosy myre and fylthe whiche of the water remayned, grete

70

multitude of myse out of syssures and ruptures of the erthe in many
places was engendrid: whiche in maner is an euydence approuyd
that of the prymordiall begynnynge of the world in lyke wyse alle
maner of lyuynge creatures was engendrid. And semblably, they
saye, at the begynnynge men were engendryd; and that they sought
their sustenaunce in the wylde felde, nakedly lyuynge in the busshy
wyldernesse; vnto whome herbes and fruytes of the tre of their owne

75

natural growynge mynystred their dayly fode and repaste; and
how wylde bestes and rauenous were toward this people, of cruelte
moeued, passynge noyous; whome to resiste and withstonde, they
accompanyed theym-self to-gydre for drede and wele encomyne,
eche of theym dyde other assiste and supporte, ordeyned places for

80

theym-self to enhabyte; and where-as claterynge and noyse whiche
they made in maner was but confuse, afterward it grewe vnto a
parfyght voys and language intelligyble, and so they aptly applyed
vnto euery thynge the very propre name. But for-as-moche as they
were situated in dyuerce places of the world, men saye, they spack

85

not all after one language. Whereupon appiered varyaunce of speche
and dyuerse carrecters and figures of lettres. And how the first
confluence of men to-gyder encompanyed, they saye, was the first
orygynal of their nacion and people.

Notes

2   **pagans . . . paynyms** (Lat. *paganus*; OF *paienime*)   The use of etymological doublets, such as these, and paired synonyms lends weight to the
expression.

5   **inmortalite**   This form, using the Latin prefix -*in*, is a learned reconstruction. The two nasals, /n/ and /m/, had been assimilated to produce
immortalitas even in classical times. See also *inperfection* (59).
       touchynge   The word is commonly used as a connective device in
formal and official prose. The technique derives from French administrative prose.

11   **remotyue** 'remote, distant'   The use of the suffix -*yue* (Lat. -*ivus*) is
normally restricted at this time to formations on a French or Latin base,
but here is not justified by the existence of a Latin parallel (classical Lat.
remotus). Moreover, the suffix is normally used to form adjectives from a
verbal base.

13   **iudicial** 'judicious'   The modern sense of pertaining to a judge or legal
matters had been established for more than a century. *OED* records a very
few uses with Skelton's sense in the sixteenth and seventeenth centuries.
See note to line 15.

Standardisation of the written language, based upon the language used by the clerks of Chancery during the fifteenth century, proceeded further, but considerable variation in spelling persisted throughout the period of Early Modern English. Within the spoken language, the prestige of London speech began to assert itself. Already, in the late fifteenth century, Caxton had acknowledged the provinciality of a Kentish dialect, and in 1580 George Puttenham, in his *Arte of English Poesie*, recommended that would-be authors use 'the usual speach of the Court, and that of London and the shires lying about London within sixty myles and not much above'. Echoing the Latin rhetorical origins of much of the synchronic study of English, opinions on its pronunciation pre-date those on its vocabulary and grammar. John Palsgrave (1530) and Sir Thomas Elyot in his *The Governour* (1531) both agree that English is subject to variation in the perceived worth of pronunciations. The latter applies to sociolinguistic and historical developments in the everyday spoken language those rhetorical ideas of the vices of letter and syllable which Chaucer had thought appropriate only to verse composition 150 years earlier. Such emphasis on English elocution led to the study of phonetics and spelling. John Hart's *An Orthographie* (1569), like Gil's *Logonomia Anglica*, is prescriptive in spirit and somewhat fanciful in its representation of phonetic facts, but by the mid seventeenth century the study of the phonetics of English emerged with a more scientific spirit in the works of John Wallis (*Grammatica Linguae Anglicanae*, 1653) and Charles Cooper (*Grammatica Anglicana*, 1685). The eighteenth century brought popular works on the subject, such as the dictionary of pronunciation by an ex-actor, John Walker, first published in 1791 and repeatedly reprinted.

The most striking linguistic developments during the Early Modern period also concern the pronunciation of the language, and may be viewed as continuing the series of raisings of the Great Vowel Shift. By 1750 the sound system of standard English possessed seven long-vowel phonemes – /iː/, /eː/, /uː/, /ɔː/, /oː/, /ɛː/, /aː/ – and the diphthongs /ʌi/, /aʊ/, /ɔi/, /juː/, /oʊ/. Changes among the consonants include the loss by 1630 of initial /k/, /g/ and /w/ in words like *knight*, *gnaw* and *write*, and of post-vocalic /l/ in *walk* and *folk*. Post-vocalic /r/ was lost in words like *arm* and *earth* by about 1800.

Morphological changes in the period were much more limited than those which distinguish Middle English from Old English, but there was considerable variation in both morphology and syntax and some important developments in the latter sphere. The loss in Middle English of extensive noun inflexion and the simplification of the pronoun system led to a syntactical rather than morphological perception of the possessive genitive marker: -(e)s was in effect released from its place in the paradigm. In the sixteenth century it was freely attached to nominal groups, and 'group genitives' such as *the king of England's law* emerged alongside (and then displaced) the older type: *the king's law of England*. Ascham and Lyly frequently substitute an inflected pronoun, *his*, for the apostrophe *s*. The third-person-singular possessive in Middle English lacked a form with which to distinguish animate from inanimate reference: *his* or *hire* was used in either case. Discrimination was possible in the subject case, where three distinct forms had long existed: *he*, *she*, *(h)it*. *Hit* was used as a possessive in the fourteenth century, and the form *its* developed analogically during the first half of the sixteenth, although it is still avoided by Shakespeare. The emergence of *you* in place of *ye* as the subject form of the second-person-plural pronoun followed a process of case simplification which had affected nouns in the Middle English period. Shakespeare was content to use the new form, retaining *ye* for passages of elevated style, but the translators of the King James Bible (1611) limited their usage to the older form. The Middle English distinction in the use of *ye/you* from *thou*, by which the former implied politeness and the latter familiarity, superiority, or contempt for the addressee, continued but was abandoned in the latter half of the seventeenth century in the South. The emergence of *who*, *which* as relative pronouns, commencing in the Middle English period, was followed in the seventeenth century by the modern distinction between personal and non-personal reference. Verbal endings in -*es* of the third-person-singular present tense can be found in London texts from the early fourteenth century, but seem to have been avoided by writers before Elizabethan times. They then begin to displace the earlier -*eth* ending. Queen Elizabeth herself used them increasingly in her letters; nevertheless the words *hath* and *doth* are usually written in this form, and may have preserved the pronunciation longer. Appearances may, however, be deceptive, since Richard Hodges comments in his *A Special Help to Orthographie* (1643) that in his time, although -*eth* was written, this was pronounced [əz], at least in multisyllabic words.

Syntactical developments also include the final abandonment of double negation in the standard language and the use of more periphrastic tense forms. Considerable fluctuation is apparent in the use of the periphrastic form with the auxiliary *do*. A simple table illustrates the usage in Shakespeare, Middle English and Modern Standard English. Parentheses indicate those usages which are currently marked or marginal.

	Declarative	*Interrogative*	*Imperative*
Do-peri.	(ME) Sh (ModE)	Sh ModE	Sh (ModE)
Plain	ME Sh ModE	ME (Sh)	ME Sh ModE

The negative is as follows:

Do-peri.	(ME) Sh ModE	Sh ModE	Sh ModE
Plain	ME (Sh)	ME (Sh)	ME (Sh)

As in other syntactical matters, the flexibility of usage permissible in Elizabethan English is apparent.

Changes in the lexicon in the Early Modern period consist in part of the continuation of Latin influence noted in Later Middle English and associated with the 'Inkhorn Controversy', but borrowings from Spanish and Italian now join these traditional sources of new vocabulary. Striking, too, is the ease with which words migrate between word-classes. The influence of Latin is strongly apparent in word-formation, where for example Latin derivational affixes are sometimes considered equivalent to those of native origin. Thus Shakespeare uses the native suffix *-ed* just as if it were the Latin *-atus*, 'having a': *mouthed wounds, stelled fires*. Nor is this restricted to poetic language: in botanical description in Culpeper's *Herbal* the leaves of the agrimony are described as *dented* (i.e. 'with teeth').

25

THOMAS WILSON,

THE ARTE OF RHETORIQUE

Thomas Wilson (*c.* 1523–81) was the son of prosperous Lincolnshire farming folk who were in a position to send him to Eton and then to King's College, Cambridge. At the first of these he would have undergone an education including the principles of Latin rhetoric, and in Cambridge he may have attended lectures on Greek given by Sir John Cheke, the chief proponent of pure English in the stylistic debates of the sixteenth century. Wilson's earliest work was completed in Latin while acting as a tutor in Cambridge, but he followed this with the first English handbook on logic, and two years later in 1553 he produced his *Arte of Rhetorique*, the first complete work on rhetoric in the English language. After suffering persecution during the reign of Queen Mary, he studied in Italy, gained legal qualifications and returned to England with the accession of Queen Elizabeth. His *Arte of Rhetorique* was reprinted in 1560. His legal career now began, and, with patronage from Archbishop Parker, it flourished. He interested himself in and published on political questions, becoming first a royal ambassador and finally a member of the Privy Council.

Rhetoric is that art which instructs on how to make effective legal and political speeches, and, by extension, how to express one's view effectively in any circumstances. Instruction in rhetoric could therefore be considered a necessary skill for public life. Wilson's *Arte of Rhetorique*, which adapted the traditional Latin treatment of rhetoric to the interests of his own time, proved popular, and went through eight editions. It was divided into six sections: on the selection of subject matter (*inventio*), structure of the speech (*dispositio*), narration (*narratio*), style (*elocutio*), techniques of memorising (*memoria*) and techniques of presentation and delivery (*pronunciatio*). The following excerpt is what Wilson has to say about simplicity or plainness, the first and most basic of Ciceronian precepts of good style. Its adaptation to the intellectual world of its time means that much of it is concerned with the debate on the place in English of lexical reinforcement from foreign sources, and especially from learned Latin. Wilson deplores the use of elaborate diction where this is merely a badge of fashion and a substitute for meaning, but acknowledges that certain registers need technical diction, and that in those registers foreign phrases have become naturalised. The supposed letter from Lincolnshire was probably never written in this form, yet almost all the words it contains have occurred in the writings of others.

Emong al other lessons, this should first be learned, that we never affect any straunge ynkehorne termes, but so speake as is commonly received: neither sekyng to be over fine, nor yet livyng over carelesse, usyng our speache as most men do, and ordryng our
5   wittes, as the fewest have doen. Some seke so farre for outlandishe Englishe, that thei forget altogether their mothers language. And I dare swere this, if some of their mothers were alive, thei were not able to tell, what thei say, and yet these fine Englishe clerkes, wil saie thei speake in their mother tongue, if a man should charge
10   them for counterfeityng the kynges English. Some farre jorneid jentlemen at their returne home, like as thei love to go in forrein apparell, so thei wil pouder their talke with oversea language. He that cometh lately out of France, wil talke Frenche English, and never blushe at the matter. Another choppes in with Englishe
15   Italianated, and applieth the Italian phrase, to our Englishe speaking, the whiche is, as if an Oratour that professeth to utter his minde in plaine Latine, would needes speake Poetrie, and farre fetched colours of straunge antiquitie. The lawyer wil store his stomack with the pratyng of Pedlers. The Auditour in makyng his
20   accompt and rekenyng, cometh in with sise sould, and cater denere, for vi.s. iiii.d. The fine Courtier wil talke nothyng but Chaucer. The misticall wise menne, and Poeticall Clerkes, will speake nothyng but quaint proverbes, and blynd allegories, delityng muche in their awne darkenesse, especially, when none can tell what thei dooe
25   saie. The unlearned or foolishe phantasticall, that smelles but of learnyng (suche felowes as have seen learned men in their daies) will so latine their tongues, that the simple cannot but wonder at their talke, and thynke surely thei speake by some Revelacion. I knowe them that thynke Rhetorique, to stande wholy upon darke
30   woordes, and he that can catche an ynke horne terme by the taile,

hym thei compt to bee a fine Englishe man, and a good Rhetorician. And the rather to set out this folie, I will adde here suche a letter, as Willyam Sommer himself, could not make a better for that purpose. Somme will thinke and swere it to, that there was never any
35   suche thyng written, well I wil not force any man to beleve it, but I will saie thus muche, and abide by it to, the like have been made heretofore, and praised above the Monne.

A letter divised by a Lincolneshire man, for a voide benefice, to a gentilman that then waited upon the lorde Chauncellour, for the
40   tyme beyng.

Ponderyng, expendyng, and revolutyng with my self your ingent affabilitee, and ingenious capacitee, for mundane affaires: I cannot but celebrate and extolle your magnificall dexteritee, above all other. For how could you have adepted
45   suche illustrate prerogative, and dominicall superioritee, if the fecunditee of your ingenie had not been so fertile, and wounderfull pregnaunt. Now therfore beeyng accersited, to suche splendent renoume, and dignitee splendidious: I doubt not but you will adivuate suche poore adnichilate
50   orphanes, as whilome ware condisciples with you, and of antique familiaritie in Lincolne shire. Emong whom I beeyng a Scholasticall panion, obtestate your sublimitee to extoll myne infirmitee. There is a sacerdotall dignitee in my native countrey, contiguate to me, where I now
55   contemplate: whiche your worshipfull benignitee, could sone impetrate for me, if it would like you to extend your scedules, and collaude me in them to the right honorable lorde Chauncellor, or rather Archigrammacion of Englande. You knowe my literature, you knowe the pastorall promo-
60   cion, I obtestate your clemencie, to invigilate thus muche for me, accordyng to my confidence, and as you know my condigne merites, for suche a compendious livyng. But now I relinquishe to fatigate your intelligence with any more frivolous verbositie, and therfore he that rules the
65   climates be evermore your beautreux, your fortresse, and your bulwarke. Amen.

Dated at my Dome, or rather Mansion place, in Lincolnshire, the penulte of the moneth sextile. *Anno Millimo, quillimo, trillimo. Per me Johannes Octo.*

70   What wise man readyng this letter, will not take him for a very
      Caulfe, that made it in good earnest, and thought by his ynkepot
      termes, to get a good personage. Doeth wit reste in straunge wordes,
      or els standeth it in wholsome matter, and apt declaryng of a
      mannes mynd? Do we not speake, because we would have other to
75   understand us, or is not the tongue geven for this ende, that one
      might know what another meaneth? And what unlearned man can
      tell, what half this letter signifieth? Therfore, either we must make
      a difference of Englishe, and saie some is learned Englishe, and
      other some is rude Englishe, or the one is courte talke, the other is
80   countrey speache, or els we must of necessitee, banishe al suche
      affected Rhetorique, and use altogether one maner of language.
      When I was in Cambrige, and student in the kynges College, there
      came a man out of the toune, with a pinte of wine in a pottle pot,
      to welcome the provost of that house, that lately came from the
85   court. And because he would bestow his present like a clerke,
      dwellyng emong the schoolers: he made humbly his thre curtesies,
      and said in this maner. Cha good even my good lorde, and well
      might your lordship vare: Understandyng that your lordeship was
      come, and knowyng that you are a worshipfull Pilate, and kepes a
90   bominable house: I thought it my duetie to come incantivantee,
      and bryng you a pottell a wine, the whiche I beseche your lordeship
      take in good worthe. Here the simple man beyng desirous to amende
      his mothers tongue, shewed hymself not to bee the wisest manne,
      that ever spake with tongue.
95   Another good felowe in the countrey, beyng an officer, and
      Maiour of a toune, and desirous to speake like a fine learned man,
      havyng just occasion to rebuke a runnegate felow, said after this
      wise in a greate heate. Thou yngram and vacacion knave, if I take
      thee any more within the circumcision of my dampnacion: I will so
100   corrupte thee, that all vacacion knaves shall take ilsample by thee.

Notes

2   **ynkehorne termes**   'Inkhorn' or 'Inkpot' were the epithets used by
      opponents of the practice to castigate the use of learned foreign borrow-
      ings. The earliest use of this kind in *OED* is in 1543.
6   **mothers**   The possessive has lost the unstressed *e* of the ME inflexion
      -*es*, but the *s* is still written as though perceived as an inflexion. No apos-
      trophe is printed.

8   **clerkes**   Wilson conservatively writes <er> in most occurrences, but see the spelling *farre* (ME *ferre*) in line 10.

10   **counterfeityng**   The image comparing language with coinage is traditional in the rhetorical tradition. Cf. Horace, *Ars Poetica*, 58–59.

farre jorneid   Although this phrase is not hyphenated in the text, its function as a modifier and its syntactic pattern parallel to that of many contemporary exocentric compounds suggest that it would be understood as a compound. Cf. *farre fetched* (17–18).

12   **oversea**   This is not a new compound but rather a case of conversion from an adverb to adjectival function. The adverbial phrase goes back to Old English, but the adjectival function belongs to the sixteenth century.

15   **Italianated**   The two derivational suffixes (-*ate* and -*ed*) here perform the same function, converting the adjective to a quasi-passive participle. Their sense is something like 'caused to have the qualities of'. The former is from the Latin passive participle ending in -*atus*, and its use is restricted to Franco-Latin bases in Middle English. It becomes more widely productive in the sixteenth century, and with the native past participle inflexion -*ed* is used to create adjectives from nouns as well as verbs.

17   **needes**   Historically an adverb formed by the addition of the -*es* inflexion to a noun base: 'of need'.

21   **Chaucer**   Presumably a reference to the opinions of the archaisers who contended that English style could be improved by the readoption of words and phrases from earlier times. The poet Spenser was later influenced by such views.

25   **smelles**   Wilson usually uses the -*eth* inflexion of the third-person singular in his more earnest discourse, but in his illustration of comic failures in the art of *pronunciatio* he produces a racy list in which all the third-person verbs, singular and plural, end in -*es*. See also *kepes* (89). Despite this distinction, there is little doubt that, except in formal situations, it would have been natural for Wilson to use the -*es* type.

29   **thynke . . . to stande**   This clause imitates closely the Latin accusative and infinitive construction.

31   **compt**   In the French of the fifteenth century, and subsequently in English, the *p* of Latin *computare* was restored to the spelling of a word which had previously existed as ME *counte*.

33   **Sommer**   The court fool to Henry VIII from 1525 to 1547.

41   **expendyng**   Lat. *expendere*, 'to weigh'.

42   **ingent affabilitee** 'enormous approachability'   Both words previously recorded in the late fifteenth century. As with all the words in this letter, the senses are those of the Latin forms from which they are derived.

mundane 'of the world'   Lat. *mundanus*.

44   **adepted** 'achieved'   From Lat. *adeptus*, 'having attained'. The earliest recorded use of a rare word.

45   **illustrate . . . dominicall** 'illustrious . . . lordly'   The letter is well sprinkled with words exhibiting the Latin-derived suffixes -*ate* and -*all*.

47   **accersited** 'summoned'   Lat. *accersitus*, past participle of *accersere*.

49   **adnichilate** 'reduced to nothing, annihilate'   Medieval Latin form of a verb which had previously been borrowed from Old French. The verb has been remodelled on the past participle inflexion -*atus*.

52   **panion**   An aphetic (that is, with loss of initial unstressed vowel) form of *companion*.

      obtestate   Lat. *obtestare*, 'call to witness'.

53   **extoll**   Lat. *extollere*, 'raise up'.

56   **impetrate**   Lat. *impetrare*, 'obtain by request'.

57   **scedules** 'letters'   Medieval Lat. *scedula*, 'a slip or roll of parchment containing writing'.

62   **condigne** 'wholly worthy'   Perhaps through French from Latin *condignus*. The word was popular in late fifteenth-century aureate verse.

      compendious 'advantageous'   Lat. *compendiosus*. The -*ous* suffix is associated with stylistic elevation since, before the sixteenth century, it derived adjectives only from French or Latin bases.

67   **Dome** 'house'   Lat. *domus*.

71   **Caulfe** 'idiot'   The <au> spelling testifies to diphthongisation of ME /ɑ/ before /lf/. This was followed during the sixteenth century by the loss of /l/, but this development is not apparent from the spelling.

72   **Doeth**   In Middle English interrogatives were formed by subject–verb inversion. The use of auxiliary *do* for this purpose and in negatives developed rapidly during the earlier sixteenth century.

78   **a difference**   Wilson is proposing that English may be stylistically variable. The opposite assumption is the untenable one that English consists of a single style (*maner*).

87   **Cha**   A reduced form of a phrase with the south-eastern dialect form of the pronoun I (*ich*). Usually means 'I have'. Used by Elizabethan writers as an index of rural unsophistication. Compare *King Lear* IV. vi. 235. The grammar seems strange here, and the symbolic associations of the phrase may be paramount.

88   **vare**   Illustrates the initial voicing of /f/ found in Middle English throughout the South and south-west Midlands.

91   **the whiche**   This type of connective, although originally part of an elevated written style, was evidently well enough known by this time to be selected by this kind of speaker.

97   **runnegate** 'renegade'   But a popular form in the sixteenth and seventeenth centuries as a more general term of abuse. This form derives through Middle English and French from Latin *renegatus*. The modern form is derived from Spanish.

98   **yngram** 'ignorant'   The variant is recorded from Wilson's time until the nineteenth century.

100   **vacacioun**   Derived from the past participle of Latin *vacare*, 'to be empty'.

26

THE DIARY OF HENRY MACHYN

The diary kept between 1550 and 1563 by Henry Machyn, a member of the Guild of Merchant Taylors of the City of London, is of linguistic importance because it gives us access to a milieu which is generally closed to later investigations. He was not an important author, a graduate of the universities or a member of the court, but a relatively successful tradesman and an ordinary citizen of London. With regard to his language a *caveat* is necessary. Some features of his language suggest that he was not a Londoner by birth, and it has recently been shown that he was probably raised in south-west Yorkshire, and was one of the numerous immigrants into London (Britton forthcoming). Additionally, it would be naive to assume that the written language of his diary is a mirror reflection of his everyday speech, unaffected by cultural values more common in sophisticated circles; nevertheless, his diary exhibits features peculiar to everyday London usage, especially in the confusion of initial <v> with initial <w>.

The value of the diary is further limited by the limitations of interests displayed. Machyn's business was the supply of trappings for elaborate funerals, and his descriptions of these ceremonies occupy the greater part of his writings. However, although his diary begins as a catalogue of funeral pomp, he quickly begins to include records of other great occasions and lesser happenings such as the burning of a neighbour's house, or the escape of a bear at a bear-baiting.

The manuscript of Machyn's diary (BL MS Cotton Vitellius F. v) was, like that of the Anglo-Saxon *Battle of Maldon* and *Beowulf*, one of those damaged in the Cottonian library fire of 1731. A transcript of parts of it had, however, been made ten years earlier, and the portions in modern spelling in parentheses [ ] in the following excerpts derive from this source.

[The xx day of March the earl of Bedford, lord privy-seal, who died
at his house beside the Savoy, was carried to his burying-place in
the country, called Chenies, with three hundred horse all in black.
He was carried with three crosses,] with mony clerkes and prestes,
[till they came to the hill] a-boyffe sant James, and ther returnyd
[certain of them] home; and thay had torchys and armes and money
gyven them. And after evere man sett in aray on horssebake. First
on red in blake bayryng a crosse of sylver, and serten prestes on
horsebake wayryng ther surples; then cam the standard, and then
all the gentyllmen and hed officers; and then cam haroldes, on
beyryng ys elmet, and the mantylls, and the crest, and anodur ys
baner of armes, and anodur ys target with the garter, and anodur ys
cott armur; and anodur ys sword: and then master Garter in ys ryche
cott armur and then cam the charett with vj banars rolles of armes,
and a-bowt the charett iiij banars of ymages, and after the charet a
gret horsse trapyd in cloth of gold with the sadyll of the sam; and
then cam mornars, the cheyffe (of whom) my lord Russell ys sune,
and after my lord trayssorer, and the master of the horse, and
dyver odur nobull men all in blake; and evere towne that he whent
thrughe the clarkes and prestes mett ym with crosses; and thay had
in evere parryche iiij nobuls to gyffe to the pore, and the prest and
clarke of evere parryche xs., tyll he cam to ys plasse at Cheynes; and
the morowe after was he bered, and a grett doll of money; and ther
the deyn of Powlles mad a godly sermon; and after a grett dener,
and gret plenty to all the contrey a-bowt that wold com thether.

The xxv day of Marche, the wyche was owre lade [day], ther
was as gret justes as youe have sene at the tylt at Vestmynster; the
chalyngers was a Spaneard and ser Gorge Haward; and all ther
men, and ther horsses trymmyd in whyt, and then cam the Kyng
and a gret mene all in bluw, and trymmyd with yelow, and ther
elmets with gret tuyffes of blue and yelow fether, and all ther veffelers
and ther fotemen, and ther armorers, and a compene lyke Turkes
red in cremesun saten gownes and capes, and with fachyons, and
gret targets; and sum in gren, and mony of dyvers colers; and ther
was broken ij hondred stayffes and a-boyff . . .

The xvij day of Aprell was a commandment [from the bishop
of London that every] parryche in London shuld have the sam day,
and the morowe, durge and masse and ryngyng for pope Jully [the
third] of that name, and for all crystyn solles.

40   The xiiij day of Aprell, the wyche was [Ester day,] at sant
Margatt parryche at Westmynster, af[ter masse] was done, one of
the menysters a prest of the ab[bay] dyd helpe hym that was the
menyster [to] the pepull who wher reseyvyng of the blessyd
sacrement of [the lord] Jhesus Cryst, ther cam into the chyrche a
45   man that was a monke of Elly, the wyche was marryed to a wyff;
the sam day ther that same man sayd to the menyster, What doyst
thow gyff them? and as sone as he had spokyn he druw his wod-
knyffe, and hyt the prest on the hed and struck hym a grett blowe,
and after ran after hym and struck hym on the hand, and cloyffe ys
50   hand a grett way, and after on the harme a grett wond; and ther
was syche a cry and showtt as has not byne; and after he was taken
and cared to presun, and after examynyd wher-for he dyd ytt.

The xx day of Aprell was raynyd at Powlles a-for the bysshope
of London and many odur and my lord cheyffe justys and my lord
55   mayre and the shreyffes; ys name was (master Fowler, alias Branch);
he was a monke of Ely; and ther was a goodly sermon, and after he
was cast and condemnyd to have ys hand that hurt the prest cut off
or he shuld suffer, and after dysgracyd, and after cared to Nuwgatt.

The xxj day of Aprell ther was wypyd at a cart-hors iij, j man
60   and ij women, and anodur man a-lone, ij old men with whyt berdes,
and on was for carehyng . . .

[The xxiijd day of April, being saint George's day, at Hampton
Court, the King, with other lords and knights of the garter, went
in their robes on procession, with three] crosses, and clarkes and
65   prestes, and my lord chancellor, the cheyff menyster, metered, and
all thay in copes of cloth of tyssue and gold, syngyng *Salva fasta
dyes* as thay whent a-bowt; the Quen('s) grace lokyd owt of a
cassement, that hundereds dyd se her grace after she had taken her
chambur; and arolds gohyng a-bowt the Kyng('s) grace.

70   The xxiij day of Aprell was the sam man cared to Westmynster
that dyd hurt the prest, and had ys hand stryken of at the post, and
after he was bornyd aganst sant Margett chyrche with-owt the
cherche-yerde.

Notes

6   **armes**   Read 'alms'. If this misspelling suggests the homophony of the
two words, it pre-dates the accepted homophony by at least a century. ME
[ɑlm] developed through [ɑʊm] to [ɑː] by the later seventeenth century,
and [ar] to [ɑː] not much before 1800.

27

JOHN LYLY, *EUPHUES OR*
THE ANATOMY OF WIT

John Lyly (?1554–1606) was intimately associated with the secular human-
istic Latin learning which emerged in the fifteenth century and flourished in the sixteenth. He was the grandson of a significant literary figure,
William Lily, a noted grammarian, and represented the third generation of
his family to profit from an education at Magdalen College, Oxford. Little is
known of his early life, but he probably attended the Cathedral School in
Canterbury where his father was an ecclesiastical official. He received his
MA from Oxford in 1575 and moved to London, where he received patronage from the Earl of Oxford. In 1578 he published his *Euphues*, which was
an immediate success and was followed in 1580 by *Euphues and his England*.
By 1630 the two separate works had gone through twenty-six editions. Lyly's
characteristic style became temporarily so fashionable that the royal court is
reported to have sought to speak in Euphuisms.

The excitement generated at court by the style of *Euphues* is understandable, since artificial prose deriving from the earlier 'curial style', with
its elaborate Latinisms and endless sentences, had been developed specifically within the written medium. Here, in *Euphues*, was an artistic style
affiliated with the spoken language. It was one founded on the patterns of
Latin rhetoric and seems to have had distant connections with both the
Latin of the Church Fathers and with Cicero, but to have been created by
Lyly by anglicising some of the features of Latin lectures he had encountered in Oxford. The major feature of the style is the use of clauses of
moderate length brought into relationship by the exploitation of certain
formal features of the language. Two or more clauses of the same syntactic
structure are related by some semantic (opposition or synonymy), phonetic
(rhyme, assonance or alliteration) or lexical (verbal repetition) device so as
to achieve an effect of balance or parallelism. Extended similes derived from
handbooks of natural history abound and, like the use of proverbs, they

7   **evere** 'every'   Machyn uses final -*e* to represent a final unstressed vowel
        in several words where Modern English would have final -*y*. See also *cared*
        (58).

8   **on red** 'one rode'   The unhistorical final -*e* is frequently not written in
        the word 'one' (OE *ān*). The preterite *red* is not easily explicable.

11   **ys elmet**   The pronunciation of initial *h*- is markedly unstable in
        Machyn's language. He spells such words both with and without *h*-. Com-
        pare *harme* (50), *haroldes* (10), *arolds* (69).

17   **my lord Russell ys sune**   The genitive inflexion -*ys* (OE -*es*) has
        become a syntactical marker of possession which may be attached to
        groups. It is sometimes erroneously interpreted as the genitive third-
        person pronoun.

20   **clarkes**   The standard spelling was *clerkes* (4), but Machyn often writes
        <er> as <ar>, reflecting a pronunciation which had developed in the
        North in the fifteenth century but which was resisted by many authors,
        since it seems to have lacked prestige.

23   **bered** 'buried' (OE *byrgian*)   The *e*-spelling suggests the survival of a
        pronunciation descending from the south-eastern origins of the London
        language, where WS *y* was written *e*.

26   **the wyche**   This form of the relative, dependent as it is on the usage
        of administrative French prose, implies some familiarity with the official
        written English of the period.

27   **Vestmynster**   Machyn frequently writes initial w- as <v> (cf. *veffelers*,
        31, 'one . . . employed to keep the way clear at a procession', *OED* s.v.
        'whiffler').

43   **who**   The use of the pronoun *who* as a personal relative is still com-
        paratively unusual at this period. In OE and in Chaucer, *who* occurs only
        as an interrogative or with indefinite reference. During the fourteenth
        century it begins to be used as a relative in the North and it is found in
        its inflected forms, *whose* and *whom*, in the South during the fifteenth
        century.

53   **raynyd**   An aphetic (see p. 158, note to line 101) form of *arraynyd*, also
        used by Machyn.

57   **cast and condemnyd**   Possibly a tautological pair, but *cast* probably
        means 'found guilty'.

58   **or he shuld suffer** 'before he should suffer death'.

59   **cart-hors**   Elsewhere *cart-ars*, 'the cart-tail', or back of a cart.

68   **hundereds dyd se**   The use of the periphrastic construction with the
        verb 'to do', distinct from the causal construction, is rare before the mid
        fifteenth century but common during the sixteenth.

may be arranged into lists. Rhetorical questions are also frequent. The narrative is heavily sententious and didactic, recounting the emotional adventures of a young 'Athenian', Euphues, his infatuation with and then rejection of the faithless Lucilla. The passage occurs when Euphues first finds himself alone with his lady.

Despite its enormous impact, Lyly's fashionable success was inevitably temporary. Already by 1598, Shakespeare, in 2 *Henry IV*, II. iv, is satirising Euphuistic style in the speeches of Falstaff imitating King Henry, and by the time of Lyly's death in 1606 his Euphuistic style was beginning to be considered ludicrous in more advanced quarters.

Euphues was surprised with such increadible ioye at this straunge euent, that hee had almost sounded, for seeing his coryuall to be departed, and *Ferardo* to gyue him so friendly entertainment, doubted not in time to get the good wyll of *Lucilla:* Whome findinge
5   in place conuenient without company, with a bolde courage and comely gesture, he began to assay hir in this sort.

    Gentlewoman, my acquaintaunce beeing so little, I am afraide my credite will bee lesse, for that they commonly are soonest beleeued, that are best beloued, and they liked best, whome we
10   haue knowne longest, neuerthelesse the noble minde suspecteth no guile wythout cause, neither condemneth any wight wythout proofe, hauing therefore notise of your heroycall heart, I am the better perswaded of my good hap. So it is *Lucilla*, that cōming to *Naples* but to fetch fire, as the by word is, not to make my place of abode,
15   I haue founde such flames that I can neither quench them wyth the water of free will, neyther coole them wyth wisedome. For as the Hoppe the poale beeing neuer so hye groweth to the ende, or as the drye Beeche kindled at the roote, neuer leaueth vntill it come to the toppe, or as one droppe of poyson disperseth it selfe into euerye
20   vaine, so affection hauinge caughte holde of my hearte, and the sparkles of loue kindled my liuer, wyll sodeinely, thoughe secretlye flame vp into my heade, and spreade it selfe into euerye sinewe. It is your beautie (pardon my abrupte boldenesse) Ladye that hath taken euery part of mee prisoner, and brought me to this deepe
25   distresse, but seeinge women when one praiseth them for their desertes, deeme that hee flattereth them to obteine his desire, I am heere present to yelde my selfe to such tryall, as your courtesie in this behalfe shall require: Yet will you cōmonly obiect this to such

as serue you and sterue to winne your good wil, that hot loue is
soone colde, that the Bauin though it bourne bright, is but a blaze,
that scaldinge water if it stande a while tourneth almost to yse, that
pepper though it be hot in the mouth is colde in the mawe, that the
faith of men though it frye in their woordes, it freeseth in works:
Which things (*Lucilla*) albeit they be sufficient to reproue the
lightnesse of some one, yet can it not conuince euery one of
lewdenes, neither ought the constancie of all, to be brought in
question through the subtiltie of a fewe. For although the worme
entereth almost into euery woode, yet he eateth not the *Ceder* tree:
Though the stone *Cylindrus* at euery thunder clappe, rowle from
the hill, yet the pure sleeke stone mounteth at the noyse, though
the rust fret the hardest steele, yet doth it not eate into the
Emeraulde, though *Polypus* chaunge his hew, yet yᵉ *Salamander*
keepeth his coulour, though *Proteus* transforme himselfe into euery
shape, yet *Pygmalion* retaineth his olde forme, though *Aeneas* were
to fickle to *Dido*, yet *Troylys* was to faithfull to *Cræssida*, thoughe
others seeme counterfaite in their deedes, yet *Lucilla* perswade your
selfe that *Euphues* will bee always curraunt in his dealinges. But as
the true golde is tryed by the touch, the pure flinte by the stroke of
the yron, so the loyall heart of the faithfull louer, is knowen by the
tryall of his Lady: of the which tryall (*Lucilla*) if you shall accompte
Euphues worthy, assure your selfe, hee wyll bee as readie to offer
himselfe a sacrifice for your sweet sake, as your selfe shall bee willinge
to employe hym in your seruice. Neyther doth hee desire to bee
trusted any way, vntill he shall be tried euery way, neither doth hee
craue credite at the first, but a good countenaunce til time his
desire shall be made manifest by hys desertes. Thus not blynded by
lyght affection, but dazeled with your rare perfection, and boldened
by your exceeding courtesie, I haue vnfolded mine entire loue,
desiring you hauing so good leasure, to giue so friendly an aunswere,
as I may receiue comforte, and you commendacion.

   Lucilla although she were contented to heare this desired discourse, yet did shee seeme to bee somewhat displeased: And truely
I know not whether it bee peculyar to that sex to dissemble with
those, whome they most desire, or whether by craft they haue
learned outwardely to loath that, which inwardely they most loue:
yet wisely did she cast this in hir head, that if she should yeelde at
the first assault he woulde thinke hir a lyght huswife, if she should

reiect him scornefully a very haggard, minding therefore that he
shoulde neyther take holde of hir promise, neyther vnkindenesse of
70   hir precisenesse, she fedde him indifferently, with hope and dispayre,
reason and affection, lyfe and death. Yet in the ende arguing wittily
vpon certeine questions, they fell to suche agreement as poore
Philautus woulde not haue agreed vnto if hee had bene present, yet
alwayes keepinge the body vndefiled. And thus shee replyed.

75   　　Gentleman as you may suspecte me of Idelnesse in giuing eare
to your talke, so may you conuince me of lyghtenesse in answering such toyes, certes as you haue made mine eares glowe at the
rehearsall of your loue, so haue you galled my hart with the remembrance of your folly. Though you came to *Naples* as a straunger,
80   yet were you welcome to my fathers house as a friend. And can you
then so much transgresse ye bounds of honour (I will not say of
honestie) as to solicite a sute more sharpe to me then deathe?
I haue hetherto God bethancked, liued wythout suspition of
lewdenesse, and shall I nowe incurre the daunger of sensuall lybertie?
85   What hope can you haue to obtayne my loue, seeing yet I coulde
neuer affoord you a good looke? Doe you therefore thinke me
easely entised to the bent of your bow, bicause I was easely
entreated to lysten to your late discourse? Or seeing mee (as finely
you glose) to excell all other in beautie, did you deeme that I would
90   exceed all other in beastlynesse? But yet I am not angry *Eupheus*
but in an agony, for who is shee that will frette or fume with one
that loueth hir, if this loue to delude mee bee not dissembled. It is
that which causeth me most to feare, not that my beautie is vnknown
to my selfe but that commonly we poore wenches are deluded
95   through lyght beliefe, and ye men are naturally enclined craftely to
leade your lyfe. When the Foxe preacheth the Geese perishe. The
Crocodile shrowdeth greatest treason vnder most pitifull teares: in
a kissing mouth there lyeth a gallyng minde. You haue made so
large proffer of your seruice, and so fayre promises of fidelytie, that
100   were I not ouer charie of mine honestie, you would inueigle me to
shake handes with chastitie. But certes I will eyther leade a Uirgins
lyfe in earth (though I leade Apes in hell) or els follow thee rather
then thy giftes: yet am I neither so precise to refuse thy proffer,
neither so peeuish to disdain thy good will: So excellent alwayes are
105   ye giftes which are made acceptable by the vertue of the giuer. I did
at the firste entraunce discerne thy loue but yet dissemble it. Thy

wanton glaunces, thy scalding sighes, thy louing signes, caused me
to blush for shame, and to looke wanne for feare, least they should
be perceiued of any. These subtill shiftes, these paynted practises (if
110 I were to be wonne) woulde soone weane mee from the teate of
Vesta, to the toyes of *Venus*. Besides this thy comly grace, thy rare
quallyties, thy exquisite perfection, were able to moue a minde
halfe mortified to transgresse the bondes of maydenly modestie.
But God shielde *Lucilla*, that thou shouldest be so carelesse of thine
115 honour as to commit the state thereoff to a stranger. Learne thou
by me *Euphues* to dispise things that be amiable, to forgoe delightfull
practises, beleeue mee it is pietie to abstayne from pleasure.

Notes

1   **surprised** 'seized'   The use of the verb *surprised* (OF *surprendre*) to
express emotional experience has a very long history in romance writing.
The idiom is found in twelfth-century French romance.

2   **sounded** 'swooned'   A variant of 'swoon' recorded from the fourteenth
century but surviving only in dialect use.
coryuall   The earliest recorded use of this adoption from a rare Latin
form *corrivalis*. The prefix *co-* serves to intensify the relationship expressed
by the base. In the sense 'rival in love', it was obsolete by the end of the
seventeenth century.

10   **suspecteth**   Lyly avoids the use of the *-es* inflexion of the third-person-
singular present tense, which was by this time common in speech and used
by contemporary writers (see Queen Elizabeth's letter, Excerpt 28, and
Machyn's diary, Excerpt 26). It is likely that Lyly's literary background
encouraged him to believe that *-eth* was the established and correct form.

13   **hap** 'fortune' (ON *happ*)   Although Euphuistic style readily employs
Latinate vocabulary, such vocabulary is less overwhelming than in fifteenth-
century aureate style. Lyly draws on a much wider range of sources, bringing his rarer words into more striking relief.
cōming   The print bar over *o* here, and in *cōmonly* (28), is a frequent
abbreviation for a vowel followed by *n* or *m*. It continues the practice of
medieval scribes, and could serve early printers by assisting them in justi-
fying the line. See also Excerpt 29.

23   **abrupte** 'unannounced, hasty' (Lat. *abruptus*, past participle of *abrumpere*)
This occurrence pre-dates *OED*'s example in Shakespeare's *2 Henry IV*.

29   **sterue** 'die'   Still retains the OE sense 'to die' rather than the narrowed
sense 'to die of hunger'. Lyly very rarely writes <ar> for earlier <er> (cf.
hart, 78), perhaps regarding it as incorrect, much as he did *-es* for *-eth*.

35   **some one**   The phrase still retains the sense of the OE adjective *sum*, 'a particular (one)'.

       conuince 'convict'   Lat. *convincere* had the sense in legal contexts of 'to convict of a crime'.

41   **fret** 'eat, consume, corrode' (OE *fretan*)   The senses 'corrode' and 'worry' were figurative extensions of the earlier sense. The former of these was discontinued during the eighteenth century.

47   **curraunt**   This is the earliest recorded occurrence in the sense 'genuine' (obsolete by the mid eighteenth century). It is used of currency in figurative opposition to 'counterfeit'.

50   **of the which tryall**   Lyly employs as a feature of formal expression a type of connection developed in French administrative prose and first encountered in English in the late fourteenth century.

58   **entire** 'whole and perfect'   The French and Latin antecedents had strong moral associations of purity and perfection, which seem to be implied here.

62   **did shee seeme**   The use of periphrastic *do* serves to place sentence stress on *seeme*, while allowing a verb–subject inversion after the adverb *yet*. Negation is found both with (41) and without (38, 63) the use of periphrastic *do*.

67   **a lyght huswife**   In early ME this had much the same sense as modern 'housewife' but it developed a pejorative sense by 1546. *OED* records this sense last in 1705. From the mid seventeenth century the pejorative sense had begun to be adopted by the phonetically reduced form *hussy*. The development occurred first in collocations like that found here, where *lyght* means 'foolish and unchaste'.

68   **haggard**   Earlier sense, 'a wild hawk caught in her adult plumage', but here the earliest example of a figurative use also favoured by Shakespeare: 'a wild and intractable person [difficult to catch or retain]'.

77   **toyes** 'trifling speeches'   The history of this word is mysterious. It is recorded once in ME but not again until it becomes very frequent in a range of senses from about 1530. The senses have in common a dismissive attitude to the thing referred to, associations with amusement, and frequently eroticism. It seems to have rapidly become an Elizabethan vogue word, but its origins are obscure.

94   **wenches**   The choice of this word is intended to be endearingly self-deprecating. The word is a shortened form of ME *wenchel*, which meant a young person of either sex. The restriction to females developed early, and two connected pejorative senses developed alongside it from the mid fourteenth century: 'serving girl' and 'wanton woman'. Although the sense 'young girl' continued, it was not unprejudiced by the socially and morally pejorative senses. Therefore, the word is inevitably dismissive.

102   **follow thee**   To this point, Lucilla has studiously used *you* as her address form; she now switches to *thou*. *You* (originally accusative and dative) has replaced *ye* as the ordinary subject form, and this plural form had been used in polite society for formal address since the mid thirteenth century. The switch to the familiar *thou* marks the admission of Lucilla's warm feelings for Euphues.

28

LETTERS OF QUEEN ELIZABETH I AND KING JAMES VI OF SCOTLAND

The Renaissance achieved what in the Middle Ages had very often been merely a pious wish – that the occupant of the national throne should exhibit a respect for learning and an interest in literary culture. Although Queen Elizabeth was by no means the financier of literature that might have been desired, and although she encouraged writers such as John Lyly only to prove reluctant to recompense them, yet her interest and encouragement made patronage available from other sources and ensured the fashionable acceptance of literary production and learning. She herself claims notice as the only monarch other than King Alfred to attempt a translation of Boethius's *De Consolatione Philosophiae*.

She employed her literacy also in writing her own letters, of which many survive including a series written to James VI of Scotland, through which she sought to manipulate diplomatic relations between the two countries. These letters are especially interesting because James's replies often survive also, and these make a striking contrast in both attitude and style as well as in language. Elizabeth's letters are written in the London standard of the day, with one or two peculiarities characteristic of her, such as the tendency to write *the* for both 'they' and the definite article; James's are in the contemporary Scots which had developed from the earlier northern Middle English into a quasi-standard. In the following excerpt, written in 1587, perhaps a week before the execution of Mary, Queen of Scots, Elizabeth seeks to justify her decision to have James's mother put to death. Perhaps reflecting the nature of the circumstances, the style is unusually tortuous, and the first sentence becomes almost unintelligible as the result of a sequence of digressive qualifications. James's letter, which like Elizabeth's is in his own hand, is a draft which may never have been sent but is a well-turned piece of diplomatic correspondence, in effect a letter of credit for its bearer.

A   Queen Elizabeth's letter

To my deare brother and cousin, the kinge of Skotz.

Be not caried away, my deare brother, with the lewd perswations of
suche, as insteade of infowrming you of my to nideful and helpeles
cause of defending the brethe that God hath given me, to be better
spent than spilt by the bloudy invention of traitors handz, may
5   perhaps make you belive, that ether the offense was not so great, or
if that cannot serue them, for the over-manifest triall wiche in
publik and by the greatest and most in this land hathe bine manifestly proved, yet the wyl make that her life may be saved and myne
safe, wiche wold God wer true, for whan you make vewe of my
10   long danger indured thes fowre – wel ny fiue – monethes time to
make a tast of, the greatest witz amongs my owne, and than of
French, and last of you, wyl graunt with me, that if nide wer not
mor than my malice she shuld not have her merite.
    And now for a good conclusion of my long-taried-for answer.
15   Your commissionars telz me, that I may trust her in the hande of
some indifferent prince, and have all her cousins and allies promis
she wil no more seake my ruine. Deare brother and cousin, way in
true and equal balance wither the lak not muche good ground
whan suche stuf serves for ther bilding. Suppose you I am so mad
20   to truste my life in anothers hand and send hit out of my owne?
If the young master of Gray, for curring faueur with you, might
fortune say hit, yet old master Mylvin hath yeres ynough to teache
him more wisdome than tel a prince of any jugement suche a
contrarious frivolous maimed reason. Let your councelors, for your
25   honour, discharge ther duty so muche to you as to declaire the
absurditie of such an offer; and, for my part, I do assure myselfe to
muche of your wisdome, as, thogh like a most naturall good son
you charged them to seake all meanes the could deuis with wit or
jugement to save her life, yet I can not, nor do not, allege any fault
30   to you of thes persuations, for I take hit that you wil remember,
that advis or desiars aught ever agree with the surtye of the party
sent to and honor of the sendar, wiche whan bothe you way, I
doute not but your wisdome wil excuse my nide, and waite my
necessitie, and not accuse me ether of malice or of hate.
35   And now to conclude. Make account, I pray you, of my firme
frindeship loue and care, of which you may make sure accownt, as

one that never mindz to faile from my worde, nor swarve from our
league, but wyl increase, by all good meanes, any action that may
make true shewe of my stable amitie; from wiche, my deare brother,
40   let no sinistar whisperars, nor busy troblars of princis states, persuade to leave your surest, and stike to vnstable staies. Suppose them
to be but the ecchos to suche whos stipendaries the be, and wyl do
more for ther gaine than your good. And so, God hold you ever in
his blessed kiping, and make you see your tru frinds. Excuse my
45   not writing sonar, for paine in one of my yees was only the cause.
      Your most assured lovinge sistar and cousin,
                                        ELIZABETH R.

B   King James's letter

Madame and dearest sister, Quhairas by your lettir and bearare,
Robert Carey youre seruand and ambassadoure, ye purge youre
self of yone unhappy fact. As, on the one pairt, considdering your
rank and sex, consanguinitie and longe professed good will to the
5   defunct, together with youre many and solemne attestationis of
youre innocentie, I darr not wronge you so farre as not to iudge
honorablie of youre unspotted pairt thairin, so, on the other syde,
I uishe that youre honorable behauioure in all tymes heirafter may
fully persuaide the quhole uorlde of the same. And, as for my pairt,
10   I looke that ye will geue me at this tyme suche a full satisfaction,
in all respectis, as sall be a meane to strenthin and unite this yle,
establish and maintaine the treu religion, and obleig me to be, as of
befoire I war, youre most louing.
                                        [unsigned]
This bearare hath sumquhat to informe you of in my name, quhom
I neid not desyre you to credit, for ye knou I loue him.

Notes

Elizabeth

1   **lewd perswations**   *lewd* has the OE sense 'ignorant' persuasions.
2   **to nideful and helpeles** 'too necessary and unaided'   The spelling of
nideful probably represents the raising of /eː/ to /iː/ which had taken place
during the fifteenth century as part of the Great Vowel Shift. Cf. *bine* (7).
7   **hathe**   The third-person-singular present tense of 'to have' retains the
-th inflexion long after *-es* has been adopted for other verbs. As late as the

eighteenth century this form is found in the written language, although it had then vanished from spoken usage.

9   **you**   The use of the plural form of the second-person pronoun is, of course, a normal courtesy in these circles. Note, however, the use of the form *you*. Originally this form was proper to object and oblique functions, but it has now displaced *ye* in use as subject also.

13   **mor than my malice**   *Mor* is used in the sense 'greater' (cf. *most*, 7). Elizabeth argues that necessity is more pressing than her personal feelings in demanding that Mary receive her just deserts. Although this extended sentence breaks down syntactically, various rhetorical devices of balance and repetition help to preserve its sense.

14   **long-taried-for**   Ready productivity in phrasal compounds becomes a striking feature of Elizabethan poetic language also.

15   **telz**   Perhaps simply a slip, since this plural inflexion is understandable only as a feature of northern dialect.

19   **Suppose you**   An interrogative clause is still formed, as in OE and ME, by the reversal of subject–verb order. In less formal contexts, however, the use of the auxiliary *do* is emerging in questions.

21   **curring faueur**   The phrase is first recorded in 1510, but as *curry Favel* from about 1400. The original meaning, used figuratively, was to groom or smooth down the chestnut horse (called Favel). The word *favel* consequently developed metaphorical associations with flattery and duplicity. Formal resemblance between *favel* and *favor* encouraged the development of the modern phrase.

22   **fortune say hit** 'chance to say it'   The plain infinitive is used rather more widely than in Modern English. Cf. *than tel* (23).

26   **I do assure**   The use of the *do-* periphrasis seems here to carry some suggestion of a marked assertion: 'I am too confident . . .'

33   **waite** 'consider'   This sense is archaic. *OED* does not record it after 1430.

37   **swarve**   (OE *sweorfan*). The spelling <ar> for earlier <er> demonstrates that the associated sound change had penetrated into the highest circles. But the spelling is rarer in Elizabeth's letters than in Machyn's diary.

44–45   **my not writing**   The creation of nominal (gerund) from a negated verb illustrates a further facet of Elizabethan freedom in language use.

James

1   **Quhairas**   The northern ME spelling <quh> of the reflex of OE <hw> is the standard spelling in Scots. In the spelling <ai>, as also the spellings <ei> (*heirafter*) and <oi> (*befoire*), *i* indicates that the preceding vowel is long.

2   **ye**   James uses the earlier form of pronoun in contrast to *you* in Elizabeth's letter.

3   **yone**   Developed from the rare OE adjective *geon*. The word is predominantly, although not exclusively, northern in ME.

11   **sall**   Forms with initial *s* in ME are generally found to the north of a line from Morecambe Bay to the Wash.

     strenthin   The use of <i> or <y> spellings in the unstressed vowels of inflexions is found from the north Midlands northwards. The loss of velarity in the nasal is widespread.

13   **I war**   (ON *váru*) The form belongs to the areas of heavier Scandinavian settlement.

29

GEORGE PUTTENHAM,
THE ARTE OF ENGLISH POESIE

*T*he *Arte of English Poesie* appeared anonymously in 1589 but is attri-
buted to Puttenham (*c.* 1529–91) with reasonable certainty. The book
is thought to have existed in manuscript for as long as two decades before
its appearance. It consists of three parts, the first a review of the history
and purpose of poetry in the process of civilisation, in which Puttenham
represents Chaucer as a learned associate and beneficiary of Richard II,
scorns Skelton as a satirical clown, and praises Sir Philip Sidney and 'that
other Gentleman who wrate the late Shepheardes Callender'. Book II
is concerned with form and metre, and the third book with the ornaments of style. What he has to say on this last topic is drawn from the
Latin rhetorical tradition, but he makes some effort to accommodate it
to English practice, and enlivens his teaching with anecdotes; the principle of stylistic decorum is illustrated by the story of an inappropriate
ale-house tale delivered as a speech at the opening of Parliament by a
Yorkshire MP.

Whether or not the anecdote is apocryphal is irrelevant to its purpose
of demonstrating provincial ineptitude in eloquence. The underlying suggestion is taken up overtly in the discussion of the language most suited
to poetry, which is printed below. The passage presents evidence that the
earlier medieval assumption of the equality of English varieties – already
being questioned in the fourteenth century – was approaching its end.
English was divisible geographically and socially as well as according to
technical domain (cf. Excerpt 25). It was divided up along lines already
laid down in the treatment by Latin rhetoric of the subject of verbal choice,
where the poet was urged to avoid words characteristic of the provinces, the
lower classes of Roman society, extreme archaisms, inappropriate domains
and genres.

Of language

Speach is not naturall to man sauing for his onely habilitie to speake, and that he is by kinde apt to vtter all his conceits with sounds and voyces diuersified many maner of wayes, by meanes of the many and fit instruments he hath by nature to that purpose, as a broad and voluble tong, thinne and mouable lippes, teeth euē and not shagged, thick ranged, a round vaulted pallate, and a long throte, besides an excellent capacitie of wit that maketh him more discip-linable and imitatiue then any other creature: then as to the forme and action of his speach, it commeth to him by arte and teaching, and by vse or exercise. But after a speach is fully fashioned to the common vnderstanding, and accepted by consent of a whole countrey and natiō it is called a language, and receaueth none allowed alteration, but by extraordinary occasions by little and little, as it were insensibly bringing in of many corruptiōs that creepe along with the time; of all which matters, we haue more largely spoken in our bookes of the originals and pedigree of the English tong. Then when I say language, I meane the speach wherein the Poet or maker writeth be it Greek or Latine, or as our case is the vulgar English, and when it is peculiar vnto a countrey it is called the mother speach of that people: the Greekes terme it *Idioma*: so is ours at this day the Norman English. Before the Conquest of the Normans it was the Anglesaxon, and before that the British, which as some will, is at this day, the Walsh, or as others affirme the Cornish: I for my part thinke neither of both, as they be now spoken and pronounced. This part in our maker or Poet must be heedyly looked vnto, that it be naturall, pure, and the most vsuall of all his countrey: and for the same purpose rather that which is spoken in the kings Court, or in the good townes and Cities within the land, then in the marches and frontiers, or in port townes, where straungers haunt for traffike sake, or yet in Vniuersities where Schollers vse much peeuish affectation of words out of the primatiue languages, or finally, in any vplandish village or corner of a Realme, where is no resort but of poore rusticall or vnciuill people: neither shall he follow the speach of a craftes man or carter, or other of the inferiour sort, though he be inhabitant or bred in the best towne and Citie in this Realme, for such persons doe abuse good speaches by strange accents or ill shapen soundes, and false ortographie. But he shall follow generally the better brought vp sort, such as the

Greekes call [*charientes*] men ciuill and graciously behauoured and
bred. Our maker therfore at these dayes shall not follow *Piers*
plowman nor *Gower* nor *Lydgate* nor yet *Chaucer*, for their language is now out of vse with vs: neither shall he take the termes of
Northern-men, such as they vse in dayly talke, whether they be
noble men or gentlemen, or of their best clarkes all is a matter: nor
in effect any speach vsed beyond the riuer of Trent, though no man
can deny but that theirs is the purer English Saxon at this day, yet
it is not so Courtly nor so currant as our Southerne English is, no
more is the far Westerne mās speach: ye shall therfore take the
vsuall speach of the Court, and that of London and the shires lying
about London within lx. myles, and not much aboue. I say not this
but that in euery shyre of England there be gentlemen and others
that speake but specially write as good Southerne as we of Middlesex or Surrey do, but not the common people of euery shire,
to whom the gentlemen, and also their learned clarkes do for
the most part condescend, but herein we are already ruled by
th'English Dictionaries and other bookes written by learned men,
and therefore it needeth none other direction in that behalfe. Albeit
peraduenture some small admonition be not impertinent, for we
finde in our English writers many wordes and speaches amendable,
and ye shall see in some many inkhorne termes so ill affected
brought in by men of learning as preachers and schoolemasters:
and many straunge termes of other languages by Secretaries and
Marchaunts and trauailours, and many darke wordes and not
vsuall nor well sounding, though they be dayly spoken in Court.
Wherefore great heed must be taken by our maker in this point
that his choise be good. And peraduenture the writer hereof be in
that behalfe no lesse faultie then any other, vsing many straunge
and vnaccustomed wordes and borrowed from other languages: and
in that respect him selfe no meete Magistrate to reforme the same
errours in any other person, but since he is not vnwilling to
acknowledge his owne fault, and can the better tell how to amend
it, he may seeme a more excusable correctour of other mens: he
intendeth therefore for an indifferent way and vniuersall benefite
to taxe him selfe first and before any others.

These be words vsed by th'author in this present treatise,
sciētificke, but with some reason, for it aūswereth the word *mech-*
anicall, which no other word could haue done so properly, for when
hee spake of all artificers which rest either in science or in handy

craft, it followed necessarilie that *scientifique* should be coupled
80   with *mechanicall*: or els neither of both to haue bene allowed, but
in their places: a man of science liberall, and a handicrafts man,
which had not bene so cleanly a speech as the other *Maior-domo*:
in truth this word is borrowed of the *Spaniard* and *Italian*, and
therefore new and not vsuall, but to them that are acquainted with
85   the affaires of Court: and so for his iolly magnificence (as this case
is) may be accepted among Courtiers, for whom this is specially
written. A man might haue said in steade of *Maior-domo*, the French
word (*maistre d'hostell*) but ilfauouredly, or the right English word
(*Lord Steward*). But me thinks for my owne opinion this word
90   *Maior-domo* though he be borrowed, is more acceptable thā any
of the rest, other men may iudge otherwise. *Politien*, this word also
is receiued from the Frenchmen, but at this day vsuall in Court
and with all good Secretaries: and cannot finde an English word to
match him, for to haue said a man politique, had not bene so wel:
95   bicause in trueth that had bene no more than to haue said a ciuil
person. *Politien* is rather a surueyour of ciuilitie than ciuil, and a
publique minister or Counseller in the state. Ye haue also this worde
Conduict, a French word, but well allowed of vs, and long since
vsuall, it soundes somewhat more than this word [leading] for it is
100   applied onely to the leading of a Captaine, and not as a little boy
should leade a blinde man therefore more proper to the case when
he saide, *conduict* of whole armies: ye finde also this word *Idiome*,
taken from the Greekes, yet seruing aptly, when a man wanteth to
expresse so much vnles it be in two words, which surplussage to
105   auoide, we are allowed to draw in other words single, and asmuch
significatiue: this word *significatiue* is borrowed of the Latine and
French, but to vs brought in first by some Noble-mans Secretarie,
as I thinke, yet doth so well serue the turne, as it could not now be
spared: and many more like vsurped Latine and French words: as,
110   *Methode, methodicall, placation, function, assubtiling, refining, compendious, prolixe, figuratiue, inueigle*. A terme borrowed of our common Lawyers, *impression*, also a new terme, but well expressing the
matter, and more than our English word. These words, *Numerous,
numerositee, metricall, harmonicall*, but they cannot be refused,
115   specially in this place for description of the arte. Also ye finde these
words, *penetrate, penetrable, indignitie*, which I cannot see how we
may spare them, whatsoeuer fault wee finde with Ink-horne termes:
for our speach wanteth wordes to such sence so well to be vsed: yet

120
in steade of *indignitie*, yee haue vnworthinesse: and for *penetrate*, we may say *peerce*, and that a French terme also, or *broche*, or enter into with violence, but not so well sounding as *penetrate*. Item, *sauage*, for wilde: *obscure*, for darke. Item these words, *declination*, *delineation*, *dimention*, are scholasticall termes in deede, and yet very proper. But peraduenture (and I could bring a reason for it)

125
many other like words borrowed out of the Latin and French, were not so well to be allowed by vs, as these words, *audacious*, for bold: *facunditie*, for eloquence: *egregious*, for great or notable: *implete*, for replenished: *attemptat*, for attempt: *compatible*, for agreeable in nature, and many more. But herein the noble Poet *Horace* hath

130
said inough to satisfie vs all in these few verses.

> *Multa renascentur quæ iam cecidere cadentque,*
> *Quæ nunc sunt in honore vocabula si volet vsus*
> *Quem penes arbitrium est & vis & norma loquendi.*

Which I haue thus englished, but nothing with so good grace, nor
135
so briefly as the Poet wrote.

> *Many a word yfalne shall eft arise*
> *And such as now bene held in hiest prise*
> *Will fall as fast, when vse and custome will*
> *Onely vmpiers of speach, for force and skill.*

Notes

1
onely   OE *ānlīc*, 'unique'. The suffix *-līc* forms both adjectives and adverbs in OE. A few *-ly* adjectives (*comely*, *costly*, *ghostly*) survive in modern English.

5
voluble 'moving easily and quickly'   The earliest record of this sense.

6
shagged 'jagged'   Again the earliest record of this sense.

7–8
disciplinable and imitatiue 'amenable to teaching and capable of imitating'   Both are Franco-Latin types. The suffix *-able* was perceived to be stylistically marked, since it was used only with Romance bases in ME. The suffix *-ative* was not productive in ME except in the word *talkative*, first recorded in 1420. The sense of *imitative* here is not recorded by *OED* before the mid eighteenth century.

11–12
whole countrey . . .   Puttenham is defining, in this distinction between *language* and *speach*, much what modern linguists would call 'standard language' and 'speech'.

12–13
none allowed   The form of negative with retention of final *-n* (OE *nān*) occurs before a following vowel.

18   **maker**   The word is used as a synonym of *poete*, as Puttenham explains in his opening sentence. The word *poete* is derived from the Greek *poiein*, 'to make'.

24   **neither of both** 'neither of the two'.

26   **heedyly** 'with attention'   Obsolete by the mid seventeenth century.

31   **peeuish affectation**   The word *peeuish* is of unknown etymology; it appears first before 1400 but becomes common only in the sixteenth century. Puttenham regards the learned love of recondite archaisms as perverse.

33   **rusticall . . . vnciuill** 'country . . . unrefined'   The use of these words echoes a Latin contrast between coarse country-dwellers (cf. *rustici*) and urbane and sophisticated city-dwellers (*cives, civilis*). The form *rusticall* is derived from French or medieval Latin.

37   **ortographie**   Used in the sixteenth century of both pronunciation and spelling.

38   **brought vp**   First used in the sense 'to raise (a child)' about 1400.

47   **currant** 'universally acceptable'   The image is of coinage or currency.

48   **ye**   Puttenham uses the earlier form of the second-person-plural pronoun. Contemporaries frequently use *you*, a form derived from the OE dative and accusative.

52   **specially write as good Southerne**   The ability to write the London language was apparent already among outsiders in the fourteenth century. Immigrants tended to modify their spellings towards those acceptable in the city. The claim that outsiders adopted the southern pronunciation should be regarded sceptically. Sir Walter Raleigh, a favourite at the royal court, spoke with a broad Devonshire accent. Nevertheless, this passage is of great importance, since it is an early statement of the association of dialect speech with social status.

56   **English Dictionaries**   The first true English dictionary was Robert Cawdrey's *Table Alphabeticall* (1604). Puttenham is referring to dictionaries as guides not to word meaning but to spelling and pronunciation. Such works were produced by Sir Thomas Smith, *De recta et emendata Linguae Graecae* (1568), and John Hart, *An Orthographie* (1569), at about the time Puttenham was writing.

62   **straunge termes** 'foreign words or phrases'.

63   **darke wordes** 'words whose meaning is unclear'.

76   **sciētificke** 'concerned with the liberal arts' (as opposed to crafts) (Latin and French).   The earliest recorded occurrence of the word. The word *mechanicall* is recorded from 1432.

82   **Maior-domo**   The first recorded occurrence of the word.

85   **iolly**   Used from the early decades of the sixteenth century as a vaguely approving epithet. Cf. modern 'jolly good'. Puttenham is here making the point that certain foreign and unusual terms are appropriate to and unremarkable in certain domains and contexts.

89   **me thinks**   An impersonal construction. The third-person singular is here written -*s* (*soundes*, 99). Puttenham usually has -*eth*.

90–94   **he . . . him**   No personification is intended. Puttenham tends to use *he* and *him* in preference to *it* when the pronoun refers anaphorically (backwards) to the topic of the sentence.

96   **Politien**   A common word in Elizabethan texts, but first recorded only in 1588. *Surueyour* here means 'supervisor' and *ciuilitie* means 'government, political system'.

98   **Conduict** 'command (of an army)'   The word was used in the later fifteenth century in this sense. Earlier ME *conduite* was derived from French, but in both French and English the *c* of Latin *conductus* was restored in the fifteenth century. The form here derives from Latinised French; the modern form *conduct* is direct from Latin, and the modern *conduit* through ME from earlier French.

109   **vsurped Latine and French**   All these words were clearly recognisable to Puttenham as of foreign origin, but not all are recent borrowings: *compendious, prolixe, figuratiue, metricall, penetrable, inueigle* are all learned fourteenth- or fifteenth-century borrowings. *Impression*, said to be a new term, is recorded from the late fourteenth century. *Numerositee*, 'rhythmical quality', and *assubtiling*, 'making subtle', are first recorded here.

115   **arte**   The art of poetical composition. These are technical terms.

136   **yfalne**   Puttenham's verse makes liberal use of archaisms. This past participle has the southern ME prefix *y*-. Both *eft* and *held in prise* are by now poetic (?Chaucerian) archaisms.

30

THOMAS NASHE

Thomas Nashe (1567–1601) was born in Lowestoft, attended St John's
College, Cambridge, where, as 'a little ape', he says, he thought Lyly's
Euphues was the last word; but he entered London literary society in 1588, and
by 1592 had learned to scorn Euphuism, seeking his own mode of expression. His career was a stormy one since many of his writings were polemic
or satirical in tone. He was involved in the Marprelate Controversy on the
side of the bishops, but more notable is his continuing feud with Gabriel
Harvey which expressed itself in a heated debate on literary style and mutual
accusations of the use of Inkhorn terms (see Excerpt 25). In *The Unfortunate
Traveller* (1594) he presents a caricature of inflated oratory in the person of
a 'bursten belly inkhorne orator called *Vanderhulke*', a luminary of the
University of Wittenberg (McKerrow 1904–10: 247–9). Nashe denies, in his
introductory address to readers of the second edition of his *Christs Teares over
Jerusalem* (1594), that this has any connection with any English university
man save perhaps Harvey, and goes on to discuss the accusations which have
been levelled against his own style in that work, which is particularly free
in lexical creativity. That defence forms the first excerpt. The second excerpt
is an illustration of his descriptive style in *The Unfortunate Traveller*, in
which he relates the picaresque adventures of one Jack Wilton, an adventurer
living on his wits. The passage forms part of his account of the seductive
luxury of life among the wealthy inhabitants of contemporary Rome.

A   From the Preface to *Christs Teares over Jerusalem*

The ploddinger sort of vnlearned Zoilists about London exclaim
that it is a puft-vp stile, and full of prophane eloquence: others
obiect vnto me the multitude of my boystrous compound wordes,
and the often coyning of Italionate verbes which end all in Ize,

as mummianize, tympanize, tirannize. To the first array of my clumperton Antigonists this I answer, that my stile is no otherwise puft up, then any mās should be which writes with any Spirite; and whom would not such a deuine subiect put a high rauishte Spirite into? For the prophanesse of my eloquence, so they may tearme the eloquence of Sainct *Austen, Jerome, Chrysostome*, prophane, since none of them but takes vnto him farre more liberty of Tropes, Figures, and Metaphors, and alleadging Heathen examples and Histories.

To the second rancke of reprehenders that complain of my boystrous compound wordes, and ending my Italionate coyned verbs all in Ize, thus I replie: That no winde that blowes strong but is boystrous, no speech or wordes of any power or force to confute or perswade but mustbee swelling and boystrous. For the compounding of my wordes, therein I imitate rich men who, hauing gathered store of white single money together, conuert a number of those small little scutes into great peeces of gold, such as double Pistols and Portugues. Our English tongue of all languages most swarmeth with the single money of monasillables, which are the onely scandall of it. Bookes written in them and no other seeme like Shop-keepers boxes, that containe nothing else saue halfe-pence, three-farthings, and two-pences. Therefore what did me I, but hauing a huge heape of those worthlesse shreds of small English in my *Pia maters* purse, to make the royaller shew with them to mens eyes, had thē to the compounders immediately, and exchanged them foure into one, and others into more, according to the Greek, French, Spanish, and Italian?

Come, my maisters, inure your mouthes to it, and neuer trust me but when you haue tride the commodity of carrying much in a small roome, you will, like the Apothecaries, vse more compounds then simples, and graft wordes as men do their trees to make them more fruitfull. My vbraided Italionate verbes are the least crime of a thousand, since they are growne in generall request with euery good Poet.

Besides, they carrie farre more state with them then any other, and are not halfe so harsh in their desinence as the old hobling English verbes ending in R; they expresse more then any other verbes whatsoeuer, and their substantiues would be quite barraine of verbs but for that ending. This word Mummianizd in the beginning of my first Epistle is shrewdly called in question; for no other

45   reason that I can conceiue, but that his true deriuatiue, which is
      Mummy, is somewhat obscure also: To Phisitions and their con-
      fectioners it is as familiar as Mumchaunce amongest Pages, being
      nothing else but mans flesh long buried and broyled in the burning
      sands of Arabia. Hereupon I haue taken vp this phrase of Ierusalems
50   Mummianized earth, (as much to say as Ierusalems earth manured
      with mans flesh.) Expresse who can the same substance so briefly
      in any other word but that. A man may murder any thing if hee list
      in the mouthing, and grinde it to powder extempore betwixt a
      huge paire of iawes: but let a quest of calme censors goe vpon it
55   twixt the houres of sixe and seauen in the morning, and they will
      in their graue wisdoms subscribe to it as tollerable and significant.

B   From *The Unfortunate Traveller*

      To tell you of the rare pleasures of their gardens, theyr bathes,
      theyr vineyardes, theyr galleries, were to write a seconde part of the
      gorgeous Gallerie of gallant deuices. Why, you should not come
      into anie mannes house of account, but hee hadde fish-pondes and
5   little orchardes on the toppe of his leads. If by raine or any other
      meanes those ponds were so full they need to be slust or let out,
      euen of their superfluities they made melodious vse, for they had
      great winde instruments in stead of leaden spoutes, that went duly
      on consort, onely with this waters rumbling discent. I sawe a
10   summer banketting house belonging to a merchaunt, that was the
      meruaile of the world, and could not be matcht except God should
      make another paradise. It was builte round of greene marble like
      a Theater with-out: within there was a heauen and earth compre-
      hended both vnder one roofe; the heauen was a cleere ouerhanging
15   vault of christall, wherein the Sunne and Moone and each visible
      Starre had his true similitude, shine, scituation, and motion, and,
      by what enwrapped arte I cannot conceiue, these spheares in their
      proper orbes obserued their circular wheelinges and turnings, mak-
      ing a certaine kinde of soft angelical murmering musicke in their
20   often windings and going about; which musick the philosophers
      say in the true heauen, by reason of the grosenes of our senses, we
      are not capable of. For the earth, it was counterfeited in that liknes
      that Adam lorded out it before his fall. A wide vast spacious roome
      it was, such as we would conceit prince Arthurs hall to be, where
25   he feasted all his knights of the round table together euerie penticost.

The flore was painted with the beautifullest flouers that euer mans
eie admired; which so linealy were delineated that he that viewd
them a farre off, and had not directly stood poaringly ouer them,
would haue sworne they had liued in deede. The wals round about
were hedgde with Oliues and palme trees, and all other odoriferous
fruit-bearing plants; which at anie solemne intertainment dropt
mirrhe and frankensense. Other trees, that bare no fruit, were set
in iust order one against another, and diuided the roome into a
number of shadie lanes, leauing but one ouerspreading pine tree
arbor, where wee sate and banketted. On the wel clothed boughs of
this conspiracie of pine trees against the resembled Sun beames,
were pearcht as many sortes of shrill breasted birdes as the Summer hath allowed for singing men in hir siluane chappels. Who
though there were bodies without soules, and sweete resembled
substances without sense, yet by the matheticall experimentes of
long siluer pipes secretlye inrinded in the intrailes of the boughs
whereon they sate, and vndiscerneablie conuaid vnder their bellies
into their small throats sloaping, they whistled and freely carold
theyr naturall field note. Neyther went those siluer pipes straight,
but, by many edged vnsundred writhings and crankled wander-
inges a side, strayed from bough to bough into an hundred throats.
But into this siluer pipe so writhed and wandering aside, if anie
demand how the wind was breathed; Forsoth yᵉ tail of the siluer pipe
stretcht it selfe into the mouth of a great paire of belowes, where
it was close soldered, and bailde about with yron, it coulde not
stirre or haue anie vent betwixt. Those bellowes with the rising and
falling of leaden plummets wounde vp on a wheele, dyd beate
vp and downe vncessantly, and so gathered in wind, seruing with
one blast all the snarled pipes to and fro of one tree at once. But
so closely were all those organizing implements obscured in the
corpulent trunks of the trees, that euerie man there present renounst
coniectures of art, and sayd it was done by inchantment.

One tree for his fruit bare nothing but inchained chirping
birdes, whose throates beeing conduit pipt with squared narrowe
shels, and charged siring-wise with searching sweet water driuen
in by a little wheele for the nonce, that fed it a farre of, made a
spirting sound, such as chirping is, in bubling vpwards through the
rough crannies of their closed bills.

Vnder tuition of the shade of euerie tree that I haue signified
to be in this round hedge, on delightful leuie cloisters, lay a wylde

tyranous beast asleepe all prostrate; vnder some, two together, as the Dogge nusling his nose vnder the necke of the Deare, the Wolfe glad to let the Lambe lye vpon hym to keepe him warme, the Lyon suffering the Asse to cast hys legge ouer him, preferring one
70   honest vnmannerly friende before a number of croutching picke-thankes. No poysonous beast there reposed, (poyson was not before our parent *Adam* transgressed). There were no sweete-breathing Panthers that would hyde their terrifying heads to betray; no men-imitating *Hyænaes* that chaunged their sexe to seeke after bloud.
75   Wolues as now when they are hungrie eate earth, so then did they feed on earth only, and abstained from innocent flesh. The Vnicorne did not put his horne into the streame to chase awaye venome before hee dronke, for then there was no suche thing extant in the water or on the earth. Serpents were as harmlesse to mankinde as
80   they are still one to another: the rose had no cankers, the leues no caterpillers, the sea no *Syrens*, the earth no vsurers. Goats then bare wooll, as it is recorded in *Sicily* they doo yet. The torride Zone was habitable: only Iayes loued to steale gold and siluer to build their nests withall, and none cared for couetous clientrie, or runing to
85   the Indies. As the Elephant vnderstands his countrey speach, so euerie beast vnderstood what man spoke. The ant did not hoord vp against winter, for there was no winter, but a perpetuall spring, as *Ouid* sayth. No frosts to make the greene almound tree counted rash and improuident, in budding soonest of all other; or the
90   mulberie tree a strange polititian, in blooming late and ripening early. The peach tree at the first planting was fruitfull and wholsome, whereas now, till it be transplanted, it is poisonous and hatefull: young plants for their sap had balme, for their yeolow gumme glistering amber. The euening deawd not water on flowers, but
95   honnie. Such a golden age, such a good age, such an honest age was set forth in this banketting house.

Notes

Christs Teares over Jerusalem

1   **Zoilists**   Zoilus was a Greek grammarian and critic of the fourth century BC, who was famous for his harsh criticism of Homer. In Elizabethan times the name came to mean an ill-disposed critic.

3   **boystrous compound wordes**   Compounding and derivation of a wide variety of kinds are characteristic of Elizabethan usage. The word *boystrous*,

'rough, coarse', is more than anything else a value judgement on compounds found unpleasing.

4   **Ize**   This verb-forming suffix was familiar enough in English from French sources, from which it is adopted in the form *-ise*. The *-ize* spelling derives from Latin more commonly than Italian, and became common in scientific discourse (Görlach 1991: 176–7; Gotti 1996: 44). Of the words cited, *tirannize* existed in the French form and Nashe had been anticipated in the Latin form by both Spenser and Shakespeare. The other two ('connected with a mummy' and 'to puff up') seem to be Nashe's coinages.

6   **clumperton** 'clownish'   Recorded from 1534.

7   **which writes**   Nashe uses *which* and *whom* consecutively as personal relatives. In the next clause the preposition *into* goes with *whom*. Except for *hath* and *doth*, he normally uses the *-es* form of the third-person-singular present tense.

21   **scutes** 'a coin of small value'   But earlier used for the French *écu*, so called because of the shield stamped on it. The word derives from Anglo-French *scute* and Medieval Lat. *scutum*.

28   **Pia maters purse** 'brain'   The *pia mater* is the membrane surrounding the brain. A Latinisation of an originally Arabic phrase meaning 'tender mother'. Recorded in technical contexts from 1400.

36   **vbraided**   The spelling represents a common assimilation between the voiceless and voiced consonants /p/ and /b/.

40   **desinence**   A technical grammatical term for the ending or suffix of a word. This is the earliest recorded occurrence in English.

44   **shrewdly** 'disagreeably'   The ME sense.

47   **mumchaunce**   Originally a game of dice (MLG *mummenschanze*), but had already come to mean a dumb show or mumming, and by extension, to 'play mumchance' meant to keep silent. Compare 'to keep mum'.

52   **if hee list** 'if it pleases him'   The grammar of impersonal constructions is no longer fully understood, so the nominative equivalent of *he* has replaced the dative *him*.

53   **extempore** 'on the spot' (Lat. *ex tempore*, 'arising out of the time or moment')   The word had been in use in English for about fifty years.

The Unfortunate Traveller

4   **anie mannes**, etc.   The syntax remains that of OE rather than that of the modern group genitive 'any man of account's house'.

6   **slust** 'sluiced'   The spelling with a final *-t* of the past participles (and also preterites) of Weak verbs whose stem ends in a voiceless consonant is common in Nashe. This habit was still in use in some circles in the nineteenth century.

16   **his**   Not personification, but the use of the common masculine and neuter form of the genitive third-person pronoun.

26   **beautifullest**   The modern English rule by which adjectives of more than two syllables form comparatives and superlatives by the use of *more* and *most* has not yet become established.

31   **intertainment**   The distribution of the *in-* and *en-* forms of the prefix is variable. See also *intrailes* (41), *inchantment* (57).

36   **conspiracie** 'collection, combination'   The sense is extended here a little beyond what is usual.

37   **shrill breasted**   Although here printed as two words, the pattern is that of a very common type of compound which was highly productive in the sixteenth century. Such compounds are interpreted as extensions into adjectival use (by the suffix *-ed*) of earlier nominal compounds of the type *redcoat*. Nashe's conscious creativity follows an established pattern of the time.

39   **resembled** 'simulated'   The use of the native suffix *-ed* in a function similar to that of the Latin passive participle ending *-atus* leads to the formation of numerous *-ed* modifiers from both verbs and nouns in Elizabethan English.

41   **inrinded** 'placed within the bark'   The OE word *rind* has been gradually replaced by the Scandinavian borrowing, *bark*, when referring to trees. The word *inrinded* was coined by Nashe.

45   **crankled** 'zig-zag'   The earliest occurrence of a rare word, etymologically related to both 'crank' and 'crinkled'.

64   **tuition** 'protection'   Once again the sense is extended from the usual contemporary senses by the non-personal agent.

70–71   **picke-thankes** 'flatterers'   The compound is recorded from 1412.

72   **sweete-breathing**   This type of adjectival compound, in which the present participle follows an adverb or adjective, has been common since the sixteenth century.

73–74   **men-imitating**   As with the previous type, compound adjectives with a noun followed by the present participle are found in OE and ME, but the major productivity of the type is from the sixteenth century.

31

SHAKESPEARE, *LOVE'S LABOUR'S LOST*, ACT V, SCENE I

The earliest surviving text of *Love's Labour's Lost* is the quarto dated 1598, which is claimed to be an edition 'newly corrected and augmented' of one apparently lost. Shakespeare's plays were produced for performance and the history of their texts is often complex. In many cases they first appeared in what have become known as 'bad' quartos – carelessly produced copies pirated from productions of the play or from the memory of actors. Such editions were then often followed by corrected, authorised versions, the 'good' quartos; and finally, after Shakespeare's death, his works were collected by his associates into the First Folio of 1623. The 'good' quarto of 1598 was probably assembled from Shakespeare's own papers, but although it may therefore be expected to represent his spelling as closely as any of the plays, this does not mean that it is an exact replica of what Shakespeare wrote. Compositors in Elizabethan times felt free to impose their own practices upon the author's text, so that although the text printed here corrects obvious compositor's errors in typesetting (which are particularly common in this play), it is impossible to determine which among acceptable variants are the spellings of the author's manuscript.

William Shakespeare (1564–1616) was the son of a prosperous glover and wool dealer and received an education at the King's New School in his home town of Stratford-upon-Avon. There is no evidence that he proceeded to any form of higher education. As a grammar-school boy he would have been instructed in the classics of Latin literature, trained in Latin grammar, and grounded in rhetoric. In the later stages he would have been expected to put this theory into practice, composing orations and formal letters based upon the rules of Latin literacy. Both analysis and practice in composition must have awakened him to the discrepancies between Latin and English, and to the debates about the status and improvement of English which occupied the attention of others with similar, and more extended, training. The question of Inkhorn terms and the refurbishment of English from Latin lies behind this scene in *Love's Labour's Lost*. Indeed, it has been suggested that the character Boy (Moth in the Folio) is an allusion to Nashe, and, less persuasively, that Armado and Pedant (Holofernes) may be related to Harvey.

> *Enter Holofernes the Pedant, Nathaniel the Curat, and Anthony Dull*
>
> PEDANT *Satis quid sufficit.*
>
> NATHANIEL I prayse God for you sir, your reasons at Dinner haue been sharpe and sententious: pleasant without scurillitie, wittie without affection, audatious without impudencie, learned with-
>
> 5 out opinion, and strange without heresie: I did conuerse this quondam day with a companion of the kings, who is intituled, nominated, or called, *Don Adriano de Armatho.*
>
> PEDANT *Noui hominum tanquam te,* His humour is loftie, his dis-course peremptorie: his tongue fyled, his eye ambitious, his gate
>
> 10 maiesticall, and his generall behauiour vaine, rediculous, and thrasonicall. He is too picked, to spruce, too affected, to od as it were, too peregrinat as I may call it.
>
> NATHANIEL A most singuler and choyce Epithat,
>
>   *Draw-out his Table-booke*
>
> 15 PEDANT He draweth out the thred of his verbositie, finer then the staple of his argument. I abhorre such phanatticall phantasims, such insociable and poynt deuise companions, such rackers of ortagriphie, as to speake dout *sine* b, when he should say doubt; det, when he shold pronounce debt; d e b t, not d e t: he clepeth
>
> 20 a Calfe, Caufe: halfe, haufe: neighbour *vocatur* nebour; neigh abreuiated *ne*: this is abhominable, which he would call *abbominable*, it insinuateth me of *insanire: ne intelligis domine,* to make frantique lunatique?
>
> NATHANIEL Laus deo, bone intelligo.
>
> 25 PEDANT *Bone? Boon for boon prescian,* a little scratcht, twil serue.
>
>   *Enter Armado the Bragart, Moth his Boy, and Costard the Clowne*
>
> NATHANIEL *Videsne quis venit?*
>
> PEDANT *Video, et gaudio.*
>
> ARMADO (*to Moth*) Chirra.
>
> 30 PEDANT (*to Nathaniel*) *Quare* Chirra, not Sirra?
>
> ARMADO Men of peace well incontred.

PEDANT Most millitarie sir salutation.

BOY (*aside to Costard*) They haue been at a great feast of Languages,
and stolne the scraps.

35   CLOWNE (*aside to Moth*) O they haue lyud long on the almsbasket
of wordes. I maruaile thy M. hath not eaten thee for a worde, for
thou art not so long by the head as *honorificabilitudinitatibus*:
Thou art easier swallowed then a flapdragon.

BOY (*aside to Costard*) Peace, the peale begins.

40   ARMADO (*to Holofernes*) Mounsier, are you not lettred?

BOY Yes yes, he teaches boyes the Horne-booke: What is Ab speld
backward with the horne on his head?

PEDANT Ba, *puericia* with a horne added.

BOY Ba most seely Sheepe, with a horne: you heare his learning.

45   PEDANT *Quis quis* thou Consonant?

BOY The last of the fiue Vowels if You repeate them, or the fift if I.

PEDANT I will repeate them: a e I.

BOY The Sheepe, the other two concludes it o u.

ARMADO Now by the sault waue of the meditaranium, a sweete

50   tutch, a quicke venewe of wit, snip snap, quicke and home, it
reioiceth my intellect, true wit.

BOY Offerd by a childe to an old man: which it wit-old.

PEDANT What is the figure? What is the figure?

BOY Hornes.

55   PEDANT Thou disputes like an Infant: goe whip thy Gigg.

BOY Lende me your Horne to make one, and I will whip about
your Infamie *circum circa* a gigge of a Cuckolds horne.

CLOWNE And I had but one peny in the world thou shouldst haue
it to buy Ginger bread: (*Giuing money*) Holde, there is the verie

60   Remuneration I had of thy Maister, thou halfepennie purse of
wit, thou Pidgin-egge of discretion. O and the heauens were so
pleased, that thou wart but my Bastard; What a ioyfull father
wouldest thou make me? Go to, thou hast it *ad dungil* at the
fingers ends, as they say.

65   PEDANT Oh I smell false Latine, *dunghel* for *vnguem*.

ARMADO Arts-man *preambulat*, we will be singuled from the
barbarous. Do you not educate youth at the Charg-house on
the top of the Mountaine?

PEDANT Or *Mons* the hill.

70   ARMADO At your sweete pleasure, for the Mountaine.

PEDANT I do *sans question*.

ARMADO Sir, it is the Kings most sweete pleasur and affection, to congratulate the Princesse at her Pauilion, in the *posteriors* of this day, which the rude multitude call the after-noone.

75 PEDANT The *posterior* of the day, most generous sir, is liable, congruent, and measurable for the after noone: the worde is well culd, choise, sweete, and apt I do assure you sir, I do assure.

ARMADO Sir, the King is a noble Gentleman, and my familier, I do assure ye very good friende: for what is inwarde betweene vs, let

80 it passe. I do beseech thee remember thy curtesie. I beseech thee apparrell thy head: and among other important and most serious designes, and of great import in deede too: but let that passe, for I must tell thee it will please his Grace (by the worlde) sometime to leane vpon my poore shoulder, and with his royall finger

85 thus dallie with my excrement, with my mustachio: but sweete hart let that passe. By the world I recount no fable, some certaine special honours it pleaseth his greatnes to impart to *Armado* a Souldier, a man of trauayle, that hath seene the worlde: but let that passe; the very all of all is: but sweet hart, I do implore

90 secrecie, that the King would haue me present the Princesse (sweete chuck) with some delightfull ostentation, or show, or pageant, or antique, or fierworke: Now vnderstanding that the Curate and your sweete selfe, are good at such eruptions, and sodaine breaking out of myrth (as it were) I haue acquainted

95 you withall, to the ende to craue your assistance.

PEDANT Sir, you shall present before her the Nine Worthies, Sir *Nathaniel*, as concerning some entertainement of time, some show in the posterior of this day, to be rendred by our assistance the Kinges commaund, and this most gallant illustrate and learned

100 Gentleman, before the Princesse: I say none so fit as to present the nine Worthies.

NATHANIEL Where will you finde men worthie enough to present them?

PEDANT *Iosua*, your selfe, my selfe, *Iudas Machabeus*, and this gallant

105 Gentleman, *Hector*; this Swaine (because of his great lim or ioynt) shall passe *Pompey* the great, the Page *Hercules.*

ARMADO Pardon sir, error: He is not quantitie enough for that worthies thumbe, he is not so big as the end of his Club.

PEDANT Shall I haue audience? He shall present *Hercules* in

110 minoritie: his enter and exit shalbe strangling a Snake; and I will haue an Apologie for that purpose.

BOY An excellent deuice: so if any of the audience hisse, you may cry, Well done *Hercules*, now thou crusshest the Snake; that is the way to make an offence gracious, though few haue the grace

115   to do it.

ARMADO For the rest of the Worthies?

PEDANT I will play three my selfe.

BOY Thrice worthie Gentleman.

ARMADO Shall I tell you a thing?

120   PEDANT We attende.

ARMADO We will haue, if this fadge not, an Antique. I beseech you follow.

PEDANT *Via* good-man *Dull*, thou hast spoken no worde all this while.

125   DULL Nor vnderstoode none neither sir.

PEDANT Alone, we will employ thee.

DULL Ile make one in a daunce, or so: or I will play on the Taber to the worthies, and let them dance the hey.

PEDANT Most *Dull*, honest *Dull*, to our sport: away.

Exeunt

Notes

1   **Satis . . .** 'enough is enough'   In the upper classes of the Elizabethan grammar school, pupils were expected to converse in Latin.

2   **reasons** 'phrases'   The word was used in ME to distinguish the grammatical conception of a sentence from that of its content, which was implied by the word *sentence*. Here the word is being used simply as a technical term suited to the characters.

3   **sententious** 'full of significance'   Adjective formed from the noun *sentence* in the sense above.

5   **opinion** 'arrogance'   This sense is recorded by *OED* 5c only from Shakespeare. The word tended to have bad associations from its earlier sense, 'belief not founded upon adequate grounds'.

6   **quondam** 'past'   (Lat., 'formerly, once, at one time'.)
of the kings   The apostrophe, with its origins in Greek, is a learned introduction towards the end of the sixteenth century and is not employed in this text, but it is frequently used in the Folio to mark the omission of letters unpronounced in delivery, although not for the possessive.

7   **Armatho**   The alternation in spelling with *Armado* reflects confusion brought about by two ME sound changes: (1) in which /ð/ > /d/ when immediately followed by *m, n, r* or *l* (OE *byrðen, morðrian* > ME *burden,*

murdren); and (2) a fifteenth-century change in which /d/ followed by syllabic *r* > /ð/ (OE *fæder, moder* > late ME *father, mother*). Variants in pronunciation arose and confused the spellings.

8   **Noui ...** 'I know the man as well as I know you'   The phrase may have been drawn from Lily's 1549 Latin grammar, where it appears as an example of the use of *tanquam*.

9   **fyled** 'polished'   A word often collocated with *eloquence*. See also *picked* (11), which is frequently collocated with *terms* in describing eloquence.

10–11   **rediculous, and thrasonicall** 'laughable and boastful'   Note the <e> for <i>, which represents a lowered variant in unstressed syllables common in London English of Elizabeth's time (cf. Excerpt 26). *Thrasonicall* is an adjective derived from 'Thraso', the name of the braggart soldier in Terence's *Eunuchus*. The word had been in use among literary men for over twenty years.

12   **peregrinat** 'having the air of a foreigner'   Shakespeare's is the first and only independent use of the word, but it is an etymological parallel with the use of *pilgrim* as an adjective in the Wycliffite Bible and in Excerpt 21.

16   **phanatticall phantasims** 'extravagant fantasists'   *Phantasims* is recorded only in this play, but Florio records the Italian word *fantasima* in 1611. The <ph> spellings represent the revived interest in Greek during the Renaissance.

17   **poynt deuise** 'precise'   Used by Chaucer in adverbial phrases.

18   **ortagriphie**   The word refers to the contemporary arts of pronunciation and correct writing (e.g. John Hart's *An Orthographie*, 1569) which sought Latin or, less usually, Greek etymologies to frame their rules. The words *doubt* and *debt* existed in ME as French borrowings, *doute* and *dette*, and the *b* is restored from the Latin etymology. The spellings *caufe* and *haufe* represent a stage in the phonetic development of the sequence [ɑl] > [ɑʊl] > [ɑʊ] > [ɔː] (cf. *sault*, 49). The final stage was reached in the early seventeenth century. *Neighbour* and *neigh* are given spellings which reflect the loss of the fricative consonant represented by *gh*. This occurred during the fifteenth century. The spelling *abhominable*, preferred by Pedant, derives mistakenly from a supposed Latin phrase **ab homine*, 'away from man' (suggesting revulsion), rather than the correct *abominari*, 'to deprecate as an ill omen'.

22   **insinuateth**   The sense of this is not certain. It seems that Pedant is using the word *insinuateth* to mean 'drive mad' and deriving it from an unrecorded Latin verb **insinare*, 'to go mad'. He then suggests in Latin that Nathaniel doesn't follow this, and glosses it 'to make frantic or lunatic'. At which Nathaniel praises God for the enlightenment. Pedant picks up his *bone*, used in error for *bene*.

25   **prescian**   Priscian (sixth century AD) was the author of the advanced Latin grammar most widely used in the Middle Ages and Renaissance.

29   **Chirra**   The form of address to a page from his master would be *sirrah*. This pronunciation may, however, derive from a greeting, *chaere*, in Erasmus's *Familiaria Colloquia*, used as a contemporary schoolbook.

35   **almsbasket**   The basket of scraps left over from a feast and distributed to the poor.

37   **honorificabilitudinitatibus**   Notorious in medieval and Renaissance Latinity as the longest word known.

38   **flapdragon**   A burning raisin or plum floating in punch (or similar) and snapped up by the participants in a Christmas game.

41   **Horne-booke**   A simple alphabet book, perhaps also containing numbers, elements of spelling and the Lord's Prayer, so called because it was mounted on a tablet of wood and protected by a thin sheet of horn. *OED* gives this as the earliest occurrence of the word.

45   **Consonant**   Possibly an expression related to that cited by *OED* in which a fool is paralleled with a consonant and contrasted with a mute (an unvoiced sound). Speaking when silence might have been the better policy is a traditional indicator of folly.

48   **Sheepe**   The Spanish word for 'sheep', *oueia*, was used in Vives' *Exercitatio Linguae Latinae* as a mnemonic for the vowels.

      concludes   Both 'finishes' the list of vowels and 'proves' the proposition. The *-es* inflexion is singular and is in concord with *the other*. But see the use of *-es* with the second-person singular in line 55. The loss of final *-t* is especially common in verbs whose base form ends in *-t*.

50   **venewe**   In fencing, the attack leading to a hit.

52   **wit-old**   This is a pun on the word *wittol*, 'a contented cuckold'. Apparently formed in late ME by blending the verb *witen*, 'to know', with *cokewold*.

65   **dunghel . . . vnguem**   The Latin tag referred to is *ad . . . unguem*, 'to the nail' – that is, 'exactly'.

73   **congratulate** 'greet, salute'   The word is first recorded in 1548, but this rare sense is recorded only between 1578 and 1611.

75   **liable** 'suitable, apt'   A sense recorded only during the last three decades of the sixteenth century. *Congrue* is used in the fourteenth century to refer to grammatical concord and harmonious composition, and, with the other associated epithets, is a statement of the stylistic ideal of decorum.

78–79   **I do assure ye**   The spelling of the second-person-plural pronoun here indicates unstressed pronunciation with a centralised vowel. It should not be confused with the stressed *ye* of formal discourse.

85   **excrement** 'that which grows out or forth' (Lat. *excrescere, excrementum*) First recorded in the sixteenth century, the word was obsolete by the beginning of the eighteenth, perhaps inhibited in use by its homonym.

91   **ostentation**   This is the sole use given by *OED* with the sense 'spectacular show'.

96   **Nine Worthies**   A frequent constituent of popular entertainment in Tudor London. Machyn (Excerpt 26) repeatedly mentions them as part of May games. They were Joshua, David, Judas Maccabeus, Hector, Alexander, Julius Caesar, King Arthur, Charlemagne and either Godfrey of Bouillon or Guy of Warwick. Shakespeare does not follow this traditional list, and includes Hercules and Pompey.

121   **fadge** 'succeed, turn out well'   The etymology of the word is unknown. It first occurs in 1578 and is rare after 1700.

32

THOMAS DEKKER, *THE GULS HORNE-BOOKE*

Although relatively well known for his comedy *The Shoemaker's Holiday*, Thomas Dekker could scarcely have considered himself one of the literary successes of Elizabethan London. Instead, he eked out a precarious living as a popular author, in and out of debtors' prison, writing brief works and pamphlets, collaborating with others on plays, but never achieving lasting personal success. The date of his birth is uncertain but appears to have been about 1572. A Londoner, he first came to prominence as a playwright in the early 1590s, and after 1598 he participated in the composition of more than sixty plays. He was at this time employed by the impresario Philip Henslowe. In 1612 he was committed to the King's Bench Prison for debt and remained there for seven harsh years. Critical opinion of Dekker's personality has been somewhat divided, viewing him both as a man of unfailing good humour and as one who suffered from the discrepancy between his own aspirations as author and gentleman and his humiliating experience as hack writer and prisoner. His *Guls Horne-booke* (1609) may hold beneath its superficial humour an ironic tone of indignation at the irresponsibility of the privileged young man-about-town. Its form is indeed an ironic inversion of the courtesy books produced for the guidance of those seeking entrance to fashionable society.

The Guls Horne-booke draws its title from elementary Elizabethan schoolbooks bound between plates of horn, and the word *gull* is significantly ambiguous, meaning both 'fop' and 'dupe or fool'. The pamphlet does not seem to have been popular in its own day, since it was not reprinted, but it has more recently been valued as a store of information on the street life of Elizabethan London. Linguistically, it is interesting for its cosmopolitan style, mixing recent borrowings and derivational forms (*dedicated, tripos*) of an elevated kind with technical theatrical vocabulary (*properties, hangings*), fashionable Spanish- and Italianisms (*bastinado, zany*) and colloquial and slang usage (*cockatrice, punck*). The printed text preserves some of the phrasings and assimilations of racy speech (*your Inne-a-court-man, one ath Scullery*). Dekker is inventive too in extending the senses of words for verbal play, and creative in coining disparaging compounds to refer to the common people. Also noticeable is his use of words of sound-echoic origin: *flirt, blare, mew, whew*.

The text here expands a few abbreviations but otherwise retains the original spelling and punctuation, including the abbreviation *y^e* used by the printer to fit his copy into the line.

How a Gallant should behaue himselfe in a Play-house

Mary let this obseruation go hand in hand with the rest: or rather like a country-seruingman, some fiue yards before them. Present not your selfe on the Stage (especially at a new play) vntill the quaking prologue hath (by rubbing) got cullor into his cheekes, and is ready
5 to giue the trumpets their Cue that hees vpon point to enter: for then it is time, as though you were one of the *Properties*, or that you dropt out of y^e *Hangings* to creepe from behind the Arras with your *Tripos* or three-footed stoole in one hand, and a teston mounted betweene a forefinger and a thumbe in the other: for if you should
10 bestow your person vpon the vulgar, when the belly of the house is but halfe full, your apparell is quite eaten vp, the fashion lost, and the proportion of your body in more danger to be deuoured, then if it were serud vp in the Counter amongst the Powltry: auoid that as you would the Bastome. It shall crowne you with rich
15 commendation to laugh alowd in the middest of the most serious and saddest scene of the terriblest Tragedy: and to let that clapper (your tongue) be tost so high that all the house may ring of it: your Lords vse it; your Knights are Apes to the Lords, and do so too: your Inne-a-court-man is Zany to the Knights, and (many very
20 scuruily) comes likewise limping after it: bee thou a beagle to them all, and neuer lin snuffing till you haue sented them: for by talking and laughing (like a Plough-man in a Morris) you heape *Pelion* vpon *Ossa*, glory vpon glory: As first, all the eyes in the galleries will leaue walking after the Players, and onely follow you: the simplest dolt in
25 the house snatches vp your name, and when he meetes you in the streetes, or that you fall into his hands in the middle of a Watch, his word shall be taken for you, heele cry, *Hees such a Gallant*, and

you passe. Secondly, you publish your temperance to the world, in
that you seeme not to resort thither to taste vaine pleasures with a
hungrie appetite; but onely as a Gentleman, to spend a foolish houre
or two, because you can doe nothing else. Thirdly you mightily
disrelish the Audience, and disgrace the Author: mary you take vp
(though it be at the worst hand) a strong opinion of your owne
iudgement and inforce the Poet to take pitty of your weakenesse,
and by some dedicated sonnet to bring you into a better paradice,
onely to stop your mouth.

If you can (either for loue or money) prouide yourself a
lodging by the water side: for aboue the conueniencie it brings, to
shun Shoulder-clapping, and to ship away your Cockatrice betimes
in the morning it addes a kind of state vnto you, to be carried from
thence to the staires of your Play-house: hate a Sculler (remember
that) more then to be acquainted with one ath Scullery. No, your
Oares are your onely Sea-crabs, boord them and take heed you
neuer go twice together with one paire: often shifting is a great credit
to Gentlemen: and that diuiding of your Fare wil make ye poore
watersnaks be ready to pul you in peeces to enioy your custome:
No matter whether vpon landing you haue money or no, you may
swim in twentie of their boates over the riuer, upon *Ticket*: mary
when siluer comes in, remember to pay trebble their fare, and it
will make your Flounder-catchers to send more thankes after you,
when you doe not draw, then when you doe: for they know, It will
be their owne another daie.

Before the Play begins, fall to cardes, you may win or loose (as
Fencers doe in a prize) and beate one another by confederacie, yet
share the money when you meete at supper: notwithstanding, to gul
the *Ragga-muffins* that stand a loofe gaping at you, throw the cards
(hauing first torne foure or fiue of them) round about the Stage,
iust vpon the third sound, as though you had lost: it skils not if the
foure knaues ly on their backs, and outface the Audience, theres
none such fooles as dare take exceptions at them, because ere the
play go off, better knaues then they will fall into the company.

Now sir if the writer be a fellow that hath epigramd you, or
hath had a flirt at your mistris, or hath brought either your feather
or your red beard, or your little legs etc. on the stage, you shall
disgrace him worse then by tossing him in a blancket, or giuing
him the bastinado in a Tauerne, if in the middle of his play, (bee it
Pastorall or Comedy, Morall or Tragedie) you rise with a skreud and

70
discontented face from your stoole to be gone: no matter whether the Scenes be good or no, the better they are, the more doe you distast them: and beeing on your feete, sneake not away like a coward, but salute all your gentle acquaintance, that are spred either on the rushes, or on stooles about you, and draw what troope you can from the stage after you: the *Mimicks* are beholden to you, for allowing them elbow roome: their Poet cries perhaps a pox go with

75
you, but care not you for that, theres no musick without frets.

Mary if either the company, or indisposition of the weather binde you to sit it out, my counsell is then that you turne plain Ape, take vp a rush and tickle the earnest eares of your fellow gallants, to make other fooles fall a laughing: mewe at passionate speeches, blare

80
at merrie, finde fault with the musicke, whew at the childrens Action, whistle at the songs: and aboue all, curse the sharers, that whereas the same day you had bestowed forty shillings on an embrodered Felt and Feather, (scotch-fashion) for your mistres in the Court, or your punck in the Cittie, within two houres after, you encounter

85
with the very same block on the stage, when the haberdasher swore to you the impression was extant but that morning.

To conclude, hoord vp the finest play-scraps you can get, vpon which your leane wit may most sauourly feede for want of other stuffe, when the *Arcadian* and *Euphuisd* gentlewomen haue

90
their tongues sharpened to set vpon you: that qualitie (next to your shittlecocke) is the onely furniture to a Courtier thats but a new beginner, and is but in his *A B C* of complement.

Notes

8
Tripos   Formed on the Latin *tripus* but given a Greek-looking ending. Greek carried greater prestige than Latin in the sixteenth and seventeenth centuries, being less widely known.

teston   A silver sixpenny piece. Originally the French name of a fifteenth-century Milanese coin which bore the head of the Duke Galeazzo Maria Sforza. Italian *testone* from *testa*, 'head'.

10
the vulgar 'the common people' (Lat. *vulgaris*, 'common, ordinary') This nominal usage was first recorded in 1590.

13
Counter . . . Powltry   Dekker here indulges in wordplay on the name of a debtors' prison. The Counter in the district of the Poultry was the Sheriff's prison from which Henslowe discharged Dekker on 4 February 1598 with a loan of 40 shillings.

14   **Bastome**   Perhaps a cudgel (Fr. *baston*), but in the context perhaps also the officer whose function it was to escort prisoners from the court to the Fleet prison on committal, and thereafter accompany them on any excursions from the gaol. So called from the red staff which he carried.

16   **terriblest**   The rule by which the superlative of a multisyllabic adjective is formed by the use of *most* is not yet fully established.

18   **your Lords**   The use of the second-person-plural pronoun as a quasi-demonstrative develops in Elizabethan English in informal contexts and is particularly common in dramatic works in the first decade of the seventeenth century.

19   **Zany** 'ludicrous imitator' (Italian and French *zani*)   The word is from regional Italian forms of Gianni, and is given to those servants who play the clown's role in the *Commedia dell'arte*.

21   **sented**   (Fr. *sentir*). The modern spelling with <sc> does not appear until the seventeenth century.

22–23   **Pelion . . . Ossa**   In Greek mythology, in order to reach the gods, the giants heaped Mount Pelion upon Mount Ossa and Ossa on Olympus to form a ladder.

39   **Shoulder-clapping** 'arrest, tap on the shoulder'.
Cockatrice 'whore'   This slang sense is recorded only between 1599 and the mid eighteenth century. The word has a complex sense history (see *OED*), and more usually in English from the fourteenth century refers to the mythological basilisk whose gaze could turn an onlooker to stone.

43   **Oares** 'oarsmen'   These work in pairs, as opposed to the sculler, who works alone.

48   **upon Ticket** 'on credit' (Fr. *étiquette*)   Originally referred to a brief note or label attached to something. Develops the sense of 'a promissory note, IOU' from about 1600, and the phrase 'on tick' is recorded from 1642.

54   **prize**   A fencing prize fight or public test undergone by fencers to qualify as masters of defence.

56   **Ragga-muffins** 'the common people' (OE *raggig*, 'rough, shaggy' + MDu *muffe*)   First recorded as a name in 1344, and later as the name of a devil in Langland.

58   **third sound**   Trumpets were sounded three times as a warning that the play was about to begin.
it skils not 'it doesn't matter' (ON *skilja*, 'divide, distinguish')   This impersonal construction is particularly common from about 1525 to 1670.

63   **flirt** 'jest, jeer'   A sense recorded between 1549 and 1726. The modern sense is not recorded before the mid eighteenth century.

66   **bastinado** 'beating, cudgelling' (Sp. *bastonada*)   The form used here seems to have been borrowed from French *bastonade* and mistakenly re-hispanised on the analogy of the pair *renegade–renegado*.

79   **a laughing**   Derived from OE expressions with a verbal noun (*on huntunge*). Common in the sixteenth and seventeenth centuries, this type declines in modern times.

mewe   The sound-echoic verb is recorded from the fourteenth century but the use as a derisive sound (cf. modern *hoot*) is found only in the works of Dekker.

81   **sharers** 'producers'   Properly, those who were shareholders in the theatre company.

85   **block** 'style, model'   Derived from the block of wood on which hats were formed.

89   **Arcadian and Euphuisd** (Text reads *Euphuird.*)   Affected by imitating the styles of Sir Philip Sidney's *Arcadia* (1590) and John Lyly's *Euphues* (1578). Both were passé in smart circles by this time.

33

JOHN DONNE

The excerpts from the works of Donne given here are distinct in textual history. His *Devotions*, composed during a serious illness in 1623, was published in the following year. The two poems from the collection 'Songs and Sonnets' were published in a volume edited by his son in 1633 but may have been written thirty or more years earlier.

Donne was born in 1572 in the same London street as John Milton a generation later. His father was a substantial member of the Ironmongers' Company who claimed gentle descent from a family of Welsh origin, and his mother was related to Sir Thomas More. His father died when Donne was only four, and his mother was remarried to the physician Dr John Syminges. The family were devout Catholics, and Donne received his education at the hands of private tutors who instructed him in Latin and French. He proceeded to Hart Hall (later Hertford College), Oxford, and later may have spent some time in Cambridge, but his Catholicism disqualified him from taking a degree in either university. He was admitted to Lincoln's Inn in May 1592. At some point in the middle 1590s he seems to have renounced his Catholicism and, after military expeditions in which he sailed with Raleigh, begun to pursue a career on the fringes of court society. In 1597 he became secretary to Sir Thomas Egerton, Lord Keeper of the Great Seal, but he ruined his career in 1601 by his clandestine marriage to Ann More, a niece of Sir Thomas's wife. Fourteen uncertain years followed during which he relied on friends and minor patrons, until, at the instigation of King James, he was ordained in 1615 and made Doctor of Divinity by Cambridge University. His career in the Church prospered and he became Dean of St Paul's in 1621, holding this post until his death in March 1631.

The text of the seventeenth Meditation given below is that of the third edition of the *Devotions*, which appeared in 1627. The spelling, although not quite consistent, is relatively modern, but <in> and <im> are preferred to

<en> and initially, and no apostrophe *s* is used. Morphologically, the *-th* termination is preferred in *doth* and *hath* to the otherwise general *-es* in the third-person-singular present tense, and distinct forms of *my* and *thy* persist before vowels (*mine own*, *thine own*). The use of periphrastic *do* is distinct from that of modern practice. The rhetorical conception of the style, preferring parallel, balanced short clauses, ensures that the syntax echoes the patterns of simple speech.

The verse examples illustrate the use of the apostrophe in order to aid the reader in scanning the lines, where it indicates the elision of *e* in the inflexional endings *-ed* and *-est*. The implication that, at least in verse, *e* might still be pronounced in such contexts is confirmed by the appearance of spellings like *findst* and *mixt* as an alternative means of indicating elision. Further details of Donne's pronunciation can be deduced from the rhymes (see notes).

A   Seventeenth Meditation

Perchance hee for whom this *Bell* tols, may bee so ill, as that he knowes not it tolls for him; And perchance I may thinke my selfe so much better than I am, as that they who are about mee, and see my state, may haue caused it to toll for mee, and I know not that.

5   The *Church* is *Catholike*, *vniuersal*, so are all her *Actions*; *All* that shee does belongs to *all*. When she *baptizes* a *child*, that action concernes me; for that childe is thereby connected to that *Head* which is my *Head* too, and ingraffed into that *body*, whereof I am a *member*. And when she *buries a Man*, that action concernes me;

10   All *mankinde* is of one *Author*, and is one *volume*; when one Man dies, one *Chapter* is not *torne* out of the *booke*, but *translated* into a better *language*; and euery *Chapter* must be so *translated*; *God* imploies seuerall *translators*; some peeces are translated by *age*, some by *sicknes*, some by *war*, some by *iustice*; but *Gods* hand is in euery

15   *translation*: and his hand shall binde vp all our scattered leaues againe, for that *Library* where euery *booke* shall ly open to one another: As therfore the *Bell* that ringes to a *Sermon*, calls not vpon the *Preacher* onely, but vpon the *Congregation* to come; so this *Bell* calls vs all: but how much more *mee*, who am brought so neer the

20   *doore* by this *sicknesse*. There was a *contention* as farre as a *suite*, (in which both *piety* and *dignity*, *religion* and *estimation*, were mingled)

which of the religious *Orders* should ring to prayers *first* in the
Morning; and it was *determined*, that *they should ring first that rose
earliest*. If we understand a right the *dignity* of this *Bell*, that tolls
for our *euening praier*, wee would be glad to make it ours, by rising
early, in that *application*, that it might be ours, as wel as his, whose
indeed it is. The *Bell* doth toll for him that *thinkes* it doth; and
though it *intermit* againe, yet from that *minute*, that that occasion
wrought vpon him, he is united to God. Who castes not vp his *Eye*
to the *Sunne* when it rises? but who takes off his *Eye* from a *Comet*,
when that breakes out? who bends not his *eare* to any *bell*, which
vpon any *occation* rings? But who can remoue it from that *bell*,
which is passing a *piece of himselfe* out of this *world*? No Man is
an *Iland*, intire of it self; euery man is a piece of the *Continent*,
a part of the *maine*; if a *clod* be washed away by the *Sea*, *Europe* is
the lesse, as wel as if a *Promontory* were, as well as if a *Mannor*
of thy *friends*, or of *thine owne* were; Any mans *death* diminishes
mee, because I am inuolued in *mankind*; And therfore neuer send
to know for whom the *bell* tols; It tols for *thee*. Neither can we call
this a *begging* of *misery* or a *borrowing* of *misery*, as thogh we were
not miserable enough of our selues, but must fetch in more from
the next house, in taking vpon us the *misery* of our *neighbors*. Truly
it were an excusable *couetousnes* if we did; for *affliction* is a *treasure*,
and scarse any man hath *enough* of it. No man hath *affliction*
enough; that is not matured, and ripened by it, and made fit
for *God* by that *affliction*. If a Man carry *treasure* in *bullion*, or in
a *wedge* of *gold*, and haue none coyned into *currant Monies*, his
treasure will not defray him as he trauells. *Tribulation* is *Treasure* in
the *nature* of it, but it is not *currant money* in the vse of it, except
we get neerer and neerer our *home*, *heauen*, by it. Another Man
may be *sick* too, and *sick* to *death*, and this *affliction* may lie in
his *bowels*, as *gold* in a *Mine*, and be of no vse to him; but this *bell*
that tels mee of his *affliction*, diggs out, and applies that *gold* to *me*:
if by this consideration of anothers danger, I take mine own into
contemplation, and so secure my selfe, by making my recourse to
my *God*, who is our onely securitie.

B 'Song'

Goe, and catche a falling starre,
    Get with child a mandrake roote,

Tell me, where all past yeares are,
　　Or who cleft the Divels foot,
5　Teach me to heare Mermaides singing,
　　Or to keep off envies stinging,
　　　　And finde
　　　　What winde
Serves to'advance an honest minde.

10　If thou beest borne to strange sights,
　　Things invisible to see,
Ride ten thousand daies and nights,
　　Till age snow white haires on thee,
Thou, when thou retorn'st, wilt tell mee
15　All strange wonders that befell thee,
　　　　And sweare
　　　　No where
Lives a woman true, and faire.

If thou findst one, let mee know,
20　Such a Pilgrimage were sweet;
Yet doe not, I would not goe,
　　Though at next doore wee might meet,
Though shee were true, when you met her,
　　And last, till you write your letter,
25　　　Yet shee
　　　　Will bee
False, ere I come, to two, or three.

C 'The good-morrow'

I wonder by my troth, what thou, and I
Did, till we lov'd? were we not wean'd till then?
But suck'd on countrey pleasures, childishly?
Or snorted we i' the seaven sleepers den?
5　T'was so; But this, all pleasures fancies bee.
If ever any beauty I did see,
Which I desir'd, and got, t'was but a dreame of thee.

And now good morrow to our waking soules,
Which watch not one another out of feare;

10   For love, all love of other sights controules,
    And makes one little roome, an every where.
    Let sea-discoverers to new worlds have gone,
    Let Maps to others, worlds on worlds have showne,
    Let us possesse one world, each hath one, and is one.

15   My face in thine eye, thine in mine appeares,
    And true plaine hearts doe in the faces rest,
    Where can we finde two better hemispheares
    Without sharpe North, without declining West?
    What ever dyes, was not mixt equally;
20   If our two loves be one, or, thou and I
    Love so alike, that none doe slacken, none can die.

Notes

Seventeenth Meditation

11   **translated**   A pun, since a common sense of the word from 1300 onwards was 'to transfer (from one place to another)'.

13   **seuerall** 'various'   The word is borrowed from French *several*, from the same Latin root as *separate*. The sense here is first recorded in 1509.

21   **dignity . . . estimation** 'high office . . . status'.

28   **occasion**   The word is recorded from 1789 in the sense of 'a religious function or ceremonial', *OED* 9 (a).

29   **wrought**   The OE preterite and past participle of the verb *wyrcan*, 'to work', had the form *worht-* . The metathesised form used here was common in ME, but during the fifteenth century the analogical form *worked* arose which (except as an adjective) entirely replaced the earlier form during the seventeenth century.

34   **it self**   The genitive form of the pronoun *it* is recorded as *its* (replacing earlier *his*) from the third quarter of the sixteenth century. The form *it* is that used also by Shakespeare.

47   **wedge** 'ingot'   This sense is found from OE until the early eighteenth century.

Song

2–4   **roote : foot**   Donne uses the long [uː] pronunciation of *foot*, which is the normal development from ME /oː/. Shortened variants, which are the ancestors of the Modern English pronunciation, were just emerging at this time.

7–9   **finde : winde : minde**   In the sixteenth and seventeenth centuries the word *wind* was pronounced most commonly with a diphthong derived from ME /iː/, that is [əi]. The modern form is a variant pronunciation with a short vowel which becomes widely current in the eighteenth century.

19   **if thou findst**   Donne does not preserve the distinct form of the subjunctive but adopts an indicative form after *if* (cf. line 10). However, he adopts subjunctive forms (*were*, *last*) after *though* (22, 23).

The good-morrow

1–3   **I : childishly**   The pronunciation [ləi] was common for -*ly* following a secondary stress in the sixteenth and first half of the seventeenth centuries. This and the rhyme *equally : I* (19–20) are therefore probably pure rhymes.

5   **bee**   The use of *be* as an indicative form is becoming an archaism by Donne's time. In *Song* (3) he uses *are*, which had begun to supersede *be* in this function in southern English during the earlier sixteenth century.

9   **watch not**   Periphrastic *do* may still be used in declaratives without any apparent emphasis, and to achieve rhyme (6, 16), but omitted from the negative in a manner parallel to that of Middle English.

9–11   **feare : where**   The word *fear* is recorded from this period with both close and open pronunciation. The rhyme here is with the open [ɛː].

12–14   **gone : showne : one**   The rhyme is a pure one, probably on [oː], but variants of all these words occur with the pronunciation [ɔː]

16   **plaine** 'open, guileless'   This sense is recorded from the later fourteenth until the early eighteenth century. The series of semantic shifts undergone by this word is a particularly interesting one. See Rudskoger (1970).

34

THE LETTERS OF LADY
BRILLIANA HARLEY

The letters reproduced below belong to a series written by Lady Brilliana Harley mostly from her home at Brompton Castle (modern Brampton Bryan) about twelve miles west of Ludlow. Brilliana Harley was born about 1600 while her father, Sir Edward Conway, was Lieutenant-Governor of the Brill (Den Briel, Netherlands). In 1623 she became the third wife of Sir Robert Harley, who had received a legal education, before entering a career in politics. His religious affiliations were with the Puritans and he supported the Parliamentary cause, but opposed the execution of the king in 1649.

The series of letters extends over a period of eighteen years, but most fall between the dates 1638 to 1643 and are usually addressed to her son, beginning after he leaves home to commence study at Oxford, continuing while he is in London at Lincoln's Inn, and concluding when he is an officer in the Parliamentary army.

Almost all are written in the sender's own hand, and they reveal Lady Harley to have been a woman of intelligence and culture as well as warm family affections. She shows a lively interest in the political and intellectual events of the day, both at home and abroad, but her letters are also full of practical maternal concern for the welfare of her son. Her powerful religious convictions are increasingly evident. The series of letters was written in a tragic setting, for the growing tensions of the Civil War pervade the later ones. By the time of the second letter printed here, Brilliana is facing, in her husband's absence, the prospect of the siege of Brompton by Royalist forces. Although doing much damage, the siege was lifted after six weeks. Brilliana did not live to see it resumed in the next spring. Her last letter, dated 9 October 1643, mentions that she has 'taken a very greate coold, which has made me very ill thees 2 or 3 days, but I hope the Lord will be mercifull to me, in giuing me my health, for it is an ill time to be sike in'.

The letters are written in a deceptively artful plain style, which often imitates familiar spoken language but maintains forceful control of discourse structures, achieving effects of balance and verbal parallelism. Modulations of tone are quite adroit, adopting colloquial phrasing, then rising with the urgency of the subject to more overt rhetorical vehemence. The language is fairly standardised, showing few dialectal peculiarities, but the spelling system is rather inconsistent and idiosyncratic, confusing standard forms with the writer's own phonetic spellings.

Letter A

To my deare husband Sr Robert Harley.

Deare S^r – Your two leters, on from Hearifort and the other from Gloster, weare uery wellcome to me: and if you knwe howe gladly I reseaue your leters, I beleeue you would neeuer let any opertunity pase. I hope your cloche did you saruis betwne Gloster and my
5   brother Brays, for with vs it was a very rainy day, but this day has bine very dry and warme, and so I hope it was with you; and to-morowe I hope you will be well at your journis end, wheare I wisch my self to bide you wellcome home. You see howe my thoughts goo with you: and as you haue many of mine, so let me haue some
10   of yours. Beleeue me, I thinke I neuer miste you more then nowe I doo, or ells I haue forgoot what is past. I thanke God, Ned and Robin are well; and Ned askes every day wheare you are, and he says you will come to-morowe. My father is well, but goos not abrode, becaus of his fiseke. I haue sent you vp a litell hamper, in which is
15   the box with the ryteings and boouckes you bide me send vp, with the other things, sowed up in a clothe, in the botome of the hamper. I haue sent you a partriche pye, which has the two pea chikeins in it, and a litell runlet of meathe, that which I toold you I made for my father. I thinke within this mnthe, it will be very good drinke. I
20   sende it vp nowe becaus I thinke carage when it is ready to drincke dous it hurt; thearefore, and please you to let it rest and then taste it; if it be good, I pray you let my father haue it, because he spake to me for such meathe. I will nowe bide you god night, for it is past a leauen a cloke. I pray God presarue you and giue you good sugsess
25   in all your biusnes, and a speady and happy meeting.
      Your most faithfull affectinat wife, BRILLIANA HARLEY.

Letter B

For my deare sonne Mr. Edward Harley.

My deare Ned – I longe to see you, but would not haue you come
downe, for I cannot thinke this cuntry very safe; by the papers I
haue sent to your father, you will knowe the temper of it. I hope
your father will giue me full derections how I may beest haue my
5   howes gareded, if need be; if he will giue the derections, I hope, I
shall fooloul it.
     My deare Ned, I thanke God I am not afraide. It is the Lords
caus that we haue stood for, and I trust, though our iniquitys
testify aganst vs, yet the Lord will worke for His owne name sake,
10   and that He will now sheawe the men of the world that it is hard
fighting against heauen. And for our comforts, I thinke neuer any
laide plots to route out all Gods chillderen at once, but that the
Lord did sheawe Himselfe mighty in saveing His saruants and
confounding His enimyes, as He did Pharowe, when he thought to
15   haue destroyed all Israell, and so Haman. Nowe, the intention is, to
route out all that feare God, and surely the Lord will arise to healpe
vs: and in your God let your confidence be, and I am assured it is
so. One meet Samuell and not knoweing wheare he dwelt, Samuell
toold him he was a Darbesheare man, and that he came lately from
20   thence, and so he did in discours; the papis toold him, that theare
was but a feawe puretaines in this cuntry, and 40 men would cut
them all off.
     Had I not had this ocation to send to your father, yet I had
sent this boy vp to Loundoun; he is such a rogeisch boy that I dare
25   not keepe him in my howes, and as littell do I dare to let him goo
in this cuntry, least he ioyne with the company of vollentirs, or
some other such crwe. I haue giuen him no more money then will
sarue to beare his charges vpe; and becaus I would haue him make
hast and be sure to goo to Loundoun, I haue toold him, that you
30   will giue him something for his paines, if he come to you in good
time and doo not loyter; and heare inclosed I haue sent you halfe a
crowne. Giue him what you thinke fitte, and I desire he may not
come downe any more, but that he may be perswaded to goo to
seae, or some other imployment. He thinkes he shall come downe
35   againe. Good Ned, do not tell Martaine that I send him vp with
such an intention. I haue derected theas letters to you, and I send

him to you, becaus I would not haue the cuntry take notis, that I
send to your father so offten; but when such ocations come, I must
needs send to him, for I can rely vpon nobodys counsell but his.
40   I pray God blles you and presarue you in safety, and the Lord in
mercy giue you a comfortabell meeting with
        Your most affectinat mother, BRILLIANA HARLEY.

July 19, 1642. Brompton Castell.

My cosen Dauis tells me that none can make shot but thos whous
45   trade it is, so I haue made the plumer rwite to Woster for 50 waight
of shot. I sent to Woster, becaus I would not haue it knowne. If
your father thinke that is not enoufg, I will send for more. I pray
you tell your father that my cosen Robert Croft is in the cuntry.
My cosen Tomkins is as violent as euer, and many thinke that her
50   very words, is in the Heariford resolutions. I beleeue it was M^r
Masons pening. He is gone to Yorke, for when he carried the letter
from the gentellmen in this cuntry, he was made the kings chapline.

Notes

Letter A

1   **on** 'one'   Final <e> is written or omitted inconsistently, but of course
no longer pronounced.

4   **cloche** 'cloak'   It is probable that the spelling <ch> attempts to cap-
ture the faint aspiration after the stop consonant rather than that <ch>
represents the modern sound /ʧ/.

saruis   Brilliana Harley normally writes <ar> for ME <er>.

7   **journis end**   The apostrophe *s* is not in use, and the possessive is normally indicated by the addition of -*s* to the base.

10   **miste**   The preterites and past participles of verbs whose base ends in a
voiceless consonant are written <t> only rarely. Generally <ed> is preferred.

14   **fiseke** 'medical treatment'   This ME sense became obsolete in the eighteenth century.

15   **ryteings**   The spelling acknowledges the loss of initial *w-* which occurred
in pronunciation in the seventeenth century. More usually the idiosyncratic
<rw> is used.

boouckes   This spelling suggests an accommodation between standardised spelling practice and acknowledgement of the phonetic facts: the
long /oː/ of earlier ME had been raised to /uː/ in the Great Vowel Shift in
the fifteenth century.

18   **runlet** 'a cask or vessel of varying capacity' (*OED*)   Recorded from 1333 into the later nineteenth century.

   meathe 'mead'   *OED* states that forms with medial /ð/ may be drawn from ON or from Welsh. Since this letter was written close to the Welsh border, the latter explanation seems attractive.

21   **dous it hurt** 'does it harm'   The third-person-singular present tense inflexion is -(*e*)*s*, even with the verb 'to do', but *hath* is still written.

24   **a leaven a cloke** 'eleven o'clock'.

   sugsess   The spelling illustrates a voicing of /ks/ before a stressed syllable in EModE.

25   **biusnes**   The ME spelling is normally with <i>, and <u> spellings indicate western origin. The *u*-form became very frequent during the sixteenth century, so that the spelling here may once again indicate uncertainty in spelling as much as western pronunciation.

Letter B

3   **temper** 'climate, atmosphere'   Used figuratively. Originally referred to the balance of elements or humours, but extended to refer to the weather – here, the political climate.

5   **gareded**   The intrusive vowel in this spelling emphasises that postvocalic /r/ is still pronounced at this period.

7–8   **the Lords caus**   Much of the phraseology of this second paragraph is that of the Puritans: *our iniquitys, men of the world* (with associations quite distinct from those of the modern phrase), *Gods childeren*.

9   **name sake** 'out of regard for his name or reputation'   The word *name* is a possessive. The phrase is first recorded in Tyndale's New Testament in 1521 with the -*es* inflexion. The endingless form is therefore more probably a later phonetic development than a survival of an ME phrase with endingless genitive.

13   **did sheawe**   The use of periphrastic *do* is perhaps intended as part of the rhetorical heightening of this passage, but Brilliana Harley uses it occasionally in less elevated contexts also.

15   **Haman**   A Persian enemy of the Jewish people who was overthrown after the intervention of Esther (Esther 3–7).

17   **I am assured** 'I am confident'   Used intransitively. No agent giving assurance is implied.

20   **and so he did in discours** 'and so he entered into conversation'.

28   **beare his charges vpe** 'cover his expenses'.

30   **if he come**   The subjunctive form follows *if*. Brilliana Harley is careful always to use the correct subjunctive forms.

34   **he shall**   Clearly used with the earlier sense of inevitability.

44   **whous**   The spelling represents the fifteenth-century raising of /oː/ to /uː/.

47   **enoufg**   The *f*-spelling represents a sixteenth-century development by which ME /x/ > /f/. The *g* remains, owing to the influence of standard spelling practice.

51   **He is gone**   The sequence verb 'to be' + past participle of an intransitive verb of motion was common in OE but has been in decline since the eighteenth century. It has survived most fully with the past participle *gone*. In Modern English, however, its use is usually limited to a statement of the fact of absence (*it's gone* opposed to *it's there*), with no implication of action found in this context. Where such circumstances are given, and with a personal subject, present-day English prefers *have*.

35

JOHN MILTON, FROM *PARADISE*
LOST, BOOK II

John Milton (1608–74) was born in Bread Street, Cheapside, the son of a well-to-do scrivener and composer, who was determined that his son should receive a thorough education. There are stories of the twelve-year-old Milton working into the early hours of the morning. After attending St Paul's School, whose headmaster was Alexander Gil, the author of the *Logonomia Anglica* (1619), Milton went on to Christ's College, Cambridge, taking his MA in 1632. On leaving university he embarked on a tour of Europe, then settled with his father for a period of private study in Greek, Latin and Italian. In 1641 he published a series of pamphlets against the bishops and went on to support the Parliamentary cause in the Civil War. He was appointed Latin Secretary to the Council of State under the Commonwealth. At the Restoration, he went into hiding, was arrested, fined, and released.

Milton began to write his English verse in 1628 or 1629, and his last work, *Paradise Regained*, was published in 1671. His epic *Paradise Lost* seems to have been in partial existence by the early 1640s, but was mostly composed after his blindness in 1651, and completed by 1667.

Milton was a learned author, composing in Latin and Italian as well as English, and the grand style which he employs in *Paradise Lost* has been the subject of criticism for its unidiomatic and artificial language. Milton is indeed heavily influenced by his familiarity with Latin, and this is evident both in Latin syntactical constructions such as the ablative absolute (28, 49, 77) and in his use of unfamiliar Latin forms and senses. But although he uses unusual wordforms and unfamiliar senses, although he exploits very long sentences with multiply embedded clauses, and although he shifts word classes, Milton's language is less innovative than that of many Elizabethan authors. Very few words in this passage are first recorded in Milton. Most of the unfamiliar forms are of sixteenth-century origin: among his innovations are: *abrupt* (used as a noun only by Milton), *remote* (used as an adverb), *horrent* (apparently his own adoption from Latin *horrentem* 'bristling').

The facsimile shows the beginning of Book IX of *Paradise Lost*. The printing is not elegant and carelessness in proof-reading is evident in the use of an exclamation mark (still fairly uncommon in English at this time) for lower case *l* in the word *still* (12). The line is also awkwardly truncated. Letter forms have developed from those used by Caxton, but some earlier practices survive, such as the use of the ligatures *ct* and *st*, the use of long *s* in initial and medial position. Italic script is used for personal names. Milton's own spelling practice is apparent in the careful use of apostrophes to mark vowel elision and the stressed (*hee, shee*) and unstressed (*thir*) variants of pronouns.

Devils in Hell

    Well have ye judg'd, well ended long debate,
    Synod of Gods, and like to what ye are,
    Great things resolv'd; which from the lowest deep
    Will once more lift us up, in spite of Fate,
5   Neerer our ancient Seat; perhaps in view
    Of those bright confines, whence with neighbouring Arms
    And opportune excursion we may chance
    Re-enter Heav'n; or else in some milde Zone
    Dwell not unvisited of Heav'ns fair Light
10   Secure, and at the brightning Orient beam
    Purge off this gloom; the soft delicious Air,
    To heal the scarr of these corrosive Fires
    Shall breathe her balme. But first whom shall we send
    In search of this new World, whom shall we find
15   Sufficient? who shall tempt with wandring feet
    The dark unbottomd infinite Abyss,
    And through the palpable obscure find out
    His uncouth way, or spread his aerie flight
    Upborn with indefatigable wings
20   Over the vast abrupt, ere he arrive
    The happy Ile; what strength, what art can then
    Suffice, or what evasion bear him safe
    Through the strict Senteries and Stations thick
    Of Angels watching round? Here he had need
25   All circumspection and wee now no less
    Choice in our suffrage; for on whom we send,
    The weight of all and our last hope relies.
      This said, he sat; and expectation held
    His look suspense, awaiting who appeerd

PARADISE
LOST.

BOOK IX.

Eanwhile the hainous and defpight-
full act
Of *Satan* done in Paradife , and
how
Hee in the Serpent had perverted
Eve,
Her Husband fhee, to tafte the fatall fruit,
Was known in Heav'n; for what can fcape the Eye
Of God All-feeing, or deceave his Heart
Omnifcient, who in all things wife and juft,
Hinder'd not *Satan* to attempt the minde
Of Man, with ftrength entire, and free Will arm'd,
Complete to have difcover'd and repulft
Whatever wiles of Foe or feeming Friend.
For ftill they knew, and ought to have ftil! remem-
The high Injunction not to tafte that Fruit, (ber'd
Whoever tempted; which they not obeying,
Incurr'd

Plate 5   The opening pages of Milton, *Paradise Lost*, Book IX

Paradise loft.   Book 9.

Incurr'd, what could they lefs, the penaltie,
And manifold in fin, deferv'd to fall.
Up into Heav'n from Paradife in haft
Th' Angelic Guards afcended, mute and fad
For Man, for of his ftate by this they knew,
Much wondring how the futtle Fiend had ftoln   20
Entrance unfeen. Soon as th' unwelcome news
From Earth arriv'd at Heaven Gate, difpleas'd
All were who heard, dim fadnefs did not fpare
That time Celeftial vifages, yet mixt
With pitie, violated not thir blifs.
About the new-arriv'd, in multitudes
Th' ethereal People ran, to hear and know
How all befell : they towards the Throne Supream
Accountable made hafte to make appear
With righteous plea, thir utmoft vigilance,   30
And eafily approv'd ; when the moft High
Eternal Father from his fecret Cloud,
Amidft in Thunder utter'd thus his voice.

Affembl'd Angels, and ye Powers return'd
From unfuccefsful charge, be not difmaid,
Nor troubl'd at thefe tidings from the Earth,
Which your finereft care could not prevent,
Foretold fo lately what would come to pafs,
When firft this Tempter crofs'd the Gulf from Hell.
I told ye then he fhould prevail and fpeed   40
On his bad Errand, Man fhould be feduc't
And flatter'd out of all, believing lies
Againft his Maker ; no Decree of mine
Concurring to neceffitate his Fall,
Or touch with lighteft moment of impulfe
His free Will, to her own inclining left

K k

In

30   To second, or oppose, or undertake
      The perilous attempt: but all sat mute,
      Pondering the danger with deep thoughts; and each
      In others count'nance red his own dismay
      Astonisht: none among the choice and prime
35   Of those Heav'n-warring Champions could be found
      So hardie as to proffer or accept
      Alone the dreadful voyage; till at last
      Satan, whom now transcendent glory rais'd
      Above his fellows, with Monarchal pride
40   Conscious of highest worth, unmov'd thus spake.
      O Progeny of Heav'n, Empyreal Thrones,
      With reason hath deep silence and demurr
      Seis'd us, though undismaid: long is the way
      And hard, that out of Hell leads up to Light;
45   Our prison strong, thus huge convex of Fire,
      Outrageous to devour, immures us round
      Ninefold, and gates of burning Adamant
      Barrd over us prohibit all egress.
      These past, if any pass, the void profound
50   Of unessential Night receives him next
      Wide gaping, and with utter loss of being
      Threat'ns him, plung'd in that abortive gulf.
      If thence he scape into what ever World,
      Or unknown Region, what remains him less
55   Then unknown dangers and as hard escape?
      But I should ill become this Throne, O Peers,
      And this Imperial Sovranty, adornd
      With splendor, armd with power, if aught propos'd
      And judg'd of public moment, in the shape
60   Of difficulty or danger could deterre
      Mee from attempting. Wherefore do I assume
      These Royalties, and not refuse to Reign,
      Refusing to accept as great a share
      Of hazard as of honour, due alike
65   To him who Reigns, and so much to him due
      Of hazard more, as hee above the rest
      High honourd sits? Go therfore mighty Powers,
      Terror of Heav'n, though fall'n; intend at home,
      While here shall be our home, what best may ease

70   The present misery, and render Hell
      More tollerable; if there be cure or charm
      To respit or deceive, or slack the pain
      Of this ill Mansion: intermit no watch
      Against a wakeful Foe, while I abroad
75   Through all the coasts of dark destruction seek
      Deliverance for us all: this enterprize
      None shall partake with me. Thus saying rose
      The Monarch, and prevented all reply,
      Prudent, least from his resolution rais'd
80   Others among the chief might offer now
      (Certain to be refus'd) what erst they feard;
      And so refus'd might in opinion stand
      His rivals, winning cheap the high repute
      Which hee through hazard huge must earn. But they
85   Dreaded not more th' adventure then his voice
      Forbidding; and at once with him they rose;
      Thir rising all at once was as the sound
      Of Thunder heard remote. Towards him they bend
      With awful reverence prone; and as a God
90   Extoll him equal to the highest in Heav'n:
      Nor faild they to express how much they prais'd,
      That for the general safety he despis'd
      His own: for neither do the Spirits damnd
      Loose all thir vertue; least bad men should boast
95   Thir specious deeds on earth, which glory excites,
      Or close ambition varnisht ore with zeal.
      Thus they thir doubtful consultations dark
      Ended, rejoycing in thir matchless Chief:
      As when from mountain tops the dusky clouds
100   Ascending, while the North wind sleeps, orespread
      Heav'ns chearful face, the lowring Element
      Scowls ore the dark'nd lantskip Snow, or showre;
      If chance the radiant Sun with farewell sweet
      Extend his ev'ning beam, the fields revive,
105   The birds thir notes renew, and bleating herds
      Attest thir joy, that hill and valley rings.
      O shame to men! Devil with Devil damnd
      Firm concord holds: men onely disagree
      Of Creatures rational, though under hope

110 Of heav'nly Grace; and God proclaiming peace,
Yet live in hatred, enmitie, and strife
Among themselves, and levie cruel warres,
Wasting the Earth, each other to destroy:
As if (which might induce us to accord)
115 Man had not hellish foes anow besides,
That day and night for his destruction waite.
     The *Stygian* Council thus dissolv'd; and forth
In order came the grand infernal Peers:
Midst came thir mighty Paramount, and seemd
120 Alone th' Antagonist of Heav'n, nor less
Then Hells dread Emperour with pomp Supream,
And God-like imitated State; him round
A Globe of fierie Seraphim inclos'd
With bright imblazonrie, and horrent Arms.
125 Then of thir Session ended they bid cry
With Trumpets regal sound the great result:
Toward the four winds four speedy Cherubim
Put to thir mouths the sounding Alchymie
By Haralds voice explain'd: the hollow Abyss
130 Heard farr and wide, and all the host of Hell
With deafning shout, return'd them loud acclaim.

Notes

1   **ye**   In his earlier works, Milton uses *you* and *thou*. Here, in epic context, he uses an archaising form of the second-person-plural pronoun,
which had been in retreat for half a century. The spelling <ye> is used
when it occurs in unstressed position, and <yee> in stressed position. Cf.
the forms *wee* (25), *hee* (66).

11   **gloom** 'darkness'   Milton first uses the word in this sense in 1629. It
seems to be a back formation from the adjective *gloomy*, first used by
Shakespeare. Earlier etymology is uncertain but may be related to Scots
gloaming.

13   **balme**   A number of words occur which were originally borrowed into
ME from French then re-formed on the model of Latin: *Abyss* (ME *abisme*),
doubtful (ME *douteful*), *equal* (ME *egal*). *Balme* may be considered one of
these (ME *baume*; Lat. *balsamus*). However, the sound change by which
[ɑlm] > [ɑʊlm] > [ɑʊm] may have encouraged analogical reformation
through an awareness of the relationship between *al* and *au*.

15   **tempt**   Aphetic (see p. 158, note to line 101) form of *attempt*.

19	**indefatigable** 'untiring' Recorded in 1611 from French, but rare before Milton's use of it.
21	**Ile** Milton prefers the medieval French and English form to that remodelled on Latin *insula* in French of the fifteenth century and common in English since the mid sixteenth century.
26	**suffrage** The sense 'intercessionary prayer' belongs to the fourteenth century, but the sense 'election', found here, is contemporary with the poem.
35	**Heav'n-warring** This type of endocentric adjectival compound consisting of a noun and present participle became common in the sixteenth century and is especially frequent in Shakespeare.
38	**transcendent** A technical term drawn from medieval Latin philosophy and recorded only in dictionaries before 1611.
40	**Conscious** This modern sense is not recorded until 1632.
42	**demurr** 'state of irresolution' Recorded from the sixteenth century.
45	**convex** 'vault (of heaven or hell)' (Lat. *convexum*) A learned word, but recorded as a noun from 1626.
46	**Outrageous** 'mad, furious' This sense of the French borrowing was common in Middle English but was obsolete by the mid nineteenth century.
48	**egress** 'right of exit' A term with legal associations, first recorded in 1538.
50	**unessential** 'insubstantial' The first recorded occurrence with this sense; the form recorded only from 1656.
57	**Sovranty** Milton's habitual spelling of *sovereignty* may have been influenced by the Italian *sovrano* but also served to indicate precisely the pronunciation required for the metre.
87	**Thir** The unstressed form of the pronoun. The stressed form is *their*.
102	**lantskip** The earlier and colloquial form of the word *landscape*. This was a technical term of artists, borrowed from Dutch *landschap*. First recorded in 1598.
116	**waite** 'keep watch (with hostile intent)' This Anglo-Norman borrowing was an archaism in Milton's time.
120	**Antagonist** Borrowed from Greek and first recorded by Ben Jonson in 1599.
121	**Supream** Milton uses this spelling when he wishes to indicate that the stress is to fall on the second syllable. His spelling for stress on the initial syllable is identical to that of Modern English.
125	**cry** 'proclaim, announce' Another archaism; common in Middle English.
129	**Abyss** The ME form, *abisme*, borrowed from OF, is formed colloquially as a superlative of *abyssus*, **abyssimus*, 'of profound depth'. The sixteenth-century form *abyss* restores the classical Latin form.

36

SIR ISAAC NEWTON, *OPTICKS*

The career of Sir Isaac Newton began unpromisingly: his father was dead before Newton's premature birth on Christmas Day 1642, and his mother remarried before he was four, leaving her son to be raised by his grandmother. The child was sickly and not expected to survive, and he grew up during the Civil War in a time of some uncertainty, when Woolsthorpe Manor (six miles south of Grantham) was a Royalist household in a predominantly Parliamentarian countryside. Nothing is known of Newton's early education before he entered the King's School, Grantham at the age of twelve, but legend credits him already with possession of mechanical and experimental aptitude. His schooling was interrupted by the necessity of managing his family's estate, but his outstanding abilities took him to Trinity College, Cambridge in 1661. There his talents were quickly recognised, and the existing Lucasian Professor of Mathematics generously stood down to enable Newton, at the age of twenty-six, to occupy his Chair. In 1699 he left Cambridge for London and became Master of the Mint and President of the Royal Society in 1703, holding these two offices until his death in 1727.

Newton's scientific reputation rests on three major achievements: his explanation of the laws of motion, his development of the calculus, and his work in optics. The groundwork for all was laid in a period of extraordinary creativity during his absence from Cambridge during the plague years of 1665–66. His major work, the *Principia*, was published – in Latin, as was the custom for important scientific writings – in 1687, and the *Opticks* appeared in English in 1704, with a Latin translation in 1706. A second, augmented edition appeared in 1718, and the present text is based on this, preserving its spelling, capitalisation and punctuation. The language is modern in terms of its spelling and morphology, but not entirely so in syntax and lexis. Some words (*Window-shut*) and senses (*Species* meaning 'image') are obsolete, and periphrastic *do* is both omitted and used in negatives (32, 73) and also in declaratives (13). Newton has a fondness for lengthy sentences with much embedded qualification. His style is formal but not unvaryingly so, and he will use both colloquialisms (*'tis manifest*) and metaphorical or otherwise marked lexical choices: *paint* (9), *lively* (30).

Exper. 8. In Summer when the Sun's Light uses to be strongest, I placed a Prism at the hole of the Window-shut, as in the third Experiment, yet so that its Axis might be parallel to the Axis of the World, and at the opposite Wall in the Sun's refracted Light, I
5   placed an open Book. Then going six Feet and two Inches from the Book, I placed there the above-mentioned Lens, by which the Light reflected from the Book might be made to converge and meet again at the distance of six Feet and two Inches behind the Lens, and there paint the Species of the Book upon a sheet of white Paper
10   much after the manner of the second Experiment. The Book and Lens being made fast, I noted the Place where the Paper was, when the Letters of the Book, illuminated by the fullest red Light of the solar Image falling upon it, did cast their Species on that Paper most distinctly: And then I stay'd till by the Motion of the Sun, and
15   consequent Motion of his Image on the Book, all the Colours from that red to the middle of the blue pass'd over those Letters; and when those Letters were illuminated by that blue, I noted again the place of the Paper when they cast their Species most distinctly upon it: And I found that this last place of the Paper was nearer to
20   the Lens than its former place by about two Inches and an half, or two and three quarters. So much sooner therefore did the Light in the violet end of the Image by a greater Refraction converge and meet, than the Light in the red end. But in trying this the Chamber was as dark as I could make it. For if these Colours be diluted and
25   weakned by the Mixture of any adventitious Light, the distance between the Places of the Paper will not be so great. This distance in the second Experiment where the Colours of natural Bodies were made use of, was but an Inch and an half, by reason of the Imperfection of those Colours. Here in the Colours of the Prism,
30   which are manifestly more full, intense, and lively than those of natural Bodies, the distance is two Inches and three quarters. And were the Colours still more full, I question not but that the distance would be considerably greater. For the coloured Light of the Prism, by the interfering of the Circles described in the second

35   Figure of the fifth Experiment, and also by the Light of the very
       bright Clouds next the Sun's Body intermixing with these Colours,
       and by the Light scattered by the inequalities in the Polish of the
       Prism, was so very much compounded, that the Species which those
       faint and dark Colours, the indigo and violet, cast upon the Paper
40   were not distinct enough to be well observed.
           Exper. 9. A Prism, whose two Angles at its Base were equal to
       one another and half right ones, and the third a right one, I placed
       in a beam of the Sun's Light let into a dark Chamber through a
       hole in the Window-shut, as in the third Experiment. And turning
45   the Prism slowly about its Axis until all the Light which went through
       one of its Angles and was refracted by it began to be reflected by
       its Base, at which till then it went out of the Glass, I observed that
       those Rays which had suffered the greatest Refraction were sooner
       reflected than the rest. I conceived therefore that those Rays of
50   the reflected Light, which were most refrangible, did first of all by a
       total Reflexion become more copious in that Light than the rest,
       and that afterwards the rest also, by a total Reflexion, became as
       copious as these. To try this, I made the reflected Light pass through
       another Prism, and being refracted by it to fall afterwards upon a
55   Sheet of white Paper placed at some distance behind it, and there
       by that Refraction to paint the usual Colours of the Prism. And
       then causing the first Prism to be turned about its Axis as above,
       I observed that when those Rays which in this Prism had suffered
       the greatest Refraction and appeared of a blue and violet Colour
60   began to be totally reflected, the blue and violet Light on the Paper
       which was most refracted in the second Prism received a sensible
       increase above that of the red and yellow, which was least refracted;
       and afterwards when the rest of the Light which was green, yellow
       and red began to be totally reflected in the first Prism, the Light of
65   those Colours on the Paper received as great an increase as the
       violet and blue had done before. Whence 'tis manifest, that the beam
       of Light reflected by the Base of the Prism, being augmented first
       by the more refrangible Rays, and afterwards by the less refrangible
       ones, is compounded of Rays differently refrangible. And that all
70   such reflected Light is of the same nature with the Sun's Light
       before its Incidence on the Base of the Prism, no Man ever doubted:
       it being generally allowed, that Light by such Reflexions suffers
       no alteration in its Modifications and Properties. I do not here take
       Notice of any Refractions made in the sides of the first Prism,

75   because the Light enters it perpendicularly at the first side, and
goes out perpendicularly at the second side, and therefore suffers
none. So then, the Sun's incident Light being of the same Temper
and Constitution with his emergent Light, and the last being compounded of Rays differently refrangible, the first must be in like
80   manner compounded.

Notes

1   **uses to be**   First recorded during the fourteenth century, this structure
becomes rare in the present tense by the mid eighteenth century. In plural
uses the distinction between the tenses is sometimes lost by the assimilation of -*ed* to the following *t*, and an invariant form *use* is written.

15   **his Image**   Newton's language has the possessive *its* (20), but he chooses
to personify the sun, taking its masculine gender from the Latin *sol*.

30   **full . . . lively** 'saturated . . . vivid'   The former is recorded of colour
only from 1657; the latter from the fourteenth century. The modern technical term *saturated* dates from 1853 in this use.

34   **the interfering of the Circles**   The overlapping circles of refracted light
of different wavelengths found in a spectrum derived from a pin-hole
source. The use of the deverbal noun is recorded between the sixteenth
and early nineteenth centuries, before it is superseded by *interference*.

50   **refrangible** 'subject to refraction'   First recorded in 1673 from Newton's
writings. He seems to have coined the technical term from a supposed
Latin adjective *refrangibilis* derived from *refrangere*. The correct Latin
form, however, is *refringere*.

37

ALEXANDER POPE, *THE RAPE OF THE LOCK*

Alexander Pope (1688–1744) was born off Lombard Street in London, the son of a linen importer and exporter who was a Roman Catholic. In an age when religious intolerance was rife, the young Alexander's father judged it prudent to move his family to Binfield in Windsor Forest, where the boy grew up and perhaps developed an interest in natural landscape which he indulged in his latter years in Twickenham. As a Catholic, entry to the major educational establishments was out of the question, so that although Pope had two or three years' schooling in Catholic schools, first at Twyford near Winchester and then in Marylebone, he was largely self educated. He seems to have been studious by nature and this inclination was perhaps furthered by a serious illness at the age of twelve which arrested his growth and partially crippled him. He had, however, demonstrated his metrical skills in 'Pastorals', written by the time he was sixteen, and through his friendship with Wycherley he found an entrée into London literary life. Although he wrote some lyric and dramatic verse, his talents lay in narrative and satire. His translations of the works of Homer provided him with the funding with which to develop his literary gifts.

The Rape of the Lock is an early work, first published in Lintot's *Miscellaneous Poems and Translations* in 1712, then republished in much-expanded form in 1714, adding the game of Ombre and the mythological machinery of the sylphs. The circumstances were that some time before 1712, Robert, Lord Petre, cut a lock from the hair of Arabella Fermor, to her and her family's indignation. The two families became estranged, and a mutual friend, John Caryll, suggested to Pope that he should heal the rift by composing a comic poem about the incident, to laugh them out of their hostility. This strategy was of limited practical success, since what good had been achieved was afterwards compromised by the poem's publication, but it resulted in the engaging mock-epic from which this excerpt is taken. The text is that of

the first edition of 1714. Pope's language was regarded by the Romantics at
the end of the century as consciously poetic and artificial, arising partly from
his use of archaisms, partly from his Latinism, and partly from the inflation
which here plays a comic role. This excerpt, however, is not without colloquialisms which serve comically to deflate the pretensions of the more
'poetic' language.

Close by those Meads for ever crown'd with Flow'rs,
Where *Thames* with Pride surveys his rising Tow'rs,
There stands a Structure of Majestick Frame,
Which from the neighb'ring *Hampton* takes its Name.
5   Here *Britain's* Statesmen oft the Fall foredoom
Of Foreign Tyrants, and of Nymphs at home;
Here Thou, Great *Anna!* whom three Realms obey,
Dost sometimes Counsel take – and sometimes *Tea.*
    Hither the Heroes and the Nymphs resort,
10   To taste awhile the Pleasures of a Court;
In various Talk th' instructive hours they past,
Who gave the *Ball*, or paid the *Visit* last:
One speaks the Glory of the *British Queen*,
And one describes a charming *Indian Screen*;
15   A third interprets Motions, Looks, and Eyes;
At ev'ry Word a Reputation dies.
Snuff, or the *Fan*, supply each Pause of Chat,
With singing, laughing, ogling, and all that.
    Mean while declining from the Noon of Day,
20   The Sun obliquely shoots his burning Ray;
The hungry Judges soon the Sentence sign,
And Wretches hang that Jury-men may Dine;
The Merchant from *th'Exchange* returns in Peace,
And the long Labours of the *Toilette* cease –
25   *Belinda* now, whom Thirst of Fame invites,
Burns to encounter two adventrous Knights,
At *Ombre* singly to decide their Doom;
And swells her Breast with Conquests yet to come.
Strait the three Bands prepare in Arms to join,
30   Each Band the number of the Sacred Nine.
Soon as she spreads her Hand, th' Aerial Guard
Descend, and sit on each important Card:

First *Ariel* perch'd upon a *Matadore*,
Then each, according to the Rank they bore;
35   For *Sylphs*, yet mindful of their ancient Race,
Are, as when Women, wondrous fond of Place.
    Behold, four *Kings* in Majesty rever'd,
With hoary Whiskers and a forky Beard;
And four fair *Queens* whose hands sustain a Flow'r,
40   Th' expressive Emblem of their softer Pow'r;
Four *Knaves* in Garbs succinct, a trusty Band,
Caps on their heads, and Halberds in their hand;
And Particolour'd Troops, a shining Train,
Draw forth to Combat on the Velvet Plain.
45   The skilful Nymph reviews her Force with Care;
Let Spades be Trumps! she said, and Trumps they were.
    Now move to War her Sable *Matadores*,
In Show like Leaders of the swarthy *Moors*.
Spadillio first, unconquerable Lord!
50   Let off two captive Trumps, and swept the Board.
As many more *Manillio* forc'd to yield,
And march'd a Victor from the verdant Field.
Him *Basto* follow'd, but his Fate more hard
Gain'd but one Trump and one *Plebeian* Card.
55   With his broad Sabre next, a Chief in Years,
The hoary Majesty of *Spades* appears;
Puts forth one manly Leg, to sight reveal'd;
The rest his many-colour'd Robe conceal'd.
The Rebel-*Knave*, who dares his Prince engage,
60   Proves the just Victim of his Royal Rage.
Ev'n mighty *Pam* that Kings and Queens o'erthrew,
And mow'd down Armies in the Fights of *Lu*,
Sad Chance of War! now, destitute of Aid,
Falls undistinguish'd by the Victor *Spade!*
65   Thus far both Armies to *Belinda* yield;
Now to the *Baron* Fate inclines the Field.
His warlike *Amazon* her Host invades,
Th' Imperial Consort of the Crown of *Spades*.
The *Club's* black Tyrant first her Victim dy'd,
70   Spite of his haughty Mien, and barb'rous Pride:
What boots the Regal Circle on his Head,
His Giant Limbs in State unwieldy spread?

That long behind he trails his pompous Robe,
And of all Monarchs only grasps the Globe?
75 The *Baron* now his *Diamonds* pours apace;
Th' embroider'd *King* who shows but half his Face,
And his refulgent *Queen*, with Pow'rs combin'd,
Of broken Troops an easie Conquest find.
Clubs, Diamonds, Hearts, in wild Disorder seen,
80 With Throngs promiscuous strow the level Green.
Thus when dispers'd a routed Army runs,
Of *Asia's* Troops, and *Africk's* Sable Sons,
With like Confusion different Nations fly,
Of various Habit and of various Dye,
85 The pierc'd Battalions dis-united fall,
In Heaps on Heaps; one Fate o'erwhelms them all.
    The *Knave* of *Diamonds* tries his wily Arts,
And wins (oh shameful Chance!) the *Queen* of *Hearts*.
At this, the Blood the Virgin's Cheek forsook,
90 A livid Paleness spreads o'er all her Look;
She sees, and trembles at th' approaching Ill,
Just in the Jaws of Ruin, and *Codille*.
And now, (as oft in some distemper'd State)
On one nice *Trick* depends the gen'ral Fate.
95 An *Ace* of Hearts steps forth: The *King* unseen
Lurk'd in her Hand, and mourn'd his captive *Queen*.
He springs to Vengeance with an eager pace,
And falls like Thunder on the prostrate *Ace*.
The Nymph exulting fills with Shouts the Sky,
100 The Walls, the Woods, and long Canals reply.
    Oh thoughtless Mortals! ever blind to Fate,
Too soon dejected, and too soon elate!
Sudden these Honours shall be snatch'd away,
And curs'd for ever this Victorious Day.
105 For lo! the Board with Cups and Spoons is crown'd,
The Berries crackle, and the Mill turns round.
On shining Altars of *Japan* they raise
The silver Lamp; the fiery Spirits blaze.
From silver Spouts the grateful Liquors glide,
110 While *China's* Earth receives the smoking Tyde.
At once they gratify their Scent and Taste,
And frequent Cups prolong the rich Repast.

Strait hover round the Fair her Airy Band;
Some, as she sip'd, the fuming Liquor fann'd,
115 Some o'er her Lap their careful Plumes display'd,
Trembling, and conscious of the rich Brocade.
Coffee, (which makes the Politician wise,
And see thro' all things with his half-shut Eyes)
Sent up in Vapours to the *Baron's* Brain
120 New Stratagems, the radiant Lock to gain.
Ah cease rash Youth! desist ere 'tis too late,
Fear the just Gods, and think of *Scylla's* Fate!
Chang'd to a Bird, and sent to flit in Air,
She dearly pays for *Nisus'* injur'd Hair!
125 But when to Mischief Mortals bend their Will,
How soon they find fit Instruments of Ill!
Just then, *Clarissa* drew with tempting Grace
A two-edg'd Weapon from her shining Case;
So Ladies in Romance assist their Knight,
130 Present the Spear, and arm him for the Fight.
He takes the Gift with rev'rence, and extends
The little Engine on his Fingers' Ends,
This just behind *Belinda's* Neck he spread,
As o'er the fragrant Steams she bends her Head:
135 Swift to the Lock a thousand Sprights repair,
A thousand Wings, by turns, blow back the Hair,
And thrice they twitch'd the Diamond in her Ear,
Thrice she look'd back, and thrice the Foe drew near.
Just in that instant, anxious *Ariel* sought
140 The close Recesses of the Virgin's Thought;
As on the Nosegay in her Breast reclin'd,
He watch'd th' Ideas rising in her Mind,
Sudden he view'd, in spite of all her Art,
An Earthly Lover lurking at her Heart.
145 Amaz'd, confus'd, he found his Pow'r expir'd,
Resign'd to Fate, and with a Sigh retir'd.
  The Peer now spreads the glitt'ring *Forfex* wide,
T'inclose the Lock; now joins it, to divide.
Ev'n then, before the fatal Engine clos'd,
150 A wretched *Sylph* too fondly interpos'd;
Fate urg'd the Sheers, and cut the *Sylph* in twain,
(But Airy Substance soon unites again)

The meeting Points the sacred Hair dissever
From the fair Head, for ever and for ever!
155   Then flash'd the living Lightning from her Eyes,
And Screams of Horror rend th' affrighted Skies.
Not louder Shrieks to pitying Heav'n are cast,
When Husbands or when Lap-dogs breathe their last,
Or when rich *China* Vessels, fal'n from high,
160   In glittring Dust and painted Fragments lie!
Let Wreaths of Triumph now my Temples twine,
(The Victor cry'd) the glorious Prize is mine!
While fish in Streams, or Birds delight in Air,
Or in a Coach and Six the *British* Fair,
165   As long as *Atalantis* shall be read,
Or the small Pillow grace a Lady's Bed,
While *Visits* shall be paid on solemn Days,
When numerous Wax-lights in bright Order blaze,
While Nymphs take Treats, or Assignations give,
170   So long my Honour, Name, and Praise shall live!
What Time wou'd spare, from Steel receives its date,
And Monuments, like Men, submit to Fate!
Steel cou'd the Labour of the Gods destroy,
And strike to Dust th' Imperial Tow'rs of *Troy*;
175   Steel cou'd the Works of mortal Pride confound,
And hew Triumphal Arches to the Ground.
What Wonder then, fair Nymph! thy Hairs shou'd feel
The conqu'ring Force of unresisted Steel?

Notes

1   **Meads**   The word was used in prose in Middle English but becomes progressively restricted to poetic language after the sixteenth century.

5–6   **foredoom : home**   This rhyme, which occurs already in Chaucer, presupposes a raised variant [oː] in *home*, so that the vowels in both words are identical and are raised to /uː/ by the Great Vowel Shift.

7–8   **obey : Tea**   The word *tea* made its way to Europe from Chinese by way of Malay and Dutch, *thee*, in the mid seventeenth century. Pronunciations varied between [iː] and [eː] until about 1760, when the modern pronunciation established itself.

17   **Chat**   An abbreviated form of *chatter*, which itself seems to have been an onomatopoeic formation often used of birds and implying nonsense.

Chat is recorded as a noun from 1530 to 1768 with the sense 'frivolous or idle talk', and from 1573 as 'familiar and informal conversation'.

18   **ogling**   A slang word, first appearing in the late seventeenth century, probably derived from Dutch *oogheler*, 'to flatter', and Low German *oegeln*, 'to look at'.

29–30   **join : Nine**   The word *join* was borrowed into English from two sources: Norman and Central French. The modern pronunciation derives from the latter borrowing, but the former source had a different diphthong ([ʊi] instead of [oi]) which was smoothed to [iː] in ME and underwent the same development as the ME long vowel. The pronunciation was probably [ʌi].

38   **forky**   A rare word closely associated with Pope's literary world; first used by Dryden in 1697 and also by Swift.

40   **expressive**   The wordform itself occurs from about 1400 onwards, but the sense 'serving to express, indicate or represent' was new in Pope's time, and is recorded only after 1711.

45–46   **Care : were**   The vowel of *were* existed in early ME in both open and close variants, but lowering before /r/ ensured that the former was generalised. OE *ea/a* in *cearu/caru* was lengthened in an open syllable in early ME and was later progressively fronted and raised to reach [ɛː] by 1650, when it coincided with the long open [ɛː] in *were*.

47   **Sable** 'black'   Used as a technical term in heraldry from 1352 on. Elsewhere, essentially a poetic word. This adjective is presumed to be derived from the noun, which is a rare medieval borrowing from a Slavic language (Russian *sobol*).

Matadores   The principal card in the game of Ombre. One of a number of technical terms to do with the game borrowed from Spanish. All date from the last two decades of the seventeenth century: *Spadillio* (49), the 'ace of spades' (Sp. *espadilla*), *Manillio* (51), the second-best trump (Sp. *malilla*), *Basto* (53), the 'ace of clubs' (Sp. *basto*), *Codille* (92), an expression used in Ombre to describe the circumstances in which the challenger loses (Sp. *codillo*).

48   **swarthy**   The restriction to complexion is relatively recent. The sense 'black' is recorded between 1577 and 1842.

61   **Pam** 'the jack of clubs'   Apparently an abbreviation of French *pamphile*.

62   **Lu**   A card game, Loo or Lanterloo, in which the jack of clubs was the highest card.

70   **Mien** 'bearing'   An aphetic (see p. 158, note to line 101) form of *demean(our)*, but becomes associated in form and sense with French *mine*, 'expression, look'. Recorded from 1513 on, but only in poetic contexts.

80   **strow**   The variant spellings *strew*, *strow* arise from a shift of stress on the diphthong of OE *streowian*.

94   **nice Trick**   The phrase plays on different senses of the two words. The former, derived from Latin *nescius*, 'ignorant', developed a very extended

range of senses but here probably means 'subtle' or perhaps 'trivial'. The word *trick* is recorded in the context of cards from 1599, and often with this play on the older sense, 'deception'.

102   **elate**   This form is recorded from the fourteenth century. The type with the *-ed* suffix does not occur until 1615.

106   **Berries**   Coffee *berries* are mentioned from 1626, but the *OED* has no reference to coffee *beans* before the mid nineteenth century. Coffee beans themselves were first imported in 1652.

109   **grateful** 'pleasing to the senses, agreeable'   This sense recorded between 1553 and 1866.

111–12   **Taste : Repast**   The vowel in *taste* is short. The modern pronunciation developed through ME open-syllable lengthening in the verb form.

117   **Coffee**   Appears more or less simultaneously in all European languages about 1600. Derived from Turkish *kahveh*, probably from an Arabic original.

123   **flit**   (ON *flytja*, 'to move (from one place to another)') The word had a wide range of senses to do with movement of position, but began to be restricted to the movement of birds from the mid sixteenth century.

147   **forfex**   Pope humorously elevates his style by adopting for the first (and almost last) time in English the Latin word for 'a pair of scissors'.

38

DANIEL DEFOE, *A TOUR THROUGH THE WHOLE ISLAND OF GREAT BRITAIN*

Defoe's *Tour*, published between 1724 and 1726, was based in part upon literary sources but more significantly on the experiences of an eventful life. Born in London in 1660, the son of a butcher, Defoe was the child of a Presbyterian family and, after initial schooling in Dorking, he was debarred by his religious affiliations from entering a university, instead attending Morton's Academy in Newington Green. There, rather than an education in the classics, he received instruction in English eloquence and composition, modern foreign languages and sciences. By 1680 he was a hose factor (a wholesale haberdasher) trying his hand at a range of other enterprises. His career as a commercial entrepreneur was interrupted when in June 1685 he joined Monmouth's side in an attempted revolution, an indiscretion for which he was pardoned in May 1687. By 1692 he was bankrupt with the enormous debt of £17,000, but he survived in minor government posts and through considerable income from a brick and tile factory near Tilbury which he owned. Following the publication of his first substantial work, the *Essay on Projects* (1697), he became a semi-official apologist for the policies of King William. In 1703, however, he was arrested and placed in the pillory for allegedly publishing a seditious pamphlet, *The Shortest Way with Dissenters*, but he was released and compensated, becoming a political agent for Robert Harley, Speaker of the House of Commons. He subsequently acted as an agent (sometimes a double agent) for both political factions, travelling extensively in Britain collecting information and opinions. Although Defoe was an exceedingly prolific author who is credited with 566 publications, he wrote all his major works between 1715 and his death in April 1731.

The anecdotal interest he shows here in the English language was preceded in his *Essay on Projects* by enthusiasm for standardisation by the foundation of an Academy. Here, however, he is telling entertaining stories rather than pleading a cause. Nevertheless, his account of the contemporary Somerset dialect is in most respects acceptable, even though the *ch*-forms are notoriously stage-rustic. The case of a country boy who reads standard orthography in his own dialect is a reminder that standardised speech had not been universally attained even in the early eighteenth century.

In my return to my western progress, I pass'd some little part of Somersetshire, as thro' Evil, or Yeovil, upon the river Ivil, in going to which we go down a long steep hill, which they call Babylon-Hill; but from what original I could find none of the country people to inform me.

This Yeovil is a market town of good resort, and some clothing is carry'd on, in, and near it, but not much, its main manufacture at this time is making of gloves.

It cannot pass my observation here, that when we are come this length from London, the dialect of the English tongue, or the country way of expressing themselves is not easily understood, it is so strangely altered; it is true, that it is so in many parts of England besides, but in none in so gross a degree as in this part; This way of boorish country speech, as in Ireland, it is call'd the brogue upon the tongue; so here 'tis call'd *jouring*, and 'tis certain, that tho' the tongue be all meer natural English, yet those that are but a little acquainted with them, cannot understand one half of what they say: It is not possible to explain this fully by writing, because the difference is not so much in the orthography of words, as in the tone, and diction; their abridging the speech, *cham* for *I am*, *chil* for *I will*, *don*, for *put on*, and *doff*, for *put off*, and the like. And I cannot omit a short story here on this subject; coming to a relations house, who was a school-master at Martock in Somersetshire, I went into his school to beg the boys a play day, as is usual in such cases; I should have said to beg the master a play day, but that by the way; coming into the school, I observ'd one of the lowest scholars was reading his lesson to the usher, which lesson it seems was a chapter in the Bible, so I sat down by the master, till the boy had read out his chapter: I observ'd the boy read a little oddly in the tone of the country, which made me the more attentive, because on enquiry, I found that the words were the same, and the orthography the same as in all our Bibles. I observ'd also the boy read it out with his eyes still on the book, and his head like a meer boy, moving from side to side, as the lines reach'd cross the columns of the book; his lesson was in the Cant. 5. 3. of which the words are these,

'I have put off my coat, how shall I put it on, I have wash'd my feet, how shall I defile them?'

The boy read thus, with his eyes, as I say, full on the text.

'Chav a doffed my cooat, how shall I don't, chav a wash'd my veet, how shall I moil'em?'

How the dexterous dunce could form his mouth to express so readily the words, (which stood right printed in the book) in his country jargon, I could not but admire; I shall add to this another peice as diverting, which also happen'd in my knowledge at this very town of Yeovil, tho' some years ago.

There liv'd a good substantial family in the town, not far from the Angel Inn, a well known house, which was then, and I suppose is still the chief inn of the town. This family had a dog, which among his other good qualities, for which they kept him (for he was a rare house dog) had this bad one, that he was a most notorious thief; but withal, so cunning a dog, and managed himself so warily, that he preserved a mighty good reputation among the neighbourhood; as the family was well beloved in the town, so was the dog; he was known to be a very useful servant to them, especially in the night, when he was fierce as a lion, but in the day the gentlest, lovingest creature that could be, and as they said, all the neighbours had a good word for this dog.

It happen'd that the good wife, or mistress at the Angel Inn, had frequently missed several peices of meat out of the pail, as they say, or powdering-tub, as we call it; and that some very large peices; 'tis also to be observ'd the dog did not stay to eat (what he took) upon the spot, in which case some peices, or bones, or fragments might be left, and so it might be discover'd to be a dog; but he made cleaner work, and when he fasten'd upon a peice of meat he was sure to carry it away, to such retreats as he knew he could be safe in, and so feast upon it at leisure.

It happen'd at last, as with most thieves it does, that the inn-keeper was too cunning for him, and the poor dog was nabb'd, taken in the fact, and could make no defence.

Having found the thief, and got him in custody, the master of the house, a good humour'd fellow, and loth to disoblige the dog's master, by executing the criminal, as the dog-law directs; mitigates

75 his sentence, and handled him as follows; first taking out his knife, he cut off both his ears, and then bringing him to the threshold, he chop'd off his tail; and having thus effectually dishonour'd the poor cur among his neighbours, he tyed a string about his neck, and a peice of paper to the string directed to his master, and with these witty west country verses on it.

80   To my honour'd master – Esq;
        Hail master a cham a' com hoam
        So cut as an ape, and tail have I noan,
        For stealing of beef, and pork, out of the pail,
        For thease they'v cut my ears, for th' wother my tail;
85   Nea measter, and us tell thee more nor that
        And's come there again, my brains will be flat.

I could give many more accounts of the different dialects of the people of this country, in some of which they are really not to be understood, but the particulars have little or no diversion in them, 90 they carry it such a length, that we see their jouring speech even upon their monuments, and gravestones; As for example, even in some of the church-yards of the city of Bristol, I saw this excellent poetry after some other lines –

        And when that thou doest hear of thick,
95   Think of the glass that runneth quick.

But I proceed into Devonshire, from Evil we came to Crookorn, thence to Chard, and from thence into the same road I was in before at Honiton.

Notes

8   **making of gloves**   The use of a deverbal noun followed by a genitive phrase, in which the noun may be understood as object to the verb underlying the deverbal noun, is common from ME to the early nineteenth century. This type, where the verbal quality of *making* is emphasised by the lack of a determiner, is stigmatised in the nineteenth century.

14–15   **brogue . . . jouring**   The earlier sense of *brogue* is 'shoe, sandal' (Irish *brōg*), but the sense 'marked accent' dates from 1705. *Jouring* (EDD 'jower') is quoted as a dialect verb in Shropshire, Somerset and Devon, meaning 'to grumble, mutter'. Defoe is the only authority for the sense here.

16   **meer natural** 'pure natural' (Lat. *merus*)   Used of speech commonly between the mid sixteenth and eighteenth centuries, and later in the phrase 'mere Irish'.

20   **cham**, etc.   These forms of the verbs 'to be' and 'will', arising originally from *ich am*, *ich wyl*, had long been conventional indicators of southern rustic speech. See Wilson's *Arte of Rhetorique* (Excerpt 25). *Don* and *doff* were widespread in dialect use in the nineteenth century.

40   **Chav**, etc.   The spelling <cooat> represents a non-standard diphthong; *veet* preserves the voicing of initial fricatives found in the South and South-West in ME; *moil* is recorded by *EDD* as a verb with the sense 'defile' from Worcester, Shropshire, Gloucester and Cornwall. The *a* in the past participles *a doffed* and *a wash'd* represents the survival of the OE prefix *ge-*. In ME this had survived latest in the South and South-West, spelt <y> or <i>, but was later lowered and centralised and is here spelt <a>.

53   **mighty good**   The use of *mighty* as an intensifier begins in OE, and was felt to belong to informal and colloquial register by the nineteenth century. Something of this colloquialism is already evident in the familiarity of language choice and the irony of this story of the thieving dog. Perhaps in deference to readers' sensibilities, this passage was omitted from the edition of 1778.

56   **lovingest**   The superlative of disyllabic adjectives still permits formation by the suffix -*est*.

59   **good wife**   The phrase had the idiomatic sense 'landlady, lady of the house' as early as the mid thirteenth century, and it is inconsistently written as a compound from the mid fourteenth. *OED* lists its use until the end of the nineteenth century. A reduced form, *goody*, is also recorded from 1589 onwards. Cf. *housewife* and *hussy*.

61   **powdering tub**   'A tub in which the flesh of animals is "powdered" or salted and pickled'.

62   **'tis**   A common abbreviation in this period. Perhaps indicates some relaxation in the formality of the style, but is common also in relatively formal and technical contexts (cf. Newton, Excerpt 36), and should not be regarded as so obvious a colloquialism as its appearance in a modern context would indicate.

69   **nabb'd** 'arrested, taken into custody'   A slang or colloquial expression first recorded in 1686.

73   **mitigates**   The use of the present tense in a predominantly preterite context may be considered a feature of the familiar tone of this narrative. The 'historic present' is recorded from the thirteenth century on. It was probably encouraged by French influence but is found also in other Germanic languages.

76   **effectually** 'effectively'   The noun *effect* gave rise to three derivative adjectives and associated adverbs during the fourteenth century: *effectual*,

effective and *effectuous*. The first is in retreat, surviving most obviously in *ineffectual*, and the last is not recorded after the seventeenth century.

84   **thease** 'this'   Listed by *EDD* for Hereford, Gloucester, Dorset, Devon and Cornwall.

wother 'other'   Forms with initial *w-* are recorded for Devon and Somerset. Cf. the standard pronunciation of *one*, which developed an initial *w-* by the fifteenth century in the South-West. The *w-* pronunciation began to be acknowledged by orthoepists after 1700. The western pronunciation seems never to have been widely accepted in the case of *other*.

85   **and us** 'if I'   The use of *us* as a first-person-singular pronoun is widespread in the West Country.

94   **thick** 'this'   This form is recorded from Worcester, Gloucester, Berkshire, Somerset, Devon and Cornwall.

39

FROM THE PREFACE TO JOHNSON'S DICTIONARY

Samuel Johnson (1709–84) was born in Lichfield, attended Lichfield Grammar School, and went on to Pembroke College, Oxford. His university career ended after fourteen months when shortage of funds forced his departure without a degree. His struggle for survival saw him successively as an unsuccessful schoolmaster, the proprietor of a private school, and a journalist in Birmingham. In 1737 he moved to London and supported his wife and himself by writing for *The Gentleman's Magazine*. Alongside various hack work, he made time for scholarly and literary production, and in 1747 he announced his 'Plan of a Dictionary' 'by which the pronunciation of our language may be fixed, and its attainment facilitated; by which its purity may be preserved, its use ascertained, and its duration lengthened'. The *Dictionary* was published in 1755, gaining Johnson immediate acclaim, an honorary degree from the University of Oxford, a Crown pension of £300 a year and an honoured place in the contemporary literary world.

As Johnson's remark, quoted from the 'Plan', suggests, the *Dictionary* arose from that concern for the status and function of the English language which had been part of learned debate since the sixteenth century. Men educated in Latin literature had for centuries been concerned by the variety, the expressive limitations and the changes they perceived in English, and as early as 1582 Mulcaster had called for an English dictionary as a remedy. Although English–Latin dictionaries existed in the fifteenth century, and other bilingual dictionaries followed in the sixteenth, there is general agreement that the earliest true dictionary of English is Robert Cawdrey's *A Table Alphabeticall of Hard Words* (1604), whose purpose was to enlighten its readers on the spelling and significance of the many recent borrowings into English. This 'hard word' approach evolved during the sixteenth and earlier seventeenth centuries into the conception of a scholarly dictionary with universal coverage. Johnson's work, which contained 40,000 entries whose senses were established by 114,000 quotations, was the most substantial contribution to the art and stature of lexicography before the publication of the *New English Dictionary* in 1884.

Although the passage quoted below demonstrates Johnson's awareness of the dynamic nature of language, it is clear that he does not view this fact with much satisfaction, and his methodology in compiling the *Dictionary* was more in accord with the statement in the 'Plan', and fundamentally pre-scriptive. He did not aim to be exhaustive, nor to provide sense histories; much contemporary colloquialism is deliberately excluded, and the senses of words which he establishes by quotation are mostly drawn from authors of an idealised past, from Sidney to the Restoration. Although Johnson exhibits much linguistic common sense, he does not separate himself from the assumption of the age that a regulated and stable language is a desirable, even if doubtfully attainable goal.

This is how people spoke in Johnson's circle — high style Milton like, rhetorical — *Wit → construction, artful of language* — 18th century → long

Of the event of this work, for which, having laboured it with
so much application, I cannot but have some degree of parental
fondness, it is natural to form conjectures. Those who have been
persuaded to think well of my design, require that it should fix our
5 language, and put a stop to those alterations which time and chance
have hitherto been suffered to make in it without opposition. With
this consequence I will confess that I flattered myself for a while; but
now begin to fear that I have indulged expectation which neither
reason nor experience can justify. When we see men grow old and
10 die at a certain time one after another, from century to century,
we laugh at the elixir that promises to prolong life to a thousand
years; and with equal justice may the lexicographer be derided,
who being able to produce no example of a nation that has preserved
their words and phrases from mutability, shall imagine that his
15 dictionary can embalm his language, and secure it from corruption
and decay, that it is in his power to change sublunary nature, or
clear the world at once from folly, vanity, and affectation.

1 sentence long.

With this hope, however, academies have been instituted,
to guard the avenues of their languages, to retain fugitives, and
20 repulse intruders; but their vigilance and activity have hitherto been
in vain; sounds are too volatile and subtile for legal restraints; to
enchain syllables, and to lash the wind, are equally the undertakings
of pride, unwilling to measure its desires by its strength. The *French*

language has visibly changed under the inspection of the academy; the stile of *Amelot's* translation of father *Paul* is observed by *Le Courayer* to be *un peu passé*; and no Italian will maintain, that the diction of any modern writer is not perceptibly different from that of *Boccace, Machiavel*, or *Caro*.

Total and sudden transformations of a language seldom happen; conquests and migrations are now very rare: but there are other causes of change, which, though slow in their operation, and invisible in their progress, are perhaps as much superiour to human resistance, as the revolutions of the sky, or intumescence of the tide. Commerce, however necessary, however lucrative, as it depraves the manners, corrupts the language; they that have frequent intercourse with strangers, to whom they endeavour to accommodate themselves, must in time learn a mingled dialect, like the jargon which serves the traffickers on the *Mediterranean* and *Indian* coasts. This will not always be confined to the exchange, the warehouse or the port, but will be communicated by degrees to other ranks of the people, and be at last incorporated with the current speech.

There are likewise internal causes equally forcible. The language most likely to continue long without alteration, would be that of a nation raised a little, and but a little, above barbarity, secluded from strangers, and totally employed in procuring the conveniencies of life; either without books, or, like some of the *Mahometan* countries, with very few: men thus busied and unlearned, having only such words as common use requires, would perhaps long continue to express the same notions by the same signs. But no such constancy can be expected in a people polished by arts, and classed by subordination, where one part of the community is sustained and accommodated by the labour of the other. Those who have much leisure to think, will always be enlarging the stock of ideas, and every increase of knowledge, whether real or fancied, will produce new words, or combinations of words. When the mind is unchained from necessity, it will range after convenience; when it is left at large in the fields of speculation, it will shift opinions; as any custom is disused, the words that express it must perish with it; as any opinion grows popular, it will innovate speech in the same proportion as it alters practice.

As by the cultivation of various sciences, a language is amplified, it will be more furnished with words deflected from their

original sense; the geometrician will talk of a courtier's zenith, or
the excentrick virtue of a wild hero, and the physician of sanguine
expectations and phlegmatick delays. Copiousness of speech will
give opportunities to capricious choice, by which some words
will be preferred, and others degraded; vicissitudes of fashion will
enforce the use of new, or extend the signification of known terms.
The tropes of poetry will make hourly encroachments, and the
metaphorical will become the current sense: pronunciation will be
varied by levity or ignorance, and the pen must at length comply
with the tongue; illiterate writers will at one time or other, by
publick infatuation, rise into licentiousness, confound distinction,
and forget propriety. As politeness increases, some expressions
will be considered as too gross and vulgar for the delicate, others
as too formal and ceremonious for the gay and airy; new phrases
are therefore adopted, which must, for the same reasons, be in
time dismissed. *Swift*, in his petty treatise on the *English* language,
allows that new words must sometimes be introduced, but proposes that none should be suffered to become obsolete. But what
makes a word obsolete, more than general agreement to forbear it?
and how shall it be continued, when it conveys an offensive idea,
or recalled again into the mouths of mankind, when it has once by
disuse become unfamiliar, and by unfamiliarity unpleasing.

There is another cause of alteration more prevalent than any
other, which yet in the present state of the world cannot be obviated.
A mixture of two languages will produce a third distinct from both;
and they will always be mixed, where the chief part of education,
and the most conspicuous accomplishment, is skill in ancient and
foreign tongues. He that has long cultivated another language, will
find its words and combinations croud upon his memory; and haste
and negligence, refinement and affectation, will obtrude borrowed
terms and exotick expressions.

The great pest of speech is frequency of translation. No book
was ever turned from one language into another, without impart-
ing something of its native idiom; this is the most mischievous and
comprehensive innovation; single words may enter by thousands,
and the fabrick of the tongue continue the same, but new phraseology changes much at once; it alters not the single stones of the
building, but the order of the columns. If an academy should be
established for the cultivation of our stile, which I, who can never
wish to see dependance multiplied, hope the spirit of *English* liberty

105 will hinder or destroy, let them, instead of compiling grammars and dictionaries, endeavour, with all their influence, to stop the licence of translatours, whose idleness and ignorance, if it be suffered to proceed, will reduce us to babble a dialect of *France*.

     If the changes that we fear be thus irresistible, what remains but to acquiesce with silence, as in the other insurmountable dis-
110 tresses of humanity? it remains that we retard what we cannot repel, that we palliate what we cannot cure. Life may be lengthened by care, though death cannot be ultimately defeated: tongues, like governments, have a natural tendency to degeneration; we have long preserved our constitution, let us make some struggles for
115 our language.

Notes

1   **event** 'outcome'   First recorded 1573. Borrowed from French with the Latin etymological sense of *evenire*, 'to come out'.

6–7 **with this consequence**   This adverbial is now normally used with cataphoric (forward) rather than anaphoric (backward) reference.

9   **reason nor experience**   The implied opposition of these two terms is medieval in origin, relating to deductive and inductive proof. The words are now no longer felt to be in opposition in ordinary speech.

13–14 **nation . . . their**   The concord of many corporate nouns is still uncertain, but *nation* would no longer have plural concord unless qualified by the name of the nation concerned.

16   **sublunary**   First recorded in 1592. In the sense relevant to this passage, from 1639. In the Ptolemaic conception of the universe, the earth was encased in nine concentric spheres, the lowest of which was that of the moon. All beneath the lunar sphere was subject to change and decay.

18   **academies**   The Accademia della Crusca had been founded in 1582 and produced an Italian dictionary in 1612, and the French Academy, founded in 1635, produced its dictionary in 1694.

19   **avenues**   The imagery is military. The word *avenue*, 'approach, path of entry or exit', was originally a military term borrowed from French, and was first recorded in 1600.

21   **volatile and subtile**   *Volatile* was borrowed from OF in the fourteenth century as a noun referring to birds and other flying creatures. As an adjective it is recorded applied to chemicals from the early seventeenth century. *Subtile*, with the sense 'fine, insubstantial', is a fourteenth-century refashioning, on the model of Latin *subtilis*, of OF and ME *soutil*. Both *subtile* and *subtle* occur as alternative spellings from the fourteenth to the late nineteenth century.

25   **Amelot**   Nicolas Amelot de la Houssaye (1634–1706). In 1683, he published a French translation of the *History of the Council of Trent* by Paolo Servita.

25–26   **Le Courayer**   Pierre François Le Courayer published his own translation of Servita's *History of the Council of Trent* in 1736.

28   **Boccace . . . Caro**   Three Tuscan authors: Giovanni Boccaccio (1313–75), Latin encyclopaedist and founder of Italian prose literature; Niccolò Machiavelli (1469–1527), administrator, literary man and political theorist; Annibale Caro (1507–66), translator of the *Aeneid* into Italian.

33   **intumescence** 'swelling up'   Recorded as a borrowing from French from 1656.

38   **traffickers**   The word was used from the sixteenth to the nineteenth century to mean 'merchant', not necessarily with pejorative association. But pejorative senses are found throughout that period.

53   **accommodated** 'provided for'   From 1597 onwards. The narrowed sense 'provided with lodging' is recorded only from 1715, but the noun is used in the modern sense, 'suitable lodging', from 1604.

57   **convenience** 'comfort'   This sense recorded from 1703 onwards.

64   **zenith**   Not a very new extension of the meaning of the word, since this figurative use is recorded from 1601.

65   **excentrick**   Used of a person or personal attribute from 1685.

         sanguine   Feelings of hopefulness and self-confidence were considered characteristic of the personality of those dominated by sanguine humour. The word was used figuratively to suggest these characteristics from 1673.

66   **phlegmatick**   Phlegmatic people were apathetic and not easily enthused. *OED* does not record the sense development foreseen by Johnson for this word, which seems always to be applied to persons.

70   **tropes** 'rhetorical devices' (Lat. *tropus*)   Properly one of those figures of speech that medieval rhetoricians regarded as 'difficult ornament' and which relied on the use of words with modified senses. Metaphor is one such trope.

75   **propriety** 'stylistic decorum, appropriateness'   The suitability of verbal choices to their context, both verbal and situational.

79   **Swift**   Johnson refers to Jonathan Swift's *Proposal for Correcting, Improving, and Ascertaining the English Tongue* (1712), in which he proposes the formation of an English Academy to stabilise English usage.

101   **columns**   The concept of structure belongs to later linguistic thought, but the point Johnson makes about the structural influence of one language upon another is a valid one, evident in phraseology and in modifications to the syntax of sentences.

40

FANNY BURNEY, A LETTER FROM BATH, 8 SEPTEMBER 1791

If the desire to write is innate rather than acquired, then Frances (Fanny) Burney (1752–1840) must be an outstanding example of that gift. Her earliest surviving poem, written in a precociously adult style, was composed before her twelfth birthday. When she was fifteen she made a bonfire of her early work, including the first draft of a novel which was to bring her literary recognition when published in revised form as *Evelina* eleven years later. Although she published two other successful novels, a greater and more sustained effort went into her journals which she recommenced after the bonfire and maintained until her sight failed sixty years later. At the same time she kept up a continuous correspondence with members of her family and acquaintances.

Fanny Burney was the daughter of the organist and musical historian Dr Charles Burney. Her father was considered to be the foremost music teacher in the London of his day, and he numbered among his friends Dr Johnson, David Garrick and Sir Joshua Reynolds. Fanny herself was appointed Second Keeper of the Robes to Queen Charlotte in 1786 and held the post for five years. In 1793 she married a French emigré, General d'Arblay, and thereafter lived sometimes in France, sometimes in England as political circumstances allowed.

Although she benefited from a culturally privileged environment, Fanny Burney did not receive a formal education outside the home. She was a voracious reader and largely self-educated. Early in life a family friend, Samuel Crisp, advised her never to frame 'studied letters, that are to be correct, nicely grammatical and run in smooth periods'. Her earliest letters have something of the spontaneity of speech, and this can be found in more familiar correspondence later in life; but she harboured also a growing attachment to fine writing, and this found expression in her last years in the extensive revision and even destruction of her earlier works. The letter

which follows, addressed to her elder sister, is sufficiently familiar to exploit playful punning and use some careless grammar and colloquialisms,
but is nevertheless rhetorically constructed and uses occasionally elevated
vocabulary. The text represents the spelling of the original, but punctuation
is modernised. Small capitals are used to represent larger, more emphatic
writing.

Queen Square,
Bath – Septr 8th

My dearest Esther will I know rejoice to hear how well the
Bath Water has agreed with Me. I am recovering apace, though
by no means without severe occasional draw-backs. But you will
probably have heard of me and my goings on through our Padre:
5   from whom I have had accounts of yourself and co, which though
only in *generals*, have satisfied me all essentials went on well.
    Saturday the 10th I set forward for Mickelham: – and there, my
dearest Esther, in the course of my *Month's confinement*, I shall
hope to see you. I think you will never be able to resist a little peep
10   at our Nursery. Heaven send it prosperous! – I think with our dear
Susan there is every possible good augur.
    I would send you some News – only I know none.
    I ought to give you, from this distance, a little flourish – only
I have not *de quoi* to compose one. I am certainly of opinion, after
15   deeply thinking over the matter, that the Heliconian spring did not
bring forth hot water. Apollo and the nine must have owed their
spirit to streams of more bracing qualities. The Hot water which
I quaff here has, in this respect, wholly disappointed me, for it
rather renders my ideas vapid than bright, notwithstanding the
20   reasonable expectations I had entertained of its WHETTING MY WITS.
And if it does not mend that, it has surely no chance to mend my
humour; for how can what is moist contribute to what is dry? Thus
you see, My dear sister, how small a chance you have to be a gainer
by my Bath Beverage.
25   This City is so filled with Workmen, dust, and lime, that you
really want two pair of Eyes to walk about in it – one for being put
out, and the other to see with afterwards. But as I, however, have
only one pair, which are pretty much dedicated to the first purpose,
you cannot, in reason, expect from me a very distinct description
30   of it. Bath seems, now, rather a collection of small Towns, or of

magnificent Villas, than one City. They are now building as if the
World was but just beginning, and this was the only spot on which
its Inhabitants could endure to reside. Nothing is secure from their
architectural rage. They build upon the pinnacle of Hills that only to
look up to breaks ones neck – and they build in the deepest depths
below, which only to look down upon makes one giddy. Even the
streets round the Pump room are pulling down for new Edifices,
and you can only drink from their choice stream, by wading though
their chosen mud. Their plans seem all to be formed without the
least reference to what adjoins or surrounds them, they are therefore high, low, broad, narrow, long, short, in manners the most
unexpected, and by interruptions the most abrupt; – and some of
their Houses are placed so zig-zag, in and out, you would suppose
them built first, and then dropt, to *find* their own *foundation*.
They seem seldom to attempt levelling the Ground for the sake
of uniformity, but, very contentedly, when they have raised one
House on the spot where it could stand most conveniently, they
raise the next upon its nearest and steepest aclivity, so precisely
above it, that from the Garret of one, you *Mount* into the Kitchen
of the other. One street, leading out of Laura Place, of a noble
width, and with a broad handsome Pavement, pompously labelled
at the corner JOHNSON STREET, has in it – only one House: – nor
can another be added, for it opens to Spring Gardens, and even
its vis à vis is occupied by the dead wall belonging to a House in
Laura Place. Nor can You make a visit from one street to another,
without such an ascent, or such a declivity, that you must have
the wheel of a carriage *locked* to go from neighbour to neighbour.
– You will ask me if I mean to set you up with materials for
making a model of Bath? but I am perfectly content with having
given you a *Model* of Confusion.

Certainly, unless you are advised to come hither for *Health*, I
should advise you not to see this place these 2 years, at least, for
pleasure; as the avenues to the pump Rooms will not sooner be
finished, and *walking* here in the winter must be next to impractic-
able. However, when all these works are compleated, and the
Compleaters, with the usual gratitude of the world, are driven aloof,
this City, already the most splendid of England, will be as noble as
can well be conceived.

It is impossible to tell you how kind, good and considerate
is our excellent Mrs. Ord: yet we are Daily upon the point of a

quarrel concerning my leaving her. 6 weeks is the appointed time for drinking these waters, and I shall just have halved *it*. However, I go to peace, good air, good Hours, and the best and dearest Society, and all those will more than compensate for Bath waters,
75   as my worn strength and wasted spirit want more of time and care and patience and HAPPINESS for recruit, than medicine. Mrs. ord gives you her most affectionate Love. I beg mine to Mr. Burney and all around you. Is my sweet little God Child as well and lovely as ever? A good question to a mama! – but when I want to get at the
80   simple truth, I always like to apply to impartial persons. Fanny, I hope, rapidly improves in an honourable mixture of literature and notability. sophy can do no better than persevere in her maternal studies; and Richard, I doubt not, will emulate his friend Dussec, till he will aim at his own superior Father. – Your news is good, I
85   hope, from the sweet Marianne? and poor Bessy? I shall now beg you to write to me at Mickleham, which I flatter myself I shall reach next Monday night, or Tuesday noon. I think from *thence* I shall be able to write You a MORE – a MOST welcome Letter ere long. Farewell, my ever dear sister – truly y^{rs}

F B.

Remember me kindly to dear James When you see him – and to *his*. –

Notes

3   **draw-backs**   This compound is first recorded in 1618 in a context where it refers to the behaviour of an individual and is clearly derived from a verbal phrase. In the sense 'anything which retards progress or advance' it is recorded from 1720, but the modern sense, to which it is now restricted and in which it is opposed to an advantage in reviewing some course of action, dates from the latter half of the nineteenth century.

4   **goings on**   In the sense 'actions, experiences', this was first recorded in a letter by Dr Johnson written in July 1775, but the verb is used by Defoe to mean 'to get on (with someone)'. There is here no implication of censure.

8   **confinement**   Fanny's younger sister, Susan, gave birth to her third child shortly after this letter. The word is used punningly, exploiting its general sense, dating from the mid seventeenth century, for Fanny's proposed stay at Mickleham, and the more restricted sense (recorded only from the 1770s) for Susan's time in childbed.

16   **the nine**   The nine muses, representing the arts, who lived by the spring on Mount Helicon whose water gave inspiration in Greek mythology.

19   **vapid** 'dull, insipid' (Lat. *vapidus*)   Originally borrowed as a semi-technical term to refer to flavour and used of drinks from 1656. The figurative extension to ideas and speech is first recorded in Johnson (1758). The word *bracing* (17) is also first recorded in 1750 to describe the effects of a tonic medicine.

31–32   **as if . . . was**   In more formal letters the writer is careful to use the subjunctive in similar clauses.

37   **are pulling down**   This type of expression (cf. *the house is building*) has been called the 'passival' and is common from ME until the end of the nineteenth century, when it is increasingly replaced by the type 'being built'. The history of the passival form is confused with that of the type *the house is a-building*, descended from OE expressions with *on* followed by the verbal noun in *-unge*. The coexistence of the two types caused some disagreement among contemporary literary men: Dr Johnson preferred *a-building*, but the majority opinion among grammarians was for *building*.

43   **zig-zag**   Of uncertain etymology, although borrowed immediately from French. The word may exploit sound symbolism, the two vowels suggesting movement in two different directions. First recorded as a noun in 1712.

48   **aclivity** 'upward slope'   First recorded in 1614, from Latin *acclivitatem* 'steepness'.

54   **vis à vis** 'opposite'   An eighteenth-century borrowing, recorded first in 1753 with very specific reference to a particular type of carriage in which the occupants sat face to face. Quickly extended to include other 'face to face' contexts.

66   **aloof**   Earlier written as a phrase *a loof* (see Dekker, Excerpt 32), this word has a nautical origin. Sixteenth-century occurrences mean to 'turn to windward' and 'sail close to the wind'. A range of senses involving physical and then metaphorical distance develops. Perhaps borrowed direct from Dutch *loef*, 'windward'.

MODERN ENGLISH

(1800–1920)

The history of English takes on an entirely new dimension after about 1800. No longer is it simply one of the varieties of the Germanic language family, nor subsidiary in its own homeland to French and Latin. Neither, for that matter, is it the symbol of English nationalism, whose merits are trumpeted in order to conceal misgivings about its true value in comparison with the classical languages. In the nineteenth century, English becomes largely standardised at home, expands beyond national boundaries, and is as a result more various in its overseas function as a world language.

The transfer of English outside its historical homeland begins with imperial expansion whose roots can be traced back to the settlements in America and the formalisation of trading relations with India at the end of the sixteenth century, but it is not until the nineteenth century that the languages of these ex-colonies, diverging significantly from that of the mother country, begin to return an influence upon the development of English at home. This relatively recent development, although important and interesting, lies outside the scope of this collection.

In England during the nineteenth century, forces for standardisation were strong. Most notable among them was the great expansion of primary education, the purpose of which was to teach children to read and write and, of course, to spell correctly. It has been calculated that, in 1818, about 600,000 out of some 2,000,000 children were attending some kind of school. The earliest national movements for elementary education were the 'National' and 'British' schools sponsored by religious bodies, but from the 1830s the Government gave financial support to the foundation of schools, and in 1870 the Elementary Education Act enabled the provision of schools by local authorities from an education rate. The expansion of popular education was accompanied by the foundation of Mechanics' Institutes in 1823 to bring instruction to working men, and the 1870s and 1880s saw the foundation of a number of university institutions in the larger industrial cities of the North.

As awareness of a correct form of the written language was promoted by increased literacy, the breakdown of old dialect distributions was hastened by easier communication and the mixing of population. The Industrial Revolution created great new cities – Leeds, Sheffield, Birmingham, Manchester, Glasgow – which developed their own urban dialects from the mixture of immigrants attracted to them. Population movement was greatly facilitated by the expansion of the railway system in the 1840s, and the trend to readier mobility and freer mixing of the population was continued in the next century by the development of both road and air transport, but above all by radio communications. The rapid development in public broadcasting after about 1920 led in England and abroad to the establishment of BBC English as a *de facto* spoken standard. This standard, alternatively known as Received Pronunciation, is that of a social and educational elite, originally developed from the manner of speech approved by the nineteenth-century public schools, and concurrently by the universities of Oxford and Cambridge.

The establishment towards the end of the nineteenth century of an approved standard for pronunciation and its subsequent promotion by broadcasting ensured that non-standard or dialect variants would henceforth be considered sub-standard – that is, not simply different, but inferior. The tendency to assess the social status of speakers from the accidentals of their speech is universal in linguistic history, but becomes oriented in Modern English into an opposition between dialect speech and the use of the standard. Although still current, in very recent times this opposition has been mitigated by a change in political sentiment on the one hand, and by the development of the objective study of language on the other.

The study of English has always incorporated two distinct traditions and purposes. Indisputably the most familiar and widely followed is the pursuit of communicative effectiveness in the use of the language, both written and spoken. Thomas Wilson's *Arte of Rhetorique* is an early textbook in this tradition, the Fowler brothers' *Modern English Usage* a more recent one. The student's purpose within this tradition is to achieve command of a kind of English to which no one can object, and by which the hearer will be both easily informed and readily impressed. It is a tradition which *prescribes* what may be judged as correct in spelling and grammar, and what is acceptable in aspects of style. A second tradition, which can also be traced back to the sixteenth century and antiquarian interest in the early history of English, is concerned less with prescribing the contemporary uses of English than with describing those uses, their historical derivation and the attitudes of speakers to them. Thus, the academic study of English is characteristically *descriptive* in its orientation. This scientific, descriptive spirit inspiring the study of the English language reached maturity in the nineteenth century, and is represented (admittedly to a debatable extent) in the compilation of the *Oxford English Dictionary*. It is true that the *Dictionary* is relatively weak in its coverage of non-literary and non-standard forms, but the expressed attitudes and practices of its editors should be compared with those of nineteenth-century grammars pressed into service in the burgeoning schools. James Beattie, in *The Vulgarities of Speech Corrected* (1826), gives his opinion, regardless of Shakespearian usage, that 'Nothing is more common, nor more offensive than such . . . expressions as *more greater, most beautifullest, more prettier, most commonest*.' Even in the late 1920s, G. H. McKnight, an American scholar, reveals how his early school instruction in grammatical proprieties has irresistibly moulded his responses. Although he, as a scholar, is able to list examples of its use from about 1500 onwards, he still finds that the British use of *their* to refer back to a single individual 'grates on the ear of the American grammatically trained'. McKnight's position demonstrates an important fact: that prescriptive and descriptive approaches to language are not utterly distinct. Not only can the same individual often accommodate both attitudes, but works such as the *OED*, whose original purpose may have been predominantly investigative and descriptive, are inevitably adopted as authoritative, and are reused to prescribe correctness and acceptability. Finally, it should not be forgotten that during the nineteenth century, and even today, standard language itself admits some variation both in pronunciation (the stressing of multisyllabic words such as *controversy*, the alternative pronunciations of *either* and *economics*) and in spelling (*paid, payed*; *-ise, -ize*; *focussing, focusing*; *learned, learnt*; *despatch, dispatch*). If frequency of use, rather than the dictionary which supposedly records it, were to be the arbiter, it is even arguable that the seventeenth-century spelling *seperate* should once again be regarded as an alternative to the 'correct' form *separate*.

By comparison with earlier periods, the changes in the English language since 1800 have been relatively superficial. There has been no major systematic change in morphology to compare with the loss of inflection in Early Middle English, nor in phonology to compare with the Great Vowel Shift. Changes to the syntax and especially to the lexicon are more notable, but not so striking as those which took place in Early Modern English.

In the phonology, a number of distinctions have been lost. Except in certain Scottish pronunciation, the distinction between /w/ and /ʍ/ (*wight* and *white*), which was the last survivor of a set of initial consonant groups (*hw, hr, hl, hn*) descended from Old English, had been lost by the late eighteenth century. As an initial consonant, [h] has been unstable since Early Middle English, but objections to its omission as 'h-dropping' date only from about 1800 and the continuing struggle for supposed correctness. This attitude may account for the later restoration of the distinction between /w/ and /ʍ/, which is still heard occasionally. The conception of correctness driving both these examples is one dependent on traditional spellings. The same reasoning has restored the [l] in *falcon*, the [w] in *woman*, and the second *i* [j] in *Christian*. The pronunciation [ɪŋ], considered vulgar in 1801, extended rapidly after the 1820s, so that the [ɪn] pronunciation of *-ing*, widespread in the first decades of the nineteenth century, itself came to be regarded as sub-standard.

Syntactically, the widening use of the prop-word *one(s)* to substitute for repetition of a noun has been noted since the early nineteenth century in expressions with a determiner, such as *this book is the one I want*, or in interrogatives and plurals, such as *which ones are they?* Some further erosion of morphological contrasts has taken place. The demise of the oblique form of the relative pronoun *whom* was predicted by Sapir in 1926, but the process has been slow and it still survives among careful speakers. The distinction between the present indicative and the subjunctive has further declined in use, so that for most people, the latter occurs only in a few fixed expressions (*if I were you*). By contrast, the periphrastic formation of verb tenses has become more extensive and complex from the Early Modern period onwards. From the late nineteenth century the passival construction *the house is building*, whose origins can be traced in Old and Early Middle English, is gradually replaced by the type *the house is being built*, which first appeared in the late eighteenth century. This was extended in the twentieth century to the perfective durative type *it has been being built*. In Early Modern English the perfect of intransitive verbs could be formed freely with the verb *to be* (*the messenger is come from the king*). But in such uses, *have* has been steadily generalised and captured the last surviving main verb, *become*, during the nineteenth century. The use of *get* as an auxiliary followed by the past participle is first recorded in the mid seventeenth century, but during the later nineteenth and twentieth centuries has encroached rapidly on the use of *to be* in forming passive constructions where there is an implication of a state of affairs coming into existence (*he got arrested*; *she got promoted*).

The lexicon of English has expanded greatly during the past two hundred years, partly by borrowing but also extensively by word-formation. Many new compounds have been produced on patterns which go back to the earliest periods of English, and a new type, the reduplicative compound, has added a few examples: *hush-hush*; *fifty-fifty*; *pretty-pretty*. A considerable number of compound verbs has emerged since the nineteenth century by a process of back-formation from nominals: *shoplift* (1820), *housekeep* (1842), *moonlight* (1887) and, more recently, *dryclean*, *doublepark* and *wordprocess*. Although some suffixes have become newly productive (*-ish*, *-ism*, *-ist*) and a few new ones become productive for the first time (*-ette*), prefixes have been more prolific. During the nineteenth century, scientific studies introduced many new prefixes from neo-Latin and Greek and extended the use of others to combine with native bases, among them *micro-*, *ante-*, *intra-*, *meta-*, *mono-*, *hypo-*, *para-*, *tele-*, *multi-*, *retro-* and *semi-*. Words formed by shortening or 'clipping' words and phrases are numerous. Nineteenth-century examples are *bus* (from Latin *omnibus*, 'for all'), *vet*, *van* (from *caravan*), *exam*, *lab*, *photo*, *fan* (from *fanatic*), *express* (from *express train*) and *pants* (from *pantaloons*). Deliberate word-creation also plays a part, through blending, as with *mingy* (1928) or Lewis Carroll's *chortle* and *slithy*, and, less consciously, through the adoption of trade, personal or place names: *colt*, *hoover*, *boycott*, *shrapnel*, *bayonet*.

Borrowing, however, is the most fertile source of additions to the lexicon. French and Latin continue to contribute heavily but are joined by borrowings from other, more distant European languages, of words with varying degrees of assimilation into the ordinary English word-stock. The nineteenth century saw the Italian loans *vendetta, mafia, salami, risotto, studio, replica, prima donna* and *inferno*. Spanish loans, often by way of America, are *guerrilla, mustang, bronco, bonanza, patio, cafeteria, rodeo, pueblo*. German contributed *poodle, dachshund, lager, leitmotiv, kindergarten, seminar, hinterland, zeitgeist*, and Russian was the source of *vodka, samovar, tundra* and *polka*. Extended trade and colonial contacts, which began to contribute vocabulary to a significant extent in the final decades of the eighteenth century, continue to be an important source in the nineteenth, too. From contact with Hindustani in India, we have *thug, khaki, cashmere, pyjama, chutney, gymkhana, polo*; from Sanskrit, *nirvana, yoga* and *swastika*. The African colonies contributed few words (*gorilla, ju-ju* and *tsetse* are examples), but a number were borrowed from Afrikaans: *veldt, commando, trek, commandeer* and *spoor*. Australian words in this period include *wombat, boomerang* and *budgerigar*. *Kiwi* is first recorded in 1835. The opening up of Japan gave the words *tycoon, geisha, hara-kiri* and *ju-jitsu*.

Although this introduction seeks to indicate some of the linguistic developments during the period from 1800 until the date of the latest excerpts in about 1920, it should not be forgotten that linguistic variety and change are always present, affecting the language of today just as they did that of the past. Change today may not seem as dramatic as the major developments of the past, but historical events, scientific discoveries and social movements still influence the language. It is worth considering in the light of past change what may be the effects on the English language of some developments during the last three-quarters of a century: the virtual abandonment of grammar teaching in primary schools, the rise of feminism, immigration into Britain of settlers whose mother tongue is not English, the electronic revolution with (American) English as its mother tongue, the continuing spread of the use of English overseas, and the growing probability of some political unity in Europe. All these may be expected to leave their mark on the English language, and in retrospect may seem to future generations as spectacular in their effect as any of the developments which have been illustrated by the excerpts in this collection.

41

THOMAS CARLYLE, *SIGNS OF THE TIMES*

Thomas Carlyle (1795–1881) was born at Ecclefechan, Dumfriesshire, the son of a stonemason. He attended Annan Academy and went on to Edinburgh University. His family intended him to become a Presbyterian minister, but the intellectual life of Edinburgh dissuaded him from this calling and he instead supported himself by teaching, reviewing and literary work. He studied German literature and published a number of studies, anthologies and translations. In 1826 he married Jane Welsh, the daughter of a doctor, to whom he had acted as tutor in German. She was well equipped intellectually and temperamentally to support her husband's literary career, and later became famous as a literary hostess and correspondent of many of the contemporary literati.

Carlyle and his wife at first found life financially difficult, and they had to withdraw from Edinburgh to Jane's farm at Craigenputtock. It was here that he wrote *Signs of the Times*, which was first published in the *Edinburgh Review* in 1829. This was followed by *Sartor Resartus*, published in *Fraser's Magazine* (1833–34). The Carlyles then moved to Chelsea, where Thomas's reputation was established first by his *History of the French Revolution* (1837) and then by a series of lectures delivered to a fashionable audience during 1840 on *Heroes, Hero-Worship and the Heroic in History*. From here, Carlyle went on to become an admired pundit on matters social and historical, and his idealising evocations of pre-industrial, pre-capitalist medieval society inspired John Ruskin and William Morris.

Although his reputation in the late nineteenth century was very high, the anti-democratic elitism which accompanied his romanticism caused a decline of his reputation in the twentieth century. Contemporary critics found his style worthy of comment and even ridicule. His love of apostrophe, emphatic use of capitals and italics, eccentric punctuation, archaisms and lexical creativity earned it the title 'Carlylese'. Of the lexical creations recorded in *OED*, many exploit the derivational possibilities of English rather than represent new base forms: thus *abortional, absolvable, absolvent, assassinative,* or the use of *adze* as a verb. Many of these formations achieved no lasting circulation, but Carlyle is the first recorded user of a large number of words now in familiar use, among them *admonitorily, affordable, alleviatory, animalism, anonymity, approvingly, approximately, autobiographical* and *baggy*.

5

10

15

In fact, if we look deeper, we shall find that this faith in Mechanism has now struck its roots down into man's most intimate, primary sources of conviction; and is thence sending up, over his whole life and activity, innumerable stems, – fruit-bearing and poison-bearing. The truth is, men have lost their belief in the Invisible, and believe, and hope, and work only in the Visible; or, to speak it in other words: This is not a Religious age. Only the material, the immediately practical, not the divine and spiritual, is important to us. The infinite, absolute character of Virtue has passed into a finite, conditional one; it is no longer a worship of the Beautiful and Good; but a calculation of the Profitable. Worship, indeed, in any sense, is not recognised among us, or is mechanically explained into Fear of pain, or Hope of pleasure. Our true Deity is Mechanism. It has subdued external Nature for us, and we think it will do all other things. We are Giants in physical power: in a deeper than metaphorical sense, we are Titans, that strive, by heaping mountain on mountain, to conquer Heaven also.

20

25

30

The strong Mechanical character, so visible in the spiritual pursuits and methods of this age, may be traced much farther into the condition and prevailing disposition of our spiritual nature itself. Consider, for example, the general fashion of Intellect in this era. Intellect, the power man has of knowing and believing, is now nearly synonymous with Logic, or the mere power of arranging and communicating. Its implement is not Meditation, but Argument. 'Cause and effect' is almost the only category under which we look at, and work with, all Nature. Our first question with regard to any object is not, What is it? but, How is it? We are no longer instinctively driven to apprehend, and lay to heart, what is Good and Lovely, but rather to inquire, as on-lookers, how it is produced, whence it comes, whither it goes. Our favourite Philosophers have no love and no hatred; they stand among us not to do, nor to create anything, but as a sort of Logic-mills to grind out the true

causes and effects of all that is done and created. To the eye of
a Smith, a Hume or a Constant, all is well that works quietly.
An Order of Ignatius Loyola, a Presbyterianism of John Knox, a
Wickliffe or a Henry the Eighth, are simply so many mechanical
phenomena, caused or causing.

The *Euphuist* of our day differs much from his pleasant predecessors. An intellectual dapperling of these times boasts chiefly of
his irresistible perspicacity, his 'dwelling in the daylight of truth,'
and so forth; which, on examination, turns out to be a dwelling in
the rush-light of 'closet-logic,' and a deep unconsciousness that
there is any other light to dwell in or any other objects to survey
with it. Wonder, indeed, is, on all hands, dying out: it is the sign
of uncultivation to wonder. Speak to any small man of a high,
majestic Reformation, of a high majestic Luther; and forthwith he
sets about 'accounting' for it; how the 'circumstances of the time'
called for such a character, and found him, we suppose, standing girt
and road-ready, to do its errand; how the 'circumstances of the time'
created, fashioned, floated him quietly along into the result; how,
in short, this small man, had he been there, could have performed
the like himself! For it is the 'force of circumstances' that does
everything; the force of one man can do nothing. Now all this is
grounded on little more than a metaphor. We figure Society as a
'Machine,' and that mind is opposed to mind, as body is to body;
whereby two, or at most ten, little minds must be stronger than
one great mind. Notable absurdity! For the plain truth, very plain,
we think is, that minds are opposed to minds in quite a different
way; and *one* man that has a higher Wisdom, a hitherto unknown
spiritual Truth in him, is stronger, not than ten men that have it
not, or than ten thousand, but than *all* men that have it not; and
stands among them with a quite ethereal, angelic power, as with
a sword out of Heaven's own armory, sky-tempered, which no
buckler, and no tower of brass, will finally withstand.

But to us, in these times, such considerations rarely occur. We
enjoy, we see nothing by direct vision; but only by reflection, and
in anatomical dismemberment. Like Sir Hudibras, for every Why
we must have a Wherefore. We have our little *theory* on all human
and divine things. Poetry, the workings of genius itself, which in all
times, with one or another meaning, has been called Inspiration,
and held to be mysterious and inscrutable, is no longer without its
scientific exposition. The building of the lofty rhyme is like any

other masonry or bricklaying: we have theories of its rise, height, decline and fall, – which latter, it would seem, is now near, among
75   all people. Of our 'Theories of Taste,' as they are called, wherein the deep, infinite, unspeakable Love of Wisdom and Beauty, which dwells in all men, is 'explained,' made mechanically visible, from 'Association' and the like, why should we say anything? Hume has written us a 'Natural History of Religion;' in which one Natural
80   History all the rest are included. Strangely too does the general feeling coincide with Hume's in this wonderful problem; for whether his 'Natural History' be the right one or not, that Religion must have a Natural History, all of us, cleric and laic, seem to be agreed. He indeed regards it as a Disease, we again as Health; so far there is
85   a difference; but in our first principle we are at one.

Notes

3   **thence** 'from there'   Carlyle also employs *whence*, 'from where', and *whither*, 'to what place' (30). The group of adverbials expressing motion to and from a place – *thence, hence, whence, thither, whither* and *hither* – is already archaic and consciously literary. The last three descend from OE forms *þider, hwider* and *hider*. The former three are thirteenth-century formations employing the adverbial-forming inflexion *-es* (on *thenne, henne* and *whenne*).

34   **Smith**, *et al.*   Adam Smith (1723–90), Scottish philosopher and socio-economic theorist, was the author of the *Theory of Moral Sentiments* (1759) and the *Wealth of Nations* (1776), both developed as lectures at Glasgow University. He was a friend of the Edinburgh philosopher David Hume (1711–76), who was the author of a *Treatise of Human Nature* (1740). Benjamin Constant (1767–1830) was a French-born political philosopher who was also temporarily resident in Edinburgh, and like the other two was concerned with questions of human personality and moral and religious feeling. Carlyle is objecting to a tendency of all three to explain human personality in terms of environmental experience rather than innate ability, and the operations of associations rather than reason. By comparison, Ignatius Loyola, founder of the Jesuit order, and John Knox, Wickliffe and Henry VIII, jointly seen as instigators of the Reformation, are considered inspired men of vision.

38   **Euphuist**   Properly, one who imitates the rhetorical style of Lyly's *Euphues* (see Excerpt 27), but here used ironically of an author who affects impressive style without significant substance.

39   **dapperling** 'a little dapper fellow'   The only previously recorded use of this scornful epithet is in Cotgrave's Anglo-French dictionary of 1611.

47   **accounting**   *OED* gives 1768 as the earliest occurrence of the sense 'to explain'. Earlier senses are more closely related to the idea of arithmetical calculation; therefore Carlyle's dislike of this term probably arises from a strong awareness of these 'mathematical' associations, and the implied claim of irrefutable proof made by its use.

48–49   **girt and road-ready**   *OED* notes that the verb *gird* is confined largely to rhetorical (often biblically influenced) contexts throughout its history. The earliest sense of *gird* is to 'surround or encircle (with a belt etc.)', sometimes to confine clothes preparatory to some action. Early sense developments were to 'belt on a sword', to 'saddle a horse', and to 'be prepared for action'. The compound *road-ready* is a nonce creation parallel to the contemporary *roadworthy*. Compound adjectives of this type are found in OE, but many are modern formations.

67   **Hudibras**   The main protagonist of Samuel Butler's *Hudibras* (1662–80), a satirical work in the form of a mock romance, whose narrative development is hidden by the numerous disputations and digressions of which it is largely composed.

78   **Association**   Associations deriving from environmental experience as a factor in forming moral and aesthetic judgements were argued by Hume and David Hartley (1705–57), popularised by Joseph Priestley, and adopted in Coleridge's early theorising on the role of the imagination in poetry.

79   **Natural History**   Hume was the author of a dissertation on the *Natural History of Religion*, which traced the origin and development of religions in an analytic spirit. His religious works betray a strong scepticism about the 'revealed' nature of religion, and he finds in them an echo of the human mind.

42

CHARLES DICKENS,

THE PICKWICK PAPERS

Charles Dickens was born on 7 February 1812. He spent a happy child-hood at Chatham, where his father was a clerk, but the boy's world collapsed when his father, whom he greatly admired, was imprisoned for debt. At the age of twelve, Dickens was forced to fend for himself, working for six shillings a week in a blacking factory. The misery of these months is reflected in the early part of *David Copperfield.* But there were also benefits, since it was then that he accumulated that knowledge of London street life which served him well in his later career. He returned to school after his father's release; then, aged fifteen, entered a solicitor's office as an under-clerk. He made strenuous efforts to learn shorthand, and so gained a role as a reporter of parliamentary debates. Entry into newspaper publishing led to a series of contributions to the *Evening Chronicle* and *Monthly Magazine,* which developed into his earliest work, *Sketches by 'Boz'* (1836–37). These were sufficiently popular to encourage the publishers Chapman and Hall to commission him to write a series on the activities of a fictional gentleman's club. *The Posthumous Papers of the Pickwick Club* appeared in episodes from April 1836 onwards, and were published in book form in the following year. The series achieved success with the introduction of Sam Weller into the story, so that, by the end of the year, Dickens had earned two thousand pounds. His literary career was established, and he pursued it through a series of novels, journalistic and editorial work, and in later times through readings of his works. He interested himself in philanthropic and radical causes, travelled extensively, and died unexpectedly of a stroke at his home in Rochester on 9 June 1870.

This excerpt is full of the good spirits of Christmas at Dingley Dell, expressing them in two contrasting styles: the standard English of the narrator, and Sam Weller's pastiche of Cockney dialect features. In both, humour depends in part on verbal inflation. The former exploits mock formality to describe trivial events (*this same branch, the mystic branch, appropriating to his own use*) but emphasises the incongruity by using colloquialisms also (*good long sitting, somewhere about five-and-forty, pretty certain*). The latter mingles the features of sub-standard speech (simplified consonant clusters, omission of unstressed vowels, invariable use of the third-person present tense, non-standard preterites and past participles, and malapropisms) with the same predilection for the elevated word and orotund phrase which once formed part of the eloquence of Dickens's own father.

Long before Mr. Pickwick was weary of dancing, the newly-married couple had retired from the scene. There was a glorious supper down stairs, notwithstanding, and a good long sitting after it; and when Mr. Pickwick awoke, late the next morning, he had
5   a confused recollection of having, severally and confidentially, invited somewhere about five-and-forty people to dine with him at the George and Vulture, the very first time they came to London; which Mr. Pickwick rightly considered a pretty certain indication of his having taken something besides exercise, on the previous
10   night.

     'And so your family has games in the kitchen to-night, my dear, has they?' inquired Sam of Emma.

     'Yes, Mr. Weller,' replied Emma; 'we always have on Christmas eve. Master wouldn't neglect to keep it up, on any account.'
15   'Your master's a wery pretty notion of keepin' anythin' up, my dear,' said Mr. Weller; 'I never see such a sensible sort of man as he is, or such a reg'lar gen'l'm'n.'

     'Oh, that he is!' said the fat boy, joining in the conversation; 'don't he breed nice pork!' and the fat youth gave a semi-cannibalic
20   leer at Mr. Weller, as he thought of the roast legs and gravy.

     'Oh, you've woke up, at last, have you?' said Sam.

     The fat boy nodded.

     'I'll tell you what it is, young boa constructer,' said Mr. Weller, impressively, 'if you don't sleep a little less, and exercise a little
25   more, ven you comes to be a man you'll lay yourself open to the same sort o' personal inconwenience as was inflicted on the old gen'l'm'n as wore the pig-tail.'

     'What did they do to him?' inquired the fat boy, in a faltering voice.

30 'I'm a goin' to tell you,' replied Mr. Weller; 'he was one o the
largest patterns as was ever turned out – reg'lar fat man, as hadn't
caught a glimpse of his own shoes for five-and-forty years.'

'Lor!' exclaimed Emma.

'No, that he hadn't, my dear,' said Mr. Weller, 'and if you'd
35 put an exact model of his own legs on the dinin' table afore him,
he wouldn't ha' known 'em. Well, he always walks to his office with
a wery handsome gold watch-chain hanging out, about a foot and
a half, and a gold watch in his fob pocket as was worth – I'm afraid
to say how much, but as much as a watch can be – a large, heavy,
40 round manafacter, as stout for a watch, as he was for a man, and
with a big face in proportion. "You'd better not carry that 'ere
watch," says the old gen'l'm'n's friends, "you'll be robbed on it,"
says they. "Shall I?" says he. "Yes, will you," says they. "Vell," says
he, "I should like to see the thief as could get this here watch out,
45 for I'm blessed if *I* ever can; it's such a tight fit," says he, "and
venever I vants to know what's o'clock, I'm obliged to stare into
the bakers' shops," he says. Well, then he laughs as hearty as if he
was a goin' to pieces, and out he walks agin' with his powdered
head and pig-tail, and rolls down the Strand vith the chain hangin'
50 out furder than ever, and the great round watch almost bustin'
through his grey kersey smalls. There warn't a pickpocket in all
London as didn't take a pull at that chain, but the chain 'ud never
break, and the watch 'ud never come out, so they soon got tired o'
dragging such a heavy old gen'l'm'n along the pavement, and he'd
55 go home and laugh till the pig-tail wibrated like the penderlum of
a Dutch clock. At last, one day the old gen'l'm'n was a rollin' along,
and he sees a pickpocket as he know'd by sight, a-comin' up, arm
in arm vith a little boy vith a wery large head. "Here's a game," says
the old gen'l'm'n to himself, "they're a-goin' to have another try,
60 but it won't do." So he begins a chucklin' wery hearty, ven, all of a
sudden, the little boy leaves hold of the pickpocket's arm, and rushes
headforemost straight into the old gen'l'm'n's stomach, and for a
moment doubles him right up vith the pain. "Murder!" says the old
gen'l'm'n. "All right, Sir," says the pickpocket, a whisperin' in his ear.
65 And ven he come straight agin', the watch and chain was gone, and
what's worse than that, the old gen'l'm'n's digestion was all wrong
ever artervards, to the wery last day of his life; so just you look
about you, young feller, and take care you don't get too fat.'

As Mr. Weller concluded this moral tale, with which the fat
70 boy appeared much affected, they all three wended their way to the

large kitchen, in which the family were by this time assembled, according to annual custom on Christmas eve, observed by old Wardle's forefathers from time immemorial.

75 From the centre of the ceiling of this kitchen, old Wardle had just suspended with his own hands a huge branch of misletoe, and this same branch of misletoe instantaneously gave rise to a scene of general and most delightful struggling and confusion; in the midst of which Mr. Pickwick with a gallantry which would have done honour to a descendant of Lady Tollimglower herself, took the old 80 lady by the hand, led her beneath the mystic branch, and saluted her in all courtesy and decorum. The old lady submitted to this piece of practical politeness with all the dignity which befitted so important and serious a solemnity, but the younger ladies not being so thoroughly imbued with a superstitious veneration of the custom, 85 or imagining that the value of a salute is very much enhanced if it cost a little trouble to obtain it, screamed and struggled, and ran into corners, and threatened and remonstrated, and did every thing but leave the room, until some of the less adventurous gentlemen were on the point of desisting, when they all at once found it 90 useless to resist any longer, and submitted to be kissed with a good grace. Mr. Winkle kissed the young lady with the black eyes, and Mr. Snodgrass kissed Emily; and Mr. Weller, not being particular about the form of being under the misletoe, kissed Emma and the other female servants, just as he caught them. As to the poor 95 relations, they kissed everybody, not even excepting the plainer portion of the young-lady visiters, who, in their excessive confusion, ran right under the misletoe, directly it was hung up, without knowing it! Wardle stood with his back to the fire, surveying the whole scene, with the utmost satisfaction; and the fat boy took 100 the opportunity of appropriating to his own use, and summarily devouring, a particularly fine mince-pie, that had been carefully put by, for somebody else.

Notes

15 **keepin' anythin'**   The loss of velarity in the pronunciation of *ing* begins in Late Middle English. Although a characteristic of Sam Weller's language, it is not necessarily considered lower class at this period, and is found also in the speech of Wardle. Emily Brontë does not make it a feature of Joseph's language in *Wuthering Heights*, although it was probably found in contemporary Haworth.

19   **semi-cannibalic**   The word *cannibal* is a variant of the tribal name Carib, used of a people who were credited by early travellers to the West Indies with eating human flesh. The noun is first recorded in 1553 and has several derivative adjectives – *cannibalean* (1602), *cannibalish* (1837), *cannibalistic* (1851). Dickens is the first recorded user of *cannibalic.*

26   **personal inconwenience**   Part of the comic appeal of Sam Weller's speech is in the incongruity of his peculiar pronunciation and relatively elevated diction. The confusion between [v] and [w] in his language is characteristic of Dickens's representation of lower-class London English, and is indeed found in other contemporary literature. A similar confusion was already evident in the sixteenth-century English of Henry Machyn (see Excerpt 26). In fact, this phonetic peculiarity was not restricted to London and could be found also in Essex and East Anglia.

30   **a goin**   This form of the present participle is very common in Sam Weller's speech. Although no longer normal in standard English by the nineteenth century, it was common in Early Modern English. It originates in an OE prepositional phrasal type (*on huntinge*), whose noun became confused in ME with the newly emerging participle in *-ing.*

31   **patterns** 'specimens'   The sense is last recorded by *OED* in 1829.

41   **that 'ere**   Compare *this here* (44). The demonstrative phrase is developed from *that there* by assimilation of the following fricative to the stop [t].

50   **furder**   Examples of the change of the voiced dental fricative [ð] to the voiced alveolar stop [d], when occurring between two vowels, are found also in the language of Sam's father and that of Mrs Gamp in *Martin Chuzzlewit*. Variation of this kind was responsible for the emergence of the forms *father, mother, weather* in the fifteenth century from earlier forms with a stop consonant.

51   **warn't**   This is a dialectally widespread negative form in sub-standard English. The origin of the forms in London and northern English may be different, since in areas of Scandinavian settlement, ME *ware* may be influenced by *várum*, whereas in the south-east Midlands the development of OE /æː/ to /aː/ occurred independently.

67   **artervards**   The <ar> spelling probably represents the long vowel [ɑː]. The following [f] has been assimilated to the [t].

96   **visiters**   The modern spelling, *visitor*, derives from fifteenth-century Latinisation of an originally French borrowing. Dickens is among the last authors quoted by *OED* to use the older spelling; he himself changed his practice during his later career. The spelling *misletoe* was also commonly used from the sixteenth to the early nineteenth centuries, when the modern spelling *mistletoe* restored the OE antecedent form, *mistiltān.*

43

EMILY BRONTË, *WUTHERING HEIGHTS*

Emily Brontë was born on 30 July 1818, the fifth of the six children
of Patrick Brontë, perpetual curate of Haworth, West Yorkshire. The
morbidity which contemporaries found in *Wuthering Heights* is paralleled
in the history of the family. Emily was only three when her mother died,
and her two eldest sisters were dead by the time she was seven. None of
the children attained the age of forty, and she herself died of tuberculosis
before Christmas 1848.

Except for a few months at boarding schools, a brief visit to Brussels
and some time as a governess near Halifax, her life was spent in Haworth
and its neighbourhood. Her education, therefore, was largely at home with
her sisters, through her own reading and through collaborating with them
in writing poetry and poetic drama. *Wuthering Heights* was written during
1845–46 and appeared in 1847 under the pseudonym Ellis Bell.

In this excerpt, extensive use is made of Haworth dialect forms. These
are quite accurately represented, but their purpose is the traditional literary
one of indicating social status through language choice. In addition, they
emphasise the dissociation between the malevolent old servant, Joseph, and
the narrator, an unwelcome interloper into his world. Consequently, most
of the dialect forms belong to Joseph, while Isabella speaks a rather literary
standard. Their mutual antipathy is focused in Joseph's mockery of the
word *parlour* and his scathing use of the hypercorrection *rume* in contrast
to his usual pronunciation, *rahm*. Their linguistic division is not, however,
quite complete, since the word *thible* (21), 'a smooth stick or spatula', is a
dialect form recorded only from north of the Humber–Mersey line, and
cranky (50), 'rickety', is restricted to Lancashire and Yorkshire. It is possible
that Emily was not aware, when she used them, of the dialectal status of
these words. Dialect speech is represented by standard spelling except where
segments differ from the standard in pronunciation. Here, dialect sounds

are indicated by deviant spellings based on an analogy with unambiguous representations of the particular sound in standard spelling practice: thus the sound [aː] is spelt <ah> in words where the standard would have [au], <ou> and [uː], <oo>. Shortened vowels are indicated by following double consonants: *brocken* (105). Consistency is high, and variants may represent real variation in the dialect (*ye/yah*) or the existence of unstressed forms (*yuh, bud*). A proportion of the words, phrases and pronunciations are archaic from the point of view of the standard (*barn, gang, marred, nave, desarve, froo this*), and although the dialect matches quite well that of the present day, certain words and pronunciations have now become rare or disappeared altogether – thus *ortherings* (12) and *bothom* (27) are now more common in Lancashire.

Joseph was bending over the fire, peering into a large pan that swung above it; and a wooden bowl of oatmeal stood on the settle close by. The contents of the pan began to boil, and he turned to plunge his hand into the bowl; I conjectured that this preparation
5   was probably for our supper, and, being hungry, I resolved it should be eatable – so crying out sharply, *'I'll* make the porridge!' I removed the vessel out of his reach, and proceeded to take off my hat and riding habit. 'Mr. Earnshaw', I continued, 'directs me to wait on myself – I will – I'm not going to act the lady among you, for
10   fear I should starve.'

'Gooid Lord!' he muttered, sitting down, and stroking his ribbed stockings from the knee to the ankle. 'If they's tuh be fresh ortherings – just when Aw getten used tuh two maisters, if Aw mun hev a *mistress* set o'er my heead, it's loike time tuh be flitting. Aw niver
15   *did* think tuh say t' day ut Aw mud lave th' owld place – but Aw daht it's nigh at hend!'

This lamentation drew no notice from me; I went briskly to work, sighing to remember a period when it would have been all merry fun; but compelled speedily to drive off the remembrance.
20   It racked me to recall past happiness, and the greater peril there was of conjuring up its apparition, the quicker the thible ran round, and the faster the handfuls of meal fell into the water.

Joseph beheld my style of cookery with growing indignation.

'Thear!' he ejaculated. 'Hareton, thah willn't sup thy porridge
25   tuh neeght; they'll be nowt bud lumps as big as maw nave. Thear,

agean! Aw'd fling in bowl un' all, if Aw wer yah! Thear, pale t' guilp
off, un' then yah'll hae done wi't. Bang, bang. It's a marcy t' bothom
isn't deaved aht!'

It *was* rather a rough mess, I own, when poured into the
30 basins; four had been provided, and a gallon pitcher of new milk
was brought from the dairy, which Hareton seized and commenced
drinking and spilling from the expansive lip.

I expostulated, and desired that he should have his in a mug;
affirming that I could not taste the liquid treated so dirtily. The old
35 cynic chose to be vastly offended at this nicety; assuring me, repeatedly, that 'the barn was every bit as gooid' as I, 'and every bit as
wollsome,' and wondering how I could fashion to be so conceited;
meanwhile, the infant ruffian continued sucking, and glowered up
at me defyingly, as he slavered into the jug.

40 'I shall have my supper in another room,' I said. 'Have you no
place you call a parlour?'

'*Parlour!*' he echoed, sneeringly, '*parlour!* Nay, we've noa *par-
lours.* If yah dunnut loike wer company, they's maister's; un' if yah
dunnut loike maister, they's us.'

45 'Then I shall go upstairs,' I answered; 'shew me a chamber!' I
put my basin on a tray, and went myself to fetch some more milk.

With great grumblings, the fellow rose, and preceded me in
my ascent: we mounted to the garrets; he opening a door, now and
then, to look into the apartments we passed.

50 'Here's a rahm,' he said, at last, flinging back a cranky board
on hinges. 'It's weel eneugh tuh ate a few porridge in. They's a pack
uh corn i' t' corner, thear, meeterly clane; if yah're feared uh
muckying yer grand silk cloes, spread yer hankerchir ut t' top on't.'

The 'rahm' was a kind of lumber-hole smelling strong of malt
55 and grain; various sacks of which articles were piled around, leaving
a wide, bare space in the middle.

'Why, man!' I exclaimed, facing him angrily, 'this is not a place
to sleep in. I wish to see my bed-room.'

'*Bed-rume!*' he repeated, in a tone of mockery. 'Yah's see all t'
60 *bed-rumes* thear is – yon's mine.'

He pointed into the second garret, only differing from the first
in being more naked about the walls, and having a large, low,
curtainless bed, with an indigo-coloured quilt, at one end.

'What do I want with yours?' I retorted. 'I suppose Mr. Heathcliff
65 does not lodge at the top of the house, does he?'

'Oh! it's Maister *Hathecliff's* yah're wenting?' cried he, as if making a new discovery. 'Couldn't ye uh said soa, at onst? un' then, Aw mud uh telled ye, baht all this wark, ut that's just one yah cannut sea – he allas keeps it locked, un' nob'dy iver mells on't but hisseln.'

70

'You've a nice house, Joseph,' I could not refrain from observing, 'and pleasant inmates; and I think the concentrated essence of all the madness in the world took up its abode in my brain the day I linked my fate with theirs! However, that is not to the present purpose – there are other rooms. For heaven's sake, be quick, and let me settle somewhere!'

75

He made no reply to this adjuration; only plodding doggedly down the wooden steps, and halting before an apartment which, from that halt, and the superior quality of its furniture, I conjectured to be the best one.

80

There was a carpet, a good one, but the pattern was obliterated by dust; a fire-place hung with cut paper dropping to pieces; a handsome oak-bedstead with ample crimson curtains of rather expensive material and modern make. But they had evidently experienced rough usage: the valances hung in festoons, wrenched from their rings, and the iron rod supporting them was bent in an arc, on one side, causing the drapery to trail upon the floor. The chairs were also damaged, many of them severely; and deep indentations deformed the panels of the walls.

85

I was endeavouring to gather resolution for entering, and taking possession, when my fool of a guide announced –

90

'This here is t' maister's.'

My supper by this time was cold, my appetite gone, and my patience exhausted. I insisted on being provided instantly with a place of refuge, and means of repose.

95

'Whear the divil,' began the religious elder. 'The Lord bless us! The Lord forgie us! Whear the *hell*, wold ye gang? ye marred, wearisome nowt! Yah seen all bud Hareton's bit uf a cham'er. They's nut another hoile tuh lig dahn in i' th' hahse!'

I was so vexed, I flung my tray and its contents on the ground; and then seated myself at the stairs-head, hid my face in my hands, and cried.

100

'Ech! ech!' exclaimed Joseph. 'Weel done, Miss Cathy! weel done, Miss Cathy! Hahsiver, t' maister sall just tum'le o'er them brocken pots; un then we's hear summut; we's hear hah it's tuh be. Gooid-fur-nowt madling! yah desarve pining froo this tuh Churstmas,

105

flinging t' precious gifts uh God under fooit i' yer flaysome rages!
Bud, Aw'm mista'en if yah shew yer sperrit lang. Will Hathecliff
bide sich bonny ways, think ye? Aw nobbut wish he muh cotch ye
110   i' that plisky. Aw nobbut wish he may.'

And so he went scolding to his den beneath, taking the candle
with him, and I remained in the dark.

Notes

11   **gooid**   The spelling represents the pronunciation [uːɪ]. A similar pronunciation for *foot* is implied by the spelling <fooit> (107), but modern
Haworth dialect uses the standard form for the latter word.

13   **mun hev** 'must have'   The modal auxiliary *mun* is derived from OSc
munu. *Mud*, 'might' (15), and the unstressed form *muh*, 'may' (109), are
recorded in this area in the nineteenth century, but the latter has not been
found by recent dialect workers. There is variation in the form of the verb
'to have'. The form *hae* (27) illustrates a widespread northern loss of
medial [v] (*forgie*, 97).

16   **daht** 'fear'   See the introduction for the spelling. The sense is the French
one common in ME.

24   **Thear**   Pronounced with the diphthong [iə]. Compare the forms *agean*,
deaved, *whear*.

        thah   Joseph uses the familiar (originally second-person-singular) mode
of address to the child, but the more distant (hardly *polite* in this passage)
form to his social superior.

25   **nave** 'fist'   From OSc *hnefi*. Found in Scotland, Ireland and the northern counties, as far south as Notts, Derby and Lincoln. In ME, south to
Worcester.

26   **in bowl**   The reduction of the definite article before a noun beginning with a consonant is usually represented by *t'*. Its omission here is
phonetically quite probable, but may be a misprint since the first edition
of *Wuthering Heights* was far from perfectly printed.

26–27   **pale t' guilp off** 'skim the thin liquid off'   The standard English [iː] is
in this dialect [eɪɪ] or [ɛɪɪ]: *ate* (51), *clane* (52); *Hathecliff* (66). Modern
Haworth dialect has a reduced number of words with this pronunciation.
The word *guilp* is uncertain in both meaning and origin.

27   **marcy**   The text represents a number of standard <er> or <or> spellings by <ar>: *desarve*, *wark*. The fifteenth-century development of ME
er to *ar* was earliest and most extensive in the North, and is preserved here
in words where it had never occurred, or had been replaced, in more
southerly localities. The modern standard spelling, *work*, derives from a
western form, the pronunciation from the south-east Midlands.

28   **deaved** 'smashed'   This sense is a unique occurrence, but the verb is
recorded north of the Humber, meaning 'deafen'.

36   **barn** 'child'   The Scandinavian and Anglian OE forms of this word are identical. The spelling *bairn* is Scots.

52   **meeterly** 'moderately' (OE *gemetlīc*).

60   **yon**   Derived from the OE adjectival demonstrative *geon*, and not, as is often implied by the spelling *yon*, an abbreviation of preposition and adverb *yond* (OE *geond*). Joseph's pronominal use is found from the early fourteenth century onwards but retreats into northern dialect usage after the seventeenth century.

67   **soa**   The evidence of present-day dialect suggests that this spelling represents the diphthong [uə].

69   **mells on't** 'interferes with it'   Widespread in dialectal usage. Derived from OF *meller, mesler.*

97   **marred** 'spoilt' (OE *merran*)   Widely used of spoilt children in nineteenth-century dialects. This represents a narrowing of its usage compared with ME or the language of Shakespeare.

99   **hoile** 'hole'   This pronunciation is still common in south-west Yorkshire.
      lig 'lie'   From OSc *liggja*. Found widely north of Staffs and Derbyshire.

104   **sall**   This northern form is recorded from ME onwards.

107   **flaysome** 'fearsome'   Widespread in dialectal usage.

110   **plisky** 'trick, escapade'   Used in Cumbria, Yorkshire and Scotland. Here with ironic implication.

44

CHARLES DARWIN,

THE DESCENT OF MAN

Among scientific authors of the nineteenth century, Charles Darwin has perhaps the strongest claim to have revolutionised the way in which we view the world in which we live. His theory of the evolution of species, which undertook to explain the mechanism by which the diversity of terrestrial life developed, was implicitly opposed to the scriptural account of instantaneous creation. It was very widely read and caused great anguish in the Victorian world by its implied conflict between faith and science. Darwin, a retiring and sensitive man whose health was poor, played no personal role in the ensuing controversy, leaving his cause to be fought by the biologist T. H. Huxley.

Darwin (1809–82) was born in Shrewsbury into a medical family. After attending Shrewsbury school, he studied medicine at Edinburgh University, but, revolted by contemporary surgery, entered Christ's College, Cambridge with the intention of becoming an Anglican priest. Here he came under the influence of John Stevens Henslow, Professor of Botany, and it was he who recommended Darwin as a naturalist to accompany HMS *Beagle* on its round-the-world voyage from 1831 to 1836. Inspired by Lyell's *Principles of Geology* (1830), the observations made on this voyage provided him with the material from which his theories developed. Most of this development took place in a period of intense activity from 1837 to 1839, but his ideas were not widely published until they seemed in danger of pre-emption by Alfred Russel Wallace. The *Origin of Species* (1859) did not, however, emphasise the point that mankind participated in the evolutionary rules governing the rest of the natural world, and it was only in 1871, after preparatory works by Huxley and Lyell, that Darwin published *The Descent of Man and Selection in Relation to Sex*, in which evolutionary principles were applied to the human species.

The excerpt printed here concerns the origins of language, a matter of great importance since Wallace was prepared to accept a clear distinction between the human and other species owing to the enormous gulf in intellectual subtlety, which he believed to be too great to derive from natural selection. Darwin's argument is that mental dexterity is a product of the possession of language. This echoes a traditional distinction between the human and other species going back to Isocrates, but it is here framed in terms of eighteenth- and nineteenth-century philological speculation on the origins of language.

That which distinguishes man from the lower animals is not the understanding of articulate sounds, for, as every one knows, dogs understand many words and sentences. In this respect they are at the same stage of development as infants, between the ages of
5   ten and twelve months, who understand many words and short sentences, but cannot yet utter a single word. It is not the mere articulation which is our distinguishing character, for parrots and other birds possess this power. Nor is it the mere capacity of connecting definite sounds with definite ideas; for it is certain that
10   some parrots, which have been taught to speak, connect unerringly words with things, and persons with events. The lower animals differ from man solely in his almost infinitely larger power of associating together the most diversified sounds and ideas; and this obviously depends on the high development of his mental powers.
15   As Horne Tooke, one of the founders of the noble science of philology, observes, language is an art, like brewing or baking; but writing would have been a better simile. It certainly is not a true instinct, for every language has to be learnt. It differs, however, widely from all ordinary arts, for man has an instinctive tendency
20   to speak, as we see in the babble of our young children; whilst no child has an instinctive tendency to brew, bake, or write. Moreover, no philologist now supposes that any language has been deliberately invented; it has been slowly and unconsciously developed by many steps. The sounds uttered by birds offer in several respects
25   the nearest analogy to language, for all the members of the same species utter the same instinctive cries expressive of their emotions; and all the kinds which sing, exert their power instinctively; but the actual song, and even the call-notes, are learnt from their parents or foster-parents. These sounds, as Daines Barrington has proved,

30   'are no more innate than language is in man.' The first attempts
      to sing may be compared to the 'imperfect endeavour in a child
      to babble.' The young males continue practising, or as the bird-
      catchers say, 'recording,' for ten or eleven months. Their first essays
      show hardly a rudiment of the future song; but as they grow older
35   we can perceive what they are aiming at; and at last they are said
      to sing 'their song round.' Nestlings which have learnt the song of
      a distinct species, as with the canary-birds educated in the Tyrol,
      teach and transmit their new song to their offspring. The slight
      natural differences of song in the same species inhabiting differ-
40   ent districts may be appositely compared, as Barrington remarks,
      'to provincial dialects;' and the songs of allied, though distinct
      species may be compared with the languages of distinct races of
      man. I have given the foregoing details to shew that an instinctive
      tendency to acquire an art is not peculiar to man.
45   With respect to the origin of articulate language, after having
      read on the one side the highly interesting works of Mr. Hensleigh
      Wedgwood, the Rev. F. Farrar, and Prof. Schleicher, and the celeb-
      rated lectures of Prof. Max Mueller on the other side, I cannot
      doubt that language owes its origin to the imitation and modifica-
50   tion of various natural sounds, the voices of other animals, and
      man's own instinctive cries, aided by signs and gestures. When we
      treat of sexual selection we shall see that primeval man, or rather
      some early progenitor of man, probably first used his voice in
      producing true musical cadences, that is in singing, as do some of
55   the gibbon-apes at the present day; and we may conclude from a
      widely-spread analogy, that this power would have been especially
      exerted during the courtship of the sexes – would have expressed
      various emotions, such as love, jealousy, triumph, – and would
      have served as a challenge to rivals. It is, therefore, probable that
60   the imitation of musical cries by articulate sounds may have given
      rise to words expressive of various complex emotions. The strong
      tendency in our nearest allies, the monkeys, in microcephalous
      idiots, and in the barbarous races of mankind to imitate whatever
      they hear deserves notice, as bearing on the subject of imitation.
65   Since monkeys certainly understand much that is said to them by
      man, and when wild, utter signal-cries of danger to their fellows;
      and since fowls give distinct warnings for danger on the ground, or
      in the sky from hawks (both, as well as a third cry, intelligible to
      dogs), may not some unusually wise ape-like animal have imitated

70   the growl of a beast of prey, and thus told his fellow-monkeys the nature of the expected danger? This would have been a first step in the formation of a language.

Notes

15   **Horne Tooke**   John Horne Tooke, author of the *Diversions of Purley* (1786, 1805), enjoyed a high reputation in England for half a century after its publication but had lost this authority by the time Darwin wrote. His purpose had been to demonstrate by etymology that the entire vocabulary could be reduced to names for physical objects, which had often been modified and abbreviated by use. His etymologies are, however, often fanciful. His mechanical explanation of the origins and evolution of language, and belief that language is the basis of mental activity, suited Darwin's purpose well.

23   **invented**   Rousseau had wryly pointed out that, in order to invent language and agree on its use, early man would have had to have possessed it already.'

29   **Daines Barrington**   (1727–1800). Lawyer, antiquary and naturalist, who is credited with inspiring Gilbert White to write *The Natural History of Selborne*.

33   **recording**   An example of the restriction of a word to a technical context. In ME, primary senses are 'to learn by heart' and 'to recite'. In the sixteenth century the sense begins to be restricted to the song of birds.

37   **canary-birds**   Canaries were first imported from the Canary Islands in the sixteenth century. The abbreviated form *canary* is recorded from the mid seventeenth century on but did not become the dominant form until the first quarter of the twentieth century.

42   **distinct races**   Darwin was very careful to point out that all modern men belong to the single species *homo sapiens* and vary only in race, but the association of language with race, and the failure to distinguish this from culture, is strange to modern ears (cf. *barbarous races*, 63).

43   **shew**   The spelling, which was common in the eighteenth and first half of the nineteenth centuries, had become restricted to legal language by the early twentieth century. The variants *shew* and *show* derive from forms of the OE *scēawian* with respectively a falling and a rising diphthong (Dobson (1968) ii, 245).

47   **Wedgwood**   Wedgwood was Darwin's brother-in-law and the author of a book, *On the Origin of Language* (1866). Schleicher, the prominent German philologist and Indo-European scholar, drew a parallel between evolutionary theory and language development in his book *Die Darwinische Theorie und die Sprachwissenschaft* (1863). Farrar, who became Dean of Canterbury, was the author of the very popular edifying school story *Eric*;

or Little by Little, but also wrote essays on the *Origins of Language* (1860) and *Chapters on Language* (1865). Max Müller was Professor of Comparative Philology in the University of Oxford from 1868 to 1900 and the author of two popular lecture series on the 'Science of Language'. The two theories of language origin referred to are that it originated from the imitation of animal cries (the 'bow-wow' theory) and that it was the extension into sound of physical gesture (the 'pooh-pooh' theory). Responsible linguistic opinion deplored these speculations about language origin, which were considered incapable of proof.

56   **widely-spread**   The addition of *-ly* to an adverbial form which had existed since OE, and in a compound of very well-established use, must be a piece of hypercorrection.

45

FROM THE GENERAL EXPLANATIONS TO THE *NEW ENGLISH DICTIONARY*

The first fascicle (A–ANT) of the *New English Dictionary* (after 1895, when published by OUP, the *Oxford English Dictionary*) appeared under the editorship of Dr James A. H. Murray in the spring of 1884 (see Excerpt 46). It was the beginning of a series which continued until the final fascicle in spring 1928 and afterwards, in various other forms, until the present day, when it is compiled as an electronic database. The origin of the *Dictionary* was recognition by members of the Philological Society that changes to the lexicon had overtaken existing dictionaries. But when an investigatory committee was formed in 1857, it was soon realised that advances in philological scholarship also justified not mere revision but the creation of an entirely new dictionary, planned to trace historical development and aiming at exhaustive coverage of the literary language. Work proceeded slowly at first but was supported by the efforts of hundreds of volunteers, whose task was to read widely, entering interesting words on slips of paper with notes of their context and source. By the time Murray was appointed editor in 1879, substantial collections existed, but much of the credit for ordering and augmenting the materials belongs to him.

His General Explanations, which precede the text, echo the weighty significance of the enterprise. An explicit figurative parallel is drawn between the lexicographical task and the pursuit of science. The whole is framed in very extended sentences, exploiting heavily modified and qualified nominal phrases, lexical pairing, and extended adverbials. The technical language of the appropriate sciences is also used: *nebulous, species, order, nucleus, class, aberrant forms.* This rhetorical opening is more than mere bravado. The dictionary belongs to the flourishing climate of nineteenth-century science, to a period when enormous strides had been made in etymology and it seemed that sound change could be subject to explanatory laws. In discussing semantic change, Murray again seeks the analogy of evolutionary science: but for inadequacy of sources, the ramifications of sense develop-ments might be set out like the biologists' phylogenetic trees. This concep-tion lies beneath the arrangement of senses in the dictionary itself.

In discussing the lexicon, Murray addresses himself to the uses rather than the meanings of words, noting special appropriateness to particular contexts (an ancient stylistic conception) but also emphasising from experi-ence the impracticality of making sharp distinctions in such classifications. The literary foundations of the *NED* (for which it has been criticised) are frankly acknowledged, but despite occasionally raised objections to its pre-scriptivism, it is notable that Murray regards the question of 'correctness' quite liberally, and in the light of historical development.

The Vocabulary of a widely-diffused and highly-cultivated living language is not a fixed quantity circumscribed by definite limits. That vast aggregate of words and phrases which constitutes the Vocabulary of English-speaking men presents, to the mind that
5   endeavours to grasp it as a definite whole, the aspect of one of those nebulous masses familiar to the astronomer, in which a clear and unmistakable nucleus shades off on all sides, through zones of decreasing brightness, to a dim marginal film that seems to end nowhere, but to lose itself imperceptibly in the surrounding dark-
10   ness. In its constitution it may be compared to one of those natural groups of the zoologist or botanist, wherein typical species forming the characteristic nucleus of the order, are linked on every side to other species, in which the typical character is less and less dis-tinctly apparent, till it fades away in an outer fringe of aberrant
15   forms, which merge imperceptibly in various surrounding orders, and whose own position is ambiguous and uncertain. For the con-venience of classification, the naturalist may draw the line, which bounds a class or order, outside or inside of a particular form; but Nature has drawn it nowhere. So the English Vocabulary contains
20   a nucleus or central mass of many thousand words whose 'Anglicity' is unquestioned; some of them only literary, some of them only colloquial, the great majority at once literary and colloquial, – they are the *Common Words* of the language. But they are linked on every side with other words which are less and less entitled to
25   this appellation, and which pertain ever more and more distinctly to the domain of local dialect, of the slang and cant of 'sets' and

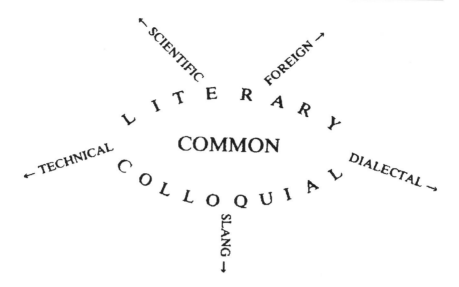

classes, of the peculiar technicalities of trades and processes, of the scientific terminology common to all civilized nations, of the actual languages of other lands and peoples. And there is absolutely no
30   defining line in any direction: the circle of the English language has a well-defined centre but no discernible circumference. Yet practical utility has some bounds, and a Dictionary has definite limits: the lexicographer must, like the naturalist, 'draw the line somewhere', in each diverging direction. He must include all the 'Common
35   Words' of literature and conversation, and such of the scientific, technical, slang, dialectal, and foreign words as are passing into common use, and approach the position or standing of 'common words', well knowing that the line which he draws will not satisfy all his critics. For to every man the domain of 'common words'
40   widens out in the direction of his own reading, research, business, provincial or foreign residence, and contracts in the direction with which he has no practical connexion: no one man's English is *all* English. The lexicographer must be satisfied to exhibit the greater part of the vocabulary of *each* one, which will be immensely more
45   than the whole vocabulary of *any* one.

   In addition to, and behind, the common vocabulary, in all its diverging lines, lies an infinite number of *Proper* or merely *denotative* names, outside the province of lexicography, yet touching it in thousands of points, at which these names, and still more

50   the adjectives and verbs formed upon them, acquire more or less
        of connotative value. Here also limits more or less arbitrary must
        be assumed.

             The Language presents yet another undefined frontier, when
        it is viewed in relation to *time*. The living vocabulary is no more
55   permanent in its constitution than definite in its extent. It is not
        to-day what it was a century ago, still less what it will be a century
        hence. Its constituent elements are in a state of slow but incessant
        dissolution and renovation. 'Old words' are ever becoming obsol-
        ete and dying out: 'new words' are continually pressing in. And the
60   death of a word is not an event of which the date can be readily
        determined. It is a vanishing process, extending over a lengthened
        period, of which contemporaries never see the end. Our own words
        never become obsolete: it is always the words of our grand-fathers
        that have died with them. Even after we cease to use a word, the
65   memory of it survives, and the word itself survives as a possibility;
        it is only when no one is left to whom its use is still possible, that
        the word is wholly dead. Hence, there are many words of which it
        is doubtful whether they are still to be considered as part of the
        living language; they are alive to some speakers, and dead to others.
70   And, on the other hand, there are many claimants to admission
        into the recognized vocabulary (where some of them will certainly
        one day be received), that are already current coin with some
        speakers and writers, and not yet 'good English', or even not English
        at all, to others.

75   If we treat the division of words into current and obsolete as
        a subordinate one, and extend our idea of the Language so as to
        include all that has been English from the beginning, or from any
        particular epoch, we enter upon a department of the subject, of
        which, from the nature of the case, our exhibition must be imper-
80   fect. For the vocabulary of past times is known to us solely from
        its preservation in written records; the extent of our knowledge
        of it depends entirely upon the completeness of the records, and
        the completeness of our acquaintance with them. And the farther
        back we go, the more imperfect are the records, the smaller is the
85   fragment of the actual vocabulary that we can recover.

             Subject to the conditions which thus encompass every attempt
        to construct a complete English Dictionary, the present work aims
        at exhibiting the history and signification of the English words
        now in use, or known to have been in use since the middle of the

90   twelfth century. This date has been adopted as the only natural
halting-place, short of going back to the beginning, so as to include
the entire Old English or 'Anglo-Saxon' Vocabulary. To do this
would have involved the inclusion of an immense number of words,
not merely long obsolete but also having obsolete inflexions, and
95   thus requiring, if dealt with at all, a treatment different from that
adapted to the words which survived the twelfth century. For
not only was the stream of English literature then reduced to the
tiniest thread (the slender annals of the Old English or Anglo-
Saxon Chronicle being for nearly a century its sole representative),
100   but the vast majority of the ancient words that were destined not
to live into modern English comprising the entire scientific, philo-
sophical, and poetical vocabulary of Old English, had already disappeared, and the old inflexional and grammatical system had been
levelled to one so essentially modern as to require no special treat-
105   ment in the Dictionary. Hence we exclude all words that had become
obsolete by 1150. But to words actually included this date has no
application; their history is exhibited from their first appearance,
however early.

Within these chronological limits, it is the aim of the Diction-
110   ary to deal with all the common words of speech and literature,
and with all words which approach these in character; the limits
being extended farther in the domain of science and philosophy,
which naturally passes into that of literature, than in that of slang
or cant, which touches the colloquial. In scientific and technical
115   terminology, the aim has been to include *all words English in form*,
except those of which an explanation would be unintelligible to
any but the specialist; and such words, not English in form, as
either are in general use, like *Hippopotamus, Geranium, Aluminium,
Focus, Stratum, Bronchitis*, or belong to the more familiar language
120   of science, as *Mammalia, Lepidoptera, Invertebrata*.

Down to the Fifteenth Century the language existed only in
dialects, all of which had a literary standing: during this period,
therefore, words and forms of all dialects are admitted on an equal
footing into the Dictionary. Dialectal words and forms which
125   occur since 1500 are not admitted, except when they continue the
history of a word or sense once in general use, illustrate the history
of a literary word, or have themselves a certain literary currency,
as is the case with many modern Scottish words. It is true that
the dialectal words are mostly genuine English, and that they are

130   an essential part of the contents of a *Lexicon totius Anglicitatis*; but the work of collecting them has not yet been completed; and, even when they shall have been collected, the phonetic variety in which they exist in different localities, and the want of any fixed written forms round which to group the variations, will require a
135   method of treatment different from that applicable to the words of the literary language, which have an accepted uniform spelling and an approximately uniform pronunciation.

Notes

4   **English-speaking men**   The phrase is perfectly possible in present-day English, but even before such uses of *men* were sensitised by the sexual politics of the 1970s, this would have been a verbose and rather portentous expression, in keeping with the opening sentences of this piece.

14–15   **aberrant forms**   The word *aberrant* is recorded from 1830, where it is used in Lyell's *Principles of Geology* (see Excerpt 44). *OED* lists its use as characteristic of natural history. The succeeding statement, that nature has drawn the line between species 'nowhere', is relevant to this linguistic context but more audacious with reference to biology than it appears today, since it implicitly accepts the Darwinian dictum of the arbitrary distinction between species, which had been so controversial in 1860.

20   **'Anglicity'**   The quotation marks identify a new formation made on the analogy of Latin *Latinitas*, 'Latinity': the stylistic ideal of correct and pure Latin, uncorrupted by errors of grammar or – more relevant here – barbarous foreign borrowings. The Latin form occurs in line 130, where the phrase may be translated as 'a dictionary of the whole of English literacy'.

27   **peculiar** 'characteristic, particular'   The sense 'strange, odd, eccentric' seems to have developed in the later nineteenth century, and was still regarded as colloquial when *OED* was compiled. The development of the senses of this word from Latin *pecus*, 'cattle', is complex and interesting. Compare also *pecuniary, fee, cattle* and *chattel.*

31   **circumference**   The author here adds the following note: 'The above diagram will explain itself, as an attempt to express to the eye the aspect in which Vocabulary is here presented, and also some of the relations of its elements typical and aberrant. The centre is occupied by the "common" words, in which literary and colloquial usage meet. "Scientific" and "foreign" words enter the common language mainly through literature; "slang" words ascend through colloquial use; the "technical" terms of crafts and processes, and the "dialect" words, blend with the common language both in speech and literature. Slang also touches on one side the

technical terminology of trades and occupations, as in "nautical slang", "Public School slang", "the slang of the Stock Exchange", and on another passes into true dialect. Dialects similarly pass into foreign languages. Scientific terminology passes on one side into purely foreign words, on another it blends with the technical vocabulary of art and manufactures. It is not possible to fix the point at which the "English Language" stops, along any of these diverging lines.'

48   **denotative**   The contrast between *denotative* and *connotative* terms reflects a technical distinction in the philosophy of John Stuart Mill, but is here used to distinguish those words which simply 'refer to' particular people or things, and those which have a more general reference together with associated attributes. Thus, it is often said that proper nouns are merely denotative labels. Murray, however, makes the point that this distinction is not always easy to maintain. Consider, for example, the associative power of names like Ferrari or Jaguar.

58   **ever** 'always'   This sense has become rare during the course of the twentieth century. It is now found mostly in phrases and formulae, such as *yours ever, ever-loving.*

78   **department** 'separate division or part of a whole'   Although this word was borrowed in the fifteenth century with the sense 'departure', the modern senses date from a separate borrowing in the eighteenth century. Johnson's *Dictionary* considers it a French word. During the last third of the eighteenth century it was used (especially in America) to refer to offices of administration and government. It is this development which, in the twentieth century, has ousted the other senses.

79   **exhibition** 'presentation'   Although the sense 'presentation, act of demonstrating' is still occasionally found, such contexts are becoming rarer, and the word seems to be becoming restricted in sense to 'public display, thing exhibited'.

85   **actual** 'contemporary'   This sense is recorded from the mid seventeenth century. Although modern dictionaries still list it, the sense which contrasts with 'potential, possible, fictional' is that which has been most familiar for some decades.

98–99   **Anglo-Saxon Chronicle**   The reference is to the *Peterborough Chronicle*, which was continued until 1154 (see Excerpt 8).

46

HENRY BRADLEY, REVIEW OF THE
NEW ENGLISH DICTIONARY

The publication in 1884 of the first volume of the *New English Dictionary* (afterwards the *Oxford English Dictionary*) was the most significant event in English lexicography after the appearance of Johnson's *Dictionary* in 1755. It represented the central achievement of nineteenth-century philology, both establishing guidelines for the historical study of the lexicon and stimulating, as its own source material, the editing from manuscript of numerous earlier texts. The origin of the Early English Text Society was intimately bound up with the Philological Society's project for a complete and authoritative dictionary of written English sources.

This publication also marked the establishment of the career of the philologist Henry Bradley, a career which is in many ways characteristic of the educational ideals of his time. Bradley was largely self-educated. Although born in Manchester in 1845, he was from a family of farmers and millers in north Derbyshire and Nottinghamshire, and he returned there the following year. He attended Chesterfield Grammar School from 1855 to 1859, where he was an outstanding scholar, but his social background did not encourage his entry to university and, after moving to Sheffield, he instead acted as tutor to the sons of two local physicians until 1863, when he joined a cutlery firm as a corresponding clerk. His studies had been begun in the library of Dr Lennard's house, and his post as a clerk left him the opportunity to broaden them. For twenty years he worked as a clerk, teaching himself modern and classical languages and even some Hebrew in his spare time, and writing a column on place names in the local newspaper. His reviews also began to establish contacts for him within the scholarly world. He had married in 1872, and when the family doctor advised that they should move south for the sake of his wife's health, Bradley was able to rely on his reputation with the editors of literary journals to ensure him some income. It was on the packing cases, unopened in his new home in

Fulham, that Bradley wrote the review of the *NED* which is quoted here, and which brought him to the attention of the dictionary's chief editor, leading eventually to his own occupation of that post and a DLitt from the University of Oxford. His work on the dictionary occupied much of his time after 1889 until his death in 1923, but his books on *The Goths* (1888) and *The Making of English* (1904) represent a peculiarly nineteenth-century amalgam of scholarly authority and popular accessibility. The latter has remained in print (in a revised version) until the present day.

It is now nearly twenty-seven years since the Philological Society commenced the collection of materials for its great English Dictionary. The number of persons who have shared in the task amount to thirteen hundred, and this great company of labourers have
5   accumulated a body of three millions of quotations, taken from over five thousand different authors. The first instalment of the work for which these unexampled preparations have been made is at length before the world, and it is now possible to judge whether the new Dictionary will be worthy of the enormous labour which has been
10 expended upon it. Happily for the credit of English scholarship, the present specimen affords every reason to hope that the skill of Dr. Murray and his assistants will prove equal to the arduous task which lies before them. It would be wonderful indeed if, in so vast an undertaking, there should not be many things to which
15 criticism might object; but it may be confidently asserted that, if the level of excellence reached in this opening part be sustained throughout, the completed work will be an achievement without parallel in the lexicography of any living language.

In comparing the Philological Society's English Dictionary with
20 the only works which can claim to be regarded as its peers – the French Dictionary of Littré and the unfinished German Dictionary of Grimm – it must be remembered that the scope of the English work is in several respects far larger than that proposed in either of the others. For one thing, the period of time embraced in the
25 English Dictionary is by several centuries longer than that surveyed by the great French and German lexicographers. The classic French language of Littré begins no earlier than the seventeenth century, and the New High German treated by Grimm goes back only to the middle of the fifteenth century. But the aim of Dr. Murray and
30 his coadjutors is nothing less ambitious than to catalogue and, so

far as the materials suffice, to discuss historically every word which
has belonged to the standard English vocabulary at any time since
the language passed out of the fully inflected stage known as Anglo-
Saxon. The epoch of this change is fixed by Dr. Murray at the year
1150. The literary barrenness of the hundred years preceding this
date happily obviates much of the inconvenience usually attending
the assignment of a definite year as the commencement of a linguistic period. The compilers of the English Dictionary have therefore to trace the development of the language through a period of
respectively three or five centuries, rich in literary remains, before
arriving at the chronological points at which the labours of Grimm
and Littré commence. Moreover, the year 1150 is not in the same
sense the beginning of Dr. Murray's work as the dates fixed by
Grimm and Littré are the beginning of theirs. It is true that both
the French and the German writers have drawn largely on the
literature of earlier centuries for the philological illustration of
the words included in their Dictionaries, but they have not done
so with anything like the fullness aimed at in the present work.
Although Dr. Murray admits no word which became obsolete before
his initial date, yet every word which he does admit is carefully
traced from its earliest appearance in 'Anglo-Saxon' writings, and
the successive variations of sense and form which it underwent in
the oldest period are discussed with the same fullness of detail and
illustration as those which took place throughout the succeeding
ages. Again, while in the French and German Dictionaries there
are many words and special senses of words for which no literary
authority is adduced, many of the illustrative examples being simply
sentences framed for the occasion, Dr. Murray in almost every case
furnishes a quotation from an English writer, with minute references
to chapter or page. The authorities quoted range in date from the
Ruthwell Cross (here assigned to A.D. 700) to the *Daily News* of
July 6, 1883.

Another point which has added to the arduousness and the value
of Dr. Murray's undertaking is that his standard for the admission
of words to dictionary rank is rightly much less rigid than those set
up by his predecessors. The Teutonic purism of Grimm led him
to reject many words which every German understands, and which
are freely used in the literature of his own and earlier times. No
doubt many of the swarm of foreign words, and of words clumsily
adapted from foreign languages by tacking on the termination

-*iren*, never ought to have become German. But their naturalization has been in fact recognized by the mass of speakers and writers of the language, and they should find a place in its Dictionary, although they might be branded with an obelus as philologically infamous. Dr. Murray has wisely gone to the extreme of admitting every word which is used by any English author, provided that the author who employs it himself regards it as standard English, and not as foreign, dialectal, or technical.

One great merit of the new Dictionary is the remarkable manner in which the convenience of readers is consulted in the typographical expedients employed to ensure facility of reference. This advantage is indeed shared to some extent by the other lexico-graphical publications of the Clarendon Press, and notably by the Etymological Dictionary of Professor Skeat; but it is here carried to a degree of perfection never before aimed at. The size of the page is identical with that adopted in Littré's Dictionary; but a page of Littré is, typographically, a chaos through which the reader must find his way as best he can, while in the English Dictionary the eye is at once directed to the object of which it is in search. Littré, for instance, prints the illustrative examples in the same type, and con-tinuously with the definitions, the only use of strengthened type being in the Arabic figures prefixed to each definition. In the present work, the standard form of each word is printed in large 'Clarendon' type, which stands out boldly from the page, so as to catch the eye at once. The various historical forms are given in 'small Clarendon', and the definitions in ordinary type. Under the definition of each sense of a word are arranged the quoted examples in a smaller letter, each quotation being preceded by its date in heavy figures, so that the chronological range over which a word, or a sense of a word, extends may be measured at a glance. In this way the several definitions of a word are spaced off from each other by an inter-vening paragraph of smaller type. The value of this arrangement in abridging the labour of consulting the Dictionary can scarcely be overestimated.

With regard to the definitions, which form the strongest point of Littré's Dictionary, and the weakest point of that of Grimm, the present work may, perhaps, be considered to hold a middle rank between the two. It can scarcely be charged as a fault that Dr. Murray has not imitated the excessive subdivision of significations into which Littré has frequently run. To give twenty-three numbered senses of the word *eau*, for instance, is an over-refinement which is rather confusing than helpful. The definitions of previous lexicographers have frequently been adopted by Dr. Murray, in many cases with due acknowledgement of their source. Here and there we notice a definition which seems incorrect or inadequate. The modern sense of *ache*, for instance, is not exactly 'a continuous or abiding pain, in contrast to a sharp or sudden one'; and when it is said that this word is 'used of both physical and mental sensation', it should have been noted that the latter use is somewhat forced and rhetorical. We speak quite naturally of a mental *pain*; but when we use *ache* in a similar sense we are consciously employing figurative language. Kingsley's phrase, 'healthy animalism', is certainly out of place as part of the definition of *Animal Spirits*; the expression (at least as Kingsley used it) denotes something quite different.

The one portion of the Dictionary which may be charged with incompleteness is what may be termed the phraseological department. Here, as in the definitions, Littré often falls into an excess of copiousness which need not be imitated. Still, a dictionary of this character ought to contain every combination of words which has any fair claim to rank as an idiomatic phrase. Thus, under the word *Acting* we may reasonably look for 'acting edition', 'acting play'; under *Agent* for 'free agent', and other similar expressions; under *Able* for 'able seaman'. None of these are formally noted in this Dictionary, though some of them appear in the quotations. Under *Alive* we miss the familiar phrase 'alive and kicking', for which literary authority could probably be found. Under *Age* the combination 'old age' of course occurs in the examples, but its idiomatic character is not properly pointed out. These deficiencies, however, are probably common to all existing English dictionaries, and the present work certainly contains an abundance of idiomatic phrases which we should fail to find in its predecessors. Among these we note the expression 'adventure school', which we had thought to be a coinage of the last few years, but which is here illustrated by a quotation dated as far back as 1834.

The most valuable feature of the new Dictionary is of course its wealth of illustrative quotations, and the skill with which these have been arranged so as to exhibit the successive changes of form and meaning which the words have undergone since the time of their earliest appearance in English. The examples, as already stated, are placed under the definition which they severally illustrate, the original sense of the words being first explained, the derivative senses following in the order of their logical descent. In the case of words of foreign origin, it does not always happen that the original

155 English sense of a word is that indicated by its etymology, as such words were often first introduced in some technical acceptation, which was afterwards extended in accordance with the wider meaning of the Latin or other original. In these cases the editor has varied his mode of treatment according to the circumstances.

160 Under the word *Advent* the ecclesiastical and religious senses of the word are mentioned first, and it is afterwards pointed out that it has been in later times applied to 'any important or epoch-making arrival', and 'poetically or grandiloquently to any arrival'. This order is justified by the fact that the earlier applications of the

165 word have given a colour to its subsequent extension of meaning. In the article *Annunciation* a different course has been followed, the etymological sense of the word being first given, and afterwards its applications to the church festival and to the event which it commemorates, although these technical senses are of earlier

170 occurrence in English.

Exception may perhaps be taken to the frequent introduction of examples from publications of the last two or three years, which may seem to savour too much of 'bringing the work down to the latest date'. It should be remembered, however, that in a few years

175 many words now current will probably have become obsolete or changed in sense; and in such instances these latest examples will be of especial value to students of the history of the language. We have noted one or two cases in which useless or misleading quotations are given, or in which examples are ranged under wrong

180 heads. Under *Advertiser* the title 'Morning Advertiser' is quoted, with the date 1882 (why not still later?). This conveys a wrong impression, as the signification which it is intended to exemplify was obsolete long before the time here indicated. In the article *Amour* the extracts from Chaucer and from R. Burney given under

185 the first definition really belong to the second. It is rather amusing to find that the only authority adduced for *Anamorphose* is a quotation from 'J. A. H. Murray, in *Mill Hill Mag.* iv. 79.' When Part II of the Dictionary appears, we shall see whether Dr. Murray is able to quote any precedent for the (certainly very convenient) word

190 *aphetized*, which he employs frequently in his etymological remarks.

We reserve for a second notice the etymology and phonology. Meanwhile, we may briefly say that in these departments, as in those already discussed, the opening part of the 'Great Dictionary' fully satisfies the high expectations which have been formed respecting it. It is earnestly to be hoped that the work will be carried to its conclusion in a manner worthy of this brilliant commencement.

Academy, Feb. 16, 1884.

Notes

5   **three millions of**   This construction, in which *million* is treated as a noun, is common from the earliest borrowing (late fourteenth century) onwards. The twentieth-century use as an adjective, and thus uninflected after a numeral, dates only from the mid nineteenth century. Bradley's usage would have been considered more correct in 1884, but compare Murray's use of the expression *many thousand words* in the General Explanations of the *Dictionary* (see Excerpt 45).

15–16   **if . . . be**   This careful observation of the use of the subjunctive form following *if* would now seem pedantic even in a scholarly review.

30   **coadjutors** 'collaborators, helpers'   This very literary word is a fifteenth-century borrowing from OF.

34   **epoch** 'assigned position in chronological sequence'   The senses of Late Latin *epocha* which connote a fixed time reference are now restricted to technical discourse (e.g. astronomy), and the more frequent senses connote a period of time.

71   **-iren**   Large numbers of verbs with a Latin base, and employing the derivative suffix *-ieren*, were adopted into German in the course of the fifteenth and sixteenth centuries.

74   **obelus** 'a symbol (÷) used in text to mark inauthenticity'.   Through Late Latin from Greek *obelos*, 'spit'.

116   **ache**   It seems doubtful that the compound *heart-ache*, recorded from Shakespeare onwards, is felt to be figurative.

180   **Advertiser**   The sense referred to is presumably that of giving public notice of an event, etc.

190   **aphetized**   Murray included the word and a definition ('to shorten by aphesis') in the second volume, but did not offer any examples of its use.

47

HENRY SWEET, *THE PRACTICAL STUDY OF LANGUAGES*

Henry Sweet (1845–1912) was described by an admiring George Bernard Shaw as 'the brainiest Oxford don of his time', and he is best known to the general public through Shaw's supposed transformation of him into the irascible phonetician Professor Higgins in *Pygmalion* and subsequently the musical *My Fair Lady*. The real Sweet was the son of a barrister at the Inner Temple. As a child he was subject to fits and was so short-sighted that he had difficulty in reading. He attended a private school in Tottenham, and then King's College School, London before moving in 1864 to study philology in Heidelberg. He then spent a brief period as a clerk before entering Balliol College, Oxford in 1869. He seems not to have been suited to the study of classical languages and achieved very poor results, although drawing attention to himself by winning the Taylorian prize in German.

Even as an undergraduate, he was engaged in scholarly publication: in 1871 his edition of the Alfredian *Cura Pastoralis* – which established the principles of OE dialectology – and his *History of English Sounds*, a year after graduation, in 1874. These were followed by a series of major works on Old English, the history of the language, English grammar and phonetics. His *Anglo-Saxon Reader* and *Anglo-Saxon Primer* formed the mainstay of undergraduate courses in Old English for a century after their publication in 1876 and 1888 respectively. Sweet's stature in the field of English Language studies was acknowledged in his own time, but he waited long for formal recognition. Although resident in Oxford from 1895 onwards, he was repeatedly disappointed in his applications for Chairs. The causes for these repeated snubs to so eminent a scholar are not clear, but are not unconnected with the abrasiveness of his personality and a sensitivity to criticism which led him into misunderstandings and feuds with the academic establishment: perhaps, in Shaw's words, 'his Satanic contempt for all academic dignitaries and persons in general who thought more of Greek than of phonetics'.

Sweet belonged to no particular school of philological thought, and much of what he has to say retains its general validity. The practical bias of his work emerges contentiously in *The Practical Study of Languages* (published in 1899 but drafted twenty-two years earlier) where he ridicules the rigidity of the scholarly establishment. 'Living philology', he insists, should be based upon the spoken word, and original fieldwork requires greater gifts than preparing endless editions of old texts. Phonetics is seen as the foundation of both language learning and dialectology, and he challenges 'some real University' to recognise that fact. In 1901 he was at last appointed to an Oxford University Readership in Phonetics.

The second main axiom of living philology is that all study of language, whether theoretical or practical, ought to be based on the spoken language.

5   The distinction between the literary and the colloquial form of the same language has considerably complicated the problem of learning languages. This distinction is not solely the result of the use of writing and printing, for even such unlettered savages as the Andaman islanders have an archaic poetical dialect which differs considerably from their ordinary spoken language; but

10   writing – and, still more, printing – have naturally increased the divergence. In many Oriental languages the divergence is so great that the colloquial is no longer a mere variation of the literary form, but the two practically constitute distinct, mutually unintelligible languages.

15   In European languages, where the difference is much less, most grammarians tacitly assume that the spoken is a mere corruption of the literary language. But the exact contrary is the case: it is the spoken which is the real source of the literary language. We may pick out the most far-fetched literary words and forms we can think

20   of, but we shall always find that they are derived from the colloquial speech of an earlier period. Even such forms as *thou hast, he hath*, were ordinary colloquialisms a few centuries ago, though they now survive only as fossil, dead colloquialisms side by side with the living colloquialisms *you have, he has*. Every literary language is, in

25   fact, a mixture of colloquialisms of different periods.

    Every literary language must indeed in its first beginnings be purely colloquial. It is certainly difficult to realize that such a

language as the classical Italian of Dante and Petrarch was originally nothing but a rough attempt to write down what were then con-
30 sidered the slovenly colloquialisms of Late Latin; but nevertheless such is the origin not only of Italian, but of all the other Romance languages as well. The tradition of the origin of Italian is still kept up in the word for 'translate', namely *volgarizzare*, literally 'make popular.'

35 Accordingly, it is now an axiom not only of Romance philology, but of philology generally, that the real life of language is better seen in dialects and colloquial forms of speech than in highly developed literary languages, such as Greek, Latin, and Sanskrit.

Important as this principle is from a scientific point of view,
40 it is still more so from a practical one, and for the following reasons: –

If we compare the written and spoken language of a given period, we shall find that the literary language is full of superfluous words and phrases, which the spoken language nearly always gets rid of. Thus in the English spoken language the idea 'sky' is expressed
45 by this word only, while in the literary language it may also be expressed by *heaven, heavens, firmament, welkin.* So also the form *hath* was still used in literary prose in the last century in such phrases as *the author hath . . .* , and it is still used in poetry and in the liturgical language of the Bible and Prayer-book, while in the
50 spoken language the only form used is *has.* Again, nothing is more difficult than to give definite grammatical rules for the use of the subjunctive mood in literary English; in the spoken language the subjunctive is not used at all except in a few perfectly definite constructions, such as *if it were.* So also in spoken French the two
55 most difficult tenses of the verb, the preterite indicative and subjunctive, have been supplanted by the perfect. So completely is the preterite obsolete that Passy, in his translation of the Gospel of Luke into modern French, discards it entirely, as in the beginning of the parable of the vineyard; œn ɔm a plāāte yn viñ, i l a
60 lwe a de viñrō, e il e parti pur lōōtā (20. 9). According to Passy (Elementarbuch, 156), it occurs only in comic imitations of the South French dialect. Even in German the complicated rules for the inflection of proper names – *Luise*, gen. *Luise'ns, Cato, Cato's,*
65 plur. Cato'ne, Leibnitz, *plur.* Leibnitz'e – are swept away bodily in the spoken language, which, as a general rule, does not inflect such words at all.

70

Again, in literature the context is often vague, as in the Homeric *méropes ánthrōpoi*, where *méropes* may mean any quality that can be predicated of men generally. So also in the Sanskrit Vēdas we have whole hymns, which, when epitomized, leave not much more than 'the bright shiner (that is, the sun) shines brightly.' In simple colloquial prose, on the other hand, the meaning of a word is generally quite clear from the context. The spoken language,

75

too, is far stricter in its use of epithets: it hardly ever introduces an adjective or other qualifier except to convey some definite information. Thus in ordinary speech we do not talk of 'the bright sun' or 'the silver moon,' simply because the epithets convey no information – tell us nothing that is not already implied in the

80

words *sun* and *moon* themselves. Even such a phrase as 'the sun shines brightly' has an uncolloquial ring about it, although it is not exactly anti-colloquial. We could say 'the moon is bright to-night,' because this really conveys information. The spoken language also prefers a simple paratactic arrangement of sentences. The complic-

85

ated periods of literary prose would, indeed, often be unintelligible in speech.

We see, then, that the advantage as regards clearness and defin-iteness is on the side of the spoken language: by starting from the spoken language we have less to learn, and we learn it accurately.

90

Everything therefore points to the conclusion that in learning foreign languages we should follow the natural order in which we learn our own language: that is, that we should begin with learning the spoken language thoroughly, and then go on to the literary language.

Notes

4

literary and colloquial   Sweet is at pains to make a distinction of some complexity. Literary language is mostly written language, and colloquial language mostly spoken; but the opposed pairs are not identical in function. Colloquial language is also defined by its use in everyday communication; literary language is consciously artful and involved with various cultural values. Colloquial language is connected with contextual situations, and is less complex in various ways than literary language, which may preserve various earlier stages in its set of expressions, as well as a wider range of registers. Sweet himself here introduces into a generally learned discourse some familiar, colloquial elements: *can think of* (19–20), *gets rid of* (44–45).

16   **grammarians**   The point is that contemporary grammars, as well as lexicographical works such as the *OED*, were based upon written, and indeed largely literary, sources. Spoken variants from the norms of such sources were therefore likely to be considered ungrammatical or sub-standard.

30   **slovenly colloquialisms**   Indeed, both Chaucer and a fourteenth-century Wycliffite commentator refer to Italian as 'corrupt Latin'.

45   **sky**   This group of synonyms forms an interesting example of the processes of lexical development. The Scandinavian borrowing *sky* replaced the OE *wolcen*, which, as *welkin*, became restricted to poetic contexts during the sixteenth century. *Firmament* was borrowed from Latin and French in technical contexts in the late thirteenth century, and has been largely restricted to poetic language from the seventeenth century. *Heaven* has become increasingly specialised in sense in religious contexts, and its plural form is now most frequent in written language.

48   **hath**   Sweet is referring to earlier eighteenth-century practice. Already in 1643, Richard Hodges had noted that this spelling was pronounced with final -*s*.

58   **Passy**   The excerpt from Passy's translation reads 'un homme a planté une vigne, il l'a louée à des vignerons, et il est parti pour longtemps'. P. Passy was the director of the International Phonetics Association, and editor of its journal, *Le Maître phonétique*. Sweet's 'Romic' phonetic notation, in which broad transcription appears in parentheses, narrow in square brackets, and which shows vowel length by doubling the vowel symbol, was the precursor of the International Phonetic Alphabet.

69   **méropes ánthrōpoi** 'men endowed with speech'   But the expression is formulaic and means little more than 'human men'.

77–78   **bright sun**   The point is one reintroduced from information science into linguistic theory in the 1950s in the work of, among others, André Martinet: meaning implies choice. If the occurrence of a form is determined by preceding context, then its occurrence contributes no additional meaning to the message. Such redundancy is not characteristic of colloquial communication.

48

SOLDIERS' LETTERS HOME
IN WORLD WAR I

The three letters which make up this excerpt are from front-line troops of very different social and educational backgrounds. The first two were written by Captain Ainslie Douglas Talbot, a regular army officer, the son of a regular army Colonel, who had been educated at Sandhurst. The first of them is addressed to his wife Dorothy, the second to his close friend Lt Col Tom Slingsby, MC, with whom he had served in India with the Lancashire Fusiliers. The third letter was written by Private David John Sweeney of the 2nd Battalion, Lincoln Regiment to his girlfriend Ivy, whom he married at the end of 1917. It was almost certainly written in July 1916. He was the son of a Clerkenwell confectioner and had become a regular soldier after being educated at the local council school. Ivy had been educated at a private school and worked as a solicitor's clerk.

Talbot's letters are written from a hospital ship at Gallipoli, where he had taken part in the ill-fated attempts to seize the Dardanelles, re-supply Russia, and take Turkey out of the war. The landings on 25 April 1915 were fiercely resisted and before the troops were finally evacuated in December there had been 252,000 Allied casualties through illness and disease as well as combat.

The first battle of the Somme (Sweeney's letter), whose purpose was to relieve German pressure on the French at Verdun, commenced on 1 July 1916 on a fifteen-mile front. The assault was on well-prepared German fortifications and casualties were heavy – as high as 60,000 in one day. Although a salient five miles deep was created, further advance proved impossible and the rains of October and November brought the battle to a close.

The letters are printed here with their original spelling and punctuation. Their style reflects both their purpose as letters home and their authors' cultural values: conversational devices (*Well, mind, by Jove* and familiar address-forms) to simulate closeness, formal evocations of religious piety in addressing their ladies, and some awkward gestures in the use of literary phrasing (*they little thought*). Despite these formalities, their style is essentially colloquial, and the coherence of the letters is often jeopardised; omission or confusion of words, errors of grammatical concord, the awkward use of cataphoric reference (reference forward in the discourse) or changes in topic, and failure to recognise sentence boundaries are found in both men. This last is especially noticeable when they are narrating stirring action in which they had been involved, and in Sweeney's letter emotional involvement is also often accompanied by the rhetorical use of capitalisation. A marked distinction between them is in their use of slang words and expressions, and especially in Talbot's fondness for intensifying adverbs (*all*, *frightfully*, *awfully*, *pretty*, *fairly*, *simply*) as well as the literary allusions by which he attempts to express depths of feeling in a way he could approve as manly.

A   Two letters from Captain Talbot

30 April 1915

Just a line Dorfie darling to let you know I am all strong. All correspondence has been stopped to an from here and this may never reach you; I am getting a wounded officer to post it at (?) where he is shortly being sent. I have a sprained ankle at present
5   but expect to be back in the firing line soon; I did it falling into a trench on the second night. I do wonder what came out in the papers about this show at home. Well girly thanks to your prayers etc. I have been most frightfully lucky so far. I long to talk a lot about it all but mus'nt. Keep up cheer mind; I know you must be
10   awfully anxious, but worrying wont help either of us; and as I have escaped so far I should be able to escape anything I think. Best love and hope this reaches you fairly soon. I must say I just can't realize that my pals, that have already been killed, are dead. I find myself quoting 'Cathcarts Hill' to myself.
15   Your loving Douglas.

2nd May. On Board *SS Alaunia*

Dear Wang,

I sent you a line yesterday via a wounded oficer; who was going to post it at the base, but as this boat is the out of mail headquarters
20   I drop a line again, as I can censor it myself. I got through the landing without a scratch thanks to my natural instinct to see cover

on a flat beach; but strained my ankle badly the second night falling into a trench in the dark. By jove it was pretty hot that Sunday
morning. I can hardly write about it yet. Poor old Porter was killed
by a hand grenade I think climbing up the cliff on my right. I am
awfully sick he got knocked over. Tom Mannsell and Tommy were
shot getting out of the boat. Clark was shot through the head sitting
in the boat. I tell you I looked pretty slippy about getting ashore I
jumped overboard into 5 feet of water I dont think the men realized
how hot the fire was they were laughing and joking till the last.

Of course you know we were under HOB as 'Screams' had been
sacked previously. Bishop is d'd good and as cool as a cucumber
under fire. Well I think we fairly made a name for ourselves as we
were the first to establish a hold on the peninsula. I only got about
five men ashore alive in my boat and not one of them could use
their rifles owing to sand jamming the bolt. Seekham did d'd well
all day. I believe he has since been hit through the shoulder. The
sniping is simply awfull here one is more likely to get a bullet in
the back than in the front. they hide all over the place. I dont think
for the first 24 hours there was a single second when you could
not hear a bullet overhead hardly.

I must say I think this kind of fighting is a bit too warm for
words. I had two horse gunner signallers who were with L battery
in France with me the first day and they said they had never
seen any thing like that first landing. We spent the night on HMS
Euryalus and landed in boats in tows early at daylight. I can tell
you the sight of the peninsula being shelled by the fleet was grand
with the sun rising above it all. We kicked off right outside the
supporting ships and went in fairly fast untill we were right under
the canons mouth. the noise of the 10″ etc: were deafening.

We never got a shot fired at us till the oars were tossed around
and then they started in earnest. The first bullet that struck the
water brought up loud jeers from our men, but poor devils they
little thought what they were in for. Brocka was the runner was in
my boat, he has a charmed life as he left his rifle on board and ran
back for it and never got touched. C. S. Wilson was about the first
man I saw hit he got out first from the boat next me and was hit in
the stomach at once I didn't need Kipling's words to stop me from
looking twice at him. Gus was hit just through the head above his
eyes I hope he wont loose his eyesight. Meekins hit his arm badly
shattered I am afraid he will have lost it. Keanly had his arm broken.
I dont know how much I am allowed to tell you of all this, but by

the time you get this you will most likely know all the casualties.
I must say I am sorry for the girls in Nuneaton, if they really cared;
65 but it will show that part of the country what a soldier does have
to go through. Well I expect to be back in the firing line in a day
or so but my foot is still bruised and although I feel an awfull
scrimshanker on this ship when I can see the battle going on on land.
I know if I go too soon my foot will go again. I could not move my
70 toes for the first day and Pirie thought it was broken. Well best
luck old chap. I am d'd glad you are not here for Mrs Wang's sake,
do try and cheer my poor girl up, I am afraid when she finds out
what the fighting is like out here it will make her feel rather sick.
Every yours, Addy.

B   Excerpt from a letter by Private Sweeney

Well dearest the 30th June was a verry busy day for us. We received
orders that Greatly supprised all of My Regt, and this is what it was
the Attack was going to be made on the 1st July and we were in
Support. on our way up to the firing line Every man had to Carry
5 something some would get Tools and Water Cans. I was rather
unlucky, I had to carry a box of 4 Stokes Shells which were no light
weight. Well the morning of the 1st July came and I was verry tired
as we had not had much rest but it had to be done no one knew
even on the Morning of the 1st what time the attack was being
10 made but the artillery started at 6.30 and at 7.30 we heard the C.O
shout The Boys are going over and where we was by getting on the
hill near us we could see the Boys going like Mad across no mans
land but we could not look for long as Fritzs artillery Observers
mite have spotted us well at 8 o clock we began to move up but we
15 had to go verry slowley up the Communication Trenches as Fritz
was shelling all of them well we got our loads and after a very hot
time we came into our owne Fire trench now was the worst part
of the Job as we had to get up the Ladders and get across to the
German trench with our loads as quick as we could how I managed
20 it I shall never be able to say but as soon as we were on top the
Germans started sending big Shrapnell Shells terrible things I heard
when we got in to the German 1st line of trenches that 15 of our
Boys were killed and wounded coming across. Well we got into his
first line we lost men killed by 1 shell buried them all I was blown
25 against the Back of the trench and just Managed to get into a

German Dugout before 3 more big Ones came well that night we had to go into the firing line and relive the Boys who had made the charge we captured 4 lines of trenches that day not so bad. Well we got into those trenches safe and we were there a few hours when he
30 started his Counter attack. We mowed them down in hundreds and he never got within 20 yards of our trench he soon got fed up and did not try again that night.

Well Dear we were in the Fire line all the Night of the 1st also 2nd and we were Relived on the Night of the 3rd by the 10th
35 Division. Well we all came out by way of a Road and we were verry [lucky] in not getting one wounded.

Well my Darling we are now out of hearing of the Guns as we have had a 26 mile Train Ride, but I dont think it will be long befor we are into them again, but at present we are not strong enough.
40 I told you Dear I was happy Well so I am, but when I think of My Poor Dear Old Chums who have fallen I could Cry I had to cry in the Trench about one of my Chums Poor Old Jack Nokes he has been out hear Since the Verry bigginning of the War and has not received a scratch he has never been home on Leave because he has
45 had a small Crime his home is at Wimbleton Poor Lad he died Game with his Mother's Name his last Word. I cryed like a Child, not only him but a lot more of my poor comrades have gone. Ivy my Darling I am sure it is You and My Poor Sister Praying for me that God has spared me. I said my Prayers at lease 1000 times a Day
50 (Please God Spare me to get out of this War safely for my dear Ivy's and my Sisters Sake). O Ivy I cannot tell you the Horrors of this War, you cannot Realise what it is like to see Poor Lads Lying about with such terrible Wounds and we cannot help them.

Notes

Talbot

7 **this show** *OED* attributes the broadened sense 'event, enterprise' to American influence, extended from the field of entertainment, and records it first in 1889. In the military context, however, the use of the word may be connected with *OED* 1c, 'a demonstration of military strength', which is recorded between 1548 and 1853.

13 **pals** Recorded from 1681 onwards, this is an adoption from Romany, where it means 'brother, mate'. It is first used in lower-life slang to mean 'accomplice, partner in crime' but is widespread in colloquial use by 1915. Cf. *chums* and *comrades* (below).

14   **'Cathcarts Hill'**   During the Crimean War, Cathcart's Hill was an observation station overlooking the city of Sebastopol. It was later the site of a cemetery and memorials to the British dead. It derived its name from General Sir George Cathcart, who was killed on 5 November 1854 at the battle of Inkerman while leading his troops up to a ridge, now heavily defended by the Russians, which he had earlier abandoned. His last words are said to have been, 'I fear we are in a mess.' I have not been able to identify the poem to which Talbot refers.

24   **Poor old Porter**   The adjectives *poor* and *old* carry with them a strong emotional charge, and their connotations of pity or affectionate familiarity are frequently exploited in these letters. The former is recorded in this shifted sense as early as the thirteenth century in Laȝamon; the latter from 1588, when it is used by Shakespeare.

28   **looked pretty slippy**   Derived from an imperative clause, an order to move quickly. *Slippy* is recorded in the sense 'quick' in colloquial and dialectal use from the mid nineteenth century.

39   **they**   The Turkish snipers. The reference of the pronoun presupposes the knowledge and involvement of the recipient of the letter. More careful textual construction would have ensured a more specific reference in the preceding clauses. Loose coherence of this kind is typical of situated conversation (cf. Sweeney's use of *he* in line 31).

51   **we never got a shot fired at us**   This structure emphasises the subjective focus as compared with a simple passive (*shots were not fired at us*). The structure would more usually occur with *have* as auxiliary. The verb *get* has greatly extended its uses as an auxiliary in speech in the modern period. Cf. *and never got touched* (56). This passive use of *get* as an auxiliary does not appear before the mid seventeenth century but is now common in spoken English, although not yet in writing.

55   **as he left his rifle**   The use of *as* with causative or resultative senses is traceable from 1400 but is rare before the twentieth century. H. W. Fowler (*Modern English Usage*, 1926) strongly disapproved of it: 'All good writers instinctively avoid it; but, being common in talk, it is much used in print also by those who have not yet learnt that composition is an art and that sentences require arrangement.' Even in spoken language it is now rare, and may sound old-fashioned, but it is particularly common in the speech-based prose of these letters.

58   **Kipling's words**   The reference is probably to some lines from one of Kipling's *Barrack-Room Ballads* (1892), 'The Young British Soldier':

> When first under fire an' you're wishful to duck
> Don't look nor take 'eed at the man that is struck
> Be thankful you're livin', and trust to your luck
>   And march to your front like a soldier.

68   **scrimshanker** 'shirker, slacker'   Recorded in army slang from 1890. The etymology is unknown.

71   **old chap**   The word *chap* is ultimately derived from *chapman* (OE *cēapman*), 'merchant, trader'. The shortened form occurs rarely in the sixteenth century and is found more widely and contemptuously in the eighteenth. Its development as a term of affection may be compared with such phrases as 'old rascal'.

Sweeney

2   **and this is what it was**   Sweeney apparently breaks the rules of grammatical concord (*orders . . . it*). However, this is perhaps best construed as a rhetorical device in which *it* is not considered to refer back to orders, but operates vaguely and cataphorically, emphasising the important information which follows.

6   **Stokes Shells**   The Stokes gun was a trench mortar, developed during 1915 by an agricultural engineer of that name and considered to be an improvement in convenience and portability when compared with previous such weapons. The word *shrapnel* (21) is also derived from the name of its inventor during the Peninsular War, General Henry Shrapnel. The original sense was that of 'a hollow shell containing bullets which are scattered by an explosive charge'. The word is now more often used to refer to the metal fragments scattered by the explosion of an ordinary high-explosive bomb or shell.

41   **Poor Dear Old Chums**   The pity and affection implied by the concatenation of modifiers is present also in the word *chum*, which is first recorded from the late seventeenth century to denote a friend with whom one shares university lodgings. It seems subsequently to have moved down the social scale, and at the time of the compilation of *OED* was found in young male society: schoolboys, criminals and convicts. It seems, like *pals*, to have been partially rehabilitated in the early years of the twentieth century.

45–46   **died Game** 'died bravely'   The expression is derived from cockfighting, in which game-cocks were pitted against each other. Both the sense 'sport' and the sense 'animals used in sport' are derived from the OE *gamen*, 'sport, merriment'. The phrase *to die game* is first recorded in 1727 in *The Beggar's Opera*.

47   **comrades**   Like *chum*, the word originally meant 'that one with whom a lodging is shared, room-mate' (Fr. *camarade*; Sp. *camarada*). It is recorded from 1591 especially in military contexts. The association with left-wing politics is, of course, a later development.

49

D. H. LAWRENCE, 'FANNY AND ANNIE'

This excerpt is taken from one of the short stories in Lawrence's second collection, *England, My England*, published in 1922 although written during 1919. Its setting is the industrial Midlands where Lawrence was born on 11 September 1885, grew up, and located much of his writing about the lives of ordinary people. The son of a Nottinghamshire miner and an ex-schoolteacher, his childhood was uncomfortable owing to the pressure on family finances of four other children, and also to the stormy relationship of his parents. Nevertheless, his mother determined that he should not follow his father into mining, and encouraged him at school. At thirteen he obtained a scholarship to Nottingham High School, but left before his six-teenth birthday to work first as a clerk in a surgical goods factory at thirteen shillings a week, and then as a teacher in Eastwood. He entered Nottingham University College in 1906 to study for a teacher's certificate, and was already writing poetry and short stories. In the three years from 1911 to 1913 he published three novels, *The White Peacock*, *The Trespasser* and *Sons and Lovers*, the last of these largely autobiographical.

During this period Lawrence struck up a relationship with the German wife of his old professor in Nottingham. After a spell in Germany, they settled during the war in Cornwall. Although Lawrence was increasingly recognised by contemporary literary circles, the publication of *The Rainbow* in 1915, which was seized as obscene, reinforced a notoriety which persisted until long after his death. After the war, Lawrence and his wife left for Italy and he spent most of the rest of his life abroad, visiting Ceylon, Australia, America and Mexico, and returning to Italy only when chronic tuberculosis was diagnosed. Attempts to find a cure proved fruitless, and Lawrence died in Venice on 2 March 1930.

'Fanny and Annie' tells of the homecoming of a lady's maid to marry the foundry-worker lover of her youth. She is smartly dressed, elegant and bright, 'such a lady' in the eyes of her aunt. He wears no cap or collar, is awkward, and she thinks he 'drags her down'. Her return is capitulation to fate. The division between the outlook of the two is symbolised in their use of language. Her future husband's mother fully appreciates this, and makes dialect speech a weapon against her new daughter-in-law, turning the knife in the wound. Some of the dialect forms used are today associated more with Derbyshire than Nottinghamshire but may well have been found in the western part of the county, where the story is set.

He stayed till about half past nine. She went to the door with him.

'When are you coming up?' he said, jerking his head in the direction, presumably, of his own home.

'I'll come tomorrow afternoon,' she said brightly. Between
5   Fanny and Mrs Goodall, his mother, there was naturally no love lost.

Again she gave him an awkward little kiss, and said good-night.

'You can't wonder, you know, child, if he doesn't seem so very keen,' said her aunt. 'It's your own fault.'
10   'Oh, Aunt, I couldn't stand him when he was keen. I can do with him a lot better as he is.'

The two women sat and talked far into the night. They understood each other. The aunt, too, had married as Fanny was marrying: a man who was no companion to her, a violent man, brother of
15   Fanny's father. He was dead, Fanny's father was dead.

Poor Aunt Lizzie, she cried woefully over her bright niece, when she had gone to bed.

Fanny paid the promised visit to his people the next afternoon. Mrs Goodall was a large woman with smooth-parted hair, a
20   common, obstinate woman, who had spoiled her four lads and her one vixen of a married daughter. She was one of those old-fashioned powerful natures that couldn't do with looks or education or any form of showing off. She fairly hated the sound of correct English. She *thee'd* and *tha'd* her prospective daughter-in-law, and
25   said:

'I'm none as ormin' as I look, seest ta.'

Fanny did not think her prospective mother-in-law looked at all orming, so the speech was unnecessary.

'I towd him mysen,' said Mrs Goodall, ''Er's held back all
30   this long, let 'er stop as 'er is. 'E'd none ha' had thee for *my* tellin'

– tha hears. No, 'e's a fool, an' I know it. I says to him, "Tha looks a man, doesn't ter, at thy age, goin' an' openin' to her when ter hears her scrat' at th' gate, after she's done gallivantin' round wherever she'd a mind. That looks rare an soft." But it's no use o'

35   any talking: he answered that letter o' thine and made his own bad bargain.'

But in spite of the old woman's anger, she was also flattered at Fanny's coming back to Harry. For Mrs Goodall was impressed by Fanny – a woman of her own match. And more than this,

40   everybody knew that Fanny's Aunt Kate had left her two hundred pounds: this apart from the girl's savings.

So there was high tea in Princes Street when Harry came home black from work, and a rather acrid odour of cordiality, the vixen Jinny darting in to say vulgar things. Of course Jinny lived in a

45   house whose garden end joined the paternal garden. They were a clan who stuck together, these Goodalls.

It was arranged that Fanny should come to tea again on the Sunday, and the wedding was discussed. It should take place in a fortnight's time at Morley Chapel. Morley was a hamlet on the

50   edge of the real country, and in its little Congregational Chapel Fanny and Harry had first met.

What a creature of habit he was! He was still in the choir of Morley Chapel – not very regular. He belonged just because he had a tenor voice, and enjoyed singing. Indeed his solos were only

55   spoilt to local fame because when he sang he handled his aitches so hopelessly.

'And I saw 'eaven hopened
And be'old, a wite 'orse –'

This was one of Harry's classics, only surpassed by the fine

60   outburst of his heaving:

'Hangels – hever bright an' fair –'

It was a pity, but it was inalterable. He had a good voice, and he sang with a certain lacerating fire, but his pronunciation made it all funny. And *nothing* could alter him.

65   So he was never heard save at cheap concerts and in the little, poorer chapels. The others scoffed.

Now the month was September, and Sunday was Harvest Festival at Morley Chapel, and Harry was singing solos. So that Fanny
was to go to afternoon service, and come home to a grand spread
70 of Sunday tea with him. Poor Fanny! One of the most wonderful
afternoons had been a Sunday afternoon service, with her cousin
Luther at her side, Harvest Festival in Morley Chapel. Harry had
sung solos then – ten years ago. She remembered his pale blue tie,
and the purple asters and the great vegetable marrows in which he
75 was framed, and her cousin Luther at her side, young, clever, come
down from London, where he was getting on well, learning his
Latin and his French and German so brilliantly.

However, once again it was Harvest Festival at Morley Chapel,
and once again, as ten years before, a soft, exquisite September day,
80 with the last roses pink in the cottage gardens, the last dahlias crimson, the last sunflowers yellow. And again the little old chapel was
a bower, with its famous sheaves of corn and corn-plaited pillars, its
great bunches of grapes, dangling like tassels from the pulpit corners,
its marrows and potatoes and pears and apples and damsons, its
85 purple asters and yellow Japanese sunflowers. Just as before, the red
dahlias round the pillars were dropping, weak-headed among the
oats. The place was crowded and hot, the plates of tomatoes seemed
balanced perilously on the gallery front, the Rev. Enderby was weir-
der than ever to look at, so long and emaciated and hairless.

90 The Rev. Enderby, probably forewarned, came and shook hands
with her and welcomed her, in his broad northern, melancholy
singsong before he mounted the pulpit. Fanny was handsome in a
gauzy dress and a beautiful lace hat. Being a little late, she sat in a
chair in the side-aisle wedged in, right in front of the chapel. Harry
95 was in the gallery above, and she could only see him from the eyes
upwards. She noticed again how his eyebrows met, blond and not
very marked, over his nose. He was attractive too: physically lovable,
very. If only – if only her *pride* had not suffered! She felt he dragged
her down.

100 'Come, ye thankful people come,
Raise the song of harvest-home.
All is safely gathered in
Ere the winter storms begin –'

Even the hymn was a falsehood, as the season had been wet,
105 and half the crops were still out, and in a poor way.

Notes

3   **presumably**   The point of the adverb is to draw attention to the unelaborated nature of Harry Goodall's speech. He relies heavily upon his interlocutor's familiarity with the circumstances and with expected etiquette.

10–11   **I can do with him** 'get on with, tolerate'   The expression meaning 'to be concerned with' goes back to the thirteenth century, but the modern colloquial sense is first recorded in use by Jane Austen in 1815.

18   **his people**   Although the use of this phrase to refer to someone's family is recorded from the fourteenth century, the *OED* (3c) remarks that it is especially prevalent as a university and public school colloquialism. Perhaps the phrase represents usage from Fanny's years of service in Gloucester.

23   **fairly hated**   The context confirms that *fairly* is here an intensifier. Although this use is now colloquial, and more common in the North, it is recorded more widely in the sixteenth and seventeenth centuries.

24   **thee'd**   The *th-* forms of the second-person pronoun are used in familiar and in scornful address in dialects from the counties of Yorkshire, Derbyshire and Cheshire northward, where forms of *thou* are used in subject position. Western Nottinghamshire shares this feature. *Th-* forms with *thee* as subject occur in the south-west Midlands and the West Country.

26   **ormin'** 'awkward' and perhaps 'foolish'   Recorded only from Nottinghamshire by *EDD*. A significant contrast is made with Fanny's hypercorrection of the form to *orming*.

    seest ta   The second-person-singular inflexion *-st*, rather than *-s*, belongs to the very west of Nottinghamshire and to much of Derbyshire but varies with the *-s* form, which is normal further north.

30   **'er**   This subject form of the feminine personal pronoun is not recorded for Nottinghamshire in the *Linguistic Atlas of England* but is found in Derbyshire.

    'E'd none   This form of negative is recorded for western Derbyshire and north Staffordshire but no longer in Nottinghamshire at the time of the Survey of English Dialects.

33   **scrat** 'scratch'   The verb is not a form of *scratch*, however, but a distinct verb-form recorded from the thirteenth century. Both OF *egrater* and Old Swedish *kratta* have been cited as parallels, but the etymology is uncertain.

    done gallivantin'   The verb is recorded from 1819 with the sense 'flirting indiscreetly', and may be a humorous development from *gallant*.

48   **It should take place**   The more usual choice of auxiliary in this environment is *would*. *Should* here implies inevitability, a significance which goes back to OE but which had been re-established by seventeenth-century grammarians and handed down in the school tradition.

58   **wite**   The comic spelling serves to emphasise the lack of aspiration in Harry's pronunciation, which corresponds with his handling 'his aitches so hopelessly'. However, aspiration in this context would not be normal in Standard English.

APPENDIX

50

ADVERTISEMENTS

A Caxton's Advertisement

It has been pointed out that the practice of advertising precedes written modes, as in the case of the green bough hung outside taverns to proclaim new wine, but we are concerned in this section only with written advertisements produced to promote trade. It may be surprising to hear that advertisements have any other purpose, but the etymological meaning of the word *advertisement* is 'that which makes someone aware of something', and early advertisements do just this. Even the earliest trade advertisements were often modelled on this announcement function, and do not seek energetically to persuade the buyer. The earliest known in English, which survives in copies in the Bodleian (see facsimile) and John Rylands Libraries, is the bill printed by William Caxton in 1477 to advertise his

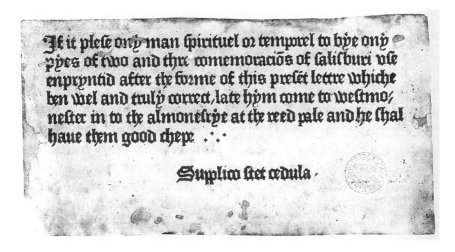

Plate 6 Caxton's Advertisement (Bodleian Library MS Arch. Ge. 37)

printing of the *Pyes of Salisbury*. Ending with an appeal *supplico stet cedula* ('I beg [you] let the bill be'), it seems to have been intended to have been pinned up, perhaps in a church porch, or some other location where it could find an appropriate audience. Its deferential style is worthy of notice. Its opening conditional *if* presumes nothing, and indeed represents a formula (the *si quis* type) adopted by many other later advertisers. In this case, the body of the text is itself a sample of the product for sale, assuring the buyer of quality by example as well as report. It gives the location where such a product can be obtained, and closes with the promise of an advantageous price. The relationship between the intended customer and the merchant is that of fair and open dealing between knowledgeable gentlemen of fairly equivalent status, and the announcement is expressed with the polite indirectness to be expected in such an interaction.

> If it plese ony man spirituel or temporel to bye ony pyes of two and thre comemoraciõs of Salisburi vse enpryntid after the forme of this presēt lettre whiche ben wel and truly correct, late hym come to Westmonester in to the Almonestrye at the Reed Pale and he
> 5   shal haue them good chepe.
> *Supplico stet cedula*

B   Two Early Newspaper Advertisements

The Publick Adviser (1657)

The earliest English newspapers belong to the 1620s, but these contained only foreign news, and few advertisements. Within a generation, however, they were joined by broadsheets and weekly publications reflecting more fully the trade interests and day-to-day life of the community of London. The advertisements of trades and professions were printed in these side by side with public notices, and, as with Caxton's earlier handbill, these often purported to inform rather than persuade. In *The Publick Adviser*, which first appeared in May 1657, attempts to reclaim lost belongings were juxtaposed with the notices of workmen, nurses and schoolmasters advertising their services. From the beginning, some of the most persistent advertisers were physicians offering cures for a wide range of diseases. The advantages of printed advertising to this profession must have been considerable, because

A Physitian.

AT *Donhead St Marie* in the County of *Wilts* at Mrs. *Lillies* liveth a Phisitian, who by his knowledge and the good success which hath ensued by Gods providence, hath cured many persons of divers diseases, which lay languishing and supposed incureable in and about the Cities of *London* and *Westminster*, which is sufficiently known unto many persons of quality in those places; Moreover he hath particular Remedies for several diseases, to cure them in a shorter time, and lesser trouble then formerly hath been known, as Convulsion, Kings-evil, Scurvey, Dropsie, Rickets, Bloody-flux, &c. besides several other diseases incident to Man and Woman not fit here to be recited, And such as are past cure (to keep them from unnecessary expences) he will deal ingeniously and tell them so. I.

A Draught of the English New Invention or Macheine.

To the Nobility and Gentry.

WHereas the first Author of the new Invention for making Chocolate, hath given a general Satisfaction to all those that ever made use of it both in City and Country, hath also contriv'd a second Invention no ways 13 Inches, grinds all Nut fine to admiration of any sort roasted or not roasted if desir'd, with that Expedition and Pleasure, that he can afford to sell it 12 d. a pound cheaper than any in *London*, and had rather sell all Nut than a mixture with Sugar. He continues to sell all Spanish Nut with Vanello 4 s. 8 d. the same without 4 s. 2 d. All Martinico Nut with Vanello at 3 s. 8 d. the same without 3 s. 2 d. both sorts made up with Sugar the finest and cleanliest that ever was made from 2 s. to 3 s. 4 d. Beware of counterfeit Inventions, until a Patent passes the Seal for the true ones. Which is to be seen, and Chocolate to be sold by none but the Author, next Door to the Bull-head in the middle of *Dean-street* near *Red-Lion-Square*. II.

Plate 7 (i) Advertisement from the *Publick Adviser* (1657)
(ii) Illustrated Advertisement from the *Daily Courant* (1703)

physicians could be charged ten shillings for an insertion such as that in Plate 7(i), as against the mere four shillings required of schoolmasters. The advertisement illustrated (*Publick Adviser*, 27 July–3 August 1657) follows a familiar pattern in reciting the doctor's past successes, an appeal to the social standing of 'persons of quality', the enumeration of various diseases treatable, as well as the convenience of the cures. Less usually, there is an engaging promise at the end to save patients' money by being frank about their chances of recovery.

The Daily Courant (1703)

Illustrations began to accompany the text of advertisements from about the middle of the seventeenth century. Plate 7(ii), which appeared in *The Daily Courant* (17 March 1703), is among the earliest known examples of the use of an illustration in a trade advertisement. Chocolate and coffee had both been introduced to the London public fifty years earlier as medicinal beverages, but had swiftly become fashionable recreational drinks in London society. The advertisement belongs to a series by one Robert Inwood, which usually began with an address line 'To the Nobility and Gentry', so that its implied audience was a restricted one of connoisseurs. The tone attempts to be factual, and the illustration is intended to support this assertion of plain truth. But there is a touch of technological magic in the secrecy of the workings of the machine, which is presented as an improvement on an earlier model by the same advertiser. This particular advertisement was provoked by competition among the suppliers of cocoa, and in particular by an attempt to copy the excellent grinder, and customers are warned against inferior imitations.

The advertisement is typographically plain, using italics for place-names, apostrophes in past participles, and capitalising referentially important nouns. Linguistically, the passage differs from present-day English mainly in its elliptical constructions, which, despite the imitation of a formal announcement in the opening *Whereas*, reflect spoken rather than written language. The passage reads more easily if commas are considered to function as parentheses and the passage is seen to be rhetorically rather than syntactically constructed. Its now unidiomatic use of articles and derivational affixes (*cleanliest*) reflect the same stylistic register. Of special interest is the reference to what we should call cocoa beans as 'nuts'. Before the nineteenth century, coffee beans were referred to as 'berries' and cocoa beans as 'nuts'. The emergence of the term *cocoa bean* is late nineteenth century, and is probably modelled on *coffee bean*, which seems to have preceded it. The motivation for the ready adoption of *cocoa bean* was probably its homonymic conflict with the word *cocoa-nut*, which denoted quite a different exotic import.

C   Eno's Fruit Salts (1889)

Eno's advertisement of 1889 continues the well-established tradition of advertising patent medicines and also introduces a sequence of the promotion of a product which was heavily advertised, reflecting cultural changes, over more than a century. Like the previous advertisement this begins with an address line, which announces its target as a mass market proud of its relatively new literacy. The headline in large, bold type proclaims the name of the product, and a sub-head in smaller type summarises some of the points made in the first paragraph, which in turn makes the essential claims for effectiveness. This is followed by a warning against competing products, advice which seeks to occupy the high moral ground by a critical quotation from an authority condemning opportunistic imitations. Three testimonials are given, which further validate the claims made, at the same time placing the product into acceptable, even exciting, social circumstances. The advertisement ends with another warning against imitations, details of where the product may be obtained, and where it is manufactured.

The advertisement is heavily textual, using a wide variety of type for sub-headings, for emphasis of telling phrases, and to foreground the product name. It is also accompanied by an illustration, which does not serve to illustrate the product on offer, but helps to identify its packet in a chemist's shop. This presents the image of a fit and healthy outdoor type, and ventures a humorous pun. Word-play of this kind frequently accompanied illustrations in advertisements meant for a mass market in the nineteenth century.

Linguistically, deviations from present-day English consist mainly in slight shifts in the senses of words and in phrasing which would now seem improbably literary. Restricting commentary to the first paragraph, it might be noted how the claims for the medicine are implied rather than stated. The

IMPORTANT TO ALL!

ENO'S "FRUIT SALT."

Sugar, Effervescing Syrups, Stimulants.

EXPERIENCE *shows that Sugar, Effervescing Syrups*, Mild Ales, Port Wine, Dark Sherries, Sweet Champagne, Liqueurs, and Brandy are all very apt to disagree; while Light Wines and Gin, or Old Whiskey, largely diluted with Soda Water, will be found the least objectionable. ENO'S "FRUIT SALT" is peculiarly adapted for any constitutional weakness of the liver. It possesses the power of reparation where digestion has been disturbed or lost, and places the invalid on the right track to health.

THE SECRET OF SUCCESS.—"A new invention is brought before the public, and commands success. A score of *abominable imitations* are immediately introduced by the unscrupulous, who, in copying the original closely enough to deceive the public, and yet not so exactly as to infringe upon legal rights, exercise an ingenuity that, employed in an original channel, could not fail to secure reputation and profit."—ADAMS.

HEADACHE AND DISORDERED STOMACH.—"After suffering for nearly two and a half years from severe headache and disordered stomach, and after trying almost everything and spending much money without finding any benefit, I was recommended by a friend to try your 'FRUIT SALT,' and before I had finished one bottle I found it doing me a great deal of good, and now I am restored to my usual health; and others I know that have tried it have not enjoyed such good health for years. "Yours most truly—ROBERT HUMPHREYS, Post Office, Barrasford."

THE ATLAS MOUNTAINS (MOROCCO), NORTHERN AFRICA.— Mr. Harold Crichton-Browne, in a letter from the Atlas Mountains, says:—"The Kaid of Demnet treated us so well that we desired on leaving to make him some acknowledgment, and presented him with a box of Huntley & Palmer's biscuits and a bottle of ENO'S 'FRUIT SALT,' with which he was much pleased."—THE WORLD, Sept. 12, 1888.

SUPERIOR TO ALL OTHER SALINES.—"Dear Sir,—Having been in the habit of taking your 'FRUIT SALT' for many years, I think it only right to tell you that I consider it a most invaluable medicine, and far superior to all other saline mixtures I have ever tried. I am never without a bottle of it in the house, as I find it possesses three most desirable qualities—namely, it is pleasant to the taste, promptly efficacious, and leaves no unpleasant after effects. I do not wish my name to appear, but apart from the publication of that you are welcome to make use of this testimonial if it is of service.—A DEVONSHIRE LADY."—Jan. 25, 1889.

CAUTION.—*Examine each Bottle, and see that the Capsule is marked* "ENO'S FRUIT SALT." *Without it you have been imposed on by a worthless imitation.*

SOLD BY ALL CHEMISTS.   PREPARED ONLY AT

Eno's "Fruit Salt" Works, Pomeroy St., New Cross Rd., London, S.E.

By J. C. ENO'S PATENT.

Plate 8 Illustrated Advertisement for Eno's Fruit Salts (1889)
ENO's Fruit Salt is a registered trade mark of Beecham Group p.l.c.

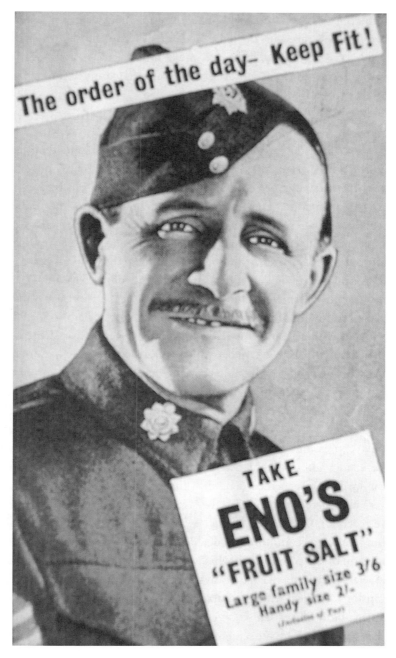

Plate 9   Illustrated Advertisement for Eno's Fruit Salts (1943)
ENO's Fruit Salt is a registered trade mark of Beecham Group p.l.c.

verb *disagree* sounds odd without the complement *with you*, and the word *largely* is now rare with the sense 'generously'. The phrase *peculiarly adapted* is now too literary for such a context, and we now rarely use the word *reparation* outside legal contexts, where it means 'compensation' (*OED* 5(d)).

D   Two Wartime Advertisements

The two final advertisements both date from 1943, and their context is World War II. Here the textual culture, which dominated advertisements until the inter-war period, has all but vanished and illustrations have replaced explanation. The Eno's advertisement continues the tradition of a healthy beneficiary of its effects. The brand is now established and the only information given is the name and pricing. The jocular heading is now appropriate to a citizenry in uniform, and the photograph is of an ordinary, approachable individual, whose sergeant's (or maybe corporal's) stripes are just visible. The advertising message is a rather abrupt imperative: 'Take Eno's Fruit Salts', contrived as an utterance appropriate to the individual depicted. There is an interesting contrast between this and the advertisement for Army Club cigarettes, which is clearly directed to a more restricted market. The slogan 'front-line cigarette' employs the tradition of punning to present a more heroic picture. The monocled smoker has a major's crown on his cap, and the captions attempt to echo his opinions stylistically in a more extended way, especially in the small type. This exploits the supposed slang expression *hit up*, but in fact this phrase is a copywriter's hypercorrection, and should read *het up*. Etymologically derived from 'heated up', this form has been recorded since the late nineteenth century. Cigarettes were considered medicinal in the stress of war. With these advertisements, we reach a point where language is subsidiary to illustration, and together they no longer communicate details of a product, but rather offer the impression of a community to which purchase of the product might admit the buyer. Advertisements had always contained assumptions about social relationships. In 1943, whilst maintaining a clear perception of socially distinct targets, both advertisements place special value on a sense of community. The emphasis of advertisements has switched from a respectful medium of information directed to individuals, and become an instrument of amicable persuasion of social groups.

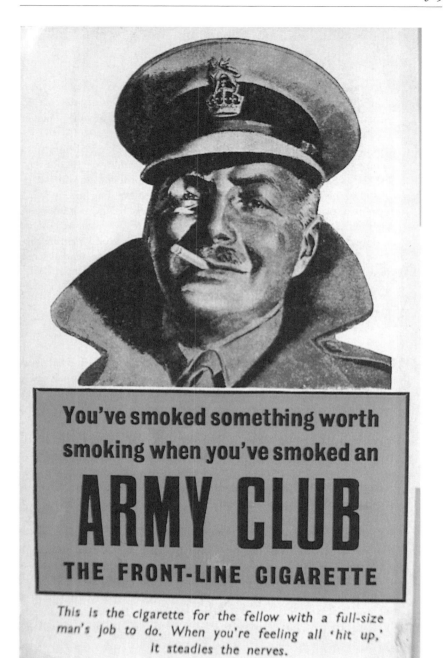

Plate 10   Illustrated Advertisement for Army Club cigarettes (1943)

Notes

A   Caxton's Advertisement

1   **If it plese**   The conventional indirectness expressed in the use of a conditional structure, subjunctive mood, and hypothetical reference to *ony man* reflects the deference required when approaching anyone of higher or equal status at this period.

1–2   **pyes ... Salisburi vse**   A pye is a clerical handbook containing rules on how to deal with more than one office or commemoration on one day. The Use of Salisbury refers to the forms of service proper to the diocese of Salisbury, the most widespread liturgy in late medieval England.

2   **enpryntid** 'printed'   A striking example of how technical innovation can lead to semantic change. In the fourteenth century, Chaucer and others used this verb to refer to the impression or imprint made on a yielding surface by a hard object. The first occurrences of the modern extended sense are in the works of Caxton, who introduced the process to Britain.

B   Early Newspaper Advertisements

The Publick Adviser

2   **liveth**   The spelling of this word and of *hath* is old-fashioned, and perhaps rather formal. Richard Hodges, *A Special Help to Orthographie* (1643) notes that although *-eth* was written, this was pronounced [əz], at least in multisyllabic words.

3   **which**   The re-distribution of the relative pronouns *which* and *who* into non-personal and personal reference respectively is not fully established here. The latter is used for a looser personal reference, or as a subordinating conjunction in the manner of fifteenth-century formal prose.

7   **persons of quality**   This phrase is first recorded by *OED* in 1579–80, and is very common in seventeenth-century advertisements. It is formed on a sense of the noun quality 'status, rank, position', which emerged in the fifteenth century.

10   **Kings-evil**   scrofula, a disease of the lymphatic glands, which was supposed to be curable by the monarch's touch. The phrase preserves a sense of the word *evil*, 'disease', which goes back to Old English.

14   **ingeniously**   A widespread malapropism in the seventeenth century, but found also in Shakespeare (*Timon of Athens*, II. ii. 230). It means 'honestly, frankly', but derives this sense from confusion with *ingenuously*.

The Daily Courant

Caption **draught** 'drawing, picture'   This sense is recorded from the late fifteenth to the end of the eighteenth century, partially surviving today in the compound *draughtsman*. The word draught has an extraordinarily wide range of senses, well worthy of investigation in terms of semantic change.

3   **hath**   In editorial matter, the third-person forms in the *Daily Courant* are modern, using *has*, but the advertisement may have been set from hand-written copy provided by Robert Inwood, who prefers the conservative *hath*.

5   **City and Country**   This inclusive phrase, which is intended to allude to gentry located both at their London and country residences, is common throughout the seventeenth and early decades of the eighteenth centuries.

6–7   **no ways**   The plural form of this phrase emerges in the fourteenth century, but is especially common in the seventeenth century. In the course of the eighteenth century, it is gradually replaced by the singular variant, which is standard today. The plural survives in dialect.

13   **Vanello** 'vanilla'   Borrowed from earlier Spanish *vaynilla* (modern Spanish *vainilla*). First recorded in English in 1662.

18   **Patent passes the Seal**   Prior to the establishment of the Patent Office in 1852, the Crown granted rights to protected manufacture. From the later fifteenth century onwards these took the form of an open letter (letter patent) marked with the King's Great Seal. This phrase derives from this procedure.

51

THE ENGLISH BIBLE

Translation of the Bible into English was first attempted in the Old
English period, when Ælfric and those associated with him produced a
version of the Pentateuch. During the tenth century also, the four Gospels
were translated into West Saxon, and in the next century the Psalter was
rendered, partly into prose, and partly into verse. Despite King Alfred's
apparent interest in the project (see Excerpt 2), no translation of the complete Bible was made. The diminished status of English after the Conquest
discouraged further attempts at translation until two versions of the Bible
were produced by the Wycliffite reformers in the late fourteenth century.
The version reproduced here is the earlier, and more literal, of the two,
perhaps prepared as an exercise to facilitate the production of the later.
The translator of the next excerpt, William Tyndale, was executed for his
religious opinions in 1536. He had been forced by opposition at home to
commence publication of his work in Cologne, but may nevertheless be
considered the father of the Modern English Bible. The Authorised Version
of the Bible, which was produced with official approval by a committee of
scholars, owes much to Tyndale and his successors both in its phrasing and
in the conscious archaism of some of its forms (e.g. its use of the subject
form *ye*, the personal relative *which*, and its almost total avoidance of the
genitive pronoun form *its*).

The passages which follow have been selected to give a general outline
of developments in a thousand years of English linguistic history. Changes
in the language can most readily be recognised if the subject matter dealt
with remains constant. However, exact parallelism in the content of these
passages is subject to some disruption, both from the source material of the
translations, and from the differing intentions of the translators. The Old
English and Wycliffite versions were based upon the text of the Latin Vulgate,
whereas Tyndale and later scholars consulted Greek and also Hebrew sources.

Moreover, earlier translators revered the exact wording of their sources, whereas later translators are more concerned with making accessible to a contemporary audience the full significance of the text before them. In this respect, the New English Bible is a freer rendering than earlier ones, and does not necessarily match them word for word.

In the following passages, punctuation has been modernised in all the versions prior to that of 1611, and in the Old English passages the spelling has been regularised to conform to an Early West Saxon norm. General guidance on the periods of linguistic history represented by the passages may be found in the introductions to the main period sections.

A Mark 6: 18–30

Old English (c. 1000)

18 Ðā sǣde Iohannes Herode: 'Nis þē alȳfed to hæbenne þīnes brōðer wīf.'

19 Ðā syrwde Herodias ymbe hine, and wolde hine ofslēan, and hēo ne mihte.

20 Sōðlice Herodes ondrǣd Iohannem, and wiste þæt hē wæs rihtwīs and hāliȝ, and hē hēold hine on cwerterne. And hē ȝehīerde þæt hē fela wundra worhte, and hē lufelice him hīerde.

21 Þā se dæȝ cōm Herodes ȝebyrdtīde, he ȝeȝearwode micele feorme his ealdormannum, and þǣm fyrmestum on Ȝalilea.

22 And þā ðā þǣre Herodiadiscan dohtor inn-ēode and tumbode; hit līcode Herode and eallum þǣm ðe him mid sǣton. Se cyninȝ cwæð þā tō ðǣm mæȝdene: 'Bidde mē swā hwæt swā þū wille, and ic þē selle';

23 And hē swōr hire, 'Sōðes ic þē selle swā hwæt swā þū mē bitst, þēah þū wille healf mīn rīce.'

24 Ðā hēo ūt-ēode, hēo cwæð tō hire mēder, 'Hwæs bidde ic?' Þā cwæþ hēo, 'Iohannes hēafod þæs fulluhteres.'

25 Sōna þā hēo mid ofste inn tō þǣm cyninȝe ēode; hēo bæd and þus cwæð: 'Ic wille þæt ðū mē hrædlīce on ānum disce selle Iohannes hēafod.'

26 Þā wearð se cyninȝ ȝeunrēt for þǣm āðe, and forþǣm ðe him mid sǣton nolde þēah hīe ȝeunrētan,

27 Ac sende ānne cwellere, and bebēad þæt man his hēafod on ānum disce brōhte. And hē hine þā on cwerterne behēafdode,

28 And his hēafod on disce brōhte, and hit sealde þǣm mǣჳdene, and þæt mǣჳden hit sealde hire mēder.

29 Þā his cnihtas þæt ჳehīerdon, hīe cōmon, and his līchaman nāmon, and hine on byrჳene leჳdon.

30 Sōðlīce þā ðā apostlas tōჳædere cōmon, hīe cȳddon þǣm Hǣlende eall þæt hīe didon and hīe lǣrdon.

Wycliffite (c. 1375)

18 Sothly Johne seide to Eroude, 'It is not leefful to thee, for to haue the wyf of thi brother.'

19 Erodias forsothe leide aspies to him, and wolde sle him, and miჳte not.

20 Sothly Eroude drede John, witinge him a iust man and hooly, and kepte him. And him herd, he dide many thingis, and gladly herde hym.

21 And whanne a couenable day hadde fallun, Eroude in his birthe day made soupere to the princis and tribunys and to the firste of Galilee.

22 And whanne the douჳter of thilke Erodias hadde entride yn, and lepte, and pleside to Eroude, and also to men restynge, the kyng seide to the wenche, 'Axe thou of me what thou wolt, and I schal ჳyue to thee';

23 And he swoor to hir: 'For what euere thou schalt axe, I schal ჳyue to thee, thouჳ the half of my kyngdom.'

24 The whiche, whanne sche hadde gon out, seide to hir modir, 'What schal I axe?' And sche seide, 'The heed of John Baptist.'

25 And whanne sche hadde entrid anon with haste to the kyng, she axide, seyinge, 'I wole that anoon thou ჳyue to me in a dische the heed of John Baptist.'

26 And the kyng was sory for the ooth, and for men sittinge to gidere at mete he wolde not hir be maad sory;

27 But a manquellere sent, he comaundide the heed of John Baptist for to be brouჳt. And he bihedide him in the prison,

28 And brouჳte his heed in a dische, and ჳaf it to the wenche, and the wench ჳaf to hir modir.

29 The which thing herd, his disciplis camen, and token his body, and puttiden it in a buriel.

30 And apostlis comynge to gidere to Jhesu, tolden to hym alle thingis that thei hadden don and tauჳt.

Tyndale (1525)

18 Jhon said vnto Herode, 'It is not laufull for the, to have thy brothers wyfe.'

19 Herodias layd waite for him, and wolde have killed him, butt she coulde not;

20 For Herode feared Jhon, knowynge that he was iuste and holy, and gave him reverence. And when he herde him, he did many thinges, and herde him gladly.

21 And when a convenyent daye was come, Herode on hys birth daye made a supper to the lordes, captayns, and chefe estates of Galile.

22 And the doughter of the same Herodias cam in, and daunsed, and pleased Herode and them that sate att bourde also. Then the kinge sayd vnto the mayden: 'Axe of me what thou wilt, and I will geve it the';

23 And he sware vnto her, 'What soever thou shalt axe of me, I will geve it the, even vnto the one halfe of my kyngdom.'

24 And she went forth, and sayde to her mother, 'What shall I axe?' And she sayde: 'Jhon Baptistes heed.'

25 And she cam in streigth waye with haste vnto the kinge and axed, sayinge: 'I wyll that thou geve me by and by in a charger the heed of Jhon Baptist.'

26 And the kinge was sorye, yet for hys othes sake, and for their sakes which sate att supper also, he wolde not put her besyde her purpost;

27 And immediatly the kynge sent the hangman, and commaunded his heed to be brought in. And he went and beheeded him in the preson,

28 And brought his heedde in a charger, and gave it to the mayden, and the mayden gave it to her mother.

29 When his disciples herde of it, they cam and toke vppe his body, and put it in a toumbe.

30 And the apostles gaddered them selves to geddre to Jesus, and tolde him all thynges, booth what they had done and what they had taught.

The Authorised Version (1611)

18 For John had said unto Herod, 'It is not lawful for thee to have thy brother's wife.'

19   Therefore Herodias had a quarrel against him, and would have killed him; but she could not.

20   For Herod feared John, knowing that he was a just man and and holy, and observed him; and when he heard him, he did many things, and heard him gladly.

21   And when a convenient day was come, that Herod on his birthday made a supper to his lords, high captains, and chief estates of Galilee;

22   And when the daughter of the said Herodias came in, and danced, and pleased Herod and them that sat with him, the king said unto the damsel, 'Ask of me whatsoever thou wilt, and I will give it thee.'

23   And he sware unto her, 'Whatsoever thou shalt ask of me, I will give it thee, unto the half of my kingdom.'

24   And she went forth, and said unto her mother, 'What shall I ask?' And she said, 'The head of John the Baptist.'

25   And she came in straightway with haste unto the king, and asked, saying, 'I will that thou give me by and by in a charger the head of John the Baptist.'

26   And the king was exceeding sorry; yet for his oath's sake, and for their sakes which sat with him, he would not reject her.

27   And immediately the king sent an executioner, and commanded his head to be brought: and he went and beheaded him in the prison,

28   And brought his head in a charger, and gave it to the damsel: and the damsel gave it to her mother.

29   And when his disciples heard of it, they came and took up his corpse, and laid it in a tomb.

30   And the apostles gathered themselves together unto Jesus, and told him all things, both what they had done, and what they had taught.

The New English Bible (1961)

18   John had told Herod, 'You have no right to your brother's wife.'

19   Thus Herodias nursed a grudge against him and would willingly have killed him, but she could not;

20   For Herod went in awe of John, knowing him to be a good and holy man; so he kept him in custody. He liked to listen to him, although the listening left him greatly perplexed.

21 Herodias found her opportunity when Herod on his birthday gave a banquet to his chief officials and commanders and the leading men of Galilee.

22 Her daughter came in and danced, and so delighted Herod and his guests that the king said to the girl, 'Ask what you like and I will give it you.'

23 And he swore an oath to her: 'Whatever you ask I will give you, up to half my kingdom.'

24 She went out and said to her mother, 'What shall I ask for?' She replied, 'The head of John the Baptist.'

25 The girl hastened back at once to the king with her request: 'I want you to give me here and now, on a dish, the head of John the Baptist.'

26 The king was greatly distressed, but out of regard for his oath and for his guests he could not bring himself to refuse her.

27 So the king sent a soldier of the guard with orders to bring John's head. The soldier went off and beheaded him in the prison,

28 Brought the head on a dish, and gave it to the girl; and she gave it to her mother.

29 When John's disciples heard the news, they came and took his body away and laid it in a tomb.

30 The apostles now rejoined Jesus and reported to him all that they had done and taught.

B Matthew 7: 13–29

Old English (c. 1000)

13 ʒanʒað inn þurh þæt nearwe ʒeat; forþon þe þæt ʒeat is swīþe wīd, and se weʒ is swīþe rūm þe to forspillednesse ʒelæt, and swīþe maneʒa sind þe þurh þone weʒ farað.

14 Ēalā hū nearu and hū anʒsum is þæt ʒeat, and se weʒ þe tō līfe ʒelæt, and swīþe fēawa sind þe þone weʒ finden.

15 Warniað ēow fram lēasum wīteʒum, þā cumað tō ēow on scēapa ʒeʒyrelum, ac hīe bēoð innane rēafiʒende wulfas.

16 Fram hiera wæstmum ʒē hīe underʒietað. Cwist þū ʒaderað man wīn-berian of þornum, oððe fīc-æppla of þyrncinum?

17 Swā ælc ʒōd trēow byrð ʒōde wæstmas; and ælc yfel trēow byrþ yfele wæstmas.

18 Ne mæʒ þæt ʒōde trēow beran yfle wæstmas, ne þæt yfele trēow ʒōde wæstmas.

19 Ælc trēow þe ne byrð ʒōdne wæstm, sīe hit forcorfen, and on fȳr āworpen.

20 Witodlīce be hiera wæstmum ʒē hīe oncnāwað.

21 Ne ʒǣð ælc þāra on heofena rīce, þe cwyþ tō mē, 'Drihten, Drihten'; ac sē þe wyrcð mīnes fæder willan þe on heofenum is, sē ʒǣð on heofena rīce.

22 Maneʒa cweþað on þǣm dæʒe tō mē, 'Drihten, Drihten, hū ne wīteʒode wē on þīnum naman, and on þīnum naman wē ūt āwurpon dēoflu, and on þīnum naman wē worhton micle mihta?'

23 Þonne cwæðe ic tō him, þæt 'ic ēow næfre ne cūðe; ʒewītað fram mē, ʒē þe worhton unrihtwīsnesse.'

24 Eornustlīce ælc þāra þe ðæs mīne word ʒehīerð, and þā wyrcð, bið ʒelīc þǣm wīsan were, sē his hūs ofer stān ʒetimbrode.

25 Þā cōm þǣr reʒn and micele flōd, and þǣr blēowon windas, and āhruron on þæt hūs, and hit nā ne fēoll; sōðlīce hit wæs ofer stān ʒetimbrod.

26 And ælc þāra þe ʒehīerþ ðās mīne word, and þā ne wyrcð, sē biþ ʒelīc þǣm dysiʒan men þe ʒetimbrode his hūs ofer sand-ceosel.

27 Þā rīnde hit, and þǣr cōmon flōd, and blēowon windas, and āhruron on þæt hūs, and þæt hūs fēoll; and his hryre wæs micel.

28 Þā wæs ʒeworden, þā se Hǣlend þās word ʒeendode, þā wundrode þæt folc his lāre.

29 Sōþlīce hē lǣrde, swilce hē anweald hæfde, and nā swā swā hiera bōceras and sundor-hālʒan.

Wycliffite (c. 1375)

13 Entre ʒe bi the streyt ʒate; for the gate that ledith to perdicioun is brode, and the weye large, and ther ben many that entren bi it.

14 How streit is the ʒate, and narewe the weye, that ledith to lijf, and there ben fewe that fynden it.

15 Perceyue ʒe, and flee fro fals prophetis, the whiche cummen to ʒou in clothingis of sheepis, bot wythynne thei ben rauyshynge wolues.

16 Of her fruytis ʒe shulen knowe hem. Whether men gaderen grapis of thornys, or fijgis of breeris?

17 So euery good tree makith good fruytis; sothely an yuel tree makith yuel fruytis.

18 A good tree may nat make yuel fruytis, nether an yuel tree make good fruytis.

19 Euery tree that makith nat good fruyt, shal be kitte doun, and shal be sent in to the fire.

20 Therfore of her fruytis ȝee shulen knowe hem.

21 Nat eche man that saith to me, 'Lord, Lord', shal entre into the kyngdam of heuenes; but he that doth the wille of my fadir that is in heuenes, he shal entre in to the kyngdam of heuenes.

22 Many shul say to me in that day, 'Lord, Lord, whether we han nat prophecied in thi name, and han cast out deuelis in thi name, and han don many vertues in thi name?'

23 And than Y shal knowliche to hem, 'For I knew ȝou neuer, departe awey fro me, ȝe that worchen wickidnesse.'

24 Therfore eche man that herith these my wordis, and doth hem, shal be maad liche to a wijse man, that hath bildid his hous vpon a stoon.

25 And rayn came doun, and flodis camen, and wyndis blewen, and rusheden in to that hous; and it felle nat doun, for it was foundid on a stoon.

26 And euery man that herith these my wordis, and doth hem nat, is liche to a man fool, that hath bildid his hous on grauel.

27 And rayn came doun, and floodis camen, and wyndis blewen, and thei hurliden in to that hous; and it felle doun, and the fallyng doun therof was grete.

28 And it is maad, when Jhesus hadde eendid these wordis, the cumpanyes wondreden on his techyng;

29 Sothely he was techynge hem, as a man hauynge power, and nat as the scribis of hem and Pharisees.

Tyndale (1525)

13 Enter in at the strayte gate; ffor wyde is the gate, and broade ys the waye thatt leadeth to destruccion, and many there be which goo yn there att.

14 For strayte ys the gate, and narowe is the waye, that leadeth vnto lyfe, and feawe there be that fynde it.

15 Beware off falce prophettes, whiche come to you in shepes clothynge, but inwardly they are ravenynge wolves.

16 Ye shall knowe them by their frutes. Do men gaddre grapes off thornes, or figges of bryres?

17 Even soo evry good tree bryngethe forthe good frute; butt a corrupte tree bryngethe forthe evyll frute.

18 A good tree cannott brynge forthe bad frute, nor yett a bad tree can brynge forthe good frute.

19 Every tree that bryngethe not forthe good frute, shalbe hewne doune, and cast into the fyre.

20 Wherfore by there frutes ye shall knowe them.

21 Not all they thatt say vnto me, 'Master, Master', shall enter into the kyngdome off heven; but he that fulfilleth my fathers will which ys in heven.

22 Many will saye to me yn that daye, 'Master, Master, have we nott in thy name prophesied, and in thy name have we not cast oute devyls, and in thy name have we nott done many miracles?'

23 And then will I knowlege vnto them, That I never knewe them; 'depart from me, ye workers of iniquite'.

24 Whosoever hearethe off me these saynges, and doethe the same, I wyll lyken hyme vnto a wyseman, which byllt his housse on a rocke.

25 And aboundance off rayne descended, and the fluddes cam, and the wynddes blewe, and bett vppon that same housse; and it was not over throwen, because it was grounded on the rocke.

26 And whosoever heareth of me these sainges, and doth not the same, shalbe lykened vnto a folysh man, which bilt his housse apon the sonde.

27 And abundaunce of rayne descended, and the fluddes cam, and the wynddes blewe, and beet vppon that housse; and it was over throwen, and great was the fall off it.

28 And it cam to passe, that when Jesus had ended these saynges, the peple were astonnied at his doctryne;

29 For he taught them, as one havynge power, and not as the scribes.

The Authorised Version (1611)

13 Enter ye in at the strait gate: for wide is the gate, and broad is the way, that leadeth to destruction, and many there be which go in thereat:

14 Because strait is the gate, and narrow is the way, which leadeth unto life, and few there be that find it.

15 Beware of false prophets, which come to you in sheep's cloth-ing, but inwardly they are ravening wolves.

16 Ye shall know them by their fruits. Do men gather grapes of thorns, or figs of thistles?

17 Even so every good tree bringeth forth good fruit; but a corrupt tree bringeth forth evil fruit.

18 A good tree cannot bring forth evil fruit, neither can a corrupt tree bring forth good fruit.

19 Every tree that bringeth not forth good fruit is hewn down, and cast into the fire.

20 Wherefore by their fruits ye shall know them.

21 Not every one that saith unto me, Lord, Lord, shall enter into the kingdom of heaven; but he that doeth the will of my Father which is in heaven.

22 Many will say to me in that day, Lord, Lord, have we not prophesied in thy name? and in thy name have cast out devils? and in thy name done many wonderful works?

23 And then will I profess unto them, I never knew you: depart from me, ye that work iniquity.

24 Therefore whosoever heareth these sayings of mine, and doeth them, I will liken him unto a wise man, which built his house upon a rock:

25 And the rain descended, and the floods came, and the winds blew, and beat upon that house; and it fell not: for it was founded upon a rock.

26 And every one that heareth these sayings of mine, and doeth them not, shall be likened unto a foolish man, which built his house upon the sand:

27 And the rain descended, and the floods came, and the winds blew, and beat upon that house; and it fell: and great was the fall of it.

28 And it came to pass, when Jesus had ended these sayings, the people were astonished at his doctrine:

29 For he taught them as one having authority, and not as the scribes.

The New English Bible (1961)

13 'Enter by the narrow gate. The gate is wide that leads to perdition, there is plenty of room on the road, and many go that way;

14 But the gate that leads to life is small and the road is narrow, and those who find it are few.

15   Beware of false prophets, men who come to you dressed up as sheep while underneath they are savage wolves.

16   You will recognize them by the fruits they bear. Can grapes be picked from briars or figs from thistles?

17   In the same way, a good tree always yields good fruit, and a poor tree bad fruit.

18   A good tree cannot bear bad fruit, or a poor tree good fruit.

19   And when a tree does not yield good fruit it is cut down and burnt.

20   That is why I say you will recognize them by their fruits.

21   Not everyone who calls me "Lord, Lord" will enter the kingdom of Heaven, but only those who do the will of my heavenly Father.

22   When that day comes, many will say to me, "Lord, Lord, did we not prophesy in your name, cast out devils in your name, and in your name perform many miracles?"

23   Then I will tell them to their face, "I never knew you: out of my sight, you and your wicked ways!"

24   What then of the man who hears these words of mine and acts upon them? He is like a man who had the sense to build his house on rock.

25   The rain came down, the floods rose, the wind blew, and beat upon that house; but it did not fall, because its foundations were upon rock.

26   But what of the man who hears these words of mine and does not act upon them? He is like a man who was foolish enough to build his house on sand.

27   The rain came down, the floods rose, the wind blew, and beat upon that house; down it fell with a great crash.'

28   When Jesus had finished his discourse the people were astounded at his teaching;

29   Unlike their own teachers he taught with a note of authority.

52

THE MARRIAGE SERVICE IN ENGLISH

The liturgy of the medieval Church was conducted in Latin, but those parts of it which most closely affected the lives of lay people might contain passages in the vernacular. Thus, essential public parts of the Marriage Service – the banns, the priest's enquiry to the congregation concerning eligibility, to the couple concerning mutual agreement, and the exchange of vows – were all conducted in English before the Reformation. The earliest extant texts of the exchange of vows date from the late fourteenth century, but the practice of using the vernacular was certainly earlier than that, and echoes of the form of vows found in MS Rawlinson lit. d. 5 are exploited for literary purposes by Chaucer in 'The Merchant's Tale', 1287–9.

The service for matrimony is one of those found in a collection for parish clergy known as a *Manuale*. These little volumes varied in practice and wording according to diocese, and their liturgies followed the Uses of Bangor, Lincoln, Hereford, and York; but they were not restricted to their original diocese, and most influential and widespread of all was that of Salisbury (Sarum). After the Reformation, for political and doctrinal reasons, an attempt was made to unify the liturgy of the Church of England, and the contents of the older *Manuale* were incorporated into the *Book of Common Prayer*, approved in 1662. It was preceded, however, by the First (1549) and Second (1552) Prayer Books of Edward VI, and the marriage service printed below is from the first of these. The second varies only in minor details of spelling. The *Book of Common Prayer* makes a significant change in the second cause of matrimony, so that it reads '. . . to avoid fornication: that such persons as have not the gift of continency might marry, and keep themselves . . .', but the only other substantive variations are in the omission of the reference to *paradise* in line 3, and the alteration of *departe* in the exchange of vows to read *do part*. The Alternative version, approved in 1927, makes more far-reaching changes.

Variation between the different versions is inspired partly by social and theological motives, and partly by a concern for clarity of expression. Among the former, are the removal of references to *holi cherche* after the Reformation, and perhaps *St Paul* in 1927. The reference to the *gift of continency* in the 1662 book is a clarification of doctrine. The gold and silver 'bride price' which accompanied the ring was omitted in 1552, and replaced with a duty to the clerk, and although the bishop of Durham noted in 1661 that the gift of gold and silver was still the custom in the North (Cuming 1961: 237), it was not restored. The wife's promise to obey, and its precursors, are the most modified part of the service. *Buxsum and boneyre*, 'submissive and meek', and the verb *serue* were not found in the bride's vows in medieval York, and became *obeye . . . serve* in 1549, before disappearing from the Alternative service in 1927. There are a few other changes in this version, perhaps motivated by a sense of delicacy.

Linguistically, the passages illustrate the general development of the language, and the medieval versions reflect the dialectal diversity of their time. A Hereford Missal prefers the verb *underfynge* (OE *underfōn*) to the Scandinavian-derived *take* in the exchange of vows, and a fifteenth-century *Manuale*, probably from St Asaph, has the unusual Southern preposition *forte* 'until' in *forte deth us departe*. The York *Manuale* lacks rounding of long *a* in *hald* and *haly*, and has the Scandinavian-derived forms *layther*, *kyrk*, *sylvere*, and *gyftys*, as well as the use of <y> for <þ>, all reflecting the northern origin of the text, whereas the Sarum passages use the southern pronoun *ich*, the rounded *holden* and *holy*, and south-eastern dialect forms like *wers*, *cherche*, and *knette*; but these are accompanied by Midland ones like *han*, *þei*, *fro*, *lasten*, and *ʒeue*. The form *seluyr* is that derived from Old English rather than Scandinavian, and *ony* is common in London and Middlesex in the fifteenth century.

The compilers of English prayer books have always been constrained by a special stylistic problem: to offer doctrinal clarity whilst maintaining the gravity associated with echoes of earlier states of the language. In 1549, the decision to replace Latin with English led to an uprising in Devon, and all subsequent revisions have been met by (less vigorously) adverse criticism. These pressures have led to the creation of a special linguistic register, most notable for its persistent archaism. The alliterative phrase *to have and to hold* has descended from Old English laws, and the use of the preposition *to* in the phrase *to thy wedded wife* has not been used idiomatically to mean 'as' since Middle English. It is striking that the 1927 service follows the 1662 book in the use of the pronouns *ye* and *thou* in the sentence *I require and charge you both, as ye will answer*. This is grammatically correct for Old and Early Middle English, since *you* was then the object form and *ye* the subject; but the 1549 Prayer Book already had *as you will aunswere* – less historically correct, but perhaps better reflecting contemporary linguistic usage.

Changes in the meanings of words have led to changes in wording. The semantic restriction of the word *catel* (originally 'chattels') limits its use to the earliest texts, but *unadvisedly* (originally 'without preconsideration') has survived into the 1927 text despite its change in meaning, as also *wedded*, despite the broadening of its meaning (originally 'pledged'). The memory of the wedding gift ('dowry') survived in the word *endow* until its replacement by the verb *share* in 1927. A further insight into the conscious archaism of much of this liturgical language is afforded by notes made by members of the revising committee in the first draft of the 1662 *Book of Common Prayer*. It was acknowledged that the sense of the phrase *with my body I the worschipe* had changed since Middle English, and the replacement of *worschipe* by *honour* was recommended. But the recommendation was not adopted, and it was more than two and a half centuries before the suggestion was implemented.

Late fourteenth-century Manual of the Sarum Use (MS Bodley Rawlinson lit. d. 5)

Ich .N. take the .N. to my weddyd wyf, to han and to holden fro this day forward, for bettere, for wers, for richere, for porere, in seknesse, and in helthe, tyl deth us departe, 3yf holy cherche hit wyle ordeyne, and þer-to y plight the my treuthe.

5 Ich .N. take the .N. to my weddyd housbonde, to han and to holden fro this day forward, for bettere, for wers, for richere, for porere, in seknesse, and in helthe, to be boneyre and buxsum in bedde and at borde, tyl deth us departe, 3if holi cherche hit wyle ordeyne, and þer-to y plight the my treuthe.

10 With this ryng y the wedde, and this gold and seluyr y the 3eue, and with my body y the worschipe, and with al my wordlyche catel y the honoure.

Early fifteenth-century Manual of the York Use
(Harvard, Widener Lib. MS 1)

Here I take ye N. to my wedded wyfe, to hald and to haue at bed
and at borde, for fay[r]er, for layther, for better, for wers, in sekenes
and in hele, till ded us depart [if haly kyrk it will ordayn], and yare-
to I plyght ye my trowth.

5 Here I take ye to my wedded housband, to hald and to haue at bed
and at borde, for fayrer, for layther, for better, for wers, in sekenes
and in hele, till ded ws depart, and yare-to I plyght ye my trowth.

Wyth yis ryng I wedde ye, and wyth yis gold and sylvere I honoure
ye, and wyth my gyftys I dow ye.

Fifteenth-century Manual of the Sarum Use (BL MS 30,506)

Lo, syres, we been her gadered togedere befor god and alle his
aungelis and his seyntis, in þe sith of holi cherche, to knette togedere
two bodies, that is to sey, þis man and þis woman, to þis end, þat
from þis tyme forward þei moste be o flesch, and two sowles in þe
5 feith and in þe lawe of god, to deserue togedere euer lastyng lyf in
amendement of that þat þei haue do amys her-before: wherfor I
amones ʒow alle, that, ʒif þer be any of ʒow þat knowe any lawful
lettyng whi þis man and þis woman mai not be wedded togedere
lawfulli, þat now he sey and knowliche it.

10 Also I charge ʒow, both man and woman, þat ʒif ony of ʒow haue
made any contract priuyli before þis tyme, or any avow mad, or
ony other cause knowe, whi þat ʒe mai not come to-gedere lawfulli,
now knowliche it.

N. Wiltow haue þis woman to þin wyf, and loue here, and worshipe
15 here, and holde hire, and kepe here in seknes and in hele, as an
hosbonde owyth to his wif, and alle oþer women to forsaken for
hire, and only to drawe to hire as longe as ʒowre bothe lyues to-
gedere lasten?

N. Wiltow haue þis man to þin housbonde, to been buxum to
20 hym, and serue hym, and worshipe hym, and kepe hym in syknes
and in hele, as a wif owith to do here housbonde, and alle oþer
men forsaken for hym, and only to drawe to hym as longe as ʒowre
bothyn lyues to-gedere lasten?

I. N. take the .N. to myn wedded wyf, to haue and to holde from
þis day forward, for beter, for wers, for richere, for porere, for
fayrere, for fowlere, in seknes and in helthe, til deth vs departe, ʒif
holy chirche it wil ordeyne: and therto I plithe þe myn trewthe.

I. N. take the .N. to myn weddid housbonde, to haue and to holde
from þis day forward, for beter, for wers, for richer, for porere, for
fayrere, for fowlere, in seknes and in hele, to be boner and buxum
[as a wyf owyd to hur husbandd], til deth vs departe, as holi cherche
it [wil] ordeyne: and therto I plithe the myn trowthe.

With þis ryng I þe wedde, and þis gold and siluer I þe ʒeue, and
with al myn bodi I the worschepe, and with al myn wordlich catel
I the honowre.

The First Prayer Book of Edward VI (1549)

Deerely beloued frendes, we are gathered together here in the syght
of God, and in the face of this congregacion, to ioyne together
this man and this woman in holy matrimonie; which is an honorable estate instituted of God in paradise, in the time of mannes
innocencie, signifying unto us the misticall union that is betwixte
Christe and his Churche: whiche holy estate, Christe adorned and
beutified with his presence, and first miracle that he wrought in
Cana of Galile, and is commended of Sainct Paule to be honourable
emong all men; and therefore is not to bee enterprised, nor taken
in hande, unaduisedlye, lightlye, or wantonly, to satisfie mens carnal
lustes and appetites, like brute beastes that haue no understanding:
but reuerentely, discretely, aduisedly, soberly, and in the fear of
God. Duely consideryng the causes for the whiche matrimonie
was ordeined. One cause was the procreacion of children, to be
brought up in the feare and nurture of the Lord, and prayse of
God. Secondly it was ordeined for a remedie agaynst sinne, and to
auoide fornicacion, that suche persones as bee maried, might liue
chastlie in matrimonie, and kepe themselues undefiled membres
of Christes bodye. Thirdelye, for the mutuall societie, helpe, and
coumfort, that the one oughte to haue of thother, both in prosperitie
and aduersitie. Into the whiche holy estate these two persones
present: come nowe to be ioyned. Therefore if any man can shewe
any iuste cause why they maie not lawfully be ioyned together: Leat
him now speake, or els hereafter for euer hold his peace.

25   *And also speakyng to the persones that shalbe maried, he shal saie,*

I require and charge you (as you will aunswere at the dreadefull daye of iudgemente, when the secretes of all hartes shalbee disclosed) that if either of you doe knowe any impedimente, why ye maie not bee lawfully ioyned together in matrimonie, that ye

30   confesse it. For be ye well assured, that so manye as bee coupled together otherwaies then Goddes woord doeth allowe: are not ioyned of God, neither is their matrimonie lawful.

. . .

Yf no impedimente bee alleged, then shall the Curate saye unto the man,

35   N. Wilte thou haue this woman to thy wedded wife, to liue together after Goddes ordeinaūce in the holy estate of matrimonie? Wilt thou loue her, coumforte her, honor, and kepe her in sickenesse and in health? And forsaking all other kepe thee only to her, so long as you both shall liue?

40   ¶ *The man shall aunswere,*
      I will.

¶ *Then shall the priest saye to the woman,*
N. Wilt thou haue this man to thy wedded houseband, to liue together after Goddes ordeinaunce, in the holy estate of matrimonie?

45   Wilt thou obey him, and serue him, loue, honor, and kepe him in sickenes and in health? And forsaking al other kepe thee onely to him, so long as you both shall liue?

¶ *The woman shall aunswere,*
      I will.

50   ¶ *Then shall the Minister say,*
Who geueth this woman to be maried to this man?

And the minister receiuing the woman at her father or frendes handes: shall cause the man to take the woman by the right hande, and so either to geue their trouth to other: The man first saying.

55   I N. take thee N. to my wedded wife, to haue and to holde from this day forwarde, for better, for wurse, for richer, for poorer, in sickenes, and in health, to loue, and to cherishe, til death us departe: according to Goddes holy ordeinaunce: and therto I plight thee my trouth.

60   *Then shall they looce theyr handes, and the woman taking again*
        the man by the right hande shall say,
        I *N.* take thee *N.* to my wedded husbande, to haue and to holde
        from this day forwarde, for better, for woorse, for richer, for poorer,
        in sickenes, and in health, to loue, cherishe, and to obey, till death
65   us departe: accordyng to Goddes holy ordeinaunce: And thereto
        I geue thee my trouth.

        ¶ *Then shall they agayne looce theyr handes, and the manne shall*
        geue unto the womanne a ring, and other tokens of spousage, as golde
        or siluer, laying the same upon the boke: And the Priest taking the
70   *ring shall deliuer it unto the man: to put it upon the fowerth finger of*
        the womans left hande. And the man taught by the priest, shall say,
        ¶ With thys ring I thee wed: Thys golde and siluer I thee geue: with
        my body I thee wurship: and withal my worldly Goodes I thee
        endowe. In the name of the father, and of the sonne, and of the
75   holy goste. Amen.

The Alternative Form of the Anglican Marriage Service
(Book of Common Prayer Revised 1927)

        Dearly beloved, we are gathered here in the sight of God and in the
        face of this congregation, to join together this man and this woman
        in Holy Matrimony; which is an honourable estate instituted of
        God himself, signifying unto us the mystical union that is betwixt
5   Christ and his Church; which holy estate Christ adorned and beau-
        tified with his presence, and first miracle that he wrought, in Cana
        of Galilee; and is commended in Holy Writ to be honourable among
        all men; and therefore is not by any to be enterprised, nor taken in
        hand, unadvisedly lightly or wantonly; but reverently, discreetly,
10   soberly, and in the fear of God; duly considering the causes for
        which matrimony was ordained.
            First, It was ordained for the increase of mankind according to
        the will of God, and that children might be brought up in the fear
        and nurture of the Lord, and to the praise of his holy name.
15   Secondly, It was ordained in order that the natural instincts
        and affections, implanted by God, should be hallowed and directed
        aright; that those who are not called of God to remain unmarried,
        but by him are led to this holy estate, should continue therein in
        pureness of living.

20   Thirdly, It was ordained for the mutual society, help, and comfort, that the one ought to have of the other, both in prosperity and
adversity.

Into which holy estate these two persons present come now to
be joined.

25   Therefore if any man can shew any just cause, why they may
not lawfully be joined together, let him now speak, or else hereafter
for ever hold his peace.

· · ·

¶ *Speaking unto the persons that shall be married, the Priest shall say,*
I Require and charge you both, as ye will answer at the dreadful
30   day of judgement when the secrets of all hearts shall be disclosed,
that if either of you know any impediment, why ye may not be
lawfully joined together in matrimony, ye do now confess it. For
be ye well assured, that so many as are coupled together otherwise
than God's Word doth allow are not joined together by God;
35   neither is their matrimony lawful.

· · ·

¶ *If no impediment be alleged, then shall the Priest say unto the man,*
N. Wilt thou have this woman to thy wedded wife, to live together
according to God's law in the holy estate of matrimony? Wilt thou
love her, comfort her, honour and keep her, in sickness and in
40   health? and, forsaking all other, keep thee only unto her, so long as
ye both shall live?

¶ *The man shall answer,* I will.

¶ *Then shall the Priest say unto the woman,*
N. Wilt thou have this Man to thy wedded husband, to live together
45   according to God's holy law in the holy estate of matrimony? Wilt
thou love him, comfort him, honour, and keep him, in sickness
and in health? and, forsaking all other, keep thee only unto him, so
long as ye both shall live?

¶ *The woman shall answer,* I will.

50   ¶ *Then shall the Priest say,*
Who giveth this woman to be married to this man?

¶ *Then shall they give their troth to each other in this manner. The Priest, receiving the woman at her father's or friend's hands, shall cause the man with his right hand to take the woman by her right*
55   *hand, and to say after him as followeth.*

I N. take thee, N. to my wedded wife, to have and to hold from this day forward, for better, for worse; for richer, for poorer; in sickness and in health; to love and to cherish, till death us do part, according to God's holy law; and thereto I give thee my troth.

60   *Then shall they loose their hands; and the woman, with her right hand taking the man by his right hand, shall likewise say after the Priest,*

I N. take thee, N. to my wedded husband, to have and to hold from this day forward, for better, for worse; for richer, for poorer; in
65   sickness, and in health; to love and to cherish, till death us do part, according to God's holy law; and thereto I give thee my troth.

¶ *Then they shall again loose their hands; and the man shall give unto the woman a ring, laying the same upon the book. And the Priest, taking the ring, shall deliver it to the Man, to put it upon the fourth*
70   *finger of the woman's left hand. And the man, holding the ring there, and taught by the Priest, shall say,*

With this ring I thee wed; with my body I thee honour; and all my worldly goods I with thee share; In the Name of the Father, and of the Son, and of the Holy Ghost. Amen.

REFERENCES AND BACKGROUND READING

General

Baugh, A.C. and Cable, Thomas, *A History of the English Language*, 3rd edn (London: RKP, 1978).

Blake, N.F., *Non-standard Language in English Literature* (London: Deutsch, 1981).

—— *A History of the English Language* (Basingstoke: Macmillan, 1996).

The Cambridge History of the English Language, ed. Richard M. Hogg, 6 vols (Cambridge: Cambridge University Press, 1992, in progress).

Fisiak, J., *A Bibliography of Writings for the History of the English Language* (Berlin: Mouton de Gruyter, 1987).

Jones, Charles, *A History of English Phonology* (London: Longman, 1989).

Jones, Richard Foster, *The Triumph of the English Language* (Stanford: Stanford UP, 1953).

Marchand, Hans, *The Categories and Types of Present-Day English Word-Formation*, 2nd edn (Munich: Beck, 1969).

The Oxford English Dictionary, 2nd edn, prepared by J. A. Simpson and E. S. C. Weiner (Oxford: Clarendon, 1989).

Partridge, A.C., *English Biblical Translation* (London: Deutsch, 1973).

Prins, A.A., *A History of English Phonemes* (Leiden: Leiden UP, 1972).

Quirk, Randolph, Greenbaum, Sidney, Leech, Geoffrey and Svartvik, Jan, *A Comprehensive Grammar of the English Language* (London: Longman, 1985).

Samuels, M.L., *Linguistic Evolution with Special Reference to English* (Cambridge: CUP, 1972).

Scragg, D.G., *A History of English Spelling* (Manchester: Manchester University Press, 1974).

Smith, Jeremy, *An Historical Study of English: Function, Form and Change* (London and New York: Routledge, 1996).

Strang, Barbara M.H., *A History of English* (London: Methuen, 1970).

Tajima, Matsuji, *Old and Middle English Language Studies: A Classified Bibliography 1923–1985* (Amsterdam/Philadelphia: Benjamins, 1988).

Visser, F.Th., *An Historical Syntax of the English Language*, 3 vols (Leiden: Brill, 1970–73).

Wordsworth, C. and Littlehales, Henry, *The Old Service Books of the English Church* (London: Methuen, 1910).

Wyld, H.C., *A History of Modern Colloquial English* (Oxford: Blackwell, 1936).

Old English

Ælfric's De Temporibus Anni, ed. Heinrich Henel, EETS OS 213 (London, 1942).

Campbell, A., *Old English Grammar* (Oxford: Clarendon, 1969).

—— *The Battle of Brunanburh* (London: Heinemann, 1938).

Fowler, David C., *The Bible in Early English Literature* (Seattle and London: University of Washington, 1976).

Gneuss, Helmut, 'The Origin of Standard Old English and Æthelwold's School at Winchester', *Anglo-Saxon England* 1 (1972), 63–83.

Godden, M.R., 'Literary Language', in *The Cambridge History of the English Language*, ed. Richard M. Hogg (Cambridge: CUP, 1992), vol. 1, 490–535.

Hall, J.R.C., *A Concise Anglo-Saxon Dictionary*, 4th edn with a Supplement by Herbert Dean Meritt (Cambridge: CUP, 1960).

Hofstetter, W., 'Winchester and the Standardization of Old English Vocabulary', *Anglo-Saxon England* 17 (1988), 139–61.

Hurt, James, *Ælfric* (New York: Twayne, 1972).

Kastovsky, D., 'Semantics and Vocabulary', in *The Cambridge History of the English Language*, ed. Richard M. Hogg (Cambridge: CUP, 1992), vol. 1, 290–408.

McKinnell, J., 'On the Date of *The Battle of Maldon*', *Medium Ævum* 44 (1975), 121–36.

The Gospel of St Mark in West Saxon, ed. James Wilson Bright (Boston and London: Heath, 1905).

The Gospel According to St Mark in Anglo-Saxon and Northumbrian Versions, ed. W. W. Skeat (Cambridge: CUP, 1871).

The Gospel According to St Matthew in Anglo-Saxon and Northumbrian Versions, ed. John M. Kemble and Charles Hardwick (Cambridge: CUP, 1858).

Mitchell, B., *Old English Syntax* (Oxford, Clarendon, 1985).

Morrell, Minnie Cate, *A Manual of Old English Biblical Materials* (Knoxville: University of Tennessee, 1965).

Oman, C.W.C., *The Art of War in the Middle Ages* (Ithaca and NY: Cornell, 1953).

The Pastoral Care, ed. N.R. Ker, Early English Manuscripts in Facsimile 6 (Copenhagen: Rosenkilde and Bagger, 1956).

Salmon, Vivian, 'Some Connotations of Cold in Old and Middle English', *Modern Language Notes* 74 (1959), 314–22.

Stanley, E.G., 'Old English Poetic Diction and the Interpretation of *The Wanderer, The Seafarer* and *The Penitent's Prayer*', *Anglia* 73 (1955), 413–66.

Toon, T.E., 'Old English Dialects', in *The Cambridge History of the English Language*, ed. Richard M. Hogg (Cambridge: CUP, 1992), vol. 1, 409–51.

Venezky, Richard Lawrence and Healey, Antonette diPaolo, *A Microfiche Concordance to Old English* (Toronto: University of Toronto, 1980).

The Vespasian Psalter, ed. Sherman M. Kuhn (Ann Arbor: University of Michigan, 1965).

The Vespasian Psalter, ed. David H. Wright, Early English Manuscripts in Facsimile 14 (Copenhagen: Rosenkilde and Bagger, 1967).

Middle English

Ancrene Wisse, Parts 6 and 7, ed. Geoffrey Shepherd (London: Nelson, 1959).

Barron, C.M., 'Who Were the Pastons?', *Journal of the Society of Archivists* 4 (1972), 530–5.

Bennett, J.A.W. and Smithers, G.V., *Early Middle English Verse and Prose*, 2nd edn (Oxford: Clarendon, 1968).

The Holy Bible containing the Old and New Testaments with the Apocryphal Books ... by John Wycliffe and his Followers, ed. Josiah Forshall and Frederic Madden, 4, vols (Oxford: Clarendon, 1850).

Burnley, David, *The Language of Chaucer* (London: Macmillan, 1989).

Burnley, J.D., 'Curial Prose in England', *Speculum* 61 (1986), 593–614.

Chambers, R.W. and Daunt, M., *A Book of London English* (Oxford: Clarendon, 1931).

Diensberg, B., 'The Lexical Fields BOY/GIRL – SERVANT – CHILD in Middle English', *Neuphilologische Mitteilungen* 86 (1985), 328–36.

Dobson, E.J., *The Origins of the Ancrene Wisse* (Oxford: Clarendon, 1976).

Elliott, R.W.V., *Chaucer's English* (London: Deutsch, 1974).

English Fragments from Latin Medieval Service-Books, ed. Henry Littlehales, EETS ES 90 (London, 1903).

Hellinga, Lotte, 'The Malory Manuscript and Caxton', in *Aspects of Malory*, ed. Toshiyuki Takamiya and Derek Brewer (Cambridge: Brewer, 1981), 127–41.

Horstmann, Carl, 'Mappula Angliae, von Osbern Bokenham', *Englische Studien* 10 (1887), 1–34.

Johnston, P.A., 'English Vowel Shifting: One Great Vowel Shift or Two Small Vowel Shifts?', *Diachronica* 9 (1992), 189–226.

Jordan, Richard, *Handbook of Middle English Grammar: Phonology*, translated and revised by Eugene J. Crook (The Hague: Mouton, 1974).

Kuhn, Sherman M., 'The Preface to a Fifteenth-Century Concordance', *Speculum* 43 (1968), 258–73.

Kurath, Hans, Kuhn, Sherman M., Lewis, Robert E. *et al.*, *Middle English Dictionary* (Ann Arbor: University of Michigan, 1954, in progress).

Kyng Alisaunder, ed. G. V. Smithers, 2 vols, EETS OS 227 and 237 (1952 and 1957).

McIntosh, Angus, 'Some Linguistic Reflections of a Wycliffite', in *Medieval and Linguistic Studies in Honor of Francis Peabody Magoun, Jr*, ed. Jess B. Bessinger, Jr and Robert P. Creed (London: Allen and Unwin, 1965), 290–3.

—— Samuels, M. L. and Benskin, Michael, *A Linguistic Atlas of Late Mediaeval English*, 4 vols (Aberdeen University Press, 1986).

The Works of Sir Thomas Malory, ed. Eugene Vinaver, 2nd edn, 3 vols (Oxford: Clarendon, 1967).

The Story of England by Robert Mannyng of Brunne, ed. Frederick J. Furnivall, 2 vols, HMSO Rolls Series (1887).

Mooney, L.R., 'A Middle English Text on the Seven Liberal Arts', *Speculum* 68 (1993), 1027–52.

Mustanoja, T.F., *Middle English Syntax* (Helsinki, 1960).

The Ormulum, ed. R. M. White and Robert Holt, 2 vols (Oxford: Clarendon, 1878).

Parkes, M.B., 'On the Presumed Date of the Manuscript of the *Ormulum*: Oxford, Bodleian Library, MS Junius I', in *Five Hundred Years of Words and Sounds: A Festschrift for Eric Dobson*, ed. E. G. Stanley and Douglas Gray (Cambridge: Brewer, 1983), 115–27.

Paston Letters and Papers of the Fifteenth Century, ed. Norman Davis, 2 vols (Oxford: Clarendon, 1971; 1976).

Pearl, ed. E. V. Gordon (Oxford: Clarendon, 1953).

The Peterborough Chronicle 1070–1154, ed. Cecily Clark, 2nd edn (Oxford: Clarendon, 1970).

Polychronicon Ranulphi Higden Monachi Cestrensis, ed. Churchill Babington and J. R. Lumby, 9 vols, HMSO Rolls Series (London: Longman, 1865–86).

Samuels, M.L., 'Some Applications of Middle English Dialectology', *English Studies* 44 (1963), 81–94.

Shaw, Sally, 'Caxton and Malory', in *Essays on Malory*, ed. J. A. W. Bennett (Oxford: Clarendon, 1963), 114–45.

The Bibliotheca Historica of Diodorus Siculus, trans. John Skelton, ed. F. M. Salter and H. L. R. Edwards, EETS OS 233 (1956).

The Early South-English Legendary, ed. Carl Horstmann, EETS OS 87 (1887).

Turville-Petre, Thorlac, 'Politics and Poetry in the Early Fourteenth Century: The Case of Robert Manning's *Chronicle*', *Review of English Studies* 39 (1988), 1–28.

Vachek, Josef, 'Notes on the Phonological Development of the NE Pronoun *She*', Sborník Prací Filosofické Fakulty Brnenské University 3 (1954), 67–80.

Vices and Virtues, ed. F. Holthausen, 2 parts, EETS OS 89, 159 (1888, 1921).

Early Modern English

Abbot, E.A., *A Shakespearian Grammar* (London: Macmillan, 1870).

Bald, R.C., *John Donne: A Life* (Oxford: Clarendon, 1970).

Barber, Charles, *Early Modern English* (Edinburgh: Edinburgh University Press, 1997).

Britton, Derek, 'Henry Machyn, Axel Wijk and the Case of the Wrong Riding: The South-West Yorkshire Character of the Language of Machyn's Diary', forthcoming in *Neuphilologische Mitteilungen*.

Brook, Stella, *The Language of the Book of Common Prayer* (London: Deutsch, 1965).

The Journals and Letters of Fanny Burney (Madame d'Arblay), ed. Joyce Hemslow with Curtis D. Cecil and Althea Douglas (Oxford: Clarendon, 1972), vol 1, 1791–2.

Butterworth, C.C., *The Literary Lineage of the King James Bible 1340–1611* (Philadelphia: University of Pennsylvania, 1941).

Cuming, G.J., *The Durham Book: Being the First Draft of the Revision of the Book of Common Prayer in 1661* (London: OUP, 1961).

Corns, Thomas N., *Milton's Language* (Oxford: Blackwell, 1990).

Defoe, Daniel, *A Tour through England and Wales*, 2 vols (London: Dent, 1928).

Dobson, E.J., *English Pronunciation 1500–1700*, 2 vols, 2nd edn (Oxford: Clarendon, 1968).

Donne, John, *The Elegies and the Songs and Sonnets*, ed. Helen Gardner (Oxford: Clarendon, 1965).

Letters of Queen Elizabeth and King James VI of Scotland, ed. John Bruce (London: Camden Society 46, 1849).

Emma, Ronald David, *Milton's Grammar* (The Hague: Mouton, 1964).

The First Prayer Book of King Edward VI (1549), The Ancient and Modern Library of Theological Literature (London: Griffith Farran Okeden & Welsh, undated *literatim* reprint).

Görlach, Manfred, *Introduction to Early Modern English* (Cambridge: CUP, 1991).

Gotti, Maurizio, *Robert Boyle and the Language of Science*, Collana Blu 27 (Milano: Guerini Scientifica, 1996).

Letters of the Lady Brilliana Harley, ed. Thomas Taylor Lewis (London: Camden Society 58, 1854).

Hulme, Hilda M., *Explorations in Shakespeare's Language* (London: Longman, 1962).

Hunter, G.K., *John Lyly: The Humanist as Courtier* (London: RKP, 1962).

Hussey, S.S., *The Literary Language of Shakespeare* (London: Longman, 1982).

Hutson, Lorna, *Thomas Nashe in Context* (Oxford: Clarendon, 1989).

Lloyd, Christopher, *Fanny Burney* (London: Longman, 1936).

The Complete Works of John Lyly, ed. R. Warwick Bond, 3 vols (Oxford: Clarendon, 1902).

The Diary of Henry Machyn, ed. John Gough Nichols (London: Camden Society 42, 1858).

Mack, Maynard, *Alexander Pope: A Life* (New Haven: Yale, 1985).

The Poetical Works of John Milton, ed. Helen Darbishire (London: OUP, 1958).

The Works of Thomas Nashe, ed. Ronald B. McKerrow, 5 vols (London: Bullen/Sidgwick and Jackson, 1904–10).

Pendry, E.D., *Thomas Dekker* (London: Arnold, 1967).

Pope, Alexander, *The Rape of the Lock*, ed. Geoffrey Tillotson (London: Methuen, 1940).

Puttenham, George, *The Arte of English Poesie*, ed. Gladys Doidge Willcock and Alice Walker (Cambridge: CUP, 1936).

Richetti, John J., *Daniel Defoe* (Boston: Twayne, 1987).

Rudskoger, Arne, *Plain: A Study in Co-text and Context* (Stockholm: Almqvist and Wiksell, 1970).

William Shakespeare: The Complete Works. Original Spelling Edition, ed. Stanley Wells and Gary Taylor (Oxford: Clarendon, 1986).

Sledd, James H. and Kolb, Gwin J., *Dr Johnson's Dictionary* (Chicago: University of Chicago, 1955).

Wijk, Axel, *The Orthography and Pronunciation of Henry Machyn, the London Diarist: A Study of the South-East Yorkshire Dialect in the Early 16th Century*, Stockholm Studies in English 1 (Uppsala: Appelbergs Bocktryck, 1937).

Wilson, Thomas, *Arte of Rhetorique*, ed. Thomas J. Derrick (New York: Garland, 1982).

Modern English

Bridges, Robert, *The Collected Papers of Henry Bradley* (Oxford: Clarendon, 1928).

Brontë, Emily, *Wuthering Heights*, ed. Hilda Marsden and Ian Jack (Oxford: Clarendon, 1976).

Brook, G.L., *The Language of Charles Dickens* (London: Deutsch, 1970).

Carlyle, Thomas, *Works, The Standard Edition*, 18 vols (London: Chapman and Hall, 1839), vol. 5: 'Critical and Miscellaneous Essays'.

Chitham, Edward, *A Life of Emily Brontë* (Oxford: Blackwell, 1987).

Darwin, Charles, *The Descent of Man and Selection in Relation to Sex*, 2 vols (London: Murray, 1871).

Dickens, Charles, *The Pickwick Papers*, ed. James Kingsley (Oxford: Clarendon, 1986).

Elliott, Blanche B., *A History of English Advertising* (London: Batsford, 1962).

Howard, Jonathan, *Darwin* (Oxford: OUP, 1982).

A D. H. Lawrence Handbook, ed. Keith Sagar (Manchester: Manchester UP, 1982).

Nevett, T.R., *Advertising in Britain: A History* (London: Heinemann, 1982).

Petyt, K.M., *Emily Brontë and the Haworth Dialect* (Menston: Yorkshire Dialect Society, 1970).

George Bernard Shaw on Language, ed. Abraham Tauber (London: Peter Owen, 1965).

Sørensen, Knud S., 'Dickens on the Use of English', *English Studies* 70 (1989), 551–9.

Sweet, Henry, *The Practical Study of Languages* (London: Dent, 1899).

INDEX

Phonetic, phonological and orthographic features

Morphological features

Style and Discourse

Language Contact